Song of the *Land*

Children's Literature Association Series

Celebrating the Works of Mildred D. Taylor

Edited by Sarah Layzell, Tammy L. Mielke,
and Michelle H. Martin

University Press of Mississippi / Jackson

The University Press of Mississippi is the scholarly publishing agency of the Mississippi Institutions of Higher Learning: Alcorn State University, Delta State University, Jackson State University, Mississippi State University, Mississippi University for Women, Mississippi Valley State University, University of Mississippi, and University of Southern Mississippi.

www.upress.state.ms.us

The University Press of Mississippi is a member of the Association of University Presses.

Saidiya Hartman, "Venus in Two Acts," in *Small Axe: A Caribbean Journal of Criticism* vol. 12, no. 2 (26), pp. 1–14. Copyright 2008, Small Axe, Inc. All rights reserved. Republished by permission of the copyright holder, and the Publisher. www.dukeupress.edu.

Any discriminatory or derogatory language or hate speech regarding race, ethnicity, religion, sex, gender, class, national origin, age, or disability that has been retained or appears in elided form is in no way an endorsement of the use of such language outside a scholarly context.

Copyright © 2025 by University Press of Mississippi
All rights reserved
Manufactured in the United States of America

∞

Publisher: University Press of Mississippi, Jackson, USA
Authorised GPSR Safety Representative: Easy Access System Europe – Mustamäe tee 50, 10621 Tallinn, Estonia, gpsr.requests@easproject.com

Library of Congress Control Number: 2025015241

Hardback ISBN: 9781496858238 | Trade paperback ISBN: 9781496858245
Epub single ISBN: 9781496858252 | Epub institutional ISBN: 9781496858269
PDF single ISBN: 9781496858276 | PDF institutional ISBN: 9781496858245

British Library Cataloging-in-Publication Data available

Contents

Acknowledgments vii
Poetic Tribute: An Oriki for Mildred 3
   Y. FALAMI DEVOE
Introduction 5
   MICHELLE H. MARTIN
Poetic Tribute: Homemade Love: Sower. Weaver. Receiver. 11
   RAEN PARKER WASHINGTON

Part 1: The Self: Intersectionality and Insider/Outsider Perspectives

The Story in the Silence: Reading Between the Lines in
Mildred D. Taylor's Logan Family Saga 15
   LATRICE FERGUSON
"I Wanted to Write a Truthful History": Intersections of Critical Race
Theory and Gender Schema in Mildred D. Taylor's Work. 31
   SHELLY SHAFFER, MELISSA BEDFORD, AND ANN VAN WIG
Beyond the Veil: In Search of Duboisian Double Consciousness
in the Works of Mildred D. Taylor 52
   HELEN BOND
Racial Education and Audience in
All the Days Past, All the Days to Come. 68
   JANI L. BARKER

Part 2: The Self: Reimagining the Logans

Re(cover)y of the Logan Family Saga 89
   NGOZI ONUORA AND SABRINA CARNESI

Re/figuring the Child-Signifier and Agency in the Film Adaptation
of Mildred D. Taylor's *Roll of Thunder, Hear My Cry* 109
   DEVIKA MEHRA

How the Logans Travel to the East: Exploring the Persian Translations
of *Roll of Thunder, Hear My Cry*, *The Friendship*, and *The Well* 131
   BAHAR ESHRAQ

Part 3: The World Outside: White Supremacy, Justice, and the Land

White Supremacy and the Black Storyteller's Narrative Unveiling 161
   SUSAN BROWNE AND WANDA BROOKS

"Don't Speak for the Trees—Listen": Mildred D. Taylor's
Song of the Trees for Environmental Justice 180
   LAUREN RIZZUTO

Contested Space: The Black Agrarian Tradition in
Mildred D. Taylor's *The Land* 204
   EMILY CARDINALI CORMIER

Her Bandage Hides Two Festering Sores That Once Perhaps Were Eyes:
"Justice" in the Logan Family Saga and *To Kill a Mockingbird* 221
   CATHARINE KANE

Part 4: The World Beyond: Legacy, Activism, and Education

Disrupting Mavericks: *Roll of Thunder, Hear My Cry*, *The Hate U Give*,
and Critical Race Theory 241
   ANNETTE WANNAMAKER

Care Ethics and Activism in Mildred D. Taylor's *Roll of Thunder,
Hear My Cry* and Angie Thomas's *The Hate U Give* 257
   BRYANNA SOMERS

Blending Fact and Fiction: *All the Days Past, All the Days to Come*
as a Novel of Black Resistance 279
   JENNIFER ANSBACH

List of Contributors 301
Index 307

Acknowledgments

We would like to thank Mildred D. Taylor, whose words shaped all of us in different ways, not least by enabling us to bring together a community of scholars in this anthology and beyond.

We thank Katie Keene at University Press of Mississippi for her constant support for this book from the very beginning, both as an editor and as a proud Mississippian. Thanks are also due to Katie Turner and to the peer reviewer for their thoughtful and encouraging feedback. We are grateful to the entire team at the Press.

We would like to share our profound thanks to our contributors for their hard work, patience, and commitment to this project. We are beyond thrilled to see so much new research and creative response to Taylor's work in print, and we know that your insights will inform and inspire discussions about Taylor for years to come.

This volume was crafted by multiple voices, including students in five of Michelle's classes at two different universities as well as critical support from research assistants at the University of Washington (UW):

- LIS 564, Spring 2019 and Winter 2021, Multicultural Resources for Youth, UW
- LIS 563, Fall 2019 and Winter 2021, Cultural History of Children's and Young Adult Literature, UW
- ENG 576, Summer 2021, Critical Studies in Form/Genre: African American Children's and Young Adult Literature History, Hollins University
- The University of Washington Information School's GA Crew for both research and graphics support
- Cleary Research Assistants Emily Ready, Danette Jasper, and Sabrina Carnesi

We also benefited from the participation of the scholars who presented at and attended the symposium celebrating the fortieth anniversary of *Roll of Thunder, Hear My Cry* at the University of Cambridge in 2016, and panels on Taylor's work at ChLA 2017, ChLA 2023, and ChLA 2024. Our interest in Taylor has sparked many discussions between scholars, and we would like to especially honor the memory of Dr. Althea Tait, who drew our attention to Patrisse Cullors's mention of *The Gold Cadillac* in her writing.

Sarah would like to thank her daughter, Rosie Hardstaff, who joined us on many Zoom calls and is roughly the same age as this project, and Dr. Breanna J. McDaniel—"my friend for always," as Jeremy Simms writes to Stacey Logan—who has been with this project in spirit from the very beginning.

Michelle would like to thank her husband, Glenn Hare, who always has her back; her daughter, Amelia Hare, reader extraordinaire; Cricket, her lap-warming, four-legged canine research assistant; and the University of Washington Information School for support to pursue the research that feeds her soul.

Tammy would like to thank the countless students she has taught at different levels and in different countries, all of whom have helped to shape her teaching and writing with their inquisitive minds. She would also like to thank Sochi, her best furry companion, who will forever be her pup no matter the years. A special heart-felt thank you to Michelle and Sarah, who saw Tammy through a pandemic and career change while we were editing this collection.

Finally, we extend thanks to our readers. Although COVID-19 brought delays to our process, the renewed global attention to anti-Black racism in the US, UK, and elsewhere following the summer of 2020 gave us a sense of increased urgency in this work. We hope that you, the readers of this volume, will carry that urgency forward.

Song of the Land

Poetic Tribute

An Oriki for Mildred

Y. Falami Devoe

Oriki—*A Yoruba praise poem spoken or sung in praise of an individual*

The gifted griot of the House of Taylor
Anoints
Awakens

Readers
Listeners
Bringing forth light in darkness.

The gifted griot of the House of Taylor
Bodaciously
Beckoning
Readers
Listeners
To peer into the lens of racial injustice.

The gifted griot of the House of Taylor
Dame of Diction
Protector of the Past
Ambassador of the Ancestors
Benefactress of Stories
Conjurer of Consciousness

The gifted griot of the House of Taylor
Purposeful with the pen
Mississippi Memory Keeper
Meritable Medal holder
Planting messages of
Dignity
Hope
Unity
Pride

Introduction

Michelle H. Martin

Racism impacted the trajectory of Mildred D. Taylor's life long before she could make her own decisions. Born in Jackson, Mississippi, she was only three weeks old when her father experienced a racist incident that prompted him to leave the South that very day. As he packed to leave, Taylor's mother removed items nearly as fast as he could pack them, attempting to urge him to stay—a scene that Taylor recreates in the final Logan novel, *All the Days Past, All the Days to Come* (*Days*), when Cassie's eldest brother Stacey decides to leave, and his wife Dee urges him to stay and unpacks his bag as he packs. Dee asks him, "Robert, have you lost your mind?" He replies, "Yeah, I guess I have. I'm crazy not to have left this place long time ago . . . I'm sick to death of these white people down here. I'm going to kill one of them if they don't kill me first" (25). In a span of three months, Taylor's father had found a job and a place to live in Toledo, Ohio, and sent for Taylor, her mother, and her older sister (Fogelman).

Taylor grew up in Ohio rather than in Mississippi because her father did not want his children subject to the racism they would necessarily endure if the family had stayed in the South. Because racism has played such a significant role in Mildred Taylor's life, and she has drawn much of her fiction from her own life and the lives of her family members and ancestors, racism always acts as a character in Taylor's work—even at times when no white characters appear at all—often invisible yet ever present, insidious, invasive, and persistent. For over forty-five years, Taylor's books have made clear not just to Americans but to readers abroad as well: white supremacy and the history of the United States are inextricably linked. Racism, discrimination, and white supremacy are, indeed, key founding principles of this nation. While Taylor's books all belong to the genre of historical fiction and therefore immerse readers in a time and place decades prior to their own lived experience, the truths they tell are just as relevant today as they were in the years the books were published, starting with *Song of the Trees* (*Song*) in 1975. In 2004, Taylor commented in an interview with *Contemporary Authors*: "It is my hope that to children who read my books, the Logans will provide those heroes missing from the schoolbooks of my childhood—Black men, women, and children of whom they can be proud" (Peacock 119). Her works have done this, and they have also given young readers a window into several eras of African American history, filling in gaps that many school curricula ignore or erase, as well-written historical fiction can do so powerfully. These stories help readers *care* about what happened in times past. Informative and moving stories, wrapped in Mildred Taylor's adept storytelling, foster both understanding and empathy in readers.

This anthology has taken well over five years to complete (including through the COVID-19 pandemic), and the publication process will likely take an additional year, and we appreciate the patience of the contributors with the iterative process necessary for bringing this many voices together.

We feel that the diverse backgrounds of the contributors is an important aspect of this anthology. Had one of us written the book as a monograph, that polyphony of voices and variety of perspectives would not have emerged. This anthology has been coedited by two white scholars (Tammy is American; Sarah British) who wrote their dissertations on Taylor's work and an African American scholar (Michelle) who has written extensively on Taylor's texts. Our combined interest in Taylor's writing represents several decades of commitment.

We have undertaken the task of coediting an anthology of critical essays about the works of Mildred D. Taylor for a number of reasons. First, *Roll of Thunder, Hear My Cry* (*Thunder*) (1976), the best known of Taylor's works, was the second novel written by an African American to win the John Newbery Medal. Although the Newbery Medal celebrated its 100th anniversary in 2022, only five other African Americans have won this award: Virginia Hamilton in 1975 for *M. C. Higgins, the Great* (1974); Christopher Paul Curtis in 2000 for *Bud, Not Buddy* (1999); Kwame Alexander in 2016 for *The Crossover* (2015); Jerry Craft in 2020 for *New Kid* (2019), the first graphic novel to win the Newbery ("Celebrating"); and Amina Luqman-Dawson in 2023 for *Freewater* (2022). And since Mildred Taylor has been publishing books for young people since 1975, her books have also played a significant role in shaping late twentieth-century and early twenty-first-century children's and young adult literature. Younger Black writers like Jacqueline Woodson, Kekla Magoon, and Angie Thomas and Black Lives Matter cofounder Patrisse Cullors credit Taylor with paving the way for them and modeling what it could mean to be an African American writer.

Despite her longevity in the field, Mildred Taylor's works have received very little critical attention. At the publication of this work, we have found twelve PhD dissertations and one Master's thesis on Taylor's works. Aside from one biography, teaching guides, and two books that partially analyze Taylor's texts, this is the first critical book focusing solely on the works of Mildred Taylor. We hope that this collection on Taylor's work will help to safeguard the series' historical and still relevant place in children's and young adult literature since academic research also plays a key role in canon building.

We created this anthology in part because we don't want the Logan Family Saga to become another *Uncle Tom's Cabin*: most Americans know about this book, but very few have actually read it. Taylor's works hold a revered place in American children's literature because of *Thunder* winning the Newbery Medal, but we believe they need to be elevated to a better-informed place. While *Thunder* is often assigned in undergrad teacher preparation and children's literature programs in the US and the UK, the curricula of many of these programs default to the white canon. If the white canon is what preservice teachers know, it's what they teach when they enter the classroom. Through publishing this anthology, we hope to support the use of these texts in schools and colleges. We want readers and scholars to remember and study these texts and acknowledge their significance going forward in the same way white canonical children's literature texts are.

INTRODUCING THE ESSAYS IN THIS VOLUME

Students in several of Michelle's graduate classes—Multicultural Resources for Youth as well as Cultural History of Children's and Young Adult Literature classes at the University of Washington, and African American Children's and Young Adult Literature History at Hollins University—helped to select the essays, drafted the essays' summaries, and proposed ways to organize them. They also prepared feedback for the authors on their drafts. At the suggestion of the students in the Hollins class, we have adopted a structure for the volume that would mirror Taylor's own literary strategy of moving from a character's interior life into connections with others and the experience of being perceived by others. Still mirroring Taylor, we then move into essays that consider the structures and systems of the wider social, economic, legal, and environmental context, and, finally, essays that address the need for activism and education in response to the failings of historical American structures and systems.

After two celebratory poems and an introduction, the volume opens with a section on the self, with character interiorities that are shaped by being racialized and gendered. We see how Taylor's characters go through processes of personal development, learning from older generations and their own experiences, followed by the ways in which Taylor highlights different points of view and ways of interacting with the world. **Latrice Ferguson** explores the silences in African American family life, using the Logan family's struggles and triumphs, demonstrating how Taylor's storytelling transcends the silence Black women are expected to maintain. **Shelly Shaffer, Melissa Bedford, and Ann Van Wig** apply gender schema theory and critical race theory to *Let the Circle Be Unbroken* (*Circle*), *Road to Memphis* (*Memphis*), and *All the Days Past, All the Days to Come* (*Days*), examining how Cassie Logan navigates and understands the intersections of race and gender, highlighting the ways Taylor demonstrates Cassie's growth from childhood to an adulthood shaped by shifting beliefs about race and gender. **Helen Bond** illustrates the influence of W. E. B. Du Bois's concepts of the Veil, double consciousness, and second sight in Mildred Taylor's work. **Jani Barker** outlines Taylor's construction of different implied readers in *Days*, unearthing Taylor's use of emotional connections with readers and intellectual lessons that provide powerful, yet fundamentally different, antiracist identifications for Black readers and readers of color compared to white readers.

In the second section, authors analyze ways in which the Logans have been reimagined by illustrators, filmmakers, and translators. This section of the volume moves from interior to exterior, featuring essays that examine how Cassie and the other Logans have been depicted, adapted, and reimagined. **Ngozi Onuora and Sabrina Carnesi** specifically focus on the history of the cover illustrations of Mildred Taylor's Logan books, focusing on the three main illustrators of the series: Jerry Pinkney, Max Ginsburg, and Kadir Nelson. **Devika Mehra** discusses children's agency in the film adaptation of *Thunder* in relation to film industry changes in the 1960s and 1970s. **Bahar Eshraq** examines three of Taylor's works translated into Persian, using Juri Lotman's five stages of reception theory.

As Cassie's world expands in size and scope, her early lessons in the importance of land and the law remain central. As the chapters in the third section highlight, land and law are used as tools of white supremacy, backed by violence and false narratives. **Susan Browne and Wanda Brooks** discuss how Taylor approaches white supremacy in *Thunder*, *The Well*, and *The Friendship*, identifying core themes through which Taylor provides a counternarrative to white supremacy and ways of reclaiming the narrative. **Lauren Rizzuto's** chapter on environmental justice and **Emily Cormier's** chapter on Black agrarianism further illustrate this reclamation. **Catharine Kane's** chapter juxtaposes *Thunder* and *Circle* with Harper Lee's *To Kill a Mockingbird*, showing that Taylor gives Black characters more agency to critique and reshape the justice system than does Lee.

The final section of this volume highlights the enduring legacy of Taylor's work. Two of the chapters, those by **Annette Wannamaker** and by **Bryanna Somers**, place Angie Thomas's blockbuster debut, *The Hate U Give*, in conversation with Taylor's *Thunder*, emphasizing the activism, care ethics, and pedagogical opportunities of each text. In the final chapter, **Jennifer Ansbach** traces the representation of the civil rights movement within Taylor's work.

The writing of the Logan books is over, but the work is not done. In 2021, Taylor won the American Library Association's Children's Literature Legacy Award, and Committee Chair Junko Yokota commented: "Taylor's storytelling shows how courage, dignity, and family love endure amidst racial injustice and continues to enlighten hearts and minds of readers through the decades" (Coyne). We believe that as long as racism and discrimination exist in the US, the UK, and elsewhere, Taylor's works will be relevant. In light of the hard work that these contributors have done to help us bring this anthology to fruition, we hope that this history of activism acts as a call to action for our own readers, giving further encouragement and support to those already dedicated to fighting for change and prompting others to consider how they can take the lessons embedded in the Logan Family Saga forward in their own everyday lives and work.

WORKS CITED

"Celebrating Black Newbery Honorees and Winners." DC Public Library. (https://www.dclibrary.org/node/69142).

Coyne, John. "Peace Corps Writer of 2021—Mildred D. Taylor (Ethiopia)." Peace Corps Worldwide. https://peacecorpsworldwide.org/mildred-d-taylor-peace-corps-writer-of-2021/.

Fogelman, Phyllis J. "Mildred D. Taylor." *The Horn Book Magazine*, vol. 53, no. 4, Aug. 1977, pp. 410–14.

Khan-Cullors, Patrisse, and Asha Bandele. *When They Call You a Terrorist: A Black Lives Matter Memoir*. Canongate Books, 2018.

Peacock, Scott. "Mildred D. Taylor." *Children's Literature Review*, vol. 90, edited by Scott Peacock, Gale Group, 2004, pp. 119–49.

Taylor, Mildred D. *All the Days Past, All the Days to Come*. Viking, 2020.

Poetic Tribute

Homemade Love
Sower. Weaver. Receiver.

Raen Parker Washington

Sunken as seeds in good ground.
Seeding Promise. Sowing Intersectionality.
Weavers of wonderment. Sorrow. Joy.

Wildflowers and Forget-Me-Nots
Uncloister in a vale of trees
To ne'er forget what crawls out of your soul
Prickles like possumhaw bushes and
Sweetgum balls—reddened bark limned
By its own deceptive beauty
Playful pines needle-shaped leaves,
Royal Oak leaf varieties and majestic maple leaves
Sweet psithurism whispers and softly sings songs of the Trees.

This is our land. Our piece of heaven to:
Play. Plant. And Plow disparate thinking and wondering.
Ploy. Plains and planes of humanity till and disrupt
Rows of pride, power and purpose.
And familial glory rears and rests in its promise.

We be ancestors' prayerful dreams across waters and lands
With tucked possessions in loomed hair

Seeds of promise–in plain sight.
Of new life. Of new ways.
Of holding space to nourish souls, spirits and feed life unto family.

Oh yes with dashes of grace, mercy and side-eyed stances
Daring blossoms and incoherent uncertainties to
Bloom and Crown.
You
See
Us.

Part 1

The Self: Intersectionality and
Insider/Outsider Perspectives

The Story in the Silence
Reading Between the Lines in Mildred D. Taylor's Logan Family Saga

Latrice Ferguson

In the 2010s when tracing family ancestry was in vogue, and the PBS series *Finding Your Roots* premiered, I, like many, decided to trace my family's history. In hindsight, I acknowledge my intentional first step was not to speak with my grandmother, Yvonne Ferguson, but instead to trust the library and archives. I had already learned that there would be no stories about our family's past shared around the hearth. My grandmother was silent about her parents and never mentioned her grandparents. Of course, archives failed me as well because history favors the oppressors, not the oppressed. However, about a year ago, I learned this story about the grandmother I had lived with for most of my life. She was born in the spring of 1935 in Lexington, Mississippi, to sharecropper parents. Upon her birth, she became the responsibility of her ten-year-old sister Emmajean. Six years later, Emmajean decided to migrate to Chicago, and shortly after my grandmother was sent to live with her.

When I first read *Roll of Thunder, Hear My Cry* (*Thunder*), I found joy in the characters and the story, but upon rereading it, I also realized a large part of the series' appeal was a family history lost to me. While it is true that the Logan Family Saga can teach readers stories missing from mainstream American historical narratives, the series can also be (and likely has also been) a balm for Black Americans in search of their family's history. In the introduction to the 40th Anniversary Edition of *Thunder*, Jacqueline Woodson describes the impact that seeing herself in Taylor's first novel had on her writing. She says, "To pick up a book and find so much of myself on the pages was amazing. But more than that, *Roll of Thunder, Hear My Cry* helped me understand the story of so many people's lives over the years" (*Thunder* i). I do not think it's a stretch to imagine that some of those people included Woodson's own family members. In a 2016 article from the *Pittsburgh Post-Gazette*, Woodson describes the difficulty of putting together the pieces of her family's narrative in her memoir *Brown Girl Dreaming*. She says, "My family wouldn't talk about enslavement, wouldn't talk about sharecropping, wouldn't talk about working in White folks' kitchens, because it was such a deeply painful memory" (Hakim). My family, too, wanted to leave pain in the past, and as a young person, I learned to "stay out of grown folks' business." It has taken years for the limited details of my grandmother's story to unfold for me, and what I have already shared here is the entirety. When I first read the Logan Family Saga, set in small-town Mississippi, with its World War II veterans and northern migration story, it became easy to overlay it atop my own family narrative. However, the Logan family story is not my own, and much like Mildred D. Taylor's family narratives inspired her work, this chapter, inspired by my own family story, is attuned to how the silences function in the Logan Family Saga and explores the relationship between the story and the silence.

The story and the silence work hand in hand in the oral histories of Black families. Gaps emerge due to the frequency of premature death in Black families, forced family separation, and the privileging of patriarchal narratives; these all result in breaks in Black family histories. Those breaks widen because memory and pain at times obscure what would be considered truth or what parts of a family's narrative are passed along. In *Growing Up with the Country*, Kendra Field uses her own family archives as a primary resource for seeking information about the Black experience postemancipation. While Field followed leads through her family histories, at times, the story's details had been changed or obscured along the way. She writes about the distance between history and memory, the spoken and the silenced. The histories were carried by women, but the stories centered men while hiding the trauma and experiences of her foremothers. She calls these "hidden transcripts" (8), and they are significant in understanding the lives of Black women. Additionally, and likely, Black women remain silent because their stories often face significant critique and scrutiny. For example, in 1968 Maya Angelou released her first in a series of autobiographies, *I Know Why the Caged Bird Sings*. It garnered mostly critical acclaim and has been published in many languages around the world. However, Angelou's critics questioned the truth in her autobiographies and debated whether they should be reclassified as something other than autobiography. In some cases, her work has even been dubbed autobiographical fiction. Despite being aware of the conventions of autobiography as representations of truth, Angelou has said that she has on occasion fiddled with the facts, combining several characters for literary effect or to be considerate of people still alive. She once said in an interview with Oprah Winfrey, "I write so I can get closer to all, tell so much truth. Not facts. Because facts can obscure the truth. You tell so many facts, the places where, people who, times when, the reasons why, blah blah blah, never getting the truth" (Angelou). Despite acknowledging that her books may not be strictly factual, Angelou stands firm in her works as being truthful autobiography. Angelou is not alone in constructing her own narrative truth, despite what people might consider factual. Zora Neale Hurston's autobiography, *Dust Tracks on a Road*, has long been accused of stretching the details, along with Billie Holiday's *Lady Sings the Blues*. Much like the women in Field's family, the accounts of the past may not align with archives, but the tellings might offer a more significant truth, by Angelou's definition, or hide the pain of the past.

Black American oral histories cannot be read without being attuned to the gaps, silences, and retellings. What remains untold is just as significant as what is told. Voice and silence have long been discussed and analyzed in African American literature, particularly their significance in African American women's literature. In 1989 Mae Gwendolyn Henderson argued that "in their works, Black women writers have encoded oppression as a discursive dilemma, that is, their works have consistently raised the problem of the Black woman's relationship to power and discourse" (Henderson). The transition from silence to voice to storytelling are central to narratives of Black women. Taylor's Logan Family chronology engages in a similar relationship between silence and telling, voice and voicelessness, and agency that is impacted so significantly by the racial oppression the family experiences in their Mississippi town. Additionally, the books themselves function as a voice that talks back to the widespread histories told in classrooms in the United States. There is tension within the representation of freedom, justice, and counterhistory that silence uncovers. While the series ends with the fight for voting rights in Mississippi and a hopeful, triumphant epilogue at former President Obama's inauguration, the silences make clear that progress is not linear, nor have the concerns of the characters been resolved in the present. The ending of the series is uneasy while it can be read as progressive and triumphant, especially since its publication date was 2020. Taylor, as a part of a larger Black literary tradition, subtly troubles the progressive narrative of Black attainment. I argue that embedded within the characters themselves, as expressed in their moments of silence, the ongoing project of overcoming the impact of white supremacy within Black families and communities becomes noticeable, undermining the triumphant series conclusion. The characters in the family use silence to protect them directly from the threat of violence and white supremacy, but also to protect against strong emotions like shame, anger, and grief.

The white supremacist structure that governs the social and political environment in Mississippi weighs heavily on all nine books of the series. Many of the major conflicts across the series occur because of the dangers associated with racism and violence by white characters in the novels. A central conflict in *Thunder* is Cassie's developing understanding of the Mississippi social structure she must navigate, at times, for her own safety. While pacing on the streets of Strawberry, Cassie accidentally bumps into Lillian Jean Simms, a white girl from her town. Lillian Jean, upset with Cassie, says, "You can't watch where you going, get in the road. Maybe that way you won't be bumping into decent white folks with your nasty little self" (114). Angry and humiliated, Cassie refuses to move to the street: "I ain't nasty . . . and if you're so afraid of getting bumped, walk down there yourself" (114). When Cassie resists Lillian Jean's attempts to push Cassie into the street, Mr. Simms, Lillian Jean's father, grabs Cassie and pushes her into the street onto her bottom. He then tells her to apologize to "Miz Lillian Jean." Cassie expects that her grandmother, Big Ma (Caroline), will come to her rescue, and they will leave the scene. Instead, Big Ma makes Cassie apologize to Lillian Jean.

This familiar scenario offers a great model to consider the silences wrought by white supremacy and the way that silence serves as a response. Mr. Simms enforces the white social hierarchy from which Cassie had, up until then, been mostly sheltered, especially compared to other children her age. The Simmses are poor, and for that reason, as Mama tells Cassie, "Mr. Simms [holds] on to that belief harder than some other folks because they have little else to hold on to. For him to believe that he is better than we are makes him think that he's important, simply because he's white" (129). This forceful introduction to white supremacy leaves both Cassie and Big Ma without recourse to respond or speak out in that moment. Instead, they must, out of fear, bottle up their feelings about the injustice and remain silent in response to Mr. Simms's racism. Despite experiencing this event together and Cassie's confusion about Big Ma's response, it is Mama, not Big Ma, who explains to Cassie what occurred and what Big Ma must be feeling. Big Ma does not speak to Cassie at all about the experience or their shared shame and anger. Mama tells Cassie that Big Ma "did what she had to do," and "she didn't like doing it one bit more than you did" (125). After explaining to Cassie what has happened, Mama says that Cassie "has done enough growing up for one day" (130). Black parents, like Caroline and Mary, hope to shield their children from the pain of racism while also preparing them to live within racist structures. Cassie's mother and grandmother struggle to navigate the dichotomy between maintaining their children's innocence and keeping them safe in the Jim Crow South. Cassie makes clear that her mother and grandmother do not coddle her and her siblings. "They said the whippings were to keep us alive, for we needed to know and follow rules, and that no Black person in Mississippi could survive without following those rules" (*Days* 15). The women frequently care for Cassie and her brothers as David often works away from the family home to make sure the family can pay the mortgage. Black mothers frequently bear the burden of responsibility for Black people's assumed delinquency. Wider society often portrays Black women as emasculators, enablers, immoral, and lascivious (Giddings 30). Throughout the series, the burden to maintain the home and secure the land, while David works in different locales, falls on Mary and Caroline. Clearly, they find protecting the land, caring for the children, and maintaining the farm difficult, but they rarely speak of their anger, sadness, shame, and fear. They do this to keep the children from worrying and because their emotions have no solutions. When Caroline demands that Cassie apologize to Lillian Jean Simms after Mr. Simms pushes her into the street, Cassie's anger extends to her grandmother as well as to her perpetrators. She does not perceive Big Ma's fear and shame at the injustice, and Cassie never learns of it from Big Ma. The grandmother and granddaughter do not get the opportunity to process their anger and shame together. Instead, Big Ma leaves Cassie to reconcile their shared experience, Cassie's first encounter with the harshness of white supremacy, without her.

By looking at the series through the silences, these examples illustrate what the family members feel is worth talking about and what is not. Mary Logan has taught at Great Faith Elementary for over fourteen years. Although she has over a decade of experience, the other teachers perceive her as a "disrupting maverick" and "a bit too radical" (*Thunder* 31). She wants to teach her children and her pupils to be critical thinkers. When Miss Crocker, Cassie and Little Man's teacher, accuses Mary of spoiling and not teaching the children "how things are" in Mississippi, Mary responds, "that doesn't mean they have to accept them" (30). And Cassie and Little Man do not. When Miss Crocker gives the children "new" books, Cassie and her brother refuse them because, along with being incredibly damaged and in "poor" condition, the inside cover says they are designated for "nigra" children. Miss Crocker punishes them for disrupting the class, but Mary understands their indignation because she has taught them to value themselves. In response, Mary glues paper to the inside book covers to hide the offensive condition and negative labels. When she teaches history, she does not shy away from "the cruelty of it; of the rich economic cycle it generated as slaves produced raw products for the factories in the North and Europe; how the country profited and grew from the free labor of a people still not free" (228). Mary speaks out against the lies in the textbook seemingly without fear even when two white men from the school board, Harlan Granger and Kaleb Wallace, arrive to observe what she teaches in her class. For Mary, the importance of the lesson justifies the risk. Harlan Granger, Kaleb Wallace, and another member of the school board fire her and take away her public platform to teach the children a history counter to that represented in the board-approved textbook.

Much like the aftermath of Big Ma and Cassie's trip to Strawberry, Mary keeps silent about her grief at losing her position at the school. Papa tells the children how much teaching means to their mother. He tells Cassie and her siblings "she's born to teaching like the sun is born to shine. And it's gonna be hard on her not teaching anymore. It's gonna be real hard 'cause ever since she was a wee bitty girl down in the Delta she wanted to be a teacher" (187). David tells the children the sacrifices Mary's father made to get her through school to achieve her dream. Throughout the rest of the series, Mary's love of teaching surfaces in her interaction with her children but also in her dedication to helping others in the community study for the Mississippi Constitution test. Similar to Big Ma's silence about the Strawberry incident, Mary keeps her grief and anger about losing her teaching job to herself. When David must leave to work to pay the taxes on the land, the women must be strong to secure the farm. While they struggle with a variety of fears and emotions, rarely do they express them with their children or even with other adults. Since Cassie narrates the story, perhaps those emotions get expressed beyond the realm of Cassie's knowing, but the reader can see that Caroline and Mary cope by simply moving forward. Cassie's two mother figures do what needs to be done regardless of the stress.

The decision to be silent rather than speak can, in addition to shielding shame and grief, contain feelings too complex for words. *The Land*, the first in the series chronologically and set in the 1800s, highlights the specific dangers at the intersection of Blackness and womanhood. Paul-Edward Logan, this book's narrator, is born to Deborah, a Georgia enslaved woman and her enslaver, Edward. In the early chapters of the book, Paul-Edward struggles to understand the nature of his parents' relationship, and it causes him significant strife. Edward teaches his Black children to read and write, and each day his white children share what they learn in school with their Black siblings. The children, Cassie (the first), Paul-Edward, Hammond, George, and Robert share dinners together whenever Edward does not have guests in their home. Although Deborah, Paul-Edward and Cassie's mother, serves as a cook and housekeeper, she never shares meals with the family, even after Edward's wife dies. Only after being dismissed from his father's dinner table at eleven does Paul-Edward grow resentful of his place within the family. "That was truly the first time I felt unwanted in my daddy's family. My daddy hadn't even bothered to tell me himself not to sit at his table. He had left that to my mama, and I resented not only him for it, but her too" (*Land* 50). Paul-Edward's resentment toward his father and mother echoes Cassie's towards Big Ma.

Deborah keeps silent about her experience with Edward. Readers understand only through conversations that Paul-Edward has with his siblings that Deborah has never consented to her "relationship" with Edward. The enslaver/enslaved power relationship thus silences Deborah's ability both to choose the father of her children and to speak out against him. Deborah says little directly about the nature of her relationship with Edward, but Cassie and Hammond both share with Paul-Edward what they were told. Hammond says: "Let's just say she told me my daddy, when he was a young man, was at first same as any fox in a henhouse where the hens couldn't get out, and she asked me if I'd be any different than my daddy if the war hadn't come and all the young chicks were still in the henhouse with no say in their taking" (55).

Cassie is much more forthright: "You're talking as if you think she had a choice about the thing.... Paul, she was his property, just like everything else around here" (61). Through these conversations, we understand that Deborah, like many enslaved women, was subject to sexual violence and rape at the hands of her enslaver. While Deborah does not speak about the nature of her relationship with Edward, in past conversations and observances, Paul mentions that his mother refuses to sit at the table at dinners. He learns that when Edward's wife died, Deborah, unwilling to take on the role of mother for Edward's other children, did not nurse Robert, born shortly after Paul. Deborah finds ways to assert her agency first as an enslaved person and then as a free woman who knows that if she tries to leave, Edward would come after her and her children (61). Silence offers Deborah both freedom and power within the narrative. When Deborah does not speak in detail about her relationship with Edward, the reader cannot assume that she feels shame, joy, pain, or love. A level of freedom comes with silence because she does not have to explain, apologize, or make amends. It does not matter, nor it is anyone's business, why she stays on Logan land postemancipation or why she will not share a meal with the family but will join Edward for a drink at the table. What does matter to Deborah is giving her children something of their own. Deborah's narrative reveals that silence can contain the complex and, perhaps, contradictory emotions that people are capable of experiencing at once, and that Black women are often denied in mainstream representation. Silence around sexual violence against Black women extends beyond *Land* through decades and generations of Logan women to the last book in the series.

Black women may find solace in silence, but they also learn silence to protect themselves from the impact that racism and sexism can have on their lives. While working as a secretary, Cassie (the second) finds herself in a potentially dangerous situation with her supervisor. While Deborah's vulnerability accompanies her enslaved status, Cassie's vulnerability as a Black woman trying to make a living results from working for Mr. Tomlinson, a Black man, who has more power than she. Cassie made the decision to live with and work for Mr. Tomlinson and his wife for both economic and safety reasons to avoid the dangers of being a single woman living alone. Unfortunately, she does not find safety in their home. While knowledgeable of Cassie's precarity, her coworker keeps silent about the dangers Cassie faces as his secretary who also lives in his home. Justine only hints, suggesting that if Cassie "had a man, maybe Mr. Tomlinson wouldn't be so interested" (*Days* 149). Tomlinson makes advances that Cassie cannot directly defy. She also cannot speak out against him because he controls both her job and her housing. Justine might want to help Cassie but cannot actively confront Tomlinson on Cassie's behalf without risking her own job. Instead, she finds other, more subtle, ways to help keep Cassie safe. After Mr. Tomlinson attempts to sexually assault her in the office, Cassie does not confront Tomlinson or tell his wife of his advances. Like many Black women, Cassie does not report him to the authorities for fear of racism while seeking help, and adherence to Black cultural expectations to protect Black male offenders (Washington 1257). Instead, she protects herself from his advances while also keeping quiet, because to speak out could have significant consequences for her work and would likely be met with disbelief or inaction. Due to the direct impact of racism, Justine and Cassie have to navigate their precarity in silence or face negative impacts on their livelihoods. According to 2013 statistics from the US Department of Justice, for every Black woman who reports rape, fifteen will not ("Female Victims"). It is not a stretch to imagine that the numbers would be much higher nearly sixty years prior to this statistic. Cassie, Justine, and Deborah's silence within Taylor's texts represent the ways that Black women navigate the power structures within which they live.

Much like her mother and grandmother have done before her, as Cassie gets older, she learns from the women in her life to prioritize talking about injustice over her personal feelings of grief and heartbreak. As the series develops, speaking out against injustice, despite the cruelty of white supremacy, takes precedence over discussing personal, painful emotions. Emotional sacrifice dominates narratives about Black women. Those controlling images and stereotypes cast Black women as perpetually strong and dominant. Those descriptions often cast Black women as having "inordinate strength, with an ability for tolerating an unusual amount of misery and heavy, distasteful work. This woman does not have the same fears, weaknesses, and insecurities as other women" (Wallace 107). Cassie, and the women she emulates, in many ways embody this strength. However, they do it not because they are somehow stronger or more capable of bearing superhuman burdens but rather because society demands that Black women take on labor with few avenues for additional support. Much of the support that Cassie does receive comes from her family and the community, and from Great Faith Church, which is an important gathering place within the community. Cassie's two major sources of support also function to stifle her self-expression about emotionally significant moments in her life.

As a direct consequence of the impact of white supremacy upon Black women's bodies, Cassie's sexuality exists at the intersection of her faith and the controlling image of the Jezebel. The trope of the Jezebel characterizes Black women as sexual deviants. Respectability offered one tactic that Black women utilized to combat that interpretation of their bodies. As theorized by Darlene Clark Hine, Evelyn Brooks Higgenbotham, and, more recently, Brittney Cooper, Black women used respectability as a tool to navigate a hostile white America and reduce potential threats of violence and assault. Cassie deals with the misconceptions about Black women's sexuality on multiple occasions throughout the series. During a doctor's visit, she is humiliated when the physician tells her to get into position. When the doctor sees Cassie's confusion, he says, "come now, a pelvic exam has nothing to do with knowing the position. All colored girls know it, married or not" (*Days* 43). However, Cassie, because of her faith and the influence of her mother and grandmother, lives a chaste and Christian life. Cassie's mother and grandmother never speak with her about love or passion; instead she "had always been protected by [her] Papa, Mama, Big Ma by [her] brothers" (160). A large aspect of that protection is faith-based. While dating her future husband, Flynn, she says, "the teachings throughout my life forbade me from having sexual relations until I was married. To do so was not only considered a sin, but would have brought disgrace upon the family if it were known" (194). Flynn de Baca, a former Catholic, does not believe in organized religion, and Cassie's parents hope that she will marry both someone local and certainly someone Christian. Cassie, because of her faith and commitment to her family, is reluctant to introduce Flynn to them. Upon Flynn's accidental death, Cassie does not share her grief with family or anyone else. "To think of Flynn, to dwell on him, was too painful. When thoughts of Flynn came rushing in, I pushed them out again. I tried to concentrate on the now" (248). She does not speak about him even when her family asks, and she feels certain she will never marry or even love again after his death. Losing their baby early in their marriage compounds Cassie's grief as well. Her family insists, however, that she will find someone else and have children, but Cassie's unexpressed grief consumes her and leads to a breakdown. She cries alone in her family's woods where no one is there to comfort her. The only thing that takes her mind off her grief is her growing commitment to fighting for justice.

Black women often have their grief, other emotions, and mental health silenced in favor of social justice, their families, their children, and more. Black women frequently grapple with the expectation that they continue to labor in the face of grief and to be strong despite overwhelming circumstances. Among the reasons Black women do not report sexual assault is a sense of responsibility toward the Black community. Black women, at times, want to protect Black men from the justice system even if they are victimized by Black men (Washington 1257). Additionally, Black women scholars and authors have written about the consequences of their own self-sacrifice and silences. In *We Want to Do More Than Survive: Abolitionist Teaching and the Pursuit of Educational Freedom* (2019), Bettina Love mentions experiencing panic attacks after her children were born. She was sure that she was dying, but test results all returned normal. "But normal results only caused more stress. I was committed to the idea that I was dying a slow death" (149). After talking with her own mother, she realized her symptoms developed in response to the burden of Black motherhood and the pressure on Black women to be superhuman in the midst of the sometimes-overwhelming weight of racism, sexism, and poverty. Audre Lorde also discusses her silences and the stress she experienced after receiving a troubling diagnosis. She most regretted her silence because it did not offer any protection from the violence perpetrated against her as a Black woman (Lorde 41). The narrative around Black women as self-sacrificing superhumans has endured with significant consequences for Black women's mental and physical health and the perceptions surrounding their needs in society. Deborah, Caroline, Mary, and Cassie endure and sacrifice much without room to express their grief, pain, anger, or frustration because their labor keeps the family whole. However, their self-sacrifice has consequences. Their health and relationships suffer because they shelve their feelings. The fight for racial justice and group uplift eclipses the women's self-care and attention to their own wellbeing.

Cassie's character embodies the ways that the narrative prioritizes speaking against injustice and racial violence over expressing personal, internal emotion. Cassie stands firm against injustice at her job in Boston. As an attorney, she fights against unjust medical practices that Black people face. When she returns to Mississippi, she helps other activists who try to register community members to vote. The family speaks candidly with the children about the breeding of enslaved people, lynching, and rape, but so often personal and interpersonal emotions go unexpressed and unacknowledged. It is no surprise that Cassie eschews the attempts to settle into a domestic life in favor of a legal career that enables her to fight for justice. As Cassie grows up, her family pays more attention to the clothing she wears, the boys with whom she talks, and her future as a wife and mother. She resists those conversations and goes hunting with her brothers and holds her own with them. Cassie does not have any close female friends and frequently shows little patience for the female friends she does have, such as Sissy and later Justine. The women in her life are all mothers and wives. While Cassie does fall in love, marry, and get pregnant, she never fully embodies the role of a wife or mother. Her marriage ends abruptly with the death of her spouse, and her pregnancy ends in a miscarriage. She does not discuss her grief but instead buries it in her studies and work. Her pursuits lead to distance between her and her family, and by extension the South. In Boston, Cassie, though isolated, has access to spaces previously denied to her and can fight for Black equality using white resources. She dates a white man but is even more reluctant to speak about their relationship because of vocal resistance from her family.

For years, Cassie does not return home and only occasionally writes to her parents. Only the fight for justice brings her back and allows her to reconnect with her family, and this reconnection to the land fulfills her. Cassie's return to the South is a part of a larger trend back to Southern roots for many Black people. If the Great Northern Migration from 1916 to 1970 marked the movement of six million Black Americans northward for economic opportunities and hopes for equality, Cassie's return South, looking to reconnect with her family history, was an early forerunner to the trend of Black Americans heading back to the South during the 1970s and into the present (Commander 190; Frey 107). Hence, while she does not return to traditional womanhood in the form of marriage and motherhood, she does return home to the South and finds rejuvenation in her pursuit of justice. *All the Days Past, All the Days to Come* ends with Cassie grieving amongst the trees, committed to staying in Mississippi to fight for equality while she remains silent about her grief and intentional in her desire to protect herself from future pain.

The men of the series drive home Kendra Field's aforementioned "hidden transcripts." Even though Taylor centers the narratives of women in the series, the men seem more likely to express themselves in nuanced ways both at home and publicly. However, when they choose silence, it reveals significant differences in the ways masculinity and femininity function in the text and broader society. The men, particularly David and Hammer, share their thoughts and emotions with the members of the family. David does not fit easily into the box of a stoic father and provider. Instead, David's first appearances in *Song of the Trees* and *Roll of Thunder, Hear My Cry* starkly differ from each other in their representation of this Logan patriarch. In *Song*, David threatens to blow himself and everyone else up to keep Andersen and his lumber men from cutting down more of the trees. He says, "One thing you can't seem to understand Andersen . . . is that a Black man's always gotta be ready to die. And it don't make me no difference if I die today or tomorrow. Just as long as I die right" (43). The men cutting down the trees describe him as "crazy" (44) and "mean as an ole jackass" (22).

Alternatively, David appears in *Thunder* as a loving father, hugging and kissing his children and wife after a long time away. In *Let the Circle Be Unbroken*, he shares his grief about Stacey's disappearance with the other children when Mary does not. He says to them, "[Y]ou think I don't know how y'all feeling? . . . Got a great big empty spot that aches all the time and can't nothing fill it 'cept for Stacey to come home? Well, I know it 'cause I got it myself" (293). These two versions of David unearth the significance of the public and the private for Black men. In the public sphere, white supremacy excludes Black men from traditional access to masculine success. Black men were unable to achieve economic, political, and social successes associated with masculinity. When the fight for racial equality moved into the public sphere during the civil rights movement of the 1950s and '60s, the assertion "I am a Man" and well-dressed Black men in suits visually reintroduced a Black manhood that countered traditional stereotypes (Estes 7). For David, his public face illustrates power and the assertion of manhood. Alternatively, in a survey of Black men considering what manhood means to them in the present, economic success and caring for family were high on the list of attributes for manhood (Hammond and Mattis 120). Like the men surveyed, David's concern is caring for his family financially. The public, assertive manhood and private, family-oriented persona are at odds at times. Often it is the public-facing persona that men keep from the women in their lives. In *Song*, David does not tell his wife, mother, or children, aside from Stacey, that he has arrived and if the lumber men do not acquiesce to his demands that they leave, he will end his life, the lives of the people threatening his property, and unknowingly the children's lives too. The short story concludes with an end to the standoff, leaving only hollow silence. David's assertion that Black men must be ready to die alludes to more current and significant ideologies in the present. Black death during David's present as well as in contemporary America is commonplace, so much so that being ready to die and the expectation of death are ever present. Claudia Rankine describes the proliferation of Black death on television and cell phone screens as a recapitulation of what has always been. Black bodies: "dying in ship hulls, tossed into the Atlantic, hanging from trees, beaten, shot in churches, gunned down by the police or warehoused in prisons: historically, there is no quotidian without the enslaved, chained or dead Black body to gaze upon or to hear about or to position a self against" (Rankine).

While David's land offers him hope and something worth fighting for, the ubiquitous presence of death threatens Black hope. Cornel West argues that at times throughout history there were "powerful buffers to ward off the nihilistic threat, to equip Black folk with cultural armor to beat back the demons of hopelessness, meaninglessness, and lovelessness" that are always present in the fight for equality and justice (14). Black men and their silences seem to emerge from the conflicts between public and private expressions of masculinity and the struggle for hope when death feels ever present.

Silences between Black women and men highlight an ongoing and painful struggle and interaction between racial equality and gender equality. Throughout the series, the camaraderie between the men and women seems positive. Cassie and her siblings support each other, and husband and wife pairs seem to work together to raise their families. However, moments of rupture also surface throughout the series. Masculinity under an oppressive state often causes those ruptures. Cassie feels incredibly close to her brother Stacey, but as he gets older, the distance between them begins to widen. She notices changes in him. He becomes private and quiet, choosing to spend time away from his younger siblings. Cassie asks her mother about this, and her response is that "he's looking for room. He's changing and he's looking for his life to change too" (*Circle* 253). The change that Stacey seeks comes with assuming traditional masculine responsibility within the family. He sees his family's financial struggles and believes it is his responsibility to take care of them while his father is away despite his young age. Once he is older, he decides to leave Mississippi, leaving his wife, Dee, and two children—both under two—with the extended family for a time. Dee's brother, Ola, tells her why Stacey leaves so suddenly. Stacey refuses to talk with Dee beyond saying he plans to go whether she likes it or not while she unpacks the things he's packing. The silence between them represents the larger, at times, dichotomous relationship between Black men and women, spawned and cultivated by racism and patriarchy. David and Mary have conversations like Dee and Stacey: men leave for opportunities to support their families. While they are gone, the women in their lives feel their absence. Mothers miss sons, and wives miss husbands. Mildred Taylor, no doubt a product of her time, was aware of prevailing narratives perpetuated by the Moynihan Report that villainized Black women for larger problems preventing African American advancement. As a product of the South and a listener to family stories, she complicates the narrative of absent Black fathers and dominant Black mothers. The men must leave to support their families, and women must be strong to protect their children from potential white terrorist violence. Black couples struggle at times to communicate while facing such violence.

Only two characters in the Logan family are not bound by the silencing nature of white supremacy—Ma Rachel and Hammer—but even so, they are framed in significantly different ways. Cassie and her siblings warmly embrace their Uncle Hammer in his first appearance in the series, despite that Cassie describes him as having "an aloofness in him which the boys and I could never quite bridge" (*Thunder* 119). Hammer, unlike David, does not seem to have a public and a private masculine persona. Instead, he overtly, dangerously, stands up against white supremacy. While Hammer expresses more emotion, in many ways, than some other members of the family, he remains largely emotionally unreachable. Ma Rachel, too, is incredibly vocal and emotionally vulnerable with her family, but the family often silences her for her safety and theirs. They describe her as "touched in the head," a euphemism for what we now understand as dementia. In *The Well*, after a much younger David and Hammer get into trouble with neighboring white boys, the sheriff and the boys' father, McCallister Simms, arrive with the intent to punish the Logan boys. The sheriff and Simms demand that Caroline whip David and Hammer in front of them. While Caroline does what the sheriff tells her to do to protect David and Hammer, Ma Rachel yells, "[D]on't cha whip them boys, Caroline!" and "We's free now!" Despite Ma Rachel's fervor, her exclamations are ignored, not just by Caroline, who does what she must, but also by the white men, who dismiss her forthrightness as insanity. Ma Rachel's voice and emotional expression only seem to be allowed because she's framed as demented and is an older woman.

The Logan Family Saga's longest, most baffling silence lies in the gap between the death of David Logan and Cassie's attendance at the inauguration of President Barack Obama. Taylor's decision to include the election in her narrative is likely meant to feel like a resolution and a triumph. Ultimately though, the silences prohibit a reading that is finite, triumphant or progressive. While Cassie had fought for voting rights in Mississippi in 1963 and her ride to Washington DC in 2008 follows the route of the Freedom Riders of 1961, progress during that time has been limited and frequently undermined by the continued tide of racism. Black people collectively struggle to overcome the trauma of the past at the macro level—collective legislative advancement—and the micro level—healing the selves. The Logan family series may have helped me imagine the story of my family's history, but it was not my family's narrative, and the gaps still remain. The work for freedom and justice did not end with the election of the first Black president. It is necessary to engage in the silence and the anger, melancholy, and doubt that hide within it because, in the case of Taylor's series, there is more history to be learned between 1963 and 2008. Also, the characters grapple with heavy emotions that many Black people still struggle to manage and speak about. The notion of racial progress espoused by this text illustrates how authors overlay American democratic rhetoric within narratives of Blackness in children's literature. Paying attention to silences shows the inability to resolve the tensions within the series' own narrative arc. The Logan Family Saga offers a more detailed view of the Black experience in America often excluded from mainstream American textbooks. The series, like many histories, adheres to the ideology of history's upward trajectory, but reading the silences in the series illustrates that history's trajectory is neither linear nor completely progressive. Sadness, pain, violence, labor, and resilience occur in the dash between 1963–2008. In *Hope Draped in Black: Race, Melancholy, and the Agony of Progress*, Joseph R. Winters argues: "The category of progress—even as it has been used in different contexts to galvanize struggles for a better, more just world—harbors a pernicious side. This all-too-familiar concept often functions in public discourse to downplay tensions, conflicts, and contradictions in the present for the sake of a more unified and harmonious image of the future" (6).

Following the Logan family's journey through Cassie's encounter in Strawberry, Mary's termination from the school, Cassie's experience at the doctor's office, and the numerous painful and unjust encounters that family and community endure under white supremacy, ending the series in Washington in 2008 feels unfulfilling.

Reading the silence and the story offers an understanding of American history as significantly relevant to the present. In 2001 in Savannah, Georgia, a statue was erected to honor the history and horror of the transatlantic slave trade with a quote by author Maya Angelou. It reads, "We were stolen, sold and bought together from the African continent. We got on the slave ships together. We lay back to belly in the holds of the slave ships in each others' excrement and urine together, sometimes died together and our lifeless bodies thrown overboard together" (Contemporary Monuments). After protest from white residents, Angelou was asked to add an addendum to the quote that read "today we are standing up together, with faith and even some joy" (Commander 188). In a 2020 article for *The Horn Book* entitled "Our Modern Minstrelsy," Kekla Magoon argues that "Black creators . . . are constantly, inevitably engaging with white expectations for how we portray Blackness." She adds, "[F]or a long time now, the publishing industry has expected books about Black people to have a certain tone, cover certain ground and adhere to a particular narrative" (Magoon). White supremacy compels silence, evident in the addendum added to a statue about a brutal history and the challenges Black people face with being able to tell particular histories. Historical and oppressive silences have led to interpersonal silences around grief, love, and mental health as evidenced by Cassie's own inability to grapple with those emotions. The silences of the series echo the real experiences of Black people in America. My grandmother's early life is largely a mystery to me because there are some things that Black people struggle to share. Narratives of Blackness do not fit easily within the American narrative of progress, but because white supremacy compels silences both historically and interpersonally, they fit far more easily than they should.

WORKS CITED

Angelou, Maya. Interview by Oprah Winfrey. *Oprah's Super Soul Conversations*, May 19, 2013, https://www.bullhorn.fm/oprahssupersoulconversations/posts/2bVMQT3-dr-maya-angelou-part-2-best-advice-she-ever-received.

Commander, Michelle D. *Afro-Atlantic Flight: Speculative Returns and the Black Fantastic.* Kindle ed., Duke UP, 2017.

Contemporary Monuments to the Slave Past. https://www.slaverymonuments.org/items/show/1158.

Estes, Steve. *I Am a Man!: Race, Manhood, and the Civil Rights Movement.* U of North Carolina P, 2006. HeinOnline.

Field, Kendra Taira. *Growing Up with the Country: Family, Race, and Nation After the Civil War.* Yale UP, 2017. deGruyter eBooks Complete.

Frey, William H. *Diversity Explosion: How New Racial Demographics Are Remaking America.* Brookings Institution Press, 2015. JSTOR, https://www.jstor.org/stable/10.7864/j.ctt6wpc40.

Giddings, Paula. *When and Where I Enter.* Bantam Doubleday Dell Publishing Group, 2003.

Gill, Gurvinder, and Imran Rahman-Jones. "Me Too Founder Tarana Burke: Movement is Not Over." *BBC Newsbeat*, BBC, July 9, 2020.

Hakim Azzam, Julie. "Author Jacqueline Woodson Listens to Silences and History." *Pittsburgh Post-Gazette*, Feb. 24, 2016.

Hammond, Widom Powell, and Jacqueline S. Mattis. "Being a Man About It: Manhood Meaning Among African American Men." *Psychology of Men and Masculinities*, vol. 6, no. 2, 2005, pp. 114–26. *APA Psychnet*, doi: 10.1037/1524-9220.6.2.114.

Henderson, Mae. *Speaking in Tongues and Dancing Diaspora: Black Women Writing and Performing*. Oxford UP, 2014.

Lorde, Audre. *Sister Outsider: Essays and Speeches*. Crossing Press, 1984.

Love, Bettina. *We Want to Do More than Survive: Abolitionist Teaching and the Pursuit of Educational Freedom*. BEACON, 2019.

Magoon, Kekla. "Our Modern Minstrelsy." *The Horn Book*, June 17, 2020. https://www.hbook.com/story/our-modern-minstrelsy.

Rankine, Claudia. "The Condition of Black Life is One of Mourning." *The New York Times*, June 22, 2015. www.nytimes.com/2015/06/22/magazine/the-condition-of-Black-life-is-one-of-mourning.html?_r=0.

Sharpe, Christina Elizabeth. *In the Wake: On Blackness and Being*. Duke UP, 2016.

Taylor, Mildred. *All the Days Past, All the Days to Come*. Viking, 2020.

Taylor, Mildred D. *The Land*. Puffin Books, 2016.

Taylor, Mildred D. *Let the Circle Be Unbroken*. Puffin Books, 2016.

Taylor, Mildred D. *Roll of Thunder, Hear My Cry*. Dial Books for Young Readers, 2016.

Taylor, Mildred D. *Song of the Trees*. Illus. Jerry Pinkney. Puffin Books, an imprint of Penguin Random House, 2016.

US Department of Justice. "Female Victims of Sexual Violence," 1994–2010 (NCJ 240655). 2013.

Wallace, Michele. *Black Macho and the Myth of the Superwoman*. Kindle ed., Verso, 2015.

Washington, Patricia A. "Disclosure Patterns of Black Female Sexual Assault Survivors." Violence Against Women, vol. 7, no. 11, Nov. 2001, pp. 1254–1283, doi:10.1177/10778010122183856.

West, Cornel. *Race Matters*. New ed., e-book, Beacon Press, 2018.

Winters, Joseph Richard. *Hope Draped in Black: Race, Melancholy, and the Agony of Progress*. Duke UP, 2016.

"I Wanted to Write a Truthful History"

Intersections of Critical Race Theory and Gender Schema in Mildred D. Taylor's Work

Shelly Shaffer, Melissa J. Bedford, and Ann Van Wig

In Mildred D. Taylor's 1977 Newbery Award acceptance speech, she spoke about how her Logan family books "mirror a black child's hopes and fears from childhood innocence to awareness to bitterness and disillusionment" (qtd. in *Circle* v). In this chapter, we examine how characters change from childhood into adulthood through experiences that challenge their innocence. Analyzing Taylor's texts through multiple critical lenses offers an opportunity to unpack how these moments are impacted by character beliefs about gender and race.

We explore Taylor's *Let the Circle be Unbroken* (*Circle*) (1981), *The Road to Memphis* (*Memphis*) (1990), and *All the Days Past, All the Days to Come* (*Days*) (2020) using critical race theory (CRT) and gender schema theory (GST) to examine the intersectionality of how race and gender impact character identity. The texts selected represent key periods in the lives of Taylor's characters: childhood, adolescence, and adulthood. As the characters mature, their experiences become pivotal moments in the development of their identity. An example of the impact of these incidents is evident in the reflection by Cassie Logan included in *Days*. As Cassie reflects in the chapter "Time of Change (1960–1961)," several of the key events that she looks back on illustrate the connections between these novels.

> I thought about all the times I had put my pride aside, had tolerated the insults of whites, had been denied the rights all white folks had just because of the color of my skin . . . I thought often of when we were on

the [road to Memphis] to take Moe to the train to escape Mississippi and how I wanted to use the restroom at a gas station, a restroom for white women. I thought often of how I was so frightened by white men when they saw me standing in front of that restroom door that I fled in fear, slipped, and fell into the mud. I thought often of the white children taunting us as their school bus passed by my brothers and me, splashing muddy water over us, and how we had to scamper up the banks of the roadside to avoid being soaked [*Thunder*]. I thought often of all the insults, about all the days of humiliation. (*Days* 353–54)

By examining when critical race theory and gender schema theory intersect in Cassie's life, we analyze the ways Cassie's character has changed because of these interactions.

We begin by outlining scholarship related to critical race theory, specifically some of the key tenets that are relevant to our analysis of Mildred Taylor's work. The literature review includes a review of scholarship related to gender, specifically Black women and Africana womanism, and ends with key work related to intersectionality.

INTERSECTIONS OF CRITICAL RACE AND GENDER SCHEMA THEORY

As white and white-presenting scholars, our analysis of Mildred Taylor's novels—*Circle*, *Memphis*, and *Days*—relies on two major theories that intersect throughout these works: critical race theory and gender schema theory. There are times when one theory or the other begs more attention in each work; however, Taylor's characters often struggle with both racism and gender norms, illustrating the intersectionality that occurs between these two facets of society.

Critical Race Theory

When analyzing Taylor's novels, CRT offers an insight into many of the characters' experiences. With a foundation developed in legal studies, CRT examines race in conjunction with systemic issues related to power, injustice, and oppression (Ledesma and Calderon; Crenshaw, "Twenty Years"). CRT purports that racism is the norm within American culture and "a fundamental way of organizing society" (Sleeter 157). Christine Sleeter, as well as Jessica DeCuir and Adrienne Dixson, has identified key tenets of CRT. The tenets employed for this analysis are interest convergence, critique of

Table 1

Tenets of Critical Race Theory (CRT)	
Tenet of CRT	Description
Interest convergence	Relationships between race and the interests of white individuals; advancements had by people of color occur only when there are benefits for white people.
Critique of liberalism	Assertions of "neutrality" and "color blindness" are façades, concealing privilege and power, and maintaining the advantages of whites (Sleeter 160).
Experiential knowledge and counter-storytelling	Stories predominantly include the voices of the masses and "white worldviews" (Sleeter 162), while silencing the voices of people of color; the need for counter-stories comes from experiential knowledge of individuals viewed as marginalized.
Permanence of racism	The "realist view" that, as Bell states, "racism is a permanent component of American life," and that racism shapes governing domains, including politics, economics, and societal norms (as cited in DeCuir & Dixson 27).

Sources: DeCuir, Jessica T., and Adrienne D. Dixson. "'So When It Comes Out, They Aren't That Surprised That It Is There': Using Critical Race Theory as a Tool for Analysis of Race and Racism in Education." *Educational Researcher*, vol. 33, no. 5, 2004, pp. 26-31.; Sleeter, Christine. E. "Critical Race Theory and the Whiteness of Teacher Education." *Urban Education*, vol. 52, no. 2, 2017, pp. 155-169.

liberalism, experiential knowledge and counterstorytelling, and permanence of racism (see Table 1).

The racial injustices presented in *Circle*, *Memphis*, and *Days* impact the lives of both white and Black characters, and Taylor challenges readers to explore how power, injustice, and oppression shape their identities. Applying the tenets of CRT to Taylor's novels adds to our analysis by mapping specific episodes that illustrate how race is related to power, injustice, and ultimately, oppression. For example, in *Memphis*, Stacey returns to Strawberry as the proud owner of a beautiful car, but white and Black Southerners constantly question him about the car, including whether he has the *right* to own it. Stacey provides a counternarrative and challenges the white people's maintenance of the status quo of Black upward economic mobility, illustrating two CRT tenets: counterstorytelling and interest convergence. Stacey's car ownership counters the concept of interest convergence, which seeks to suppress Black economic status, as Stacey's ownership of a luxury car resists white people's concept of a limited economic status they believe Black people ought to occupy.

Gender Schema Theory

Gender schema theory (GST) (Bem; Starr and Zurbriggen) proves useful in examining the ways Taylor's characters enact gender within the narratives. According to Christine Starr and Eileen Zurbriggen, GST examines how people become gendered from an early age and the impact this gendering has on cognitive and categorical processing throughout their lifetimes (567). As children learn from their experiences, they generate "gender schema," which foster ideas about what it means to be masculine or feminine.

While scholarship employing GST to children's and young adult literature is limited, aspects of gender, such as gender roles and feminism, have been examined. Mary Trepanier-Street and Jane Romatowski examined the potential impact of children's literature on young children's perceptions of gender roles, noting that in early childhood, children have "gender-stereotypic" views of jobs assigned to "males and females" (158); however, they found that after exposure to nonstereotypical gender roles in children's literature, children had a more flexible view of occupational roles. Scholars have also employed a feminist lens to analyze gender within children's literature, finding the need for counterstories to assist in the "further [deconstruction of] hegemonic notions of gender" (Earles 384).

In addition to GST's application to children's literature, gender schema and norms have also been studied in Black feminist scholarship. Jasmine Abrams, Morgan Maxwell, and Faye Belgrave highlight the shared "complex and painful history of racial exclusion, discrimination, injustice, and economic hardship" (151) between Black women and men. These factors have influenced Black women and men's gender schema and their "gendered perceptions and roles" (151) that have been fostered within their community (Sharp and Ispa; Tenenbaum and Leaper). Abrams, Maxwell, and Belgrave continue by noting, "how Black women perceive and engage Black men is a byproduct of the interaction between shared environmental conditions and culturally specific gendered perceptions" (152). In their study, Randi Cowdery and colleagues found Black men and women often upheld gender roles, while also maintaining a balance, when in the best interest of the family. However, in regard to the concept of *power*, because Black men are often the recipients of negative treatment and lack power within larger society, Black women neutralize negativity by affording Black men more power within their culture.

While Black women negotiate their identities in relation to Black men within their communities, Clenora Hudson-Weems identified the concept of Africana womanism, and how women of African descent have their own "unique experiences, struggles, needs, and desires," within their culture (24). This includes an emphasis on the idea of "motherhood," which holds historical and cultural significance in Black culture (Pellerin 77). The identity of a woman of African descent is shaped by her race and her gender, including any oppression she faces for being female. The struggle of the Black community outweighs that of the Africana woman, so her racial identity takes precedence when it comes to overcoming oppression and fighting injustice. In her study, Pellerin found that Africana women frequently rejected media portrayals of Black women and wanted more "multidimensional representations of Africana womanhood" (84).

Rachelle Washington and Michelle Martin present an examination of women in Taylor's novels through the lens of Africana womanism. For example, as Cassie Logan finds her voice, she stands up and speaks out against injustice, with race rather than gender at the forefront; however, because she is a Black woman, this empowers other Black women to speak up. For example, in *Days*, Cassie speaks up and takes action in the women's restroom at the theater, where bathroom stalls are still segregated. Other Black women accept the injustice, but Cassie does not. Not only does Cassie use a white-only stall, but her friend uses one as well; Cassie's bravery empowers the other Black women in the restroom, which demonstrates Africana womanism. As Cassie matures throughout the Logan novels, she learns to navigate a racist society and to operate "in subversive modes" compared to more blatant defiance, which allows her to work the system in a way that garners further attention to inequalities and oppression (Washington and Martin 54).

Washington and Martin determine that female characters in the novels "embody a womanist perspective through their investment in African roots and traditions, as well as their advocacy of resistance and social justice" (40). While Cassie challenges these gender roles, she also tries to uphold cultural expectations. One example of this occurs in *Memphis* when Cassie insists on going on a hunt with the boys. This leads to an argument with Big Ma, who says, "I done told y'all and told y'all time and time again, a hunt ain't no place for a young lady! This girl, she got no business goin' huntin'! That's what menfolks s'pose to do!" (47). Big Ma argues that Cassie needs to start "taking on womanly ways," and Cassie responds, "I got womanly ways . . . I cook and wash dishes" (48). Eventually, Mary and David agree to allow Cassie to go hunting with her brothers. Before leaving, Cassie appeases Mary and Big Ma by trying on dresses for church to see which one "shows [Cassie] off best" (58). Soon it is time to go hunting, and Mary tells Cassie to wear an old skirt instead of pants because, "Hunting is one thing, but wearing pants at your age is another" (59). Ironically, it is acceptable for Cassie to go hunting with her brothers but unacceptable for her to wear pants. This example demonstrates two ways Cassie complies with gender norm expectations in her family: (1) doing household chores and (2) wearing skirts.

Furthermore, instances of Black men exerting male dominance are also present in Taylor's works. For example, Stacey and the other boys insist on protecting Cassie during their journey in *Memphis* or when Cassie must be escorted on a double date in *Days*. When discussing the disparity between male and female roles within Black culture, Devon Carbado states, "[W]hatever the status of Black girls, it is Black boys . . . who have the potential to become strong Black men, the potential to save themselves and thus the Black community" (7). Meanwhile, Black women are held to specific societal standards and experience oppression for both their race and gender. Through careful analysis of these novels, one can see how gender is enacted by both male and female characters in ways that support and challenge gender schema.

Intersectionality

To address connections between the multiple dimensions of identity, we draw on Kimberlé Crenshaw's work on intersectionality. Crenshaw coined the term *intersectionality*, first applying the word to the way "race and gender interact to shape the multiple dimensions" experienced by Black women ("Mapping the Margins" 1244). Referred to by many monikers, such as the "race-class-gender matrix," "interlocking systems of oppression," and the "intersectional approach" (Berger and Guidroz 1), intersectionality highlights and stresses the connections, or intersections, between concepts commonly associated with oppression. When employing intersectionality, the relationship between multiple identities such as a female (GST) person of color (CRT) is highlighted, bringing attention to the layers of oppression one person, or group of people, may face. Intersectionality also highlights the danger of "single-axis thinking," particularly when addressing social justice issues (Cho, Crenshaw, and McCall 787).

Within this chapter, the intersection between CRT and GST is examined to determine how it shapes the identities of various characters in these three Taylor novels. Examples include how characters change due to systemic issues of racism as well as gender issues through childhood, adolescence, and adulthood. Our chosen books span the lives of the Logan children, affording the opportunity for readers to see the evolution of Taylor's characters and their identities in relation to the intersectionality between CRT and GST.

METHODS OF INVESTIGATION

As we analyzed the intersectionality ("Mapping the Margins") between CRT and GST, we employed thick description (Geertz) to describe the way characters in the novels interpret, think about, and change due to their experiences with race and gender. The following table shows our combined analysis of the three novels using CRT, GST, and intersectionality. While a number of examples of CRT, GST, and intersectionality are present in Taylor's three novels, only the noted excerpts (see bolded items) will be further discussed and analyzed in this chapter.

Table 2

Novel	Critical Race Theory	Gender Schema Theory	Intersectionality
Let the Circle Be Unbroken	• TJ receives a guilty verdict from an all-white jury	• Mama talks to Papa about leaving for the railroad • Cassie feels jealous of Stacey paying attention to other girls	• **Mrs. Lee Annie Lees attempts to vote** • Cassie carries a picture of Jeremy Simms • David Logan (Papa) tells Cassie to never mix races in relationships • Black and white men flirt with Suzella, and Cassie is jealous • **Stuart punishes Uncle Bud for fathering Suzella with a white woman** • **Little Man uses the term "gal"** • Stuart/other white boys approach Jacey • **Uncle Hammer goes after Stuart after he talks to Jacey**
The Road to Memphis	• whites question Stacy's car ownership • Stuart/friends hunt Harris • Clarence suffers medical emergency	• Cassie wears pants instead of dresses • Cassie develops a crush on Solomon Bradley • Sissy gets pregnant	• **Cassie experiences discrimination at the gas station** • Moe escapes Strawberry
All the Days Past, All the Days to Come	• Cassie is the only Black lawyer in her firm • Civil rights incidents occur • Lawyer Tate experiences harassment for buying a house in a white neighborhood	• Cassie double dates until she's married • Cassie's boss in California sexually harasses her • Cassie is told again and again to get married	• **Cassie experiences discrimination at the movie theater** • Cassie dates a white man • **Cassie experiences harassment by the doctor in Toledo**

Coding Table for Mildred Taylor's *Circle*, *Memphis*, and *Days*. Bolded items are analyzed in the chapter.

INTERSECTIONS: "MISS LOGAN, I UNDERSTAND YOU'RE THE INSTIGATOR OF ALL THIS"

The following analyses discuss key scenes from the three chosen novels. These incidents were chosen because gender and race both play a role and influence the situation in important ways.

"I figure I's deserving of doing something I wants to do, white folks like it or not": A Black Woman's Right to Vote

Throughout the Taylor novels, systemic racism upheld by unjust laws is brought to the forefront. A particularly evocative instance occurs when Mrs. Lee Annie Lees attempts to register to vote in *Circle*. During this episode, characters in the text struggle with several tenets of CRT (i.e., permanence of racism, interest convergence, and counterstorytelling), along with gender roles within the community and society.

In *Circle*, readers meet Mrs. Lee Annie Lees, an African American woman close to the Logan family. One day, Mrs. Lee Annie Lees informs Mary Logan, Big Ma, and others, "I thinks I wants to vote" (*Circle* 192). Mrs. Lee Annie Lees's insistence on voting involves both CRT and GST: (1) Black people in Mississippi are technically allowed to vote, but the process of registering, due to Jim Crow laws, is basically impossible (i.e., poll taxes and voter tests); and (2) Black women in Mississippi have never been allowed to vote, since the law after Reconstruction only applied to Black men.

Mrs. Lee Annie Lees exclaims, "I knows what I gotta do to take that test," and describes the process for registering to vote, including the poll tax and voting test. She is asked, "[H]ow many colored folks you know vote," and she replies: "Ne'er a one. But part of that's 'cause these ole white folks think ain't no colored folks gon' come down to their ole voting places to vote. Well, this here ole aunty gon' strut right down there and show them I knows the law. Ole Lee Annie Lees gon' vote jus' like her daddy done" (*Circle* 194).

This excerpt illustrates the role of race in suppressing the Black vote in fictional 1930s Spokane County where not one Black person is registered. However, Mrs. Lee Annie Lees is determined to challenge the permanence of racism by trying to register.

Although actively discouraged from registering, Mrs. Lee Annie Lees has a different story, a counternarrative, that challenges the dominant narrative occurring in Mississippi. She remembers her father voting. She says, "Course now, my papa voted. Back in the times of the Reconstruction when the black men got the vote—women didn't have no vote. Walked right up to that votin' place and made his X. Didn't hafta take no test back then" (*Circle* 114). This counterstory provides testimony to Mrs. Lee Annie Lees's father's voting experience and illustrates how *rules* in the South differ in the 1930s compared to the time immediately after the Civil War.

During this conversation, someone mentions Harlan Granger, the owner of the land on which Mrs. Lee Annie Lees lives, fearful Granger won't take kindly to "one of 'his' colored people" (*Circle* 195) going out and trying to vote. Mrs. Lee Annie Lees states, "[A]ll my life whenever I wanted to do something and the white folks didn't like it, I didn't do it. All my life, it been that way. But now I's sixty-four years old and I figure I's deserving of doing something I wants to do, white folks like it or not. And this old body wants to vote . . ." (*Circle* 195).

This statement illustrates Mrs. Lee Annie Lees's determination to change her story. She recognizes the role racism plays in society and that oppression keeps many Black people from voting. She also challenges the permanence of racism and equips herself with knowledge to fight the status quo.

Under Mary's tutelage, Mrs. Lee Annie Lees and Cassie learn about the Mississippi Constitution, an experience that further shapes Cassie's identity. When Cassie learns about the words in the constitution and witnesses Mrs. Lee Annie Lees's determination to combat the permanence of racism and provide a counternarrative to the oppression of Black voters, her future is foreshadowed. Hamida Bosmajian states, "In the Mississippi of [Cassie's] childhood and adolescence, custom and unjust statutes of segregation have institutionalized racism" (143). This becomes clear when Cassie witnesses the consequences of challenging institutional racism, which puts the interests of whites over Blacks. Cassie's childhood experiences contribute to her "growing consciousness of the liberating power of just laws" (Bosmajian 141); in fact, Cassie mentions her knowledge of the constitution in *Days* (345, 385), citing the experience with Mrs. Lee Annie Lees. As readers learn in *Days*, Cassie pursues a law career and eventually engages in civil rights activism, illustrating how this experience impacts her future.

In chapter 13 of *Circle*, Mrs. Lee Annie Lees makes her long-awaited trip to the courthouse with Mary, Cassie, and another friend, Mrs. Leora Ellis. Although escorted to town by men, the four Black women decide to enter the courthouse alone, saying the presence of Black men "could prove too threatening" (355). This circumstance illustrates Black women using gender to their advantage to navigate an already tense situation, with Black men still possessing power and enacting their role of protector.

Once in the courthouse, the situation quickly shifts, and gender no longer protects the women; they are back in the battle of racism. Granger, coincidentally at the courthouse, persuades the registrar to let Mrs. Lee Annie Lees take the test, reminding the registrar of his power to decide whether she passes. This scene recalls the CRT concept of interest convergence: Black voting is not in the interest of whites. If Black voters register, it challenges the status quo and the power of whites in Spokane County—and throughout Mississippi. While Granger instructs Boudein, the registrar, to let Mrs. Lee Annie Lees take the test since she paid her poll tax, he also notes taking the test and registering "are two different things" (360). Granger and Boudein appear to comply with the law by allowing Mrs. Lee Annie Lees to pay the poll tax, but these white men ultimately have the power to decide Mrs. Lee Annie Lees's voting fate, regardless of whether she pays the fee and passes the test.

Throughout the testing process, the white people in the office comment on Mrs. Lee Annie Lees's intelligence as related to her race: "Can't no darky understand the complexities of the constitution" and "the older they [Black people] get, the more childlike they become . . ." (360–61). The white landowners and community members in Spokane County believe the *story* that Black people are less intelligent than whites, even though Mrs. Lee Annie Lees attempts to create a counternarrative. This is evidenced by Boudein commenting on Mrs. Lee Annie Lees's mental capabilities regarding her understanding of the constitution. Through dramatic irony, Taylor reveals to readers that Mrs. Lee Annie Lees has learned the constitution and its principles, and, if given a fair chance, would have passed the voting test. Her counternarrative is silenced by the dominant white story. Mrs. Lee Annie Lees's experience with attempting to register to vote becomes a pivotal moment in Cassie's life.

"She pulled a pretty good one": The Penalty of Passing

One character whose experiences revolve around both her race and gender is Suzella, the Logan children's cousin. The following example shows how Suzella challenges the CRT tenets of permanence of racism and interest convergence due to her being able to *pass* as a white woman; however, once her cover is blown, her father must physically pay the price, as she watches in shame.

Suzella is introduced to readers in *Circle* as a light-skinned adolescent whose father, Cassie's Uncle Bud, is Black and whose mother is white. Because her skin is light, she is able to pass for white, which readers—and the Logans—discover she has been doing in New York. This challenges the notion of the permanence of racism. Because Suzella can pass as white, she is not permanently subjected to the racism that Cassie and other characters cannot escape; because Suzella is able to conceal her Blackness, she can reap the benefits of being white; and because Suzella looks white, she receives different treatment from both Black and white men compared to other Black women. Suzella's complicity in her own oppression may not be immediately apparent to her during the events in *Circle*; however, as noted by Cheryl Harris's piece *Whiteness as Property*, the act of passing as white and suppressing one's Black identity has both positive and negative consequences, and Suzella's suppression of her identity may have long-term repercussions on her psyche. Up North, Suzella can pretend to be white with few consequences; however, in Misssissippi, the permanence of race is legislated: interracial marriage and not acknowledging your race are both illegal—meaning Suzella's very existence is illegal. Though at times she is able to escape personal, physical attacks, she is still on the periphery of racist acts; she witnesses harm and hate afflicted on others and experiences the same anger and fear when racists target her family. Suzella's need to pass as white in the first place illustrates her knowledge of systemic racism; it serves her material interest in certain situations, though it bears a psychic and social cost.

The permanence of race and interest convergence are illustrated in the following scene in Strawberry, Mississippi, where Cassie, Suzella, Christopher-John, and Little Man encounter Stuart Walker, a local white boy. When Stuart begins flirting with Suzella, she plays along but quickly realizes her mistake upon hearing Stuart's disrespect to her cousins. Stuart's interaction with Suzella is (1) a result of her being female, which the reader can easily infer by his flirting, and (2) a result of her light skin, which makes her appear white. Cassie and her brothers immediately feel betrayed and angered that Suzella passes for white and does not claim to be their cousin. This challenges the norms in the South, where Black women do not get involved with white men, due to historical abuse and power differentials linked to aspects of interest convergence and the permanence of racism. It is not in whites' interest for Blacks to assume a white identity because this type of subversive behavior would unsettle the white power in the South. In this situation, Suzella uses her light skin to her advantage but in the process realizes that race impacts every interaction in the South, where she cannot deny her heritage without consequences. Suzella and Cassie have contrasting experiences as Black women in the South, and because Suzella's life has been so different from Cassie's, each character struggles with the other's reality, which is influenced both by race and gender, further highlighting the intersections between these concepts.

When Stuart discovers that Suzella has tricked him, he decides not to take it out directly on her but on her father, Bud. Readers witness the consequences Black people in Mississippi face for challenging the CRT tenets of interest convergence and the permanence of race. In retaliation for Suzella's "[pulling] a pretty good one" on Stuart (342), Stuart and his friends stop Bud's car. Cassie warns her uncle not to pull over, having predicted "it was not going to be very pleasant when [Stuart] realized what he had done" (245), referring to Stuart's mistake in treating Suzella as if she were a white woman. After Bud stops the car, Stuart and friends make him get out, harass him, and interrogate him about Suzella's parentage. Bud lies, insisting that Suzella's mom is a light-skinned Black woman. Mocking Bud and exerting white power, Stuart orders Bud to take off his clothes, leaving him in nothing but his undershorts. As Bud stands there, emasculated and trembling, Stuart grabs his face, still demanding an answer to his question about Suzella's mother. If Bud had confessed his wife's race, it would have threatened Stuart's construction of white womanhood as something to be exclusively owned by white men, which connects gender to the CRT notion of whiteness as property. Bud's experience connects GST and CRT as he is targeted by Stuart (1) for being Black, (2) for his daughter's trespass, and (3) for daring to have a sexual relationship with a white woman. While Suzella gets off easy after Stuart learns the truth, her father suffers consequences that impact his gender identity as a strong Black man and a male protector. These young white boys intentionally humiliate and exert power over Bud despite his seniority, simply because they are white and he is Black. This illustrates the systemic racism that permeated life in the South. Even though Bud crosses boundaries of race in the North, Southern whites remind him that race is always permanent, especially in Mississippi. Suzella, on the periphery, witnesses her father being the recipient of a hate crime because she falsely presented her heritage. She encounters an impossible situation—one controlled by the larger system—resulting in Suzella's having to make decisions to ensure her survival. While Taylor does not revisit Suzella's story in the Logan Family Saga, readers can infer that passing acts as a form of self-annihilation, which may have negatively impacted her future identity with her realization that passing actually contributed to her own oppression.

"THAT GIVE US ALL THE MORE REASON TO RESPECT 'EM": THE BLACK MAN AS PROTECTOR

Several key events in the Logan novels demonstrate the intersection of race with the gender norm of Black men possessing power and being the protector of Black women and families. While battling 1930s Mississippi community standards that uphold racism and powerlessness, men in the Logan series struggle to enact their roles as strong, Black men.

In *Circle*, this norm transpires as Mr. Morrison, Stacey, Cassie, Christopher-John, and Little Man are working on the farm. When Morrison notices Cassie struggling a bit while moving a hay bale, he signals to Christopher-John and Little Man to give her a hand. Exhibiting some braggadocio, Little Man exclaims, "Move, gal. Let some real muscles in" (251). Morrison quickly chastises Little Man for using the word "gal," noting it is a "white folks'" term (251–52). According to Morrison, "White folks don't respect our female folks, so that give us all the more reason to respect 'em and don't be speaking to 'em the way the white folks do" (252). Not only does this illustrate Little Man's respect toward Morrison because he is an elder who should be listened to, but this exchange also signifies ways people in the Black community can resist assimilation to white practices. Morrison points out that Black men both need to protect and respect Black women, illustrating the notion that they are fighting the same battle—the battle of intraracial as well as interracial racism. Morrison also creates a counternarrative to the oppressive words used toward Black women by white men; he tries to rewrite the narrative for Little Man by pointing out the oppressive intention behind words like "gal."

In *Memphis*, another event demonstrates the norm of Black men possessing power and needing to protect Black women. After driving for several hours, Cassie, Stacey, and three friends—Moe, Willie, and Clarence—stop at a remote gas station. The permanent impact race has on Black people's experiences in the South surfaces when Cassie needs to use the restroom, but the gas station has "whites-only" bathrooms; the closest facility for Black customers is a local woman's home or in the woods behind the station. Cassie becomes frustrated and ventures toward the door of the "whites-only" restroom, contemplating whether she should challenge the rules. As she stands on the threshold, a white woman returns and reports Cassie to the shop owner, who screams at Cassie and kicks at her "like somebody with no heart would kick a dog" (179). The shop owner sees a Black person, and Cassie's gender prompts him to use violence against her without fear of retaliation, likely due to the unequal distribution of social, physical, and racial power.

Cassie's experience exemplifies how both racism and gender norms impact this event. Cassie lies, saying she fell while searching for a spot in the bushes to urinate, knowing that the truth would result in serious consequences to the boys' gender schema: (1) their male ego would be impacted by the decision to let the incident go; or (2) their role as male protectors would put them in danger if they returned to the gas station to seek justice. Cassie knows that if she had told her older brother and friends that the gas station owner kicked her, they might retaliate, illustrating the common gender norm of the male protector, but there is no way for the group to enact justice in the Jim Crow South. Additionally, her gender impacts her in this situation. The gas station owner knows he can mistreat Cassie without fear of retaliation because he is a white man, and she is a Black woman.

This resembles another altercation in *Circle* when Uncle Hammer wants to attack Stuart after Stuart comments, "What other business we'd have with a nigger bi—," (146) in reference to Jacey Peters, a local Black girl. David holds Hammer back and signals to Joe Billy to get Stuart into the car. Stuart eyes David and Hammer, knowing "[his] power was in the color of his skin" and that Hammer could not touch him (146). The permanence of race impacts this experience, as Stuart, who is much younger, can assert authority over older men like Hammer and David, respected figures in the community, simply because of Stuart's whiteness.

Both examples—the gas station and the Jacey Peters incident—show that if the Black men had retaliated against their white oppressors, the larger systems of power and race would have won, leaving the Black men's engendered need to protect useless; any retaliation against the white men would have resulted in violence and quite possibly the death of Cassie's friends and relatives. The intersectionality of race and gender are evident in these examples; by not being able to protect those in their family or community from disrespect, and even violence, Stacey, Hammer, David, and others in the Logan Family Saga suffer from a discord between societal norms and their identities as Black men.

"UP HERE, THIS WAS SUPPOSED TO BE LIKE THE PROMISED LAND": RACE AND GENDER DISCRIMINATION IN THE NORTH AND THE SOUTH

Even when Cassie becomes an adult, living in other parts of the US, her experiences continue to be impacted by both race and gender. In her most recent novel, Taylor continues to illustrate the tension created by the intersectionality of race and gender on her characters; when characters must deal with both race expectations and gender norms, this often creates struggle.

During a doctor's visit, Cassie is in the waiting room in Detroit with both white and Black patients, and while this seems progressive, upon closer look, Cassie notes the office staff, nurses, and doctors are all white. She discovers that the North is just as racist, though less conspicuous, as the South (i.e., white and Black patients sit together in the waiting room, yet doctors and staff give Black patients inferior treatment). This demonstrates the permanence of racism, even in Northern society where Black and white people are supposed to be more equal.

After a long wait, Cassie enters the examination room, where her encounter with the white, middle-aged doctor reveals similar racism and sexism as in the South. Throughout her visit, Cassie demands respect from the white doctor, but he responds with thinly veiled discrimination, relating to the permanence of race. For instance, rather than calling her "Miss Logan," the doctor refers to Cassie by her first name (*Days* 40). This familiarity should not have been appropriate in a professional situation like the doctor's visit; however, since Cassie is a Black woman, the doctor does not feel the need to treat her with the same decency or respect that he would show the white women he treats. This episode hearkens to the gendered history around white enslavers and enslaved Black women. It is immediately clear to readers that race influences the doctor's treatment of Cassie.

He continues to belittle Cassie, both because she is Black and a woman, when he replies to Cassie's inquiry about her blood pressure: "How is it?," the doctor states, "Fine." Cassie replies, "I mean what was the reading" (41–42). The doctor's reply, "Fine," assumes Cassie does not know or understand how to interpret the reading, illustrating his feeling of white, male superiority. The doctor treats Cassie according to the narrative that he believes: she is less-knowing and less-deserving. The counterstory suggests that Cassie can interpret her blood pressure results, and the fact that she is a Black woman does not determine her level of intelligence.

Despite Cassie's attempts to tell her counterstory, he continues to make assumptions based on Cassie's race and gender. When the doctor insists on giving Cassie a pelvic exam, rather than providing professional instructions, he says, "I'm sure you know the position" (43). In an ultimate act of disrespect, the doctor refuses to allow a nurse in the room for a pelvic exam. Readers wonder if a full examination of a male patient would have been as invasive as the exam the doctor wants to complete. Even worse, the doctor implies that all Black women are sexually promiscuous when he says, "[A]ll you colored girls know it, married or not" (43), again revealing the story of Black women he believes to be true. The doctor's response to Cassie's request for a nurse and question about why a nurse cannot be present is nothing more than, "Because I said so" (44). In disbelief, Cassie gets down from the table, saying, "I don't think I'll take the exam" (43).

Connecting to the permanence of racism and GST (i.e., masculinity and gender roles), the doctor treats Cassie like she is sexually promiscuous because she is (1) Black and (2) a woman. The reader infers what might have happened to Cassie if she had not refused the exam (i.e., being sexually assaulted by the white doctor), although the doctor insists, "You think I want something from you? You don't have anything I haven't seen before" (44). The doctor's retort denotes his acknowledgement of Cassie being a woman due to her anatomy, but he does not want anything from her due to her race. It is apparent that this doctor abuses his position of power with other women in the clinic, especially young, single, Black women.

Gender schema theory and Africana womanism also aid in the examination of this incident. Cassie flatly refuses the physical exam, forfeiting the possibility of a new job, and does not tell any of the men in her community what happened at the doctor's office, although she does confess the experience to her sister-in-law, Dee. Various implications can be inferred from Cassie not telling the men in her life: (1) the Black men in her life, who have the power, would want to protect Cassie due to their role as protector within the community; and (2) since Black women's roles are tied to both gender and race, as outlined in the theoretical framework of Africana womanism, talking to Dee about both the racial discrimination and sexual harassment illustrates their shared identity as Black women.

"I'M NOT ABOUT TO USE THAT TOILET AFTER SHE'S BEEN IN THERE": NORTH DOES NOT MEAN DIFFERENT

CRT and GST assist in interpreting another key event in Cassie's adult life: when she goes to the movies with Moe and another couple in *Days*. In the following examples, Cassie experiences racism that is more subtle than in the South, while also exerting power as an Africana woman when she speaks out and models resistance for other Black women.

The event begins by illustrating examples of gender norms at play; Cassie and Moe are on a double date with Henry and Brenda, "for even though [Cassie] was a grown woman, the tradition of double dating remained, and that was expected until [Cassie] married. That was simply the way things were . . ." (*Days* 44). When Cassie and her friends arrive at the theater, they see a long, integrated line heading toward the ticket window, unlike in Mississippi where "there was a separate entry for 'colored'" (45). This scene illustrates a positive racial experience for Cassie; even though she apprehensively adheres to gender norms within her culture by being on a double date, she witnesses integration between races within the public sector, when most of her life she has only seen segregation. But Cassie's positive racial experience is short lived.

As the group enters the theater and heads to the concession counter, Brenda tells Cassie she needs to use the restroom. Despite the fact that Blacks and whites mingle in the lobby and ticket line, when Cassie and Brenda enter the women's restroom, they find the stalls have not been integrated, with just one stall reserved for Black women. Cassie refuses to adhere to this discrimination, exerting her protest against the permanence of race and challenging interest convergence. Although this occurs in the North, white societal norms continue to highlight the binary that suppresses Black actions, in order to maintain white superiority. Seeing additional empty stalls, she encourages Brenda to use one of the white stalls. Brenda does, but when she exits the stall, a white woman in line says, "I'm not about to use that toilet after *she's* been in there" (*Days* 47). The white woman does not think twice about what she has said, but her response impacts Cassie and Brenda. Only Cassie has the nerve to say something to the white woman. After Cassie exits the stall she uses, she retorts, "You too good to use a toilet after a colored person, you won't be able to use this toilet either" (47). This experience illustrates a key component of CRT, that racism is an ordinary phenomenon, imperceptible to members of the dominant society while extremely perceptible to members of less privileged groups.

As discussed earlier, this example also illustrates Africana womanism, as Cassie's actions provoke her friend Brenda to act also. This occurrence changes Cassie's narrative of oppression. In *Memphis*, Cassie struggles with the oppression, powerlessness, and racism she feels from a gas station owner but does not challenge the norms. In *Days*, after numerous life experiences, she challenges the norm and uses the stalls reserved for white women in the theater despite the expectation that has been established for Black women to use the designated stall. As part of her Africana womanist identity, Cassie recognizes her role in battling the communal struggle of racism, seen in her instructing Brenda to use a whites-only stall and using one herself, an idea Cassie merely toyed with in *Memphis*. Her bravery to challenge the norm also stems from being in the North, surrounded by women, rather than in the South, where violence against Black people was not only common but extreme; if retaliation for Cassie's defiance were to transpire, she would be more likely to be arrested than die at the end of a rope. The designated stall also illustrates the permanence of racism and how de facto segregation still exists in the North, even when not upheld by law. Being in an environment that Cassie perceives as safer emboldens her to exercise her capacity to fight the permanence of racism as related to her identity as a woman of African descent.

After the incident in the restroom, Cassie and Brenda return to the main lobby and learn that the theater expects all Black patrons to sit in the balcony versus the main floor of the theater. Cassie, "sick of the bigotry" (*Days* 47), decides she will not sit in the balcony: "I think I'll sit downstairs this evening" (48). Again, Cassie takes her Africana womanist identity and uses it to address the oppression Black people face, in a place that was supposed to be the promised land. Eventually the police are called, and Moe, thinking proactively, calls Henry's father, Mr. Tate, an attorney. Only through Tate's persuasion do the white theater manager and police officers release Moe and Cassie. Outside the theater, Tate approaches Cassie and states, "Miss Logan, I understand you're the instigator of all this" (53). Cassie says, "It's the principle of the thing, Mr. Tate. All my life, living in Mississippi, it was understood everything was separate. Up here, this was supposed to be like the promised land" (53). Cassie struggles with the fact that despite the absence of Jim Crow signs, the North reveals itself to be just as racist as the South. Tate advises Cassie, "You go up against the system again, you could wind up in jail" (54). It becomes clear that the system, both in the North and the South, is not on the side of Black people, and if Cassie tries to fight it, she will most certainly lose that battle.

Tate admires the stand Cassie has taken and enquires into Cassie's teaching degree. Cassie replies, "Well, to be truthful with you, I don't know if I'll teach or not. My mother's a teacher and she loves it, but I don't feel the same as she does about teaching and I figured I ought to love whatever I do if that's what I'm going to be doing the rest of my life" (61).

Cassie's conversation with Lawyer Tate illustrates gender norms about the teaching profession, which is female-dominated. Cassie reveals that she majored in education because of her mother, not because of love for the career. The implication that she could easily get a teaching job is also evident when she says, "Only reason I got the teaching degree was because . . . I'd always have a job if I were a teacher" (111). Cassie's pursuit of this career shows how gender schema has shaped her decision.

Tate contradicts gender norms by planting the idea that Cassie could go into law; not only is law primarily a male profession; it is primarily a white profession. Tate, a Black male, has already challenged the tenet of interest convergence by pursuing a career in law. Now, switching from the role of Black male protector, again countering gender norms, he encourages Cassie to pursue a career she loves rather than continuing gendered career traditions. Additionally, Cassie's identity develops further dimensions as she considers, and eventually pursues, a law degree, building upon her desire to see change in the world, an idea planted after learning about the Constitution and witnessing Mrs. Lee Annie Lees's pursuit to vote. Cassie's multifaceted identity comes to fruition in the final novel of the Logan Family Saga.

CONCLUSION: "I WANTED TO WRITE A TRUTHFUL HISTORY"

This chapter has presented an analysis of the intersectionality of critical race theory and gender schema theory as experienced in the lives of Taylor's characters in three novels: *Circle, Memphis,* and *Days*. Critical race theory and gender schema theory are based on observations of society, which is why these theories can be used to examine the kinds of systemic injustices and personal experiences depicted in Taylor's historical fiction. Taylor's texts share stories of racism, gender conformity, and intersectionality during childhood, adolescence, and adulthood that offer a lens into a time period that moves beyond the characters' experiences to include realistic insight into ways of being for both Black and white people. In her Author's Note that opens the final novel, Taylor writes, "I wanted to show Black heroes and heroines in my books, men and women who were missing from books I read as a child . . . I wanted to write a truthful history of what life was like for Black people in America" (*Days* viii). With a rich cast of characters represented across decades and generations, Taylor illustrates a plurality of gendered experiences, multiple childhoods and adulthoods, and changes and challenges to individuals and systems alike.

Throughout Taylor's novels, numerous events illustrate the intersection between race and gender. While this chapter discusses only a few specific examples—Mrs. Lee Annie Lees's attempt to vote, Suzella passing as white, the Logan men's need to protect Black women, and Cassie's experience in the North—readers can easily peruse Taylor's books and discover additional instances in which characters experience tenets of critical race theory and gender schema theory. Race and gender shape the lives of the Logan children and their identities, through both firsthand experiences and by witnessing the struggles of others.

The patterns of intersectionality mold Taylor's characters, specifically members of the Logan family, resulting in who they become in the final novel. Cassie's character development is built by her life in Great Faith and Strawberry, where racism and gender norms influence her decisions and actions. She is shaped by her experiences in Jackson, during the road trip and as a result of her acquaintance with the handsome and successful Solomon Bradley, who reinforces and challenges her views on race and gender. Her character is further formed when she moves North and West, still experiencing racism and gender expectations despite the geographical change. While she does challenge some norms, such as learning the Constitution with Mrs. Lee Annie Lees in *Circle*, wearing pants in *Memphis*, and becoming a female lawyer in *Days*, she is still cautious in her decisions; she does not tell Stacey and the other boys what happened at the gas station (*Memphis*), and she hides that she is dating a white man (*Days*). However, as the number of injustices accrues, Cassie begins to see how she can change the narrative. In *Circle* she wants to see more equal rights for African Americans before she is as old as Mrs. Lee Annie Lees. The decision to pursue a law career and become a civil rights activist in *Days* also illustrates Cassie's counternarrative. Cassie's multidimensional identity is merely one portrayal of life for African American females in the historically truthful, decades-long saga of Mildred Taylor's Logan family.

Taylor's writing can cause productive discomfort for readers as they enter a world of America's segregated past; for some, Taylor's world is unfamiliar, and for others, Taylor's world is a reflection, illustrating the concept of windows, mirrors, and doors, as discussed by Rudine Sims Bishop. For example, Bishop found that readers may peer through the window into books; in this case, readers observe the lives of Cassie and her family and learn about America's racist past (and present) by looking through the window into these stories. Readers can also step through the door and immerse themselves in the lives and struggles experienced by the characters, allowing themselves to experience injustice and racism firsthand. Most of all, Bishop claimed that books can be mirrors; African American readers often see themselves in Taylor's stories, as the experiences reflect their lives and experiences.

Mildred Taylor's books are essential because of the insights they provide for children and other marginalized authors to interrogate issues in similar ways. Jacqueline Woodson states: "*Roll of Thunder, Hear My Cry* helped me understand the story of so many people's lives over the years. . . . I know that I am a writer because Ms. Taylor wrote this book and I saw myself inside the pages of it, the way so many thousands of readers have since seen themselves in the pages" (qtd. in *Thunder* introduction).

Taylor acknowledges the impact her books have: "Now, just as the storytellers of old, I continue to relate the truth as I have done in all my writing. [The Logan series] includes that same truth, the truth about America" (*Days* viii).

WORKS CITED

Abrams, Jasmine A., et al. "Circumstances Beyond Their Control: Black Women's Perceptions of Black Manhood." *Sex Roles*, vol. 79, 2018, pp. 151–62.

Bem, Sandra L. "Gender Schema Theory: A Cognitive Account of Sex Typing." *Psychological Review*, vol. 88, no. 4, 1981, pp. 354–64.

Berger, Michele T., and Kathleen Guidroz. Introduction. *The Intersectional Approach: Transforming the Academy Through Race, Class, and Gender*, by Berger and Guidroz. U of North Carolina P, 2009, pp. 1–22.

Bishop, Rudine Sims. "Mirrors, Windows, and Sliding Glass Doors." *Perspectives: Choosing and Using Books for the Classroom*, vol. 6, no. 3, 1990.

Bosmajian, Hamida. "Mildred Taylor's Story of Cassie Logan: A Search for Law and Justice in a Racist Society." *Children's Literature*, vol. 24, by Francella Butler et al. Yale UP, 1996, pp. 141–60.

Carbado. Devon W. "Introduction: Where and When Black Men Enter." *Black Men on Race, Gender, and Sexuality: A Critical Reader*, edited by Devon Carbado, NYU Press, 1999, pp. 1–17.

Cho, Sumi, et al. "Toward a Field of Intersectionality Studies: Theory, Applications, and Praxis." *Signs*, vol. 38, no. 5, 2013, pp. 785–810.

Cowdery, Randi S., et al. "Gendered Power in Cultural Contexts: Part II. Middle Class African American Heterosexual Couples with Young Children." *Family Process*, vol. 48, no. 1, 2009, pp. 25–39.

Crenshaw, Kimberlé. "Mapping the Margins: Intersectionality, Identity Politics, and Violence Against Women of Color." *Stanford Law Review*, vol. 43, no. 6, 1991, pp. 1241–99.

Crenshaw, Kimberlé W. "Twenty Years of Critical Race Theory: Looking Back to Move Forward." *Connecticut Law Review*, vol. 43, no. 5, 2011, pp. 1253–1352.

DeCuir, Jessica T., and Adrienne D. Dixson. "'So When It Comes Out, They Aren't That Surprised That It Is There': Using Critical Race Theory as a Tool for Analysis of Race and Racism in Education." *Educational Researcher*, vol. 33, no. 5, 2004, pp. 26–31.

Earles, Jennifer. "Reading Gender: A Feminist, Queer Approach to Children's Literature and Children's Discursive Agency." *Gender and Education*, vol. 29, no. 3, pp. 369–88.

Geertz, Clifford. "Thick Description: Toward an Interpretive Theory of Culture." *The Interpretation of Cultures* by Clifford Geertz. HarperCollins Publishers, 1973, pp. 310–23.

Harris, Cheryl I. "Whiteness as Property." *Harvard Law Review*, vol. 106, no. 8, 1993, pp. 1707–91.

Hudson-Weems, Clenora F. *Africana Womanism: Reclaiming Ourselves*. Bedford Publishers, 2004.

Ledesma, Maria C., and Dolores Calderon. "Critical Race Theory in Education: A Review of Past Literature and a Look to the Future." *Qualitative Inquiry*, vol. 21, no. 3, 2015, pp. 206–22.

Pellerin, Marquita. "Defining Africana Womanhood: Developing an Africana Womanism Methodology." *The Western Journal of Black Studies*, vol. 36, no. 1, 2012, pp. 76–85.

Sharp, Elizabeth A., and Jean M. Ispa. "Inner-City Single Black Mothers' Gender-Related Childrearing Expectations and Goals." *Sex Roles*, vol. 60, 2009, pp. 656–68.

Sleeter, Christine. E. "Critical Race Theory and the Whiteness of Teacher Education." *Urban Education*, vol. 52, no. 2, 2017, pp. 155–69.

Starr, Christine R., and Eileen L. Zurbriggen. "Sandra Bem's Gender Schema Theory After 34 Years: A Review of Its Reach and Impact." *Sex Roles*, vol. 76, 2017, pp. 566–78.

Taylor, Mildred D. *All the Days Past, All the Days to Come*. Viking, 2020.

Taylor, Mildred D. *Let the Circle Be Unbroken*. Kindle ed., Puffin Books, 1981.

Taylor, Mildred D. *The Road to Memphis*. Dial Press, 1990.

Taylor, Mildred D. *Roll of Thunder, Hear My Cry*. 40th anniversary special ed, Kindle ed., Dial Press, 2016.

Tenenbaum, Harriet R., and Campbell Leaper. "Are Parents' Gender Schemas Related to Their Children's Gender-Related Cognitions? A Meta-Analysis." *Developmental Psychology*, vol. 38, no. 4, 2002, pp. 615–30.

Trepanier-Street, Mary L., and Jane A. Romatowski. "The Influence of Children's Literature on Gender Role Perceptions: A Reexamination." *Early Childhood Education Journal*, vol. 26, no. 3, 1999, pp. 155–59.

Washington, Rachelle D., and Michelle H. Martin. "In Search Of Mildred Taylor's Womanists: Feminist Agency in the Logan Family Novels." *Critical Insights: Coming of Age*, edited by Kent Baxter, Salem, 2012, pp. 37–54. Salem Online, online.salempress.com.

Beyond the Veil
In Search of Duboisian Double Consciousness in the Works of Mildred D. Taylor

Helen Bond

Mildred D. Taylor's novels offer the racial theorist and literary critic a wide range of interpretive possibilities. While considerable overlap exists between racial theorizing and literary criticism, these two approaches can provide multiple insights into Taylor's impressive body of works. Taylor's ten books for children and young adults have explored many themes: pride, prejudice, humility, family, community, land, racial conflict, feminism, child agency, and more (Johnson 4). While writing her final sequel to the Logan family story, Taylor describes being "tapped on the shoulder" by history ("Tapped" 61). The stories of her father, grandparents, great-uncles, aunts, and other family members, as well as her own, became the impetus for her novels. Despite variations in time, place, and events, Taylor's stories are woven together in what I argue is a great Duboisian patchwork called the Veil.

Incorporating a Duboisian lens to study Taylor's work combines Du Bois's extraordinary literary genius and moral reckoning with Taylor's unflinching capacity for critical storytelling. This chapter examines the presence of the Duboisian Veil in Taylor's novels. Du Bois is mentioned once by name in *Thunder*; his trope of the Veil is useful for understanding how Cassie Logan and her family navigate a world under its shadow (Smith 23). The goal of this chapter is to use the Duboisian Veil as an interpretive lens to investigate the literary representation of one fictional Black family's lived experience in the years leading up to the Civil Right Movement. By situating Du Bois at the center of Taylor's works, I hope to show that Du Bois's ideas were central to Taylor's storytelling and to the ideas she wished to convey.

DEFINING THE DUBOISIAN VEIL

W. E. B. Du Bois (1868–1963) is considered the foremost thinker and writer of the African American experience (Du Bois, Gates, and Oliver xii). Historian Eric Foner acknowledged Du Bois as a "scholar, poet, agitator, father of Pan-Africanism, founder of the NAACP, [and] pioneer of modern sociology and African American history" (130). Henry Louis Gates, Jr. has described Du Bois as a race man and a man of letters who is as relevant today as he was in his time (Du Bois, Gates, and Oliver xxxvii). Du Bois's works are as notable as the man. James Weldon Johnson, author of *The Autobiography of an Ex-Colored Man*, wrote that *The Souls of Black Folk* was not only a remarkable book but second only to *Uncle Tom's Cabin* in its impact and portrayal of African American life (Johnson 34).

In *The Souls of Black Folk*, Du Bois introduces the defining theories of his legacy: conceptions such as the Veil, double consciousness, and second sight. Du Bois's construct of the Veil is defined as a metaphor for the color line, or a fog that not only separates the races but obscures and distorts their interactions and perceptions of one another (10). He further explains that literary texts help him rise above the Veil and see through the fog that excludes Black people from the polity (14–15). David Levering Lewis authored two biographies on Du Bois. He explains that Du Bois's trope of the Veil is both noun and verb (90). He recounts that it is a way of knowing and being but also manifests as a physical object that Rodino Anderson, in "Poetically Dwelling with the Veil," describes as a "thought thing" (276). Du Bois uses the Veil as both a literary trope and as a metaphor to describe the racial boundaries of the period and its impact on the Negro:

> The Negro is a sort of seventh son, born with a veil, and gifted with second-sight in this American world—a world which yields him no true self-consciousness, but only lets him see himself through the revelation of the other world. It is a peculiar sensation, this double consciousness, this sense of always looking at one's self through the eyes of others, of measuring one's soul by the tape of a world that looks on in amused contempt and pity. One ever feels his twoness—an American, a Negro; two souls, two thoughts, two unreconciled strivings; two warring ideals in one dark body, whose dogged strength alone keeps it from being torn asunder. (*Souls of Black Folk* 4)

In *Darkwater: Voices from Within the Veil*, Du Bois refers to his life story as being within the "shadow of the veil" (14). In *The Art and Imagination of W. E. B. Du Bois*, Rampersad notes that "[t]he most striking device in *The Souls of Black Folk* is Du Bois's adoption of the veil as the metaphor of black life in America" (79).

Du Bois argued that living a veiled existence resulted in a duality of experience for African Americans (Du Bois, Gates, and Oliver 11). This notion of duality and a veiled existence can be used to explore the relationships, interactions, and contradictions that coexist in the works of both Taylor and Du Bois. Applying Du Bois's scholarship and keen observations of Black life to Taylor's award-winning novels of the Logan family is not only relevant but purposeful. Entangling Du Bois's use of autobiography, metaphor, emotion and moral clarity with Taylor's family stories of uplift and perseverance heard around the kitchen table and front porch enables readers to grasp the depth of the social, economic, and political forces at play in rural Mississippi and across the nation in the 1930s.

Entanglement works in both directions. Du Bois's ideas can be entangled with Taylor's without sacrificing their poetic persuasiveness and metaphysical quality. Nor does applying Du Bois's framework of the Veil distract from the compelling narratives that Taylor weaves with the voice of nine-year-old Cassie Logan. Neither suffers from the analysis. Scholars have adapted the concept of entanglement from Karen Barad to show that more than particles can become entangled. People can become enmeshed, connected, or entangled with ideas, differing histories and cultures, literary texts, and other people. Barad shows that making meaning of these entanglements can be very revealing (2–5).

Shafag Dadashova characterizes the power of autobiography found in both authors' work as a form of life-writing and epiphany (231). Du Bois effectively uses both to evoke the trope of the Veil and the death of his son. He describes how the Veil shadowed the "wee thing" with his olive-colored skin and curly hair (*Darkwater*, ch. 1). His only harkening was that the child would not have to live under its shadow. Wilson Jeremiah Moses describes Du Bois's Veil as a metaphor for black skin (Moses 167). It has also been likened to Paul Lawrence Dunbar's trope of the Mask. Dunbar's poem "The Mask," like the Veil, draws on symbolic imagery of invisibility, exclusion, and misperception (Dunbar 8), all elements identifiable in Taylor's works. Comparisons have also been made to Frantz Fanon's first book, *Black Skin, White Masks*, which analyzes racial consciousness in the Black and white imagination (Khalfa 527). The concept of the Veil does suffer from the multiplicity in definition and use. However, it doesn't lose its moral clarity and force in defining life under relentless oppression and discrimination in either text.

Critics of Du Bois in his day recognized this quality in his work, warning readers not to be seduced by its emotional appeal (Du Bois, Gates, and Oliver 228). Langston Hughes, reflecting on the texts to which he turned for comfort and inspiration in his early days, sought the Bible and *The Souls of Black Folk* (Hughes, Rampersad, and Roessel 3). In an anonymous review in *The Nation* on June 11, 1903, a writer warns, "The back of this there is careful knowledge of past and present conditions in the South, clear insight into their meanings, a firm intellectual apprehension of their tendency, which is something to be reckoned with . . ." (Gates and Oliver 228). Shamoon Zamir's influential and important work *Dark Voices: W. E. B. Du Bois and American Thought, 1888–1903* comes to much the same conclusion. Zamir compares *The Souls of Black Folk* with the works of a number of important thinkers and philosophers, such as Hegel's seminal *Phenomenology of Mind*. Zamir finds that Du Bois's work is informed by a number of thinkers but ultimately is distinctive and unique in its analysis and impact (12). While Hegel discussed the individual and unhappy consciousness, he suggested that self-consciousness occurred when the Veil lifted (49). Du Bois argued that in a racist society, the lifting of the Veil simply exposes one to the racist gaze of the very society that imposed it (*Darkwater*, ch. 1). Classicist Tom Hawkins argues that the roots of Du Bois's Veil lie in the classical tradition of Plato, whose work Du Bois studied in high school. He argues that Du Bois uses the Veil as a metaphysical likeness to Plato's Cave that chains its prisoners in ignorance and darkness, whereas Du Bois's Veil cloaks its prisoners in a fog of exclusion and invisibility (Hawkins 39–42). This alienation provokes the need for the development of outsider vision or second sight.

Rampersad notes in his analysis that the Veil and the dual nature of consciousness were central to Du Bois's perception—even though double consciousness was in use as a medical term during Du Bois's time (79). Du Bois eventually gravitated from the concept of double selves to being truer selves (Rampersad 73–75).

THE EPIPHANY OF THE VEIL

Du Bois describes how he encountered the contemptuous Veil in *The Souls of Black Folk*. He explains it formed a chasm between himself and his classmates growing up in Massachusetts. He retells a merry scene that takes place in a wooden schoolhouse and the exuberance of buying and exchanging greeting cards with his fellow classmates. The scene is happy until a girl in his class, whom he describes as a "tall newcomer," refuses his card (*The Souls of Black Folk* 2). Du Bois felt the rejection so sharply that he immediately felt the sting of twoness—of double consciousness. He is a fellow classmate yet an outsider. He evokes the Veil as he describes the incident later in life: "Then it dawned upon me with a certain suddenness that I was different from the others; or like, maybe, in heart and life and longing, but shut out from the world by a vast veil" (4).

Born in Great Barrington, Massachusetts, in 1868, just five years after the Emancipation Proclamation, young Du Bois lived what he calls a "rollicking boyhood." This boyhood was interspersed with a growing awareness that he was different. Du Bois recounts how the Veil shadowed him from Great Barrington to Atlanta and beyond. He asks, "Why did God make me an outcast and stranger in mine own house?" (2).

However, the suddenness of the rebuff of his classmate's rejection set Du Bois's epiphany of the Veil into motion. The refusal of a ten-cent card was not only painful but drew a line—a color line. In the foreword of *The Souls of Black Folk*, Du Bois describes that "the problem of the twentieth century is the problem of the color-line" (v), which the tall newcomer felt she could not cross. Out of this incident and others unnamed emerged one of Du Bois's most vivid and salient concepts of race: the great Veil (Fertik and Hanses 3).

Taylor's novels, read through the lens of Du Bois's trope, allow a means to deconstruct how the Logan family responds to conflict, solves problems, and utilizes their agency while living what Du Bois calls a veiled existence. The Veil, symbolized as the color line, helps to reveal the salience of race and resistance in interactions between Black people and white people in Taylor's novels (Schrager 560). Du Bois's lens helps readers pull back the obscurity of the Veil, enabling them to visualize the nature of this racial violence and how movement around the color line evokes such a disproportionate response in Taylor's novels (Bosmajian 141). Du Bois's corollary concept of double consciousness, which results from living a veiled existence, can help readers to understand the internal conflict with which members of the Logan family struggle as they must make decisions with far-reaching consequences (Shaw 34).

VEIL WORK

Du Bois was interested in unveiling power structures through storytelling intended to empower the next generation. Du Bois's publication of *The Brownies' Book* in 1920–1921 aimed to empower African American youth through stories, poems, and history (Du Bois, "The True Brownies" 286). Through the magazine, Du Bois hoped to contribute to the agency and resilience of Black children and families in a society torn apart by racial violence as depicted in the *Crisis* magazine, the official publication of National Association for the Advancement of Colored People (NAACP) (Vaughn-Roberson and Hill 495). In *The Brownies' Book*, Du Bois urged parents not to raise their children "ignorant of their true identity and peculiar situation" ("The True Brownies" 285). Du Bois also included a section in the journal entitled "As the Crow Flies," where he reported on the accomplishments of Black people ("The True Brownies" 286) as a source of pride and empowerment for the "Children of the Sun," an endearing term he used for Black children.

Taylor, like Du Bois, also wanted to portray strong, determined Black communities (Hayes 32). She is doing "Veil work," as her stories helped reveal a Black existence that lay hidden beneath layers of prejudice and exclusion that not only separated the races but obscured and distorted their understandings of each other. Taylor does Veil work when she uses her early recollections of her childhood and family stories to expose the complex relationships that form the foundation for the Logan family series ("Talking with Mildred D. Taylor"). She described the oral tradition of storytelling for passing these stories on to future generations (Magoon 51). Though mostly told through the voice of Cassie Logan, the intergenerational narratives in *Roll of Thunder, Hear My Cry* reveal a slice of African American life that was not included in the schoolbooks Taylor read as a child (Taylor, Legacy Award 47). Taylor states that Cassie's voice is the gendered voice of her aunt, sister, and herself and is the voice that seemed to speak most clearly to Taylor's revelations of her family struggles. In her acceptance speech for the 2021 Children's Literature Legacy Award, Taylor stated: "I wanted to show Black people as heroes and heroines missing from the schoolbooks of my childhood" (49). Taylor and Du Bois are both engaged in Veil work as they peel back the layers to reveal not only Black struggle, but also Black resilience along the color line.

What was missing from the schoolbooks of Taylor's youth were stories of courage like that told in the 1995 novella, *The Well*. David Logan narrates the story of two families living within a mile of each other in the sweltering heat of Mississippi with dwindling water. The Simmses are white tenant farmers on a plot of forty acres with a dry well. The Logans own two hundred acres of land with a well that has what Sheriff Peterson Rankins calls the "[f]inest water in the county" (10). The Logans share their water freely with the Simmses—despite mutual tensions between them. Taylor strives to tell a more complicated story as she pulls back the Duboisian Veil to reveal tensions within the household regarding sharing the cool, sweet water, an act that the sheriff calls "a mighty Christian thing" (44).

Conflict continues over the scarcity of water that eventually spills over the color line in *Well*. Hammer talks back to Charlie Simms, a white boy, and then has the nerve to hit him as well. Whether it was her second sight or her double consciousness, Mama knows it is safer to diffuse the situation than to have Old Man McCalister Simms have his way with Hammer and David for hitting Charlie. She satisfies his blood lust by whipping her boys herself with a leather strap in McCalister's presence, while the sheriff looks on. Mama knows a much worse fate than a strap awaits if Old Man McCalister Simms were to punish her sons (*Well* 59). Taylor's depiction of this incident gives readers a taste of how precarious life was along the color line and how natural disasters like droughts can exacerbate racial violence. This incident demonstrates how the Veil, that is the racialized artificial barrier between Black and white Americans, creates an imbalance of power that leaves Mama with the dubious task of inflicting harm on her sons as a way of preventing an even greater harm to them, done by others—white others.

The conflict continues as Charlie and Ed-Rose poison the Logans' well, after which their father forces them to clean out the dead animals they have thrown into the well. Since the only source of water in the community is now polluted, everyone suffers. Taylor ends the novel with the draining and replenishing of the Logans' well for clean water in the future. Taylor describes how both Black folks and white folks came for the water, except for the Simmses, who never ask for water again.

DOUBLE CONSCIOUSNESS

The state of double consciousness results from adapting to life within the Veil. Du Bois defines it as the tension, or internal striving brought about by being an American citizen—an insider, yet also an outsider, to the benefits of that citizenship. Double consciousness can also embrace multiple identities, in the form of an intersectional analysis.

Taylor often describes her early life in Toledo, Ohio—a hardscrabble town in the North that never let her and her family forget that they were different. Taylor was born in 1943 in Jackson, Mississippi, and migrated with her family to Toledo at the tender age of three months. She is the great-granddaughter of a former enslaved man who was the son of an African and Native American woman and a white landowner. Her parents had ties to landownership and a desire to move into more integrated neighborhoods, which whites resisted. First- and even second-generation migrants often resided in urban areas that were more racially and ethnically segregated than their Southern counterparts during the initial Great Migration in 1940 when Black families left the South in droves (Leibbrand et al. 30). While Taylor describes racism as more subtle in the North and more explicit in the South, it nevertheless existed in both places, shaping the lessons she communicates in her novels. In the Author's Note of *All the Days Past, All the Days to Come,* Taylor recounts how racial epithets were as familiar to her ear in Toledo as they had been in Jackson (vii).

The Veil in Taylor's work is not in the language of Du Bois but in the spirit of Du Bois. Taylor evokes a vision of the Veil using the voice of Cassie Logan, nine-year-old narrator of *Thunder* (7). Leona Fisher argues that Cassie draws readers into an emotionally riveting experience of racism that enables the reader to empathize with the Logan family and characters through narrative focalization (158). In other words, Taylor disturbs the Veil by inviting readers into the life of the Logan family in a way that enables them to "inhabit positions in history, ethnicity, or class that may at first seem alien" (Fisher 159).

OUTSIDER VISION

These positions in history seem alien to readers because they have been veiled—that is, they have been obscured by the dynamics of race and hierarchy that place some on the top and others at the bottom. These positions are veiled through time, distance, experience, class, identity, intersectionality, and prejudice. The language and imagery of the scenes painted in the text are intended to help readers see more clearly, to help them develop what Du Bois calls outsider vision or second sight.

This enables readers to understand and even share in the satisfaction felt by the Logan children in *Thunder* when the whites-only school bus gets trapped in a ditch the Logan children have dug. The imagery of the four Logan children lying flat on their bellies in the brush, crowing with laughter, is a peek from underneath the Veil. When Mr. Grimes, the bus driver, announces that the bus has a broken axle (30), it conjures up Anderson's "thought thing," a description he uses for the Veil. The bus becomes such a "thing," a manifestation of the color line as it speeds along, casting dust and mud on children living on one side of the color line while providing comfort and transportation to those on the other. But not today. The broken axle will take time to repair, and those who ride must now walk like the Black children do, or find other transportation. When Big Ma and Mama state that they are glad that no one got hurt, yet also glad that it happened, this reflection peels back a layer of double consciousness. Big Ma, generally careful since history has taught her the consequences of unbridled actions, joins with Mama, the "disrupting maverick" in sharing late-night laughter at the bus getting stuck in the mud (30).

Duboisian double consciousness is an outcome of living in the shadow of the Veil. The concepts of double consciousness and second sight are intimately connected to the Veil as functions of living within its gravity. The theory of double consciousness organizes the social relationships between those on opposite sides of the color line very differently. This differential positioning results in lack of mutual understanding and consequences of situations with a racial component, like that of the school bus. Big Ma and Mama interpret and respond to the bus getting stuck in the mud according to their positioning as both citizen and noncitizen, American and Negro, and both insider and outsider. They make meaning of the situation in a way that helps them and their loved ones refute and resist the shame that is associated with their subordinated social status.

In her acceptance speech for the 1997 Assembly on Literature for Adolescents of NCTE (ALAN) Award, Taylor describes her intentions for writing the stories told by her family. The ALAN Award honors those who have made significant contributions to the field of adolescent literature. "I envisioned presenting an aspect of American history which during my own childhood was not presented in the history books. I envisioned presenting a family united in love and self-respect, and parents, strong and sensitive, attempting to guide their children successfully without harming their spirits, through the hazardous maze of living in a discriminatory society" ("Acceptance Speech"). Taylor is articulating the need to tell stories that would pull back the Veil to show a family united in love and resilience, trying to guide their children while living under the shadow of racism.

Taylor most notably exposes the Veil and its manifestations in the form of double consciousness and second sight in a scene at Great Faith Elementary and Secondary School in *Thunder* (McDowell 216). The school is one of the largest Black schools in the county and what Cassie calls a "dismal end to an hour's journey" (*Thunder* 15). Little Man gets into trouble with Miss Daisy Crocker, a teacher at the school, when he refuses his textbook, calling it dirty. Textbooks are rare at Great Faith, and Ms. Crocker is incensed at his ingratitude. Little Man finally accepts the book only to open it and then throw it onto the floor. He refuses to pick it up after Miss Crocker orders him to do so.

As the protective older sister, whose class is temporarily sharing classroom space due to an absent teacher, Cassie opens her book to the inside cover and discovers why Little Man is so upset. On the inside cover is a chart that details the issuance of the textbooks and to whom, and their corresponding condition. New books and books in the best condition are issued to white children. Books in very poor condition are issued to the "nigra" (*Thunder* 25). Cassie tries to explain this to Miss Crocker, who refuses to listen. Miss Crocker dutifully reminds the class that they must be grateful for the books regardless of the condition. Cassie feels torn between acceptance of books they need and outrage at their condition. Herein lies the double consciousness, the tension that arises when treated unfairly. This injustice results in both Cassie and Little Man ending up on Miss Crocker's whipping chair.

Cassie vows to tell Mama, but Miss Crocker gets to the desk of Mary Logan first. Miss Crocker is doubly incensed by Mama's lukewarm response to her children's actions. Miss Crocker eyes her suspiciously—after all, Mary grew up in the Mississippi Delta and not in Spokane County like everybody else who teaches at Great Faith. As Mary papers over the chart on the inside of the damaged books, despite Miss Crocker's objections, Cassie watches through the doorway. She silently evokes her outsider vision or her ability to almost clairvoyantly grasp the social undertones of racialized situations, which allows her to intuitively know that her mother understands. The tension between intersecting identities results from living under the shadow of the Veil. Outsider vision enables one to recognize this clash of consciousness. Mary Logan from the Delta, the teacher who papers over the books, also dares to keep a copy of Du Bois's book *The Negro* tucked away in her room.

Du Bois is mentioned only once in any of Taylor's novels. In *Thunder*, T.J. slips away to look for his cap. Cassie, Stacey, Christopher-John, and Little Man set out to look for him and find him in Mama's room at her desk. They suspect he is deflecting suspicion from his search for test questions from his teacher by explaining his interest in the book. While T.J. certainly has an interest in getting an advanced copy of the test, I argue that he also has an interest in those Black kings of early Africa. T.J. claims, "Aw man, I ain't done nothin' Jus' lookin' at Miz Logan's history book, that's all. I'm mighty interested in that place called Egypt she's been tellin' us 'bout and them black kings that was rulin' back then" (*Thunder* 76). The same teacher who refused to be outraged at Little Man's behavior may also have spoken of the independence of Ethiopia and the empires of Timbuktu in Mali, West Africa, that inspire T.J.

Du Bois's book *The Negro*, originally published in 1915, was considered one of the most comprehensive histories of Africa and the diaspora at the time. The color line was not just relevant to the American South but was applied to the Global South and colonizers around the world. Du Bois would write four additional books on Africa. In *The Negro*, he argues that race is a social construct with no basis in biology. In the closing chapter, he projects into the future. "What do Negroes themselves think of these their problems and the attitude of the world toward them? First and most significant, they are thinking" (XII). The inclusion of *The Negro* in Taylor's *Thunder* demonstrates a sense of interconnectedness to not only Africa but to the wider diaspora.

Feminist author Deborah King might argue that no single overriding factor or identity would explain Mary Logan's actions. Black women's circumstances vary depending on the situation under consideration and the peer groups to whom they belong and to which they are compared. In some situations, class may be omnipresent. In other cases, race or gender, or sexual orientation, may be the motivating factors. Double consciousness may be too limiting as a construct to characterize the tensions of Black life underneath the Veil. King argues that this requires a multiple consciousness approach as Black women have always realized that the "interactive oppressions that circumscribe their lives provide a distinctive context for black womanhood" (King 49). This approach is not in contradiction with Du Bois's double consciousness but adds layers of context to Taylor's depiction of Mary's experience as a wife, mother, teacher, and an outsider.

CONCLUSION

Du Bois describes conditions in which he can transcend circumstances by rising above the Veil. Du Bois's outsider vision and construct of double consciousness help readers of Taylor's novels transcend the Veil to not only "see" but empathize with the lives of the Logan family. Sociologist and leading race theorist Howard Winant describes Du Bois's conception of the Veil as one of the most powerful theories of race and racism ever developed (315). Winant explains that Du Bois's concept of the Veil is sociohistorical; that is to say its construction is both social and historical, which in turn creates the self-aware actor or agent. He argues that the concept of the Veil is as relevant today as it was during the time Du Bois lived. Structural inequality and systemic discrimination perpetuate the existence of the Veil.

The struggles and triumphs that Taylor was hoping to reveal within her novels were also influenced by Du Bois's impact on her father, Wilbert Taylor (Davis, ch. 1). Pamela Davis suggests that Taylor's father and Du Bois had similar values that may have found their way into Taylor's writings (58). Davis also finds evidence of personal correspondence in which Taylor recounts briefly how Du Bois's writings and life did impact her work (63). Du Bois muses that the emergence of double consciousness and second sight occur as functions of living along the color line, the physical manifestation of the Veil. Taylor uses the voice of young Cassie Logan and other youth to demonstrate agency in many of her characters. In each of the stories, their actions help pull back the Veil, allowing the reader a peek along and behind the color line. Davis also argues that Taylor's work shifted from a racial lens to a more multicultural lens. Davis describes how Taylor expressed writing stories in ways that revealed how the children of all backgrounds might perceive a more realistic representation of themselves through the Black experience. Taylor used the African American experience as a lens through which other ethnic or Indigenous groups might also seek self-determination.

What else might be visible beyond the Veil? Readers might find the self-aware agent that Winant raises regarding Du Bois's conception of the Veil. Taylor's novels have been studied for the development of agency, as well as a focus on the land, family, and community. The Logan family fight to maintain their dignity and the ownership of their land and sometimes their lives. The land is representative of empowerment, along with the trees in *Song*, and the water in *Well*. Sarah Hardstaff's 2015 essay examines Taylor's signature novel, *Thunder*, for child agency. Hardstaff compares the linguistic and literary interpretations of the novel from Cassie's perspective. While living a veiled existence tends to stifle agency, Taylor's characters manage to still exercise theirs within their limited spheres of influence.

Taylor also wanted to make visible a more complex and holistic conception of Black lives that resembled the rich tapestry of life she and her family lived. The stories that were retold on front porches, in the kitchen, around the fireplace, and on long car rides did not resemble the sad sagas that Taylor recalled from textbooks and lessons in school (Legacy Award 47).

Her stories were influenced by the lives of her extended family of aunts, uncles, and cousins and the steady migration of her immediate family between Mississippi and Toledo, Ohio (Hayes 33). She described in an American Library Association interview that there was a general lack of common knowledge of Black people's lived experiences and history, which she felt was mostly informed by stereotypes ("Acceptance Speech"). Taylor's mother's and father's families were landowners since the 1800s, and she wanted to portray through her stories that Black lives mattered.

Du Bois held similar sentiments. He also hoped that readers of *The Brownies' Book* would come to "know that colored children have grown into beautiful, useful, and famous persons" ("The True Brownies" 286). He used the Veil as a signifier or a proxy for the invisibility of Black lives. The Veil draws on symbolic imagery of invisibility, exclusion, and misperception.

For example, in *Let the Circle Be Unbroken* (*Circle*) the Veil provides the context for Moe Turner's statement that this year, unlike years past, his family may earn enough to break free from sharecropping, a system that exchanges work for a share of the profits from the crops. Moe's family had sharecropped on the Montier plantation since the 1880s and despite bountiful harvests, the Montiers had managed to find a way to keep them indebted and working for them. Cassie refers to his dream as Moe's "sharecropping hallucinations" and is shushed quiet by her brothers when she dares to break his spell of hopefulness (*Circle* 90). Yet Moe is undeterred. His belief that this year may be the year his family breaks free is duplicitous or an example of double consciousness. Despite his repeated desire for his family to earn enough in a system that is designed to cheat them, he remains optimistic.

Moe tries to rise above the situation, like Du Bois rises above the Veil, and to remain hopeful. This scene takes place within a certain labor relationship between Black and white people—a veiled relationship where the planter class benefited at the expense of the laboring class. The outcome of such a relationship was known and even expected with children as young as the Logans able to understand its dynamics.

In the closing chapter of *Thunder*, Cassie takes stock of T.J.'s predicament, understanding its cruel dynamics. While David intervenes to keep T.J. from being hanged, his future is still uncertain. The enormity of the event is not lost on young Cassie, nor on her family. This realization is like Du Bois's epiphany of the Veil when the tall newcomer refused his card at school that day in Great Barrington. This incident parallels the profound ordinariness with which Cassie carries on with her life in the absence of T.J. She wakes up the next day and the day after that, running in the woods, dabbling in the pond, and walking barefooted to school with the boys. Even the grim reminder of the Jefferson Davis school bus speaks to the banality of life in the shadow of the Veil. While Cassie admits she never really liked T.J., the writer of cheat notes in Stacey's class, she also acknowledges the unfairness of what happened to him. She cries for him and for herself, as she experiences the impact of the shadow of the Veil. She vividly describes the experience on the last page of *Thunder*: "What happened to T.J. in the night I did not understand, but I know that it would not pass. And I cried for those things which had happened in the night and would not pass. I cried for T.J. For T.J. and the land" (276).

In Taylor's last book, *All the Days Past, All the Days to Come,* Cassie ends her journey much the way she began it in *Song*. Her journey down the winding trail to the pond and then to the trees that were felled during her childhood mirrors her journey to Ohio and then California, Colorado, Massachusetts, and back to Mississippi, where the Veil seems intact. Her epiphany is that racism and discrimination, like the great Veil, simply reappear in different forms in different places where there are no signs, but the rules and expectations remain. While Cassie realizes that some things do not pass, at least easily, she bears witness to change. Taylor's concluding novel of the saga ends with real people and fictional characters: Vivian Malone and James Hood admitted to the University of Alabama; Ralph Bunche, a close follower of Du Bois, appointed as ambassador to the United Nations; Morris killed; and Papa dead.

Taylor grew up listening to voices of those who were born with a veiled existence and gifted with second sight. Applying Du Bois's theories to Taylor's collective works reveals the resilience and strength of Black people but also their vulnerability, pain, and circumstance. Throughout Taylor's novels, readers witness the inner workings of Black families who are never monolithic in how they approach problems, understand the world, and battle inner and outer demons. She depicts the hot head, the risk taker, the loner, the talker, the compromiser, the mediator—"Ain't gonna be no shootin,'" Mama said without anger in her voice (*Well* 15)—and the other. There is always an outcast.

Each character shares a set of circumstances they carry, like a backpack, meaning that these circumstances are easily accessible and ever present. These characters are like everybody else in the world except for this backpack that can grow heavy or light depending on the situation. For example, a big black Hudson swerves to a stop near a group of children in *Circle*, and a man gets out and leans across the shiny hood, asking for Dubé Cross using a racial slur (300). The backpack is like a set of circumstances ready to deploy at the slightest provocation, with little warning or forecast. Something as odd as the rejection of a greeting card or raising one's voice to the wrong person could unleash a torrent of unsuspecting violence, or just an odd feeling of being different.

After a while, the characters in Taylor's novels adapt, like all the seventh sons before them. They develop vision and perception so acute, they can sense when a situation is serious and when it is not. They can spot a look across the room. As a result of living a veiled existence, Taylor's characters develop varying levels of second sight and the angst of double consciousness that goes along with it. Yet they also laugh, work hard, make time for family and friends, have fun, make mistakes, and after Christmas breakfast, get dressed and go to church. They develop resilience through community and then tell stories about it so that the rest of us will never forget.

WORKS CITED

Anderson, Rodino F. "Poetically Dwelling with the Veil: The Intellectual, Moral, and Aesthetic Dimensions of W. E. B. Du Bois's Educational Philosophy." *Philosophy of Education Yearbook*, vol. 61, 2005, pp. 275–83.
"Author Profile: Mildred D. Taylor." *World Literature Today*, vol. 78, no. 2, May 2004, p. 3.
Barad, Karen. *Meeting the Universe Halfway: Quantum Physics and the Entanglement of Matter and Meaning*. Duke UP, 2007.
Bosmajian, Hamida. "Mildred Taylor's Story of Cassie Logan: A Search for Law and Justice in a Racist Society." *Children's Literature*, vol. 24, 1996, pp. 141–60.
Davis, Pamela M. *Shifting Ideology in Mildred D. Taylor's Books*. 2013. Middle Tennessee State U, PhD dissertation.
Dunbar, Paul Laurence, "We Wear the Mask." *The Complete Poems of Paul Laurence Dunbar*, Dodd, Mead, 2010, p. 8.
Du Bois, W. E. B. (William Edward Burghardt). *Darkwater: Voices From Within The Veil*, Kindle ed., Harcourt, Brace and Howe, 1920.
Du Bois, W. E. B. *The Negro*. The Project Gutenberg EBook of The Negro 1915. https://www.gutenberg.org/files/15359/15359-h/15359-h.htm.
Du Bois, W. E. B. *The Souls of Black Folk; Essays and Sketches*. A. G. McClurg, 1903. Kindle ed., Johnson Reprint Corp., 1968.
Du Bois, W. E. B. "The True Brownies." Editorial. *Crisis*, Oct. 1919, pp. 285–86.
Du Bois, W. E. B. *The Brownies' Book*. 1920–21. Retrieved from the Library of Congress, <www.loc.gov/item/22001351/>.
Du Bois, W. E. B. *The Souls of Black Folk, A Norton Critical Edition*, edited by Henry Louis Gates Jr. and Terri Hume Oliver, 1st ed., W. W. Norton, 1999.
Fertik, Harriet, and Mathias Hanses. "Above the Veil: Revisiting the Classicism of W. E. B. Du Bois." *International Journal of the Classical Tradition*, vol. 26, no. 1, Mar. 2019, pp. 1–9.
Fisher, Leona W. "Focalizing the Unfamiliar: Laurence Yep's Child in a Strange Land." *MELUS*, vol. 27, no. 2, June 2002, p. 157.

Foner, Eric. "Review of The Remarkable Life of W. E. B. Du Bois, by David Levering Lewis." *The Journal of Blacks in Higher Education*, no. 30, 2000, pp. 130–33. *JSTOR*, https://doi.org/10.2307/2679119.

Hayes, Regina. "Mildred D. Taylor." *The Horn Book Magazine*, vol. 96, no. 4, July 2020, p. 32.

Hardstaff, Sarah (Layzell). "'Papa Said That One Day I Would Understand': Examining Child Agency and Character Development in *Roll of Thunder, Hear My Cry* Using Critical Corpus Linguistics." *Children's Literature in Education*, vol. 46, no. 3, Sept. 2015, pp. 226–41.

Hawkins, Tom. "The Veil, the Cave and the Fire-Bringer." *International Journal of the Classical Tradition*, vol. 26, no. 1, Mar. 2019, pp. 38–53.

Johnson, Dianne. "A Tribute to Mildred D. Taylor." *World Literature Today*, vol. 78, no. 2, May 2004, p. 4.

Khalfa, Jean. "Frantz Fanon's 'Black Skin, White Masks': New Interdisciplinary Essays." *The Modern Language Review*, vol. 102, no. 2, Apr. 1, 2007, p. 527.

King, Deborah K. "Multiple Jeopardy, Multiple Consciousnesses: The Context of a Black Feminist Ideology." *Signs*, vol. 14, no. 1, 1998, pp. 42–72.

Leibbrand, Christine et al. "The Great Migration and Residential Segregation in American Cities During the Twentieth Century." *Social Science History*, vol. 44, no. 1, 2020, pp. 19–55. *PubMed*, doi:10.1017/ssh.2019.46.

Lewis, David Levering. *W. E. B. Du Bois: Biography of a Race, 1868–1919*. Henry Holt, 1993.

Magoon, Kekla. "Our Foundation, Our Springboard: The Trailblazing Work of Mildred D. Taylor and Jacqueline Woodson." *The Horn Book Magazine*, vol. 97, no. 4, July 2021, pp. 50–53.

McDowell, Kelly. "*Roll of Thunder, Hear My Cry*: A Culturally Specific, Subversive Concept of Child Agency." *Children's Literature in Education*, vol. 33, no. 3, Sept. 2002, pp. 213–25.

Moses, Wilson Jeremiah. *The Golden Age of Black Nationalism, 1850–1925*. Archon Books, 1978.

Rampersad, Arnold. *The Art and Imagination of W. E. B. Du Bois*. Harvard UP, 1976.

Schrager, Cynthia D. "Both Sides of the Veil: Race, Science, and Mysticism in W. E. B. Du Bois." *American Quarterly*, vol. 48, no. 4, Dec. 1996, pp. 551–86.

Shaw, Stephanie J. *W. E. B. Du Bois and The Souls of Black Folk*. The John Hope Franklin Series in African American History and Culture. U of North Carolina P, 2013.

Smith, Karen Patricia. *A Chronicle of Family Honor: Balancing Rage and Triumph in the Novels of Mildred D. Taylor. African American Voices in Young Adult Literature*. Scarecrow, 1994.

"Talking with Mildred D. Taylor," American Library Association, https://www.ala.org/aboutala/offices/resources/taylor. Accessed Aug. 11, 2021.

Taylor, Mildred D. "Acceptance Speech for the 1997 ALAN Award." https://scholar.lib.vt.edu/ejournals/ALAN/spring98/taylor.html.

Taylor, Mildred D. *All the Days Past, All the Days to Come*. Kindle ed., Viking Press, 2020, vii.

Taylor, Mildred D. "Children's Literature Legacy Award Acceptance." *The Horn Book Magazine*, vol. 97, no. 4, July 2021, pp. 47–49.

Taylor, Mildred D. *The Land*. Phyllis Fogelman Books, 2001.

Taylor, Mildred D. *Let the Circle Be Unbroken*. 1981. Kindle ed., Puffin, 1991.

Taylor, Mildred D. "My Life as a Writer." *World Literature Today*, vol. 78, no. 2, May 1, 2004, p. 7.

Taylor, Mildred D. *Roll of Thunder, Hear My Cry*. Dial. 25th anniversary ed., Phyllis Fogelman Books, 2001).

Taylor, Mildred D. *Song of The Trees*. Puffin, 1975.

Taylor, Mildred D. "Tapped on the Shoulder." *World Literature Today*, vol. 88, no. 5, Oct. 2014, pp. 60–61.
Taylor, Mildred. *The Well*. Kindle ed., Penguin Young Readers Group, 1995.
Vaughn-Roberson, Courtney, and Brenda Hill. "The Brownies' and Ebony Jr.!: Literature as a Mirror of the Afro-American Experience." *The Journal of Negro Education*, vol. 58, no. 4, Oct. 1989, pp. 494–510.
Winant, Howard. "The Dark Matter: Race and Racism in the 21st Century." *Critical Sociology*, vol. 41, no. 2, Mar. 2015, pp. 313–24.
Zamir, Shamoon, and Vilna I. Bashi. "Dark Voices: W. E. B. Du Bois and American Thought, 1888–1903." *American Journal of Sociology*, vol. 102, no. 1, 1996, pp. 267–69.

Racial Education and Audience in *All the Days Past, All the Days to Come*

Jani L. Barker

Mildred D. Taylor's Logan Family Saga, begun with *Song of the Trees* (1975), comes to a bittersweet end with *All the Days Past, All the Days to Come* (*Days*) (2020). Cassie Logan again serves as narrator, no longer the naïve child of *Song* or the Newbery Medal–winning *Roll of Thunder, Hear My Cry* (*Thunder*) (1976), but an adult, more knowledgeable about the realities of racism, although no less outraged by them. This sweeping finale tells of the Logan family's life and the nation's racial history from 1944–1963, plus a brief 2009 epilogue. The scope goes beyond the Mississippi Logan land to encompass Cassie's life in the North and on both coasts, as well as her brothers' families and her own loss of an expected child and her beloved husband. The novel also shows the psychological priming for change that being drafted to fight for America against white Europeans in World War II had on Black veterans, the strengthening civil rights movement, and the costly victories that were early tipping points of political change. The inextricable intertwining of personal and racial history for the Logans, and African Americans more generally, is illustrated by an episode late in the novel in which the family gathers at David's death bed, holding hands and praying in an "unbroken" circle (481). Meanwhile, through the window Cassie can see the sheriff who had tacitly supported the white men who had shot at the Logan siblings, attempting to run them off the road earlier in the day as they tried to attend the funeral of murdered civil rights activist Medgar Evers (482).

In *Days* the intimate narrator-reader relationship established in earlier Logan novels continues to engender readers' strong investment in the Logan family, connecting author, narrator, text, subject matter, and reader (real and implied). Given the variable reading responses of actual readers, which may reveal as much about individual readers as about *Days*, this paper focuses on the "implied reader," as theorized by Wolfgang Iser—a construct rooted in "the structure of the text" that guides the reading process, embodies all the "predispositions" required for a literary text "to exercise its effects," and "prestructures the role to be assumed by each recipient" (Iser 34). Literary and rhetorical elements in Taylor's text prestructure several overlapping audiences, starting with implied readers with limited knowledge of and potential misconceptions about the nation's racial past. Education is at the heart of this novel, as is typical of African American youth literature (Johnson 2)—not simplistic didacticism, but nuanced instruction through the storytelling of an author and a narrator who bring readers into the Logans' world, letting them witness the impact of racism. Additionally, the novel awakens memories for long-time Logan fans through frequent references to events of previous Logan books, adding a feeling of homecoming. The allusions to earlier stories evoke a rich backdrop for readers being introduced to the Logans, perhaps stimulating a desire to read and learn more. The adult protagonist-narrator, sexual content, and complexity of *Days* suggest an older target audience, although nothing precludes middle-grade readers from reading *Days*. Additionally, the Logans' race-based interactions with characters suggest mixed-race implied audiences. Implied readers of all races are drawn into the lives of the Logans, inspired to care about them and feel their frustration, fear, rage, pain, loyalty, and love. However, Cassie's repeated recognition of the pervasiveness of racism in America will resonate with Black and other nonwhite readers, while an intellectual tension is structured into the reading experience of white implied readers that creates strong emotional identification with the Logans while reminding critical white readers that racism has distanced people like them from the family.

Using critical race theory as a lens through which to view the novel's depictions of race relations, this essay explores how *Days* educates its implied audiences on racism in mid-twentieth-century America and pays homage to those who worked for civil rights. It also explores the novel's structuring of race-based identifications for implied readers of color, especially Black readers, and for the white implied reader, arguing that the novel uses the emotional connections it evokes and intellectual lessons it provides to promote strong, but distinct, antiracist identifications for these audiences.

CRITICAL RACE THEORY AND THE MATERIAL AND PSYCHIC EFFECTS OF RACISM IN *DAYS*

Through her experiences, Cassie Logan realizes that "[b]eing colored was a way of life in America" (125). Her comment encapsulates much of what critical race theorists argue about race and racism, especially anti-Black racism. Critical race theory (CRT) views race as central to understanding power, ideology, and societal functioning in a range of legal, economic, educational, and social areas. Racism, according to CRT theorists such as Derrick Bell, Richard Delgado, and Jean Stefancic, is deeply embedded in American institutions and the nation's mindset, viewed as "ordinary, not aberrational" (Delgado and Stefancic 8), so normal as to be practically imperceptible to most of the dominant society unless racist actions are extremely blatant. For members of less privileged groups, however, racism is experienced almost ubiquitously and is, as Cassie notes, a way of life. CRT also shares with Taylor's novels an emphasis on activism that "not only tries to understand [the] social situation, but to change it" (Delgado and Stefancic 3). Finally, CRT argues for the potential of storytelling to make a positive difference for members both of outgroups who voice their stories and the dominant group (Delgado 2436–37). Thus, and as we can see elsewhere in this volume, CRT serves as a useful lens for analyzing Taylor's writing, as it explains much that the Logan novels show. In a 2009 article, Wanda Brooks applies three tenets of CRT in her analysis of *The Land*: (1) the use of counterstories through which African Americans "voice and validate their life circumstances" and "respond to racism and its dominant ideology by calling into question normative depictions of everyday living that ignore or discount structural barriers to equality"; (2) "the role of property rights in US society and its relationship to whiteness"; and (3) "institutionalized racism" (38). Similarly, in a 2010 article, I use CRT to undergird an analysis of *Thunder* and its depiction of racism as pervasive and normalized in the "educational, legal, and economic lives of those in the Logans' community" (Barker 125). CRT also illuminates how the novel advocates strategic resistance to racism and serves as a valuable counterstory to dominant cultural narratives (Barker 125). Critical race theory is equally applicable to the other Logan books.

In *Days*, Cassie's experiences and reflections teach readers that racism throughout the nation is multifaceted, pervasive, and both materially and psychologically damaging. These two categories of damages correlate well with two basic camps within CRT: the "realists" and the "idealists." The "realists" or "economic determinists" camp of CRT thinkers holds that "racial hierarchies determine who gets tangible benefits" (Delgado and Stefancic 21). For these materialists, changing "the physical circumstances of minorities' lives" is the central focus in combating racism (Delgado and Stefancic 25). In contrast, the "idealists" view "racism and discrimination" as "matters of thinking, mental categorization, attitude, and discourse" and argue that racism can be remedied most effectively by "changing the system of images, words, attitudes, unconscious feelings, scripts, and social teachings" that send cultural messages about the relative values of different groups of people (Delgado and Stafancic 21).

Days, like Taylor's previous books, provides ample examples of the material, tangible race-based deprivations that the "realist" CRT camp emphasizes. The prologue shows Man (Clayton Chester, known previously as Little Man) and Cassie, on Man's final leave before shipping out for World War II, at the back of a bus with a segregating curtain moved back as needed to increase space for white passengers. This opening reminds long-time Logan fans of previous bus-related racism, including the lack of a school bus for the Black children and the delight the driver and students in the white school's bus took in deliberately splashing the Black children with mud and running them off the road (*Thunder* 43). Other discriminatory policies abound: signs in the South proclaim, "Whites Only. Colored Not Allowed" (*Days* 83, 294); Black citizens are prohibited from eating in restaurants, staying at motels, or visiting the "white only" library; forced to drink from "nasty-looking" water fountains designated for "colored" use (84, 293–94); refused the right to try on clothes before buying (230, 293); and segregated in hospitals (86) or refused medical care (251). On seeing Cassie's race, a California landlady falsely claims an apartment is unavailable, wishing her "[g]ood luck finding a place in your own neighborhood" (213–14). Readers are thus taught that before laws were enacted to forbid them, such overt discriminatory practices were widespread.

The realist consequences of anti-Black racism are most starkly evident in the physical violence—tolerated or upheld by legal authority—that is a ubiquitous threat, especially for those defending themselves or challenging the social order. In a biographical incident based on Taylor family history, Stacey is hit by a white man and restrained by Black coworkers because, as his brother-in-law explains, "Boy'd be in jail, or dead, he'd've hit that white boy" (Taylor, "My Life" 8; *Days* 25). As in earlier novels, the Logan family and friends share stories of tragic oppression, such as a Black soldier shot in the head for refusing to move over to let a white man pass (320). As voter registration drives gain momentum, leaders, including the Logans' friend Morris Turner, are arrested and even killed for their involvement in activities viewed as "inciting folks toward riot" (403). Arsonists burn down Great Faith Church, site of registration classes (404–5). Taylor intermingles stories of fictional characters (often based on Taylor family history) with historical figures such as Herbert Lee of Amite County, killed by his white neighbor, a Mississippi legislator and relative of the sheriff, for working on a registration drive. Although Mr. Lee was shot in front of ten witnesses, a coroner's jury acquitted the white killer the same day (406–7). These horrific accounts provide historical backdrop, while more vividly recounted narratives of characters with whom we identify draw readers into vicarious participation in the oppression. In an especially tense scene, the Logan siblings are endangered by white longtime adversaries who surround the Logan car, forcing Stacey to decide whether to try to outrun them and risk being shot or be run off the road (466–69). When bullets hit the car during their desperate attempt to avoid being forced onto a back road, Cassie notes, "There was no terror greater for black folks than being chased by white folks on a back country road" (469). Later that day, white strangers try to overturn their car as they are stuck in Jackson traffic (471), another reminder of the pervasiveness of the material, physical dangers of being Black in the American South.

Although *Days* never directly addresses the "realist" versus "idealist" debate within CRT, and the activism shown by Logan family members and friends fits within the "realist" camp, *Days* also amply illustrates the racist attitudes, ways of thinking, discourse, and representation in images and stories that, according to the "idealists" camp of CRT thinkers, lies at the heart of racial discrimination (Delgado and Stefancic 21). The novel itself provides positive representation for Black people and antiracist modes of thinking that counter the bigotry that pervades daily life for the Logans and the community. Cultural messages intended to drive home the designated inferiority of Black people are everywhere. At a theater restroom, when Cassie and a friend decline to wait for the stall unofficially designated for colored people, a white woman refuses to use a toilet after a Black woman (*Days* 47). As police escort Cassie, Moe, and Stacey from the movie theater, a white movie goer comments "Damn niggers! Think they can do anything they want!" (*Days* 52). Racial slurs like this assault Black people throughout the nation (125, 198, 372, etc.). Augmenting the psychic damage of these ongoing assaults, racial stereotypes incessantly remind people of color that others view them as lesser. Cassie notes that media depicts "the American Negro as enslaved, shiftless, ignorant, usually following behind or at the will of some white person" (291).

Moreover, both realist and idealist, material and psychological, aspects of racism intertwine. The "white flight" after Stacey buys a house in the midst of white-occupied properties (32) attests to the racist thinking that is the "idealist" side of the "realist" housing discrimination coin. The "realist" discrimination of bus segregation leaves Man "fuming" over the humiliation of sitting in "a soldier's uniform behind a black curtain so that white folks would not have to be reminded of his existence" (3), while a more insidious damage is suggested when, after Man walks home rather than repeatedly move back in the bus, the family fears retaliation for his quiet protest. When an Ohioan doctor refuses to call a nurse in during a pelvic exam and, invoking inaccurate racial stereotypes, implies that Cassie is sexually promiscuous, the psychic damage of the harassment is accompanied by a material consequence: Cassie loses her chance for a job by refusing to complete the required physical exam. Later, in California, Cassie is accosted by a car full of white teenagers who suggest a group rate for her sexual favors and make "obscene remarks," rendering her physically and emotionally unsafe while walking "colored in a white neighborhood" (200).

Days joins Taylor's other works, and CRT, in highlighting the psychological as well as material costs of racism and the consequent need to resist even when resistance might seem unwise or futile. Racism permeates the daily lives and psyches of Black people. Cassie reflects on "all the days of humiliation. Every colored person in the South . . . had memories of humiliation and anger" (354). The designated inferiority symbolized by the ubiquitous "whites only" signs is internalized, not for the Logans by acceptance, but by constant awareness: "Even if there were no signs on display, they were imprinted in all our thinking" (83), Cassie muses. Racism also shapes practices. The Logan parents feel compelled to be "hard" on their children to teach them the rules "the years of slavery and Jim Crow had proven" necessary for survival for Black people (16). White-mandated subservience, along with well-precedented fear of injury, leads Moe Turner to attack the Aames brothers in a pivotal scene in *The Road to Memphis*, with repercussions that persist throughout *Days*. Cassie recalls the "shame" of the Aames brothers' humiliation of a young Black soldier, as they taunt him with "racial jokes," rubbing his head for good luck; Moe's later refusal to "bow his head" for them provokes his attack and decades-long self-exile to evade arrest (62–63). Psychological assault can warrant actions that carry serious material risks. After Stacey places a huge order for take-out at a Wyoming restaurant that has refused the Logan siblings a table, then "changed his mind" in revenge for the discrimination, Cassie reflects that while this defiance "might have seemed an insignificant way of fighting back," such acts were "all that allowed us a little dignity as human beings" (125). The ever-present psychic drain caused by racism makes resistance a form of self-defense.

EDUCATING READERS ON RACISM THROUGHOUT THE US AND ON THE CIVIL RIGHTS MOVEMENT

Much of the education in racism in *Days* focuses on correcting misconceptions that racism in the United States before the civil rights movement was largely confined to the South. Stacey joins the Great Migration of Black workers "looking for better jobs, for less discrimination, for all the opportunities of the North" (34), followed by his siblings. However, while the discrimination elsewhere is less overt and usually less violent than in the South, it is still pervasive. Repeatedly, Cassie must recognize that racism permeates every hoped-for refuge. In Ohio, when the theater staff call the police after she insists on integrating the main floor of a movie theater, Cassie reflects on the hypocrisy of the Northern pretense of equality: "throughout the South, folks were direct and honest.... The signs were everywhere.... But here in Toledo, ... [i]t was simply understood. *Whites Only. Colored Not Allowed*" (56). When the Logan siblings encounter car trouble and seek lodging, with Cassie noting that they are in Iowa, not Mississippi, the motor court manager retracts the "ROOMS AVAILABLE" sign (119). In Wyoming, after being refused a table at a restaurant, Cassie reflects, "We had thought maybe things would be different here, in the great American West. We were wrong.... For us, America remained as always, the same. *Whites Only. Colored Not Allowed*" (125–26). Again, in California, when police stop Cassie and Flynn, her future husband, as they drive through a wealthy neighborhood and arrest Flynn without justification, Cassie "stared in disbelief. This was not Mississippi. This was Los Angeles" (198). When refused continuing services at a Colorado medical center, an exclusion she is certain is racial, Cassie feels betrayed: "I hadn't felt this way in Colorado before. It's an insult in a place I thought maybe was different..." (251). In every region of the nation, Cassie is slapped in the face with racial prejudice and material race-based discrimination.

Taylor's repeated emphasis on the protagonist-narrator's surprise and disillusionment at racism encountered throughout the nation counters a dominant narrative about America's racial history. The young Cassie's frequent shock when encountering racism in *Thunder* both reveals that she has not yet internalized racism and encourages implied readers "to identify with Cassie's subject position and thus with her outrage at deeply ingrained racism" (Barker 126). Similarly, the difficulty with which the adult Cassie relinquishes hope of finding a place where she can expect anything approaching equality shows the narrator's resilient optimism but also suggests an implied audience with an erroneously restricted view of racism in America. This audience, witnessing Cassie's repeated disillusionments, joins with her recognition that racism permeates the nation, and that being Black is not just a full-time job, but also "a full-time fight," one impossible to win alone (*Days* 255). Cassie pursues law school and later works in a Boston law firm. She still faces discrimination, being asked to leave a nightclub at which she is the only person of color aside from the entertainers (297), but by this point Cassie is no longer surprised (298).

Days also educates readers on more subtle forms of racism. Cassie, an attractive Black woman with a degree from the Boston University School of Law and a job at an established law firm, suffers the discomfort of being "the only" Black person in her class, her firm, her neighborhood. Only one classmate, Guy Hallis, befriends her. At a law school Christmas party, after some white female students sit on Santa's lap and kiss him, someone grabs Cassie, despite her dignified protests, and shoves her onto his lap, shouting, "Don't want to discriminate!" (301). The allegedly antidiscriminatory rhetoric calls attention to

Cassie's difference, accentuating the harassment. At parties with well-educated white people, Cassie wearies of finding herself, repeatedly, the "only one" and enduring laboriously polite conversation or requests to represent her race by giving her "views as a Negro" (306). As wearying as being the "lone token" is, Cassie takes advantage of coming "to the attention of people with influence, who pointed [her] out as an example of what a colored person could achieve" (291) and, fully aware of the subtle racism underlying the rare opportunities, she still "snatched every opportunity presented" (295). This willingness to exploit racism itself is another side to the resistance she employs throughout the novel.

Indeed, recognition of the need to fight back against racist oppression, to work for real change, is central to *Days*. Repeatedly, the protagonist-narrator emphasizes the need for change, doubts it ever happening, and spotlights slowly growing movements toward change and virulent resistance to these movements, along with perseverance in the costly struggle. The epilogue, set in 2009, more than sixty-eight years after the prologue and forty-five years after the final chapter, suggests the efforts are not fruitless. One paragraph tells of Barack Obama's election and Great Faith Church chartering a bus to attend his inauguration, driving through the states traveled by the 1961 Freedom Riders. Then, a single sentence concludes the series: "I was on the bus" (485).

Clearly *Days* serves, in part, as an homage to those who worked for change; its triumphant epilogue, spotlighting a very different bus ride than the one in the prologue, suggests a progressive stance. In this area, the novel might be said to diverge from CRT, which, even though it embeds an activist component, challenges the civil rights movement's vision of progressive change. As Delgado and Stefancic explain, "Unlike traditional civil rights discourse, which stresses incrementalism and step-by-step progress, critical race theory questions the very foundations of the liberal order" (3). Yet the novel leaves room both for celebration of progress and for questioning the possibility of real change in America. The realities of racism ring throughout the novel more loudly than civil rights success; the Logan family's doubts are in constant tension with their hopes of change, and the silent gap between the 2009 epilogue and the novel's publication in 2020, after the change in presidential administrations, suggests questions for the reader to fill in.

Taylor presents a complex view of Black involvement in the civil rights movement through the Logans' ambivalent views about fighting for change. No Logan questions the need for change or internalizes racist views of their rightful position in society, but family members disagree about methods and the possibility of success. When the Logan veterans of World War II return and argue in favor of fighting the white people in this country for change, Big Ma doubts it could come in their lifetime (93). Cassie, usually active in pushing against the racist status quo, resists an Ohioan lawyer's encouragement to pursue a career in law to help with the postwar opportunity for "big, big changes" (265), citing the ongoing lack of change. Yet Lawyer Tate's exhortation that she fight for "changes in race laws all across this land" (266) must resonate, as she starts law school shortly afterward. Mary Logan eagerly reports National Association for the Advancement of Colored People (NAACP) efforts to address racist violence and injustice, arguing, "[I]f we organize, take a chapter from the Montgomery boycott, we might be able to get some change" (321), but Hammer remains skeptical, reiterating the entrenched oppression in the South (322). When Stacey's daughter, Rie, excitedly talks of opportunities at Spelman College to help with "breaking the chains" (340), her protective father forbids her involvement. After she gets arrested, along with Dr. Martin Luther King and many others, for participating in sit-ins, Stacey reluctantly delays her bail to increase the attention given the activist efforts (363–64). While Mary and Cassie are committed to the voter registration drive, David refuses to be tested and judged by white men just to vote for white men and laughs at Cassie's suggestion that Black people might run for office (402). Although the novel clearly applauds activist efforts for change, it implicitly raises questions for readers about which positions they might have taken, extending to *Days* the "complexly interrogative nature" that Michelle Martin suggests creates the power of the Logan novels (6). Implied readers, viewing compelling arguments for differing positions, are denied the comfort of simple solutions to racial issues—even those easy to celebrate in hindsight.

A key difference in *Days*' education in antiracist activism compared to the other Logan novels' approaches to educating readers in racism's reality is the lower degree of intimacy and the emotional involvement evoked by the narrative. When showing the impact of racism, Taylor's novels take the reader closely into scenarios that affect the Logan community, positioning readers to feel the emotions of the narrator and her family, to see and hear events as if we were there. The implied white reader who might underestimate the reality and impact of racism in American society is positioned to experience it vicariously. While teaching about civil rights activism, in contrast, *Days* takes a broader perspective, providing an overview that at times reads more like a history lesson than a fictional narrative that positions the reader at the scene. While all the Logan novels are historically accurate, Taylor situates *Days* far more historically than her previous books. The actions of historical figures, including Martin Luther King and Medgar Evers, are described, and we learn of Logan family members' and friends' involvement in the movement, sometimes adjacent to these renowned activists. The activism of historical and fictional figures is reported with a more cognitive than emotional approach. In the same declarative way that Cassie summarizes major initiatives such as sit-ins, freedom rides, and economic boycotts and provides overviews of hard-won successes, such as the implementation of federal laws mandating desegregation, she recounts her family's efforts.

When Man decides to join the Freedom Riders to honor an Army buddy who had been killed in 1949 for refusing to move to the back of a bus (375-76), we have some emotional engagement as his siblings determine to follow his bus in solidarity (378). However, after Man is arrested, three short sentences recount his siblings' observation of Man being taken away, their decision to take his place at the white lunch counter, and others joining their impromptu protest. The limited aftermath, "We were all arrested" (381), distances readers from the scene. Far less affect appears in this episode than in the three-page account of James Meredith's attempts to enroll at the University of Mississippi, the federal support for his enrollment, Mississippi's strenuous efforts to keep the university "a bastion of white purity" and the governor's public declaration that a Negro would "Never!" be admitted. All four Logan siblings, with families gathered, watch "transfixed," as the televised accounts show the rioting that precedes Meredith's attendance. To the Logans' disbelief, he successfully enrolls (430-32).

While Taylor's texts actively promote empathy for those who suffer racism, *Days* does not position readers to feel vicarious heroism in the civil rights movement. It shows the Logans, with whom readers identify, to be relatively insignificant pawns, crediting victories to collective labor and sacrifice. The wide-angle, often overview-based portrayal of civil-rights activism that plays such an extensive part of *Days* may be a necessary result of the novel's broad scope; it may also have a calculated effect of showing the enormity of racism via the tremendous efforts required by masses of people to combat it. Almost certainly, *Days*' education in resisting racism structures the learning experiences in ways that honor those whose efforts, large and small, led to increased civil rights, without making room for any reading-dreams of glory. The novel prestructures an affective response for implied readers that promotes a sense of the urgent need for action and of respect for those who acted; it denies readers feelings of heroic satisfaction from participating vicariously in the courageous acts.

Readers are, however, engaged in narrative identification with Cassie's commitment to continuing civil rights efforts in Mississippi. After the murder of family friend Morris Turner, Cassie reflects on his unfinished task in a passage with cognitive and emotional resonance:

> Much had been accomplished to ease us toward first-class citizenship ... but there was still much to be done. Despite all of Morris's efforts, only a few people had been registered to vote.... Morris ... had refused to be beaten by the system. If one Negro could be registered, hundreds more could be registered. Thousands more. Every ... Negro person of age in the state of Mississippi could one day vote, and when that

happened it would mean equal rights for all of us. It would change the state. That was Morris's dream. Little Brother Morris. (460)

Thinking "of all who had gone before," Cassie resolves to remain and finish Morris's work (460–61). Again, the narrative spotlights the need for action and resolve to take it rather than providing readers with vicarious victories. We learn nothing of Cassie's subsequent efforts or success.

RACE AND IMPLIED AUDIENCES

Days provides a nostalgic reunion for returning Logan fans, introduces new readers to the Logans, and educates all readers in racism in mid-twentieth-century America, correcting common misperceptions in the process. Stories from earlier Logan books—most based on tales told by Taylor's family (Taylor, "My Life" 8)—extend the education in racism further into the past, illuminating its long-term effects while intensifying the connections built among readers, author, and Logan characters. Just a few examples include allusions to a fatal bus accident shortly after several Black folks were ordered off to make room for white passengers (*Bridge* and *Days* 6); Moe Turner's attack on white boys (*Memphis* and *Days* 57, 62–63); a white store owner who shot a Black man for refusing to call him "Mister" (*Friendship* and *Days* 323); eleven-year-old Cassie's attempts to help Mrs. Lee Annie gain the vote (*Circle* and *Days* 345–46); and Charlie Simms's shoving Cassie off a sidewalk (*Thunder* and *Days* 354). In addition to the connections established between reader and text, *Days* prestructures for implied audiences reading experiences influenced partially by race. Of course, ALL readers are invited into the Logans' world and encouraged to empathize with them, but the clear divide between races insisted on by the family suggests differing ways in which implied readers of different races are positioned to see themselves reflected within the novel.

For Black readers, African American literature reflects the lives of their forebears, telling stories of experiences that have shaped their own lives. It shows the courage of Black protagonists, providing positive images instead of the absent or stereotypical ones that children's literature too often has offered. Rudine Sims Bishop credits African American literature for youth with providing benefits that include celebrating "the strengths of the Black family as a cultural institution and vehicle for survival"; bearing "witness to Black people's determined struggle for freedom, equality, and dignity"; nurturing "the souls of Black children by reflecting . . . [their] beauty and competencies"; and honoring "story as a way of teaching and as a way of knowing" (*Free* 273). *Days* yields all these advantages. Bishop notes that for Taylor, "Black life is a matter of surviving and maintaining self-respect and dignity while living in a racist cultural context" (*Free* 266). Spotlighting the solidarity of the Black community, her novels offer the Black implied reader a strong sense of belonging with the Logans, a silver lining of the racist oppression. While traveling back to Mississippi, Cassie reflects on her automatic bond with unknown Black people: "All colored folks were a part of this life; none of us were strangers. We all lived under the same rules, no matter what our individual circumstances. . . . Those rules and our color bound us together" (*Days* 95). Even in the North, Cassie is certain that Attorney Tate would understand what had led Moe Turner to attack the white men who had harassed him after humiliating and injuring other Black young men because "[a]nybody of color would have understood" (62). Stacey's home symbolizes the close inclusiveness of the Black familial community, with up to fourteen people counted as family living there, plus renters on the second floor who joined them daily to enjoy music or television. The resilience to glean good even from the evils of racism is reflected in Black food heritage. Many traditional foods, such as hog-head souse, were "delicacies born in slavery" that became "rooted in our culture," Cassie explains (313). "While the white folks got the choice cuts . . . colored folks took the leavings . . . and made a feast of them" (314). Scenes of preparing and sharing feasts radiate warmth and welcome. Cassie describes the "battle for equality," with news shared through publications "by and about people of color" and through churches and speakers, as "uniting Negroes as a people and making us proud" (414–15).

Although the twenty-first-century Black implied reader lives under different rules and circumstances than Cassie, the shared experience of racial discrimination remains. In "Storytelling for Oppositionists and Others: A Plea for Narrative," Richard Delgado argues for the "psychic self-preservation" to be found through stories, even "stories about oppression, about victimization, about one's own brutalization" that can "lead to healing, liberation, mental health" and "promote group solidarity" (2437). The Logans share stories of their family's past, "long-ago stories told over and over again" (323), including tales of oppression and "stories of laughter and good times" (324), clearly gaining the healing and connecting benefits Delgado mentions. As readers listen in, those who have experienced racial oppression, including non-Black persons of color, share these healing benefits, even if their specific experiences vary.

Like the implied Black reader, the implied white reader is positioned to identify emotionally with the Black protagonists, appreciating their solidarity and strength. Intellectually, however, Logan family members' opposition to admitting white people into the family forces the white implied reader to recognize their difference from the Logans, based on racism and its legacy. In *Days*, as in previous books, Taylor strategically splits the implied white reader's identification in ways that promote antiracism. Empathy with the Logan community increases white readers' awareness of racism and its costs, while showing different positions white people can take toward racism motivates antiracist identification. Delgado argues for the need, within a white-dominated society, to engage the majority race in racial reform, using stories, "the oldest, most primordial meeting ground in human experience," to "overcome" Black people's "otherness" and form "a new collectivity based on the shared story" (2438). He also, however, is aware of the dangers of raising defensiveness of "the majority-race reader" (2434), arguing for "insinuative" and at least seemingly "noncoercive" stories and counterstories (2415). And defensiveness is likely. Social justice educator Robin DiAngelo argues that white people tend to be highly fragile when confronted with issues of race: "The smallest amount of racial stress is intolerable—the mere suggestion that being white has meaning often triggers a range of defensive responses" including "anger, fear and guilt" (2). Although unwilling to compromise on telling painful truths or to "whitewash history" (*Days*, "author's note" viii), Taylor incorporates strategies to reduce the implied white reader's defensiveness. First, she refuses the simple binary of Black as good, white as evil. Second, she depicts sympathetic, antiracist white characters, providing white readers with positive examples with whom they may choose to align themselves in contrast to the racist oppressors.

In *Days*, as in earlier Logan family books, Taylor avoids a "simplistic view of ethnicity" and forces "the reader to judge characters by their actions and not by their ethnic identities" (Martin 6). Black characters can behave despicably, as in the case of a Black supervisor who sexually harasses Cassie (*Days* 147–48, 161–63). More commonly, complex characterization mixes admirable traits with unwise attitudes and actions. When Cassie, emotionally exhausted from a day of racist insult and injury and "sick of the bigotry" (47), determines to integrate fully a Toledo theater, her impulsive action comes perilously close to getting her arrested—and Moe with her, which would have led to his extradition to Mississippi and possible execution. Reading the scene, one might be torn between sympathizing with Cassie's disillusionment at the invisible "*Whites Only. Colored Not Allowed*" signs (56) and applauding her activism, and, conversely, wanting to join Stacey in chastising her for unthinkingly taking such a risk, even for principle (56).

As the racism described above shows, white people frequently exhibit bad behavior ranging from demeaning insults to race-based murder, but the novel also depicts admirable white role models. Henry Giroux, in "White Noise: Toward a Pedagogy of Whiteness," calls for rethinking "the subversive possibility of whiteness" to include antiracist practices. While acknowledging that it is "imperative" to have "a critical analysis of whiteness address its historical legacy and existing complicity with racist exclusion and oppression," he also advocates for allowing white youth "to appropriate selective elements of white identity and culture as opposition" and to "distinguish between whiteness as a racial practice that is antiracist and those aspects of whiteness that are racist" (43). Giroux argues for a view of white racial identity that is not monolithic, but rather involved in a "complex relationship with other determining factors" that frame identity in nonessentialist ways that are not "racially innocent or intractably racist" (71). Whiteness must "be addressed within power relations that exploit its subversive potential while not erasing the historical and political role it plays in shaping other racialized identities and social differences" (71). Ideally, white individuals will move beyond the "paralysis inspired by guilt or the anxiety/fear of difference that fuels white racism" (71) and, while acknowledging their privilege, recognize their agency to make alliances and choices that lead to a more socially just society. While thoroughly exposing white racism, Taylor also includes characters who illustrate the possibility of this type of white antiracism, providing an ideal option for her implied white reader.

Wade Jamison remains the consummate white ally; Cassie describes this powerful figure as "the one white man we called our friend" (*Days* 63) and "the only white person in Mississippi we all trusted" (98). He earns this trust by openly supporting antiracist policies and actions (347). Talking with the NAACP voter registration class at Great Faith, he humbly discusses his difficult choice to oppose racism: "I had to decide if I would see people—black and white—as separate and unequal, separate and equal, or just plain equal. It's taken me a while to reach the conclusion of just plain equal. That's what all you are fighting for, and from my perspective, I want you to know there are white people here in Mississippi who understand and support you" (392).

Cassie's friend, colleague, and suitor, Guy Hallis, also helps with voter registration classes, enduring intense harassment and a near-fatal attack from other white men (395). When Mama has a stroke, Cassie's Toledo bosses, who had hired her as the first local Black cashier in a white-owned business, provide a loan to fund the Logans' trip home, refusing to take Stacey's war bonds as collateral, as he would lose money by cashing them in. The Logan family's solidarity and work ethic—which they compare to their own family character—is sufficient security (80–81). An elderly white couple escorts Cassie to a nearby drugstore when she is sexually harassed by white teens, remaining until her ride arrives. While they never exchange names, Cassie reflects, "I knew on that night, when I was alone in a white world, they had been my guardian angels. I knew now that angels came in all colors" (202). The white implied reader can see these and other examples and identify with ways of enacting antiracism.

While fully acknowledging antiracist white allies, Taylor's writing nonetheless insists that racism has created a gap between Black and white people, one impossible for the desires of well-intentioned white people to bridge. In earlier Logan novels, Jeremy Simms tries to befriend the Logan children, which earns him beatings and family rejection. He pretends he can see the Logans from the outdoor bedroom he created, seemingly imagining himself into the Logan family (*Thunder* 230). David Logan, however, cautions Stacey against accepting Jeremy's friendship because "white folks mean trouble" and interracial friendship in a society that denies Black citizens equality is too risky (158). Many engaged white readers I have known, strongly identifying with the Logans, have found Mr. Logan's stance disturbing. Understandably, actual readers of all ages, emotionally attached to the Logans, might feel hurt to realize that they, like Jeremy, would be excluded from friendship based on their race. Preservice teacher candidates, who mediate the reading experience for children, have expressed especially intense concerns. From these objectors' perspective of racism as individual racial bigotry, a view common among the white middle class, Papa's race-based rejection of a boy who is personally innocent of racist attitudes and actions instills racism within his children and teaches this racism to child readers. From the perspective of Taylor's texts and of CRT, however, racism is not just a matter of individual bias, but of mindsets, practices, and policies deeply entrenched in society and transcending individual intentions. Therefore, while Taylor intentionally works to engage and educate white readers, and while Logan family members can recognize white individuals as "good" and even "angels," within the Logans' world, white people collectively threaten "trouble," and the nation's racist legacy had rendered some relationships untenable between white—however admirable—and Black people, at least until society has fundamentally changed.

The Logans (and readers) learn in *Days* that Jeremy Simms was killed during the war (92). In this last Logan novel, it is Guy Hallis, a wealthy, white, northeastern lawyer, who is emphatically excluded from the Logan family. Logan males make their views of the folly of interracial romance clear in *Let the Circle Be Unbroken*; learning that Mama's cousin Bud married a white woman, Stacey angrily warns Christopher-John, "Can't love anybody white" (163). A Black woman's union with a white man is especially intolerable, given Logan history; Cassie's grandfather, Paul-Edward, was the result of an involuntary union between his enslaved mother and her enslaver (*Land*; *Days* 409). Knowing her family's views, Cassie hides Guy's courtship. After a surprise encounter with Guy, Stacey lectures Cassie about the history of sexual exploitation of Black women, equates interracial romance with betrayal of family and race (*Days* 289), and threatens to disown her if she becomes involved with Guy (290). Stacey's wife warns Cassie that romance with Guy would result in a "family torn apart" (335). Mama and Papa both, separately, express admiration for Guy but caution Cassie against romantic involvement (428–30). Marriage would, Cassie knows, "mean betrayal" (409). Circumstances have changed just enough that, unlike Jeremy, Guy can be accepted as a friend as well as an ally in the struggle for civil rights, but he cannot be family because a white man could never share their racial experiences. While Guy wishes Cassie would let him into more of the part of her life that deals with racial issues (359), Cassie muses, "Despite his liberal outlook and supposed understanding of what I experienced as a black person, I knew he could have no true understanding of my world. He had never walked in a black person's shoes" (361). When Guy argues, "dammit, Cassie, I want to understand!" (387), she can only reply, "This is *my* world. These are *my* people. You have no place in it" (388). Although yearning to allow Guy to help fill the emptiness in her life, Cassie rejects an interracial marriage (369). She is proud of his humble, energetic work with her people, but when, after being beaten for his voter registration work, he pleads, "I've gone into the heartland of Mississippi, seen your life and felt its brutality. What else can I do?" (409), she replies, "Nothing" (409). The message to the implied white readers: no amount of effort or vicarious identification can fully bridge the divide between those who experience racist oppression as members of the outgroup and those from the dominant race—however much they might share in the suffering racism brings. It is an uncomfortable message, but one upon which Taylor insists.

Thus tension is built into the reading experience for the implied white reader, with much of *Days* actively drawing this audience into the Logans' lives but parts of it highlighting their inability to understand these lives completely. While the implied reader is to learn from this tension, some gatekeepers resist the discomfort generated by it. Given white fragility and widespread reluctance to acknowledging the problem of racism in American society (DiAngelo; Bell; Delgado and Stefancic), Taylor's unflinching insistence that race is central to American life and that white people cannot fully understand the Black experience of racism makes some reluctant to use her books. Julie Wollman-Bonilla lists fearful subject matter, failure to "represent dominant social values or myths," and identification of racism or sexism as a "social problem" as key reasons why a "vocal minority" of teachers and teacher education candidates consider some texts "inappropriate" for use with elementary school students (289). Yet Taylor has indicated her desire to connect with "children, both Black and white," who would like her characters and identify strongly with them ("Newbery" 26) and her hope that her work would "be instrumental in teaching children of all colors" about the work done by Black people in the generation that laid the groundwork for the civil rights movement ("Newbery" 28), desires that presumably continue through *Days*. Responses to earlier Logan novels indicate her success. Pat Pinsent credits the "skill of Taylor's writing" in creating scenes that are informative and engaging enough to "heighten the child reader's empathy" and, for the "duration of reading," render it "very difficult for white readers not to feel as if they are members of the black community" (10). Sarah Hardstaff acknowledges "being allowed to share Cassie's perspective" changed her "view of the world" and argues that "perhaps Taylor's greatest achievement is in providing an opportunity for the audience to share, as the 'fifth Logan,' in acts of collaborative witness and collective agency" (240). Undeniably, Taylor's narratives engage readers deeply, both affectively and cognitively. However, the unyielding exclusion of whites from the Logans' inner circle makes it untenable for the implied white reader to assume that full membership into the Black community has been granted, whatever the feelings of actual white readers.

I would argue that *Days* simultaneously hangs a "Colored Only" sign outside the possibility of fully understanding living as a victim of racism *and* slips readers behind the sign, partially subverting the prohibition through the powerful vicarious reading experience. In her influential article "Mirrors, Windows, and Sliding Glass Doors," Bishop argues for the need for "children from dominant social groups" who are used to seeing their lives reflected in literature to have access to books that are "windows" that "help them understand the multicultural nature of the world they live in, and their place as a member of just one group, as well as their connections to all other humans." She claims these windows "are also sliding glass doors" that allow readers to imaginatively walk into and "become part of whatever world has been created or recreated by the author." Taylor's writing creates that immersive experience for the implied white reader for most of the reading experience. Her message that white people can never fully understand the lived experience of Black people in a racist society could be seen as opened blinds, providing reminders of the white reader's position on the outside, peering in, even as they imaginatively enter the Logans' world. The "open blinds" I posit differ from the "curtains" Native scholar and activist Debbie Reese adds to Bishop's analogy, signifying a means of protecting private, meaningful spaces and activities from white misunderstanding and exploitation. Taylor's visible attempts to distance white readers seem less a matter of protecting African American culture from invasive violation than a reminder to white readers that their experiences are vicarious and their access, provisional. Even as the narration reinforces the power of literature and language to "make present the felt experiences of people living in other places and at other times" (Stephens 75), it provides a reminder of the limits of the immersive reading experience.

Days offers a rich, complex education on race, racism, and the fight for change in the decades leading up to and into the American civil rights movement. For longtime readers of Taylor's Logan books, it provides a final opportunity to engage with well-loved characters and see the Logan children mature. With the brief epilogue set decades after Cassie's return to Mississippi to carry on civil rights work, readers who have grown to care about Cassie and her family have some closure: Cassie survives her commitment to civil rights activism and witnesses the once-inconceivable prospect of a Black man becoming president.

Yet in this novel that remains interrogative despite its didactic focus, this ending raises questions. What fills the forty-five-plus-year gap between final chapter and epilogue? Does Cassie ever find new love or have children after her devastating early losses? Do her brothers return to the family land after retiring, as they hoped to do if the sociopolitical climate in Mississippi changed? Perhaps most importantly, given the pervasiveness of racism shown and the doubts raised about the possibility of meaningful change, to what extent is being Black still a way of life (and sometimes death) in America? Since Taylor's writing is an homage to her family, to the generations that prepared for the civil rights movement and the gains it engendered, the epilogue ending the Logan Family Saga fittingly celebrates an achievement almost unimaginable in their lifetimes. Nonetheless, it, as so much that preceded it, leaves important questions for the reader.

WORKS CITED

Barker, Jani L. "Racial Identification and Audience in *Roll of Thunder, Hear My Cry* and *The Watsons Go to Birmingham—1963.*" *Children's Literature in Education*, 2010, vol. 41, no. 2, pp. 118–45.

Bell, Derrick. *Faces at the Bottom of the Well: The Permanence of Racism.* Basic Books, 1992.

Bishop, Rudine Sims. *Free Within Ourselves: The Development of African-American Children's Literature.* Heinemann, 2007.

Bishop, Rudine Sims. "Mirrors, Windows, and Sliding Glass Doors." *Perspectives: Choosing and Using Books for the Classroom*, vol. 6, no. 3, 1990. Reprinted by *Reading Is Fundamental*, 2015, https://scenicregional.org/wp-content/uploads/2017/08/Mirrors-Windows-and-Sliding-Glass-Doors.pdf.

Brooks, Wanda. "An Author as a Counter-Storyteller: Applying Critical Race Theory to a Coretta Scott King Award Book." *Children's Literature in Education*, vol. 40, no. 1, 2009, pp. 33–45.

Delgado, Richard. "Storytelling for Oppositionists and Others: A Plea for Narrative." *The Michigan Law Review Association*, vol. 87, no. 8, Aug. 1989, pp. 2411–41.

Delgado, Richard, and Jean Stefancic. *Critical Race Theory: An Introduction.* 3rd ed. NYU Press, 2017.

DiAngelo, Robin. *White Fragility: Why It's So Hard for White People to Talk about Racism.* Beacon Press, 2018, Kindle.

Giroux, Henry A. "White Noise: Toward a Pedagogy of Whiteness." *Race-ing Representation: Voice, History, and Sexuality*, edited by Kostas Myrsiades and Linda Myrsiades, Rowman and Littlefield, 1998, pp. 42–76.

Hardstaff, Sarah (Layzell). "'Papa Said That One Day I Would Understand': Examining Child Agency and Character Development in *Roll of Thunder, Hear My Cry* Using Critical Corpus Linguistics." *Children's Literature in Education*, vol. 46, no. 3, 2015, pp. 226–41.

Iser, Wolfgang. *The Act of Reading: A Theory of Aesthetic Response.* Johns Hopkins UP, 1978.

Johnson, Dianne. *Telling Tales: The Pedagogy and Promise of African American Literature for Youth*. Greenwood Press, 1990. Contributions in Afro-American and African Studies 139.

Martin, Michelle H. "Exploring the Works of Mildred Taylor: An Approach to Teaching the Logan Family Novels." *Teaching and Learning Literature with Children and Young Adults*, vol. 7, no. 3, 1998, pp. 5–13.

Pinsent, Pat. *Children's Literature and the Politics of Equality*. David Fulton Publishers, 1997.

Reese, Debbie. "Mirrors, Windows, Sliding Glass Doors, and Curtains." *YouTube*, Oct. 12, 2016, https://www.youtube.com/watch?v=ctOJtK-ONgo&ab_channel=WritingtheOther.

Stephens, John. "Analysing Texts: Linguistics and Stylistics." *Understanding Children's Literature*, edited by Peter Hunt, 2nd ed., Routledge, 2005, pp. 73–85.

Taylor, Mildred D. *All the Days Past, All the Days to Come*. Viking, 2020.

Taylor, Mildred D. *The Friendship*. Bantam, 1987.

Taylor, Mildred D. *Let the Circle Be Unbroken*. 1981. Penguin, 1991.

Taylor, Mildred D. *Mississippi Bridge*. Dial, 1990.

Taylor, Mildred D. "My Life as a Writer." *World Literature Today*, vol. 78, no. 2, May 2004, pp. 1976–1985.

Taylor, Mildred D. "Newbery Medal Acceptance." *Newbery and Caldecott Medal Books 1976–1985*, edited by Lee Kingman, Horn Book, 1986, pp. 21–30.

Taylor, Mildred D. *The Road to Memphis*. Dial, 1990.

Taylor, Mildred D. *Roll of Thunder, Hear My Cry*. 1976. Puffin, 1991.

Taylor, Mildred D. *Song of the Trees*. Dial, 1975.

Wollman-Bonilla, Julie E. "Outrageous Viewpoints: Teachers' Criteria for Rejecting Works of Children's Literature." *Language Arts*, vol. 75, no. 4, 1998, pp. 287–95

Part 2

The Self: Reimagining the Logans

Re(cover)y of the Logan Family Saga

Ngozi Onuora and Sabrina Carnesi

INTRODUCTION

Mildred D. Taylor's Logan Family Saga represents nonstereotypical, well-developed characters narrated through an African American girl who relates a first-person perspective on the sting of racial injustice (Hintz and Tribunella 365; McNair 101). Over the years, art from different illustrators has graced the covers of the novels in Taylor's series. Knowing that books are often judged by their covers (Publisher's Weekly), publishing companies (re)branded, or (re)covered, the books as the series expanded. Everything from the production to the promotion of a book is influenced by a need to pair the written text with compelling imagery. Libraries and bookstores spend time designing displays to attract buyers/readers, and publishing houses spend money repackaging books in new editions in hopes of garnering increased sales. A design team and illustrator(s) can communicate a lot through the size of the book, the typeface, titling, the medium used to create the cover art, the composition of the cover images, and more. All these elements work together to communicate the essence of a book's content and its underlying theme(s). The manner in which the book cover illustration communicates to the reader is precisely what attracted coauthor of this chapter Ngozi Onuora to an important book from her childhood: *Zeely* (1967) by Virginia Hamilton. An early cover of *Zeely* depicted a tall, thin, dark-skinned woman striding confidently past two Black children. For Onuora, seeing cover characters that looked like her was meaningful. Covers matter.

In this chapter, we discuss why book covers matter, what constitutes a "good" book cover, and how book cover design impacts readers, authors, and publishers. Next, we highlight three key artists who have illustrated book covers for the Logan Family Saga and use visual rhetoric as a framework to analyze and interpret them. This analysis is limited to the United States publications of eight of the ten Taylor books, particularly those that feature main characters from the Logan Family. The analysis is also limited to images of front cover art versus all the elements that encompass the paratext of the novels. We finish with a brief commentary on the overall aesthetic impression of the cover art by Kadir Nelson for Taylor's books, the most recent representation of the series.

WHY BOOK COVERS MATTER

The goal of a book cover is to attract potential readers to pick up the book and buy it or borrow it from the library (Ford 50). In a 2010 survey titled "Covers Matter," results showed that out of every six hundred respondents, mainly from the US and the UK, almost 80 percent said that covers play a decisive role in their purchasing decisions (James and Grilo). Literacy support sites, such as Reading Rockets, ask, "Is the book visually appealing?" as the first criteria for teachers selecting nonfiction picture books to use with children. Thus, an important consideration is whether the front and back covers are attractive (Gill).

In an article for the *Guardian*, Holly Connolly discusses social media's impact on book cover design. Many influential Bookstagrammers will not take photos of and post book covers they do not like (Haupt). Some will purchase multiple copies of a book if they see an edition with a more attractive cover (Connolly). Even the New York Public Library has used the Instagram platform to attract more readers to classic literature with interactive, digital covers of its InstaNovels (NYPL Staff). Another popular book promotion is video reviews posted on the TikTok app using the hashtag #booktok. Publishing houses are starting to see the broad appeal of #booktok as a helpful marketing tool, turning some contributors into paid influencers for their services (Harris). With plans for TikTok to lengthen user time limits (Chalk), what used to be a minute-long content review and cover display will be closer to a three-minute advertisement. Followers of such posts rely heavily on the #booktokkers' and Bookstagrammers' sense of judgment.

What a book represents and presents, who the implied audience is, and what readers can expect from an author are expressed through the cover image (Ford 51). The cover design is not typically within the author's purview; however, books are often judged and evaluated by the authenticity and integrity of their covers. Authenticity and integrity of a book can be questioned when publishers whitewash covers by making Black, brown, and Indigenous characters appear white. Such misrepresentation places the covers out of alignment with the book's content. An example of this was with the advanced copy cover of Justine Larbalestier's book *Liar* (2009), which featured a white girl on the cover of a book with an African American protagonist because the publishers believed they could not sell the book with a Black character on the front cover (Pride). While the publishers of Elizabeth Acevedo's award-winning book *The Poet X* did not misrepresent the protagonist's Afro Latine identity on the book cover, they published the cover with the photo of a real person who did not give permission for her likeness to be used. This resulted in a controversy related to appropriation.

"GOOD" BOOK COVERS

Because book covers matter and book packaging is serious business for publishers, publishing houses pour significant dollars into the craft of designing "good" book covers. What constitutes a "good" book cover is largely subjective; however, publishing companies hire professionals to strategically design book covers based on prevailing market trends (Barthelmess; Kreider; Rawling; Raynor; Shaina). The March/April 2014 *Horn Book* article "What Makes a Good Book Cover?" says that the effectiveness of a cover is predicated on three key responsibilities: responsibility to the book, responsibility to the publisher, and responsibility to the reader. "Responsibility to the book" considers whether the cover conveys what the book is about and what the book is like (Barthelmess). "Responsibility to the publisher" refers to the techniques marketers use to promote the book titles for readers of all ages (Watson). "Responsibility to the reader" highlights the tone set by the cover and how it communicates the essence of broader themes that may be contained within the story (Barthelmess). The practice of carrying out such responsibilities has brought about some popularized mainstream trends. According to Dena McMurdie, host of the Batch of Books blog, seven major trends prevailed in the field of book cover design for young adult literature in 2019:

1. a return to the use of illustration instead of the formerly popular photographs;
2. symbolism, particularly for the fantasy genre;
3. abstract, ornamental covers that do not provide many clues to the story's content;
4. vibrant colors such as bright pinks, reds, and yellows;
5. dark colors such as deep greens, purples, blues, greys, and blacks that stand out against the white backgrounds on websites;
6. adult-looking cover designs; and
7. big, easy-to-read titles—usually in a white or color font that contrasts with the background illustration (McMurdie).

When discussing the way children of all ages gravitate toward books that reflect relevance and with which they can identify, Jennifer Anne Ford says, "The most immediate of vehicles for that initial identification is the book cover" (54). As such, additional book cover features of importance include relevance and identification.

VISUAL RHETORIC

We analyze and interpret the book covers for the Logan Family Saga using visual rhetoric, an aspect of visual literacy that provides a framework for determining how cover illustrations function to communicate meaning, story content, and cultural and historical significance for each book. This framework has been used in the fields of communication, marketing and advertising, visual art, and in any field that desires to design visual "text" to persuade the consumer, or viewer, to think or act in specific ways ("What is Visual Rhetoric?"). Its main goal is to understand how visual text "communicates its message and meanings" and offers insight or an interpretation of the visuals based on the analysis of related elements (Purdue OWL) such as composition, color, line, texture, shape, form, size/scale, and symbolic elements. Our use of visual rhetoric analysis considers cover image depictions and why illustrators may have made particular design choices (Purdue OWL). We use the aforementioned visual elements and design principles such as balance, emphasis, movement, pattern/repetition, proportion, value, and rhythm when appropriate and apparent (ThoughtCo; Bang).

Additionally, this analysis evaluates the overall cover image for whether it conveys the essence of the book's content, tone, mood, and narrative quality (Barthelmess). Cultural assumptions influence such conveyances (Ford 50) and often account for why the same book may have vastly different covers when published in different countries (see Eshraq, this volume). The same can be said of covers created by illustrators in different time periods, which can easily be observed with the covers for the Logan Family Saga. Finally, some covers more directly convey the book's overarching theme or message than others. Children's author and illustrator Molly Bang states that because "[a]rt is a way of communicating our feelings about the peculiar and awesome situation of being alive" (133), it is more important to be concerned with a picture's effectiveness than with its attractiveness (130). We take Bang's and Ford's reasonings into consideration throughout this analysis. The books in this study have publication dates that range from 1975 to 2001 and have been produced in the United States by three lauded illustrators: Jerry Pinkney, Max Ginsburg, and Kadir Nelson. Taylor's final installment of the Logan Family Saga, *All the Days Past, All the Days to Come*, is not included in this analysis because the cover was not illustrated by any of the three featured artists in this chapter. *The Gold Cadillac* is also not analyzed because this novella does not feature Cassie or her immediate family.

THE ILLUSTRATORS

The artwork of Pinkney, Ginsburg, and Nelson has definitively contributed to the legacy of Mildred Taylor's books. Pinkney and Nelson are African American men who have strong portfolios of children's literature that they have authored and illustrated, in addition to producing artwork for the general public. Ginsburg also possesses a phenomenal body of work that is less concentrated in the world of children's books. Before analyzing the book covers of these artists, we share more about their artistry.

The Pinkney Tradition

In the fall of 2021, the world experienced the loss of illustrator Jerry Pinkney. Pinkney's children's literature art spans over half a century. Among the many accolades of this highly decorated Philadelphia native are the Caldecott Medal and Coretta Scott King book awards, and several honorary doctoral degrees (Jerry Pinkney Studio). Because Pinkney had dyslexia and struggled with reading, his drawing talent helped increase his self-esteem and ability to focus (The History Makers; Woodmere Museum YouTube Video; Jerry Pinkney Studio). Often referred to as "the Pinkney tradition" by his wife, Gloria Jean, talent abounds in the literary and fine arts arenas in the Pinkney family (Bishop, "Pinkney Family"). In addition to Gloria Jean, a children's book author in her own right, Pinkney has three sons, Brian, Scott, and Myles, and one daughter, Troy, who are all successful "creatives" (Martin 106) and "children's book people" (Bishop, *Free* 168). Troy and Scott are involved with art therapy and design, respectively. Myles, a photographer, has illustrated children's books and collaborated with his wife, author Sandra L. Pinkney (Bishop, *Free* 168). Myles and Sandra's daughter, Charnelle Pinkney Barlow, also follows the family tradition as a Georgia-based author-illustrator and surface designer (Danielson; Simon and Schuster). Pinkney's oldest son, Brian, is also an award-winning illustrator who often collaborates on book projects with his wife, Andrea Davis Pinkney. Andrea Pinkney is one of only a few African American editors employed in a major publishing house in the United States, where she holds the crucial position of vice president and editor-at-large for Scholastic.

Jerry Pinkney illustrated over one hundred books for children throughout his career. His illustrations for children's books are characterized by his opalescent watercolor technique (Bishop, "Pinkney Family"), and he often portrays African American culture in his artwork (African American Literature Book Club). Though Pinkney was known as a master watercolorist, he also loved the technique of pencil drawing (Woodmere Art Museum, "Artist Jerry Pinkney"). For Taylor's series, Pinkney illustrated the cover art and internal illustrations for *Song of the Trees* and the cover and the 25th anniversary edition of *Roll of Thunder, Hear My Cry*. As the first illustrator of the initial books of the series, Pinkney, well-established and highly lauded, contributed positively to the legacy of the Logan Family Saga.

The Social Realist

Max Ginsburg is a New York–based artist known for gritty realism depicted in oil paintings, using the alla prima technique that reflects his connection to the city in which he has lived for most of his life (Cavalier Galleries). Until the 2016 rebranding of the series, Ginsburg had illustrated more book covers for the Logan Family Saga than any other illustrator. Thus, his art has had an enormous impact on the branding of the series. He illustrated the covers of nine of the ten books by Taylor as well as the internal illustrations for *The Friendship* and *Mississippi Bridge*. The only cover Ginsburg did not illustrate is *Days*, which was illustrated by Jessica Jenkins, a designer at Penguin Young Readers (Lodge).

Ginsburg communicates the real-life intensity of social injustices and war in his art. He believes that realism is truth and truth is beauty (Cavalier Galleries), and his cover depictions get to the heart of truth-telling by capturing the overarching themes of each of Taylor's books. His cover art renders such an intense degree of realism that it is as if the reader is viewing moments of the Logan Family's lives captured through a photographer's lens instead of the stroke of a paintbrush. In an article for *The Artist Magazine*, Maureen Bloomfield describes Ginsburg as an artist who believes "one person isn't more interesting than another; each commands his/her part in the scene" (44–45). Ginsburg lives up to his belief statement, for in all his Logan Family book covers, he provides the readers with a delicious peek into the narrative by exhibiting the characters emotionally and reflectively in the roles they play in a particular plotline.

The Contemporary Urban Realist

To commemorate the 40th anniversary of *Thunder* in 2016, Dial Publisher commissioned Kadir Nelson to illustrate the covers of the first nine books in the Logan Family Saga (Burnett), which were all of the books in the series that had been published at that time. Nelson is a critically acclaimed Los Angeles–based illustrator who DreamWorks Studios employed to create the conceptual art for Steven Spielberg's Oscar-nominated film *Amistad*. His artwork has been featured on numerous album and magazine covers and is in several museums, including the Smithsonian National Museum of African American History and Culture in Washington, DC.

Nelson has also contributed significantly to children's literature. He entered the field in the late 1990s and has illustrated over thirty children's books (Bishop, *Free* 188). Many have been highly lauded, as evidenced by the numerous awards he has earned, which include the 2005 Coretta Scott King Illustrator Award for *Ellington Was Not a Street* (Scholastic), the 2009 Sibert Medal for *We Are the Ship*, and the 2020 Coretta Scott King Illustrator Award for his artwork in Kwame Alexander's *The Undefeated* (2019).

Nelson's style embodies modern urban realism, focusing on figurative paintings that highlight historical narratives and heroic figures (Kadir Nelson, Inc.). Nelson's preferred medium for painting is oil. In an interview with Artists Network, Nelson described his technique and workflow for completing a typical image: "I begin with a loose sketch, and then transfer the drawing to the surface. Photographs help in the process, as well" (Woodson). Nelson's distinctive art combines realism and abstraction to depict figures in an elongated style (Bishop, *Free* 188). He strives to highlight the human spirit and the integrity and strength in all human beings (188). In celebration of the 40th anniversary of *Thunder*, Nelson's cover illustrations have arguably done just that for the characters Taylor crafted in this series.

THE BOOK COVERS

Taylor's work has greatly influenced children's book publishing for five decades (Burnett). Since Taylor's first publication, *Song of the Trees*, the trends and methods for designing book covers have evolved. Our analysis unfolds according to the historical chronology of the plots, and we discuss the cover art for each book in the order in which the artists illustrated them: Pinkney, Ginsburg, and finally, Nelson.

The Land

As the first book chronologically for the Logan Family Saga, *The Land* begins with Paul-Edward Logan, the grandfather of Cassie Logan (protagonist of *Thunder*). Pinkney did not illustrate a cover for this book. Ginsburg's cover for *Land* features the two main characters: Paul-Edward (called Paul) and Mitchell, who lives on Paul's father's land. Paul can pass for white because he has inherited many features from his father, Edward Logan, who is the white enslaver of Paul, Paul's sister, and Paul's mother. Mitchell's father takes care of Mr. Logan's horses; and, after a brief bit of rivalry, Paul and Mitchell eventually become lifelong friends and experience a series of life transitions together. The two young men on Ginsburg's cover each hold an axe as they stand in front of a grove of trees with a clearing in the near distance—one very light-skinned with straight, brown hair and the other one dark-skinned with tightly coiled natural hair. Ginsburg's preference for muted colors is evident in the greens and earth tones of the land and the clothing Paul and Mitchell wear. The title matches the cover well in that the entire backdrop gives the impression that trees surround the two main characters, with Paul in the center of the cover while Mitchell stands off-center to Paul's left. Readers can see that Mitchell is taller and more muscular than Paul. Both characters look directly out at the reader. The scene Ginsburg depicts is one of strong determination in the facial expressions of both men. They stand under the trees as if their feet were rooted in the soil. Their set expressions show no emotion and illustrate the strength in their desire to work the land they own. It is as if they are daring someone to try and take the land from them.

Kadir Nelson also gave the land prominence on the cover of his 2016 edition, which reflects a significant aspect of the plot: the importance of the land. However, Nelson's approach to the book cover makes the land and horizon the central focus. On Nelson's cover, only one character appears with a horse. In proportion to the expanse of land, this character's small silhouette against the vastness of the land looks insignificant. The character is looking away from the reader and out toward the land with the rising (or possibly setting) sun. Readers cannot see the person's facial features, and his skin color, age, and other characteristics are not as evident as on Ginsburg's cover. However, it is assumed that this character is Paul-Edward. He stands in front of a horse, presumably the gray palomino that Paul-Edward buys from Mr. Sawyer, a man from whom he learned woodworking skills. Silhouetting Paul-Edward against his expansive four hundred acres gives readers the impression that the land and its connection to Paul are of vital importance and that Paul is part of the land, and the land is part of Paul. Whereas Ginsburg used muted earth colors, Nelson illustrates with bright golds and vibrant greens, causing the land to seem radiant and giving the impression that nothing is more important than the land.

The Well

The second book in the series chronologically features Paul-Edward and Caroline's sons: David and Hammer. *The Well* is about the contentious relationship the two Logan brothers have with the Simms brothers, Charlie and Ed-Rose. During a lengthy drought in the area, the Logans have the only well that has not run dry. Charlie Simms contaminates the well with chopped-up pieces of dead animals, jeopardizing the health of both Black and white residents in the area. Both Ginsburg and Nelson illustrated covers for this title.

Ginsburg depicts David and Hammer standing barefooted by a well, looking toward two white men (the Simms brothers) approaching on horse and carriage. The shorter of the two Logan brothers, David, holds a bucket and a crutch, with his right leg in a cast. Hammer stands near the road, defiant, with his hands in his pockets, keeping his eyes on the approaching Simms. One of the Simms brothers is saying something while pointing toward Hammer and David (or possibly the well) while guiding the horse and carriage in the direction of the Logan well. The well is located on the far left-hand side of the cover, partially blocked by David and partially off-cover. According to Bang, the closer an object is to the edge or to the center, the greater the tension (82). This story certainly contains a high level of tension throughout. This scene shows the start of *Well* when the Simms boys first come to the Logan well to get two barrels of water, setting the stage for future confrontations between Hammer and Charlie. Objects placed higher up in a picture draw the viewer's attention and feel more important or are in a stronger tactical position, while the lower portion of the picture "feels more threatened, heavier, sadder, or constrained" (Bang 70). Ginsburg's cover illustrates the power dynamics between the two characters: Charlie's higher positioning in the cover art can be equated with his higher position of privilege in the South's segregated society, while Hammer's lower position on the ground, standing barefooted in the dirt, can be equated with his status as one with less privilege. It can also mean that the characters in the bottom half of the cover are more grounded (Bang 72). Ginsburg chose to include the story's four main characters on the cover, using selected shades of blues, greens, and browns.

Kadir Nelson's cover focuses significantly on the well—along with the Logan brothers, the only characters depicted on the cover. On Nelson's cover, Hammer holds the bucket while David has a crutch and wears a cast on his left leg. The story never states which leg David hurts when he falls out of a tree, and it is interesting that Ginsburg and Nelson each chose a different injured leg. On Nelson's cover, it appears that Hammer is wearing shoes, but David's feet are not visible, except for his cast. Both Logan boys are looking off to their left, but the reader does not know what they are viewing, and their faces do not register any particular emotion. Nelson's greens are washed out, with the bright white sun coming up from behind the Logan brothers and highlighting the silvery well toward the center of the cover. This is fitting because all of the action in the story centers around the importance of the Logan family's well. In contrast to Ginsburg's rendition, Hammer and David are not standing in the dirt and dust. Rather, they are standing on a rich, lush carpet of green grass. The positioning of the young brothers in the midst of fertile, rich land is significant to the richness of the Logan family's well-being in contrast to that of other Blacks and whites in their drought-ridden community. It also emphasizes the Logan family's natural sense of place in a society that doesn't see their position as natural or acceptable.

Song of the Trees

In this novella, David is an adult, married, and with children whom we get to know more closely in *Thunder*: Stacey, Cassie, Christopher-John, and Little Man. One day while chasing each other in the forest, the Logan siblings discover that a white man, Mr. Andersen, plans to cut down all the trees on their land. Pinkney, Ginsburg, and Nelson each illustrated this title. Pinkney's version of the cover for this book shows a barefooted Black girl sitting at the base of a tree and smiling. His combination of pencil and pastel watercolor as the artistic media is noticeably similar to his future artwork for *Thunder*'s first edition (for more on Pinkney's illustrations for *Song*, see Rizzuto's essay in this volume). It is difficult to estimate Cassie's age in the illustration, but she looks older than the eight years depicted in the plot. Also, considering the circumstances regarding what happens to a portion of the trees and how much the plot identifies Cassie's love and passion for the trees, her smile and casual reclining position could misrepresent the story. While Cassie enjoys sitting among the trees, she is distraught for most of the book about the way Mr. Andersen and his crew treat her brothers and the careless, disrespectful manner in which Mr. Andersen chops down the trees. In *Picture This: How Pictures Work*, Bang discusses how two or more objects in a picture that have the same color are often integrally associated with each other (45). It is quite possible that Pinkney wanted to ensure that the reader associated the trees with Cassie in a seamless way.

Ginsburg's realistic cover art seems to capture the moments before the children spot Mr. Andersen and his crew. His cover more accurately represents a critical moment in the story's narrative, showing a forest scene in which Cassie appears in the foreground, hiding behind a large tree trunk from her two brothers, who appear in the background. An air of mystery permeates what appears to be a game of hide and seek. The puffy sleeves and Peter Pan collar of Cassie's blouse add a fragile vulnerability to the eight-year-old character that the covers of future installments in the series never again revisit. Ginsburg uses the size of the tree trunks to establish depth and to let the viewer know that Cassie's brothers are a little distance from where she is hiding. The trees as vertical structures can be viewed as monuments of kinetic energy that include the past and the future while also containing potential energy of the present (Bang 55). The order and stability in these woods (Bang 57) is in danger of being disrupted if Mr. Andersen and his crew succeed.

Nelson's cover encapsulates Pinkney's and Ginsburg's versions by including Cassie and her siblings and using the trees as a prominent focus. Nelson shows all four of David Logan's children, with Cassie front and center. With her hands clasped together, Cassie faces the reader with a look of determination and pride and with a towering tree in the forest that serves as her backbone. The boys flank Cassie, standing slightly behind the tree in front of which she stands. As Little Man looks directly at the reader, Stacey and Christopher-John look off to the left—Stacey with a serious expression and Christopher-John with a dreamy, faraway look. The surrounding trees form a canopy of protection around the children as dappled sunlight shines through the treetops.

Mississippi Bridge

This novella is the only story in the Logan family series narrated by a white character, Jeremy Simms. The Logan siblings are secondary characters to their friend, Jeremy, in this book. Unlike the rest of the Simms family, Jeremy disagrees with the way white people treat Black people during this time period. On a stormy, foggy day, the Logan children witness Jeremy working with local white men and a Black man named Josias to pull dead bodies from the wreckage of the bus the children have just watched plummet into the river.

Ginsburg illustrated two different covers for this book. One of the covers provides more visual context for what happens in the story than the other. It features Jeremy and the well-dressed Josias peering anxiously over the damaged railing of a wood-planked bridge as foaming water sprays up toward the two of them. This cover depicts the story's climax. Ginsburg's second cover shows Jeremy following closely behind the four Logan siblings as they walk across the bridge with the foaming river spraying up on either side of them. Each child's facial expression shows varying degrees of worry and concern as they cross the bridge, especially Christopher-John, who clings to Stacey for support.

Nelson's cover also shows the four Logan siblings flanked by Jeremy in the rear. The difference is that Nelson's cover shows the five characters at the far end of an intact bridge as if contemplating a crossing. All of the characters face the reader and appear to be looking out at the other end of the bridge. Perhaps they are viewing the bus disaster, but none of that is depicted on the cover. Nelson captures the haziness of the day by using muted blue tones for the rainy sky, but the cover does not indicate a violent storm that could derail a moving bus full of passengers. The Logan children wear dried calf skins to protect them from the rain. In *Thunder*, the reader learns that the children hate to wear the animal hides because of their musty smell. Although the family cannot afford raincoats, they are slightly better off than Jeremy Simms, who has nothing to shield him from the rain except for a cap as he stands next to Stacey at the rear of the group in what appears to be soaking wet clothing. Compared to Nelson's other covers in the series, this is one of the most muted scenes with the grayish-blue sky. The somber tones could represent the lives lost in the bridge accident. Nelson's penchant for vibrant colors shows in the green trees that stand at full unyielding attention as the winds and rains cause calamity. Just as the trees stand rooted in their position like pallbearers at a funeral, the Logan children stand at the edge of the bridge as if to say, "Nothing can move us. We stand against injustice, and we will survive."

Roll of Thunder, Hear My Cry

This award-winning novel is probably the most well-known book in the Logan Family Saga. All three illustrators highlighted in this chapter have created cover art for this book, as have several other illustrators. *Thunder* continues with David Logan, his wife, Mary, the four Logan children, David's mother, and the 400 acres of land inherited from his parents. Narrated by nine-year-old Cassie, the book covers the daily experiences of the Logans, ending with Mary Logan being fired from her teaching job and T.J. Avery's near lynching by an angry white mob. Most book covers for *Thunder*, including Pinkney's, Ginsburg's, and Nelson's, feature Cassie front and center.

Pinkney designed two book covers for *Thunder*—one for its original printing and the other for the 25th anniversary edition. Pinkney's original cover shows Cassie in the foreground, facing the reader with a semismile on her face. The smile, however, does not extend through her cheeks and into her eyes. Her expression could be read as a grimace or a hesitancy to react fully to a situation. The beauty of the land Cassie so loves spreads out across the background behind her with a cloud-filled sky. While Pinkney's pastels and neutral tones on the original *Thunder* book cover are evident, the 25th anniversary edition uses darker tones. The text mentions no picket fence in the Logans' yard, but Cassie stands in front of what appears to be the Logan home, draping her hands over a picket fence in front of the house. Christopher-John sits to the rear on the porch. As in Pinkney's earlier cover illustration, Cassie's expression can be read as showing a hint of a smile. A shadow seems to be cast over the porch to darken the space above Christopher-John's head. Darker backgrounds and deep shadows can suggest adversity or obstacles (Bang 47). Compared with the first cover, Pinkney shifts focus from the vastness of the land to the security of home.

Like Pinkney, Ginsburg focuses on safety. Ginsburg's cover emphasizes a significant event in the story in which David sets the fields on fire. Cassie, Christopher-John, and Little Man huddle together on the porch of a building (likely their home) while a fire blazes in the background. Cassie shields her younger siblings in her arms as they cast backward glances toward the fire.

None of the children are wearing shoes. As mentioned earlier, Ginsburg's covers capture moments in time like a photographic snapshot. Like Nelson, Ginsburg presents his subjects in more lifelike, three-dimensional ways.

Nelson's 40th anniversary cover design for *Thunder* gives prominence to the sky in the background. As Cassie stands front and center, staring directly at the reader, the greenness of the fields fans out toward the trees that will soon be overtaken by smoke from the fire her father started. Her crossed arms and expressionless face convey a sense of finality. Throughout the series, readers learn how hard the Logans have worked at holding onto their land. Readers also perceive the personal connection that Cassie has to the trees. With her father setting their cotton crop aflame to avert the mob from lynching T.J. before his trial, Cassie is further away from the fire on Nelson's cover than on Ginsburg's cover, placing her in a safer position. Her demeanor seems to demonstrate a resolve that says, "What's done is done."

The Friendship

This companion novella to *Thunder* centers around a character introduced briefly in *Land*: Tom Bee, who saved store owner John Wallace's life when he was a young boy. Due to that experience, John Wallace allows Mr. Bee to call him by his first name. While it was common in the Jim Crow South for whites to refer to Blacks of any age by their first name, Black people had to address white people—even children—using Mr., Mrs., or Miss. By 1933, John Wallace seems to better understand the power of white supremacy. He has all but forgotten his promise to Mr. Bee, but Mr. Bee has not. In this story, the Logan children witness an altercation between Mr. Tom Bee and John Wallace, ending with John Wallace shooting Mr. Bee. This incident reconfigures the social hierarchy between Mr. Tom Bee and John Wallace: the shooting clearly establishes John Wallace's power over Mr. Bee. Both Ginsburg's and Nelson's covers feature all four of the Logan children, although each artist chose a different emotion to highlight in their rendition.

Portraying a scene that occurs early in the narrative, Ginsburg's cover art depicts Stacey, Cassie, Christopher-John, and Little Man standing on the side of the road, with the Wallace store in the background. Stacey casually leans on a roadside fence that Christopher-John is sitting atop. Christopher-John seems more relaxed, while Cassie and Little Man take a more rigid stance on the ground. All are barefooted and looking attentively at Stacey. The serenity of this cover counters the shock and trauma that lie ahead.

Nelson's 2018 cover art places the four Logan siblings inside the Wallace store. Cassie, Christopher-John, and Little Man stand behind Mr. Tom Bee, who is staring down a gray-haired white man, John Wallace. Stacey appears helpless as he looks to Mr. Tom Bee for direction and strength. His younger siblings are statuelike as if holding their breath, frozen in fear. Light and shadow dominate the line of demarcation that defines the social privileges of the times. John Wallace on the right faces Mr. Tom Bee and the Logan children on the left. Both men are impeccably dressed, with neither outshining the other in quality or style, giving the appearance of being equal in stature. Mr. Bee and the Logans stand on a darker shaded side of the room, while Mr. Wallace stands next to the window, which appears to create a brighter light-filled effect. Nelson's ample use of white on the shelves of the Wallace store represents the white privilege the Wallace family exudes in their mannerisms and social behaviors.

Let the Circle Be Unbroken

This novel begins three months after the ending of *Thunder*. The Logans face a multitude of conflicts just to keep intact their life, their land, and what limited liberties the Jim Crow South allows. Ginsburg's cover art presents the Logan family gathered in a candid setting, on the front porch. Bang notes how greater tension is drawn to an object that is centralized to the middle or border of a frame (82). In her explanation, the tension indicates a destabilizing situation or danger. In the case of *Circle*'s cover art, however, the central figure focuses on a smiling David Logan, who sits on the porch steps encircled by his children, wife, and mother. By positioning David as the patriarchal center, the male head-of-family, Ginsburg alludes to the age-old societal views of the male as foundational to the family's security and well-being. All the children are barefooted. Cassie and Christopher-John wear jeans, and Stacey and Little Man wear overalls, emphasizing the casual setting. Mary holds a notebook, signifying her endeavor as an after-school tutor after being fired from her teaching job. Mary is bending at the waist, turned slightly toward her husband, as she reaches out her hand in the direction of his right shoulder, allowing the reader to visualize the family connection. The scene focuses on the title's message of love as the strength that binds a family and holds them together. David's mother, Big Ma, wearing an apron and holding the screen door, stands in the rear, smiling at the joyous scene. The muted color palette is rich in shades of blues, pinks, and purple, establishing a mood of tranquility (Bang 39).

Nelson also creates a cover that emphasizes the motif of Logan family closeness and togetherness. Nelson chooses to present the family in a portrait setting as if they were formally posing for a picture. As in Ginsburg's depiction, Bang's motif of tension (82) is seen in David Logan's sitting in the center as the focal point, drawing to mind how his positioning is a focus that destabilizes the dangers of the segregated South. David symbolizes safety, implying his role as the anchor that holds the family together. Big Ma and Mary stand behind

David, with both women placing their hand on his nearest shoulder, in a display that shows they have his back and support his position as the center of the family unit. In this image that highlights male societal positioning, David has one hand on the outer shoulders of his two oldest sons, Christopher-John and Stacey—both of whom sit with Cassie and Little Man at their father's feet. We question if it would have been more significant to have David embrace the shoulders of his two oldest children, Cassie and Stacey, since the hierarchy of sibling interaction by age is apparent in the story's narration. Though the Logan children are wearing shoes, it was common for youth to go barefooted due to Depression-era poverty, and to wear shoes only on formal occasions (Bates). In Nelson's cover, the children wear shoes, and their father wears a suit. Such formality in dress conveys the family's upwardly mobile socioeconomic status, especially given Mary's college education and their privilege as second-generation landowners in a sharecropping community. While most of the family members look somber, the slight smile on Big Ma's face can be interpreted as an expression of satisfaction and pride in the family and the ties that unquestionably bind them.

Road to Memphis

Road to Memphis takes place in 1941, seven years after the events of *Circle*. Cassie is completing high school in Jackson, Mississippi, and Stacey now works in Jackson. He has purchased a late-model, well-kept sedan and uses it to help his friend Moe escape lynching by driving him to Memphis to catch a train North. Both Ginsburg and Nelson provide cover art for this book.

Ginsburg's cover art portrays the experiences of Cassie and Stacey as they travel to Memphis. The car is parked on the side of the road with the hood raised. Cassie stands next to Stacey while either Little Willie or Moe sits on the car's bumper. Cassie strikes a matter-of-fact stance and appears to be talking while the two males look at her as she speaks. Both males are dressed professionally. The young man sitting on the bumper wears a suit coat but has loosened his tie, as has Stacey. The surrounding trees appear dense, tall, and unending—a safety net capable of hiding the stranded youths (Bang 70).

In contrast to Ginsburg's focus on a significant conflict in the story, Nelson chose to feature the car moving on the road instead of being stranded on the side of the road. The car's front faces the reader, with Stacey at the wheel and Cassie in the passenger seat. The position of the car facing the reader is similar to the way Nelson chose to have Cassie face the reader in *Thunder*, when the events taking place have put her in mortal danger. In *Memphis*, similar danger arises. With no choice to turn around or stop, Stacey must keep the car moving north to Memphis for Moe's safety. Nelson uses the horizon as a backdrop from which the car appears to emerge, heading toward an uncertain future. In contrast to Ginsburg's dominant use of the forest as dense and unending, here the open road appears endless, and the vastness of the sky looks as if it continues into perpetuity. The symbolic cover art's reference to unboundedness is apropos for the characters at this time in their lives, for they are at the precipice of new experiences that lead them further down separate roads.

CONCLUSION

Mildred Taylor is known to write in the privacy of her ranch in Colorado. She has not used modern marketing tools, such as social media, to attract readers or bolster sales. Nor does she use elaborate author websites replete with book trailers, cover reveals, personal blog posts, and links to podcasts and video interviews. Unlike many popularized young adult novels that have been made into movies—some with sequels and remakes–only *Thunder* led to a film adaptation back in 1978. Yet Taylor's work transcends those traditional marketing techniques, and her publishing house has stood firmly behind her work, based on the strength of Taylor's personal brand and reputation for compelling storytelling, adept character development, and the enduring relevance of her stories.

This chapter examined cover art for many of Taylor's Logan family books, specifically eight of the titles published in the United States and illustrated by three esteemed artists recognized for their excellent contributions to the field of children's literature. These artists form part of the rich legacy left by *Thunder*, and its sister novels and novellas, offering readers a window into the Black American experience. Albeit depicted in different ways, most of the covers by Pinkney, Ginsburg, and Nelson encapsulate the content of Taylor's fictionalized family stories in nuanced ways. From Pinkney's delicate watercolors to Ginsburg's realistic portrayals, to the recent reimagining by Kadir Nelson, each illustrated edition plays a crucial role in shaping the series' aesthetic and capturing the ideological and cultural contexts in which Taylor crafted her saga.

With the 40th anniversary redesign of the initial nine books in the Logan Family Saga in 2016, the covers aimed to introduce these stories to a new generation of readers. Nelson's distinctive illustrative style conveys the serious, poignant, and deeply powerful nature of the series (Oulton). At a time when the need for diverse books is still blatantly apparent (We Need Diverse Books) and the idea of books as mirrors, windows, and doors is still relevant (Bishop, "Mirrors, Windows"), Nelson's covers hold significant importance for their depictions of the boldness and resilience embodied by the characters as well as for providing a new unifying brand for the series.

Book covers take the essence of a book and encapsulate it into one important piece of artwork designed to make a first impression and capture a reader's attention and desire to read the book. Pinkney's cover illustrations offered an introduction into the world of the Logan Family by featuring the key protagonist of the series: Cassie Logan. To have a Black girl featured on the cover of a children's book, even in Pinkney's soft watercolors, was courageous for the mid-1970s, especially considering that we are still having debates around the whitewashing of book covers in the United States and Europe, although we have experienced a trend toward addressing this phenomenon in the American market (Pride; Durosomo; Hadden). Max Ginsburg's work stood out as pivotal cover art for the series until Kadir Nelson's redesigns. Ginsburg's covers represent an authenticity and rawness that seem to communicate sight, sound, smell, and touch to the reader. His covers pull readers into the story even before they read the first page. Nelson's poster-like oil stylizations combine a touch of old-school charm with modern flair, creating paintings that emit a soulful presence, providing a clear character focus and setting a tone that resonates with twenty-first-century readers. Appealing to those accustomed to the clean strokes of digitized graphics, Nelson's art seamlessly blends the traditional with the contemporary. In all, these three illustrators have added to the relevance of Taylor's books over the past fifty years and have kept readers engaged, allowing many of us to see ourselves and our families through these stories.

WORKS CITED

Acevedo, Elizabeth. *The Poet X*. HarperCollins Publishers (HarperTeen), 2018.
African American Literature Book Club. "Jerry Pinkney." *Aalbc.com*, 1997–2020.
Alexander, Kwame. *The Undefeated*. Houghton Mifflin Harcourt (Versify), 2019.
American Library Association. "Mildred Taylor wins 2021 Children's Literature Legacy Award," Jan. 25, 2021. https://www.ala.org/news/press-releases/2021/01/mildred-taylor-wins-2021-children-s-literature-legacy-award.
American Library Association. "Coretta Scott King Book Awards: All Recipients, 1970-Present." https://www.ala.org/rt/emiert/cskbookawards/coretta-scott-king-book-awards-all-recipients-1970-present#1988.
Association for Library Service to Children. "Newbery Medal Winners, 1922-Present. https://www.ala.org/alsc/awardsgrants/bookmedia/newberymedal/newberywinners/medalwinners.
Bang, Molly. *Picture This: How Pictures Work*. Chronicle Books LLC, 2016.
Barthelmess, Thom. "What Makes a Good Book Cover?" *The Horn Book*. Mar. 12, 2014. https://www.hbook.com/?detailStory=makes-good-book-cover.
Bates, Athan. *Barefoot in Bussell Town During the Great Depression*. American Star Books, 2010.
Bishop, Rudine Sims. *Free Within Ourselves: The Development of African American Children's Literature*. Heinemann, 2007.

Bishop, Rudine Sims. "Mirrors, Windows, and Sliding Glass Doors." *Perspectives: Choosing and Using Books for the Classroom*, vol. 6, no. 3, summer 1990, pp. ix–xi.

Bishop, Rudine Sims. "The Pinkney Family: In the Tradition," Jan. 10, 1996. https://www.hbook.com/?detailStory=the-pinkney-family-in-the-tradition.

Bloomfield, Maureen. "City Scenes and Social Commentary." *The Artist Magazine*. vol. 3, no. 5, July 2013, pp. 44–51.

Botelho, Maria Jose, and Masha Kabakow Rudman. *Critical Multicultural Analysis of Children's Literature: Mirrors, Windows, and Doors*, Routledge, 2009.

Burnett, Matia. "Celebrating 40 Years of 'Roll of Thunder, Hear My Cry.'" *Publisher's Weekly*, Feb. 18, 2016. https://www.publishersweekly.com/pw/by-topic/childrens/childrens-book-news/article/69436-celebrating-40-years-of-roll-of-thunder-hear-my-cry.html.

Cavalier Galleries. "Max Ginsburg—Bio." *Max Ginsburg*. https://cavaliergalleries.com/artist/max_ginsburg/biography/. Accessed May 1, 2020.

Chalk, Will. "Tiktok Increasing Video Length From One to Three Minutes." *BBCNews*. July 2, 2021. https://www.google.com/amp/s/www.bbc.com/news/newsbeat-57692353.amp.

Children's Book Council. "Choosing a Child's Book." *Reading Rockets*, 1995. https://www.readingrockets.org/article/choosing-childs-book#:~:text=Very%20young%20children%20are%20attracted,to%20create%20their%20own%20stories.

Connolly, Holly. "Is Social Media Influencing Book Cover Design?" *The Guardian*. Aug. 28, 2018. https://www.theguardian.com/books/2018/aug/28/is-social-media-influencing-book-cover-design

Durosomo, Damola. "Nnedi Okorafor Tells the Story of How Publishers Once Tried to Whitewash Her Book Cover." *Okay Africa*. Mar. 15, 2017. https://www.okayafrica.com/nnedi-okorafor-book-cover-whitewashed/.

Ford, Jennifer Anne. "What Students and Teachers Can Learn by Judging a Book by Its Cover." *The Australian Library Journal*, vol. 65, no. 1, 2016, pp. 50–56, DOI: 10.1080.00049670.2016.1125757.

Gill, Sharon Ruth. "What Teachers Need to Know About the 'New' Nonfiction." *Reading Rockets*. https://www.readingrockets.org/article/what-teachers-need-know-about-new-nonfiction.

Ginsburg, Max. "Young Adult Gallery." *Ginsburg Illustration*. www.ginsburgillustration.com/young/index.html#80. Accessed May 1, 2020.

Ginsburg, Max. https://www.maxginsburg.com. Accessed May 1, 2020.

Hadden, Cara. "Whitewashing in the Publishing Industry: The Book Cover Edition." *Bookstr*. June 15, 2023. https://bookstr.com/article/whitewashing-in-the-publishing-industry-book-cover-edition/

Hamilton, Virginia. *Zeely*. Macmillan Publishing, 1967.

Harris, Elizabeth. "Crying on TikTok Sells Books." *The New York Times*, Mar. 20, 2021. https://www.nytimes.com/2021/03/20/books/booktok-tiktok-video.html.

Haupt, Angela. "The Bookstagrammers and Book Tubers Changing the Way We Read." *Washington Post*, Aug. 6, 2019. https://www.washingtonpost.com/entertainment/books/the-bookstagrammers-and-booktubers-changing-the-way-we-read/2019/08/06/60b76d6a-afb6-11e9-8e77-03b30bc29f64_story.html.

The History Makers. "Jerry Pinkney—Biography," 2020. https://www.thehistorymakers.org/biography/jerry-pinkney.

James, Thea, and Ana Grilo. Book Smugglers. "Cover Matters: The Survey Results." *The Book Smugglers*. Apr. 27, 2010. https://www.thebooksmugglers.com/2010/04/cover-matters-the-survey-results.html.

Jerry Pinkney Studio. "Biography" webpage, 2019. https://www.jerrypinkneystudio.com/frameset.html.

Kadir Nelson, Inc. "The Artist." *The Art of Kadir Nelson*. 1998–2020. https://www.kadirnelson.com/about.

Kreider, Tim. "The Decline and Fall of the Book Cover." *The New Yorker*, July 16, 2013. https://www.newyorker.com/books/page-turner/the-decline-and-fall-of-the-book-cover.

Larbalestier, Justine. *Liar*. Bloomsbury, 2010.

Lodge, Sally. "Cover Reveal: Mildred D. Taylor Bids Farewell to the Logans." *Publisher's Weekly*, June 20, 2019. https://www.publishersweekly.com/pw/by-topic/childrens/childrens-book-news/article/80509-cover-reveal-mildred-d-taylor-bids-farewell-to-the-logans.html.

Martin, Michelle. *Brown Gold: Milestones in African-American Children's Books, 1845–2002*. Routledge, 2004.

McMurdie, Dena. "YA Book Cover Trends to Look for in 2019." *Batch of Books* blog.

The Mississippi Writers Page. "Mildred D. Taylor." *The Mississippi Writers Page* webpage, 2015. https://mwp.olemiss.edu//dir/taylor_mildred/.

NYPL Staff. "Insta Novels: Bringing Classic Literature to Instagram Stories." Aug. 22, 2018. https://www.nypl.org/blog/2018/08/22/instanovels?utm_campaign=instanovels.

Oulton, Emma. "The Logan Family's Back!—Cover Reveals." *Bustle* blog, Apr. 21, 2016. https://www.bustle.com/articles/156072-roll-of-thunder-book-series-gets-beautiful-new-covers-to-celebrate-the-40th-anniversary.

Pride, Felicia. "Black Faces on Covers Don't Sell Books?" *The Root*, July 29, 2009. https://www.theroot.com/black-faces-on-covers-dont-sell-books-1790882839.

Publisher's Weekly. "What Do Children's Book Consumers Want?" *Publisher's Weekly*, Jan. 31, 2011. https://www.publishersweekly.com/pw/by-topic/childrens/childrens-industry-news/article/45943-what-do-children-s-book-consumers-want.html.

Purdue Online Writing Lab. "Visual Rhetoric: Analyzing Visual Documents." https://owl.purdue.edu/owl/general_writing/visual_rhetoric/analyzing_visual_documents/index.html. Accessed May 1, 2020.

Purdue Online Writing Lab. "Visual Rhetoric." OWL Purdue YouTube Channel. Jan. 1, 2013. https://www.youtube.com/watch?v=-vJvivIzkDg&t=51s.

Rawlins, Sharon. "Copycat Covers: YA Book Covers That Make You Look Twice." *YALSA–The Hub* blog, Apr. 30, 2013. https://www.yalsa.ala.org/thehub/2013/04/30/copycat-covers-ya-book-covers-that-make-you-look-twice/.

Raynor, Madeline. "Books with Strangely Similar Covers." *Entertainment Weekly*, July 5, 2016. https://ew.com/article/2016/07/05/books-have-strangely-similar-covers/.

Scholastic. "Jerry Pinkney," 2020. https://www.scholastic.com/teachers/authors/jerry-pinkney/.

Shaina. "I Swear I've Seen That Book Before." *Provo City Library at Academy Square* blog, Nov. 9, 2017. https://www.provolibrary.com/blog/1733-i-swear-i-ve-seen-that-book-before.

Simon and Schuster. "Charnelle Pinkney Barlow," 2022. https://www.simonandschuster.com/authors/Charnelle-Pinkney-Barlow/165210336.

Taylor, Mildred. "2021 Children's Literature Legacy Award Acceptance." *The Horn Book* website. June 30, 2021. https://www.hbook.com/story/2021-childrens-literature-legacy-award-acceptance-by-mildred-d-taylor.

Taylor, Mildred. *All the Days Past, All the Days to Come*. Viking, 2020.
Taylor, Mildred. "My Life as a Writer." *World Literature Today*, vol. 78, no. 2, May–Aug. 2004, pp. 7–10. *JSTOR*, https://www.jstor.org/stable/40158381.
Taylor, Mildred. *The Friendship*. Dial Books, 1987.
Taylor, Mildred. *The Gold Cadillac*. Dial Books, 1987.
Taylor, Mildred. *The Land*. Phyllis Fogelman Books, 2001.
Taylor, Mildred. *Let the Circle Be Unbroken*. Dial Books, 1981.
Taylor, Mildred. *Mississippi Bridge*. Dial Books, 1990.
Taylor, Mildred. *The Road to Memphis*. Dial Books, 1990.
Taylor, Mildred. *Roll of Thunder, Hear My Cry*. Dial Books, 1976.
Taylor, Mildred. *Song of the Trees*. Dial Books, 1975.
Taylor, Mildred. *The Well*. Dial Books, 1995.
ThoughtCo. "The 7 Principles of Art and Design." ThoughtCo.com, May 22, 2019. https://www.thoughtco.com/principles-of-art-and-design-2578740.
We Need Diverse Books website. https://diversebooks.org/.
"What is Visual Rhetoric?" *A Research Guide*. https://www.aresearchguide.com/what-is-visual-rhetoric.html.
Woodmere Art Museum. "Artist Jerry Pinkney Discussing Illustrating Latest Book About MLK, Jr." YouTube video, 2020. https://youtu.be/gjXIFUp7Ba4.
Woodmere Art Museum. "Freedom's Journal: The Art of Jerry Pinkney," 2020. https://woodmereartmuseum.org/experience/exhibitions/freedoms-journal_4756.
Woodson, Michael. "How to Breathe Life into a Portrait: A Conversation With Oil Artist Kadir Nelson," *Artists Network* blog, Mar. 20, 2017. https://www.artistsnetwork.com/art-mediums/oil-painting/oil-artist-kadir-nelson/.

Re/figuring the Child-Signifier and Agency in the Film Adaptation of Mildred D. Taylor's Roll of Thunder, Hear My Cry

Devika Mehra

INTRODUCTION

Adaptations of children's literary texts have always been an essential part of children's cinema and add to the existing discourses on cultural texts for children and young people. In the history of adaptation within the context of children's cinema, the 1960s and the 1970s are significant decades with several noteworthy adaptations of children's novels produced during the period ranging from films such as *The Railway Children* (1971), *Sounder* (1972), *From the Mixed-up Files of Mrs. Basil E. Frankweiler* (1973), *Little Women* (1978), and *A Hero Ain't Nothin but a Sandwich* (1978), among others. In 1978, Jack Smight adapted Mildred D. Taylor's *Roll of Thunder, Hear My Cry* as a teleplay for television that was later heavily edited and shortened to a 110 minute film produced by Tomorrow Entertainment with Arthur Heinemann as the screenwriter. This chapter is the first in-depth critical analysis of the 1978 adaptation of the novel, analyzing the shift away from the strengths of the novel in this film adaptation through the lens of film history, genre studies, and adaptation theory.

This chapter also analyzes the 1978 adaptation of *Roll of Thunder, Hear My Cry* within the context of various macrostructural flows at the time of its production. The novel's adaptation in the late 1970s shifted the axis of focus from Cassie Logan to the Logan family and refigured the child signifier and agency within the film's narrative. Situating it as a family film made in the 1970s gives insight into the ideological underpinnings of the film text and its interrelationship with the literary text. This analysis attempts to understand how the child-signifier is refigured in the cinematic context to deal with issues of agency, marginalization, and racial oppression and to construct alternative images of childhood and family in American children's cinema. The interplay between the film and the novel in terms of absence and presence will be discussed to highlight whether the filmic text works as a counternarrative of subversion on a similar plane as Taylor's novel or completely undermines it.

HOLLYWOOD IN THE 1960S AND 1970S: FILM AS AN "ACT OF CONTEXTUALIZED INTERLOCUTION"

Significant socio-politico-cultural changes in the 1960s and 1970s impacted the nature of American films produced during this period. The films were "shaped by the omnipresent social and political upheavals of the era: the civil rights movement, the domestic consequences of the Vietnam War, the sexual revolution, women's liberation, the end of the long postwar economic boom, and the traumatic Shakespearean saga of the Nixon presidency" (Kirshner 4). On the one hand, there were shifts in network policy, the 1966 breakdown of Hollywood's Production Code and the emergence in 1968 of the new rating system itself, the civil rights movement, satellite television, and episodic series on TV that focused on domestic family settings (Schatz 15; E. Taylor, "Introduction" 5; E. Taylor, "From the Nelsons" 12). There was a move to experiment with a film's content, and exploring politically subversive, violent, and sexually explicit material became more permissible. On the other hand, commercial interests undermined representational politics in film and media. There was a tendency to lean toward more comprehensive outreach, a cross-racial family audience on TV, and to subdue the reality of social and cultural movements prevalent at the time.

In their turn away from the old classic Hollywood system and codes that had popularized "a universal apparatus" that diluted cultural density and muted political debate (Cripps 4), a space was created where discourses of race, gender, class, the corruption inherent in institutions, and the question of justice and injustice could be raised, even if in a limited way. The growing number of African American filmmakers and actors, the diversification of characterization, and the increasing focus on the African American experience were all instrumental in creating a market for Black Independent cinema. This market, which included the Blaxploitation films of the 1960s–1970s (Cripps; Lawrence), LA Rebellion films—a movement by young African and African-American filmmakers who studied at the UCLA Film School in the 1960s–1980s—and the Black Independents in New York from the late 1960s onward, marked a significant shift in the film industry. This cinema sought to counter the misrepresentation of Black people and Black experience in America perpetuated by Hollywood mainstream productions by experimenting with form and content to represent an alternative vision of Black life and culture. However, the intense power of the era's social movements did not always register in mainstream film productions, and the white gaze continued to hold ground in Hollywood films. Moreover, as Steve Neale notes in *Genre and New Hollywood*, post-change in the rating system in 1968, Hollywood considered family audiences and child-friendly films its most significant and most stable source of income. As opposed to the 1950s films that focused on simplistic moral symbolism, the 1960s witnessed a liberalized Black racial character image with a multilevel view of race relations in films; and the 1970s saw scrutiny of these images by Black people themselves (Pines 89). This historical context of variations in films, representational strategies, and their politics in the 1960s and 1970s reflects the structural absences (Cripps 4; Snead 147) in these film productions and provides an insight into the problematic politics of the 1978 adaptation of *Thunder*. Ella Shohat and Robert Stam argue that films are often political representations that signify an "act of contextualized interlocution between socially situated producers and receivers" (278). As with any adaptation or film, in the case of the adaptation of *Thunder*, these questions—who manufactured it, for whom, and how it was circulated—are interconnected and together facilitate a discussion of its representational politics. Shohat and Stam point out that cinema translates correlations of social power into registers of foreground and background, on-screen and off-screen, speaking and silent (278). The context and content of *Thunder*'s adaptation in light of these debates give insight into the relationalities between the novel and its adaptation that incorporate different levels of refiguring child agency, highlighting the discursive shift regarding race, childhood, and family from the novel to the film.

ROLL OF THUNDER, HEAR MY CRY: CONTEXTS AND HISTORY OF THE FILM ADAPTATION

In the introduction to *Children's Novels and the Movies*, Douglas Street argues, "The history of the cinematic adaptation of the children's novels is closely intertwined with the overall history of the movie industry, and some of cinema's first reels drew on books for the young" (ix). The transition from print to cinematic or televisual media is not a seamless translation. There is a change in signifying practices wherein the novel undergoes a series of transformations to suit a different media. This, in turn, facilitates a dialogic relationship with the literary text as well as the culture within which the adaptation is manufactured and exhibited. While the adaptation contributes to the constructions of childhood and creates a dialogue with the literary text, it transforms the political messaging of the novel, depending on different visual and aural representational strategies, casting, production team, and channels of circulation. As Robyn McCallum discusses, like other children's and family films, "[h]istorically, film adaptations of children's texts have been heavily influenced by the dominant 'Hollywood aesthetic'" (23). Certain features of novelistic expression are essential for the film to succeed; however, these markers vary depending on which elements are critical for reproducing the core meaning (Whelehan 7).

Taking adaptation as an intertextual process that is more than a repetition (Hutcheon; McCallum), filmic adaptations interact with and intersect with external factors, cinematic aesthetic codes and genre systems, and industry and audience preferences, and transform their source texts into a framework of visual representations that may demonstrate different political and cultural messages. This process and connections include negotiation with the literary source, cultural appropriations, and the hegemonic ideology of the Hollywood genre system (Cartmell 23). More specifically, the ideological hold of the dominant Hollywood narrative and aesthetic perpetuates similar and problematic images and messages that continue to resonate for a long time. One case in point is that of D. W. Griffith's *Birth of a Nation* (1915) and how it circulated and cemented "defamatory, racial caricatures and cinematic stereotypes" (Snead). Another example is the 1946 Walt Disney production *Song of the South*, rereleased several times, which through a faulty representation undercuts the suffering and racial oppression of Black people, violence, and existing power relations in America. These stereotypical representations of Black people that were popularized in American life and arts in the nineteenth and early twentieth centuries were reproduced repeatedly in Hollywood movies and perpetuated negative imagery of Black people (Lupack xiv).

Visual representations created in a particular culture are perpetuated by social agents who choose to create an image widely circulated and encoded in the cultural framework within which people base their choices (Hall). There is a strong link between social-structural patterns and cultural myths, and images on-screen represent social structure. It is important to consider some of these historical, sociopolitical, and economic conditions of production that enabled specific alternative images of Black people to be represented on the screen that were neither typecast nor reductive, attempting to defy problematic stereotypes and homogenization of Black people's lived experiences. These portrayals were not subject to the "dominant gaze" (Russell 244) that continued to produce problematic and inappropriate stereotypical images of Black people such as mammies (typecast as the Black matriarch figure looking after white children), toms (typecast as simple-minded and caring for the wellbeing of whites), and bucks (typecast as violent, strong, and lecherous). Russell argues that it is this "dominant gaze" (Russell's term) that reflects "the tendency of American popular cinema to objectify and trivialize the racial identity and experiences of people of color, even when it purports to represent them" (244), and it "invites the viewer to empathize and identify with its viewpoint as natural, universal, and beyond challenge; it marginalizes other perspectives to bolster its own legitimacy in defining narratives and images" (Russell 244). There was a slowly emerging space in American cinema for viewpoints that had been othered, silenced, caricatured, and suppressed, as can be seen in the Black Independent cinema of the late 1960s–1970s that illustrates how a diverse range of independent films by Black filmmakers radically engaged with cinematic language, form, genre, and content to provide an alternative vision of Black experience. Moreover, the emergence of these alternative images in the media challenged the earlier homogenized stereotypical images that had been circulated and solidified without question.

While these films were quite political in the messages they were disseminating, some other films that operated within the Hollywood system faced limitations to the level of radical social commentary they could exhibit. Kirshner highlights that what is most remarkable about 1970s films is that they "often had a political text, and even more commonly a political subtext, especially concerning gender, class, race, and the relationship between individuals and (corrupt or flawed) institutions" (21). This impact of 1970s film is evident in children's and family films too. Babington and Brown discuss the important influence of the Hollywood family film on children's cinema (loc 270, loc 275). They point out that these conditions "allow[ed] the wider proliferation of material deemed unsuitable for child consumption, and paralleling a broad relaxation in attitudes regarding suitability for children, resulting from factors such as earlier sexual maturing and common access to previously restricted knowledge" (loc 270, loc 275). Films, whether for adults, children, or dual audiences, had the opportunity to experiment and create new and alternative content. The gradual shift in cinematic engagement with Black racial identity and the representation of the lived experiences of Black people in America has influenced films for children, paving the way for the production of films that engage with more diverse issues and alternative portrayals. In the 1978 adaptation of *Thunder*, important political and ideological subtext is undermined due to the generic limitations of a family film and multigenerational and cross-racial television audience. The film often shifts focus to the family, not the individual. For instance, after Cassie's ordeal at the market with Lillian Jean and Mr. Simms, the bridging shot (a shot that seems continuous despite a spatial or temporal break) shows the image of a happy family enjoying breakfast together, safe and comfortable in their kitchen, skipping Cassie's traumatic processing of why Big Ma does not defend her against Mr. Simms. The focus has already transitioned from Cassie's encounter with racism to the family's happiness that Uncle Hammer did not confront Mr. Simms, and everyone is safe. The action in the film continually circles back to the visual representation of the family as a unit capable of overcoming obstacles and being happy in the comfortable space of the home. In focusing on the family instead of the individual, the power of Cassie's individual growth gets deleted as well.

FROM NOVEL TO SCREEN: REWORKING THE POLITICS IN THE PROCESS OF ADAPTATION

The film adaptation of *Thunder* focuses on a Black family living in the 1930s Depression-era South and their lived experience and is mediated and narrated by Cassie Logan as an inquisitive eleven-year-old girl. It traces the events of one crucial year for the Logan family and their struggle to fight racism along with keeping their land. The film opens with Cassie's voiceover and the eye-line shot that first shows the spectators, the four children, as a group gazing out from their window. It then cuts to the assumed focus of their gaze, the black car and the land outside. In the novel, by witnessing, participating, and acting, Cassie begins to understand the personal and communal history of racial oppression, realizes the continuous trauma of racism, and learns the importance of land and its connection with her family's dignity, while she also comes to understand the need to acquire agency to subvert or resist suppression by whites. However, the film deviates from highlighting her agency. By presenting her in a group, the film constructs her focal importance as dependent on the family unit. The film's depiction of the Logan household and its members becomes a vital example of the representation of a Black family within the oeuvre of 1970s family films for children. Paratextual features, such as the opening and closing credits and the montage sequence in the shortened version of the film, work as an exposition to the series of events that will take place and establish the danger surrounding the family. They include introductions to the family members and refer to their individual acts of resistance that occur off-screen such as Little Man's anger at the old books or the children's encounter with the bus.

Thunder is similar to what Brown and Babington term "'the literal family film', i.e. a narrative centered on the interactions of a nuclear family" (loc 2245). Although its primary focus is on the Logan family, which extends beyond the nuclear family setup and includes the grandmother, Uncle Hammer, and Mr. Morrison, who isn't related but whom the Logans treat as family, it adopts the generic system of family films with a dual address in its portrayal of an African American family in the South during the Depression era. The family setup is a unified and loving one that works as a site to negotiate the problem of racism and empower children by educating them about the alternative history of Black people in America.

While this film adaptation offers a different paradigmatic perspective on home, childhood, school, and family through a Black American family and their fight against racism, within the constraints of the generic elements and the Hollywood system of TV films (and later, digital versions), the film tends to lose the radicalism inherent in the novel. The adaptation of this novel into a film for TV and a subsequent shortened version facilitates a restructuring of various elements of the novel that co-opt certain generic elements of the family film, such as a resolution and a seemingly hopeful, happy ending, the importance of the family as a unit over individual agency, and the toning down of the violence. Even though this is an essential contribution to family films, its potential to critique existing power relations and racism is less charged than the novel.

Family films are a staple of American cinema (McCallum; Wojcik-Andrews; Babington and Brown) and include films that may or may not be child-centric but target a mixed audience of children and adult caregivers. Appreciating the profits from a loyal family audience (children and their parents will view together), prominent filmmakers soon capitalized on the potential success of the juvenile literary outpouring (Street 13). Moreover, these films served as the perfect place to promote universal family values with a limitation on the political messaging of the film. In their tendency to "reaffirm kinship ties" and "evoke comfort and reassurance" (60) and a focus on a patriarchal, heteronormative nuclear family, such family films had the power to disseminate liberal, humane values while undermining critical social problems of the time.

While the family serves as a lens through which specific social concerns and problems are depicted and analyzed, children's perspectives are interspersed with those of the adult family members. Booker argues that these films depict the modern nuclear family as a space where children learn to think of the social world as a matter of "us" (the family) versus "them" (everyone else) (185). It is interesting to note the mix of anxieties and escapism that the family film genre is capable of representing. Brown attributes the rising popularity of the family film since the 1970s to how they "address Western social anxieties regarding the condition of the 'family,' but also appeal to a very different audience group concerned predominantly with emotional uplift and escapism" (Loc 246).

It should be noted that there were mainstream and independent family films that focused on Black people and their experiences as a family. However, the portrayal of these screen families varied markedly with the changes in production and direction. Reid's analysis of Hollywood's images of the Black family and the interracial collaborations in the studios highlights that they "invite different forms of black subjectivity and different relationships between the audience and the screen image" (44). Even though a distinctive African American family film genre was established by early Black independent film producers and writers, one of the significant differences, in this case, is that this film is produced, directed, and adapted by white people. A thematic focus on universal appeals to familial love, unity, and strength transcends race and racism in line with the conventions of a family melodrama that appeals to a cross-racial audience. This dynamic is evident in how the film represents childhood, positions family as a key site where important issues such as recounting personal history, sharing stories, resisting racial attacks, among others, are negotiated and highlights ways to acquire agency within the family circle. These "remain bound by social and cultural constructions of childhood that regulate standards of acceptability" (60).

In the process of this particular adaptation, the film decenters the focus from the child to the family seen in the narrative and the visual representational strategies. Characters in the foreground and the background or on-screen and off-screen in crucial moments of the film reflect the social power relations inside and outside the film. The family is the fulcrum, and the film reinstates this through different cinematic modes such as long-shots and close-ups of the family as a unit, the family home and the kitchen/dining room as a key setting in the film for discovery and resolution of problems, the patriarchal and heteronormative ideology apparent in the intrafamily dynamics in the film, and the power dynamics and gendered representation of the children in the film. A common strategy in this film is to show the children in the background while the adults in the family try to overcome an issue, as the camera slowly captures the expressions on the children's faces using close-up shots—evident when Cassie is listening in on her parents as they discuss the mortgage. The scene visually marks the gendered hierarchy with David standing, asking to see the books, and Mary sitting while Cassie is standing in the background, working in the kitchen. A close-up shot gradually captures Cassie's understanding of the danger to the family and their home.

Some popular, successful film adaptations, representative of this emphasis on sensitivity and universality, include *Sounder*, a film in which everything contributes to the total impact, or Alice Childress's gutsy, compassionate screen adaptation of her own *A Hero Ain't Nothin' But A Sandwich* (1978) (Street), which reunited and portrayed the powerful performances of Paul Winfield and Cicely Tyson. Even in *Thunder*, there is a focus on the star power of adult actors: Claudia McNeil as Big Ma, Janet MacLachlan as Mary Logan, Robert Christian as David Logan, Rockne Tarkington as Mr. Morrison, and Morgan Freeman as Uncle Hammer. These were famous stage, television, or film performers and reflected certain representational codes. For instance, Claudia McNeil was already renowned for playing the role of the Black matriarch; Janet MacLachlan was famous as the teacher in *Sounder* who inspired the young boy to pursue his educational aspirations; and Rockne Tarkington acted in Blaxploitation films. As a genre film often relies on easily recognizable codes and elements, the use of these actors added to how the film's message was relayed to the audience. This adaptation then merges the representational codes of these actors with the genre system of the white dominant family film narrative that situates this adaptation apart from other family films made by independent African American filmmakers.

In Reid's discussion on the family film, he notes that "adaptations from black literary classics provided another source for the construction of the African American family film" (44) and "a combination of a black literary classic and the theme of African American family life" (45) became common for successful film adaptations (*Native Son*, 1951, 1986; *A Raisin in the Sun*, 1961; *The Learning Tree*, 1969) (47). These and other successful family film adaptations had a crossover appeal and a cross-racial audience. Such variations in the adaptation owe a lot to the dominant Hollywood aesthetics and genre system of the time that valued universality over race as a model of success and attempted to target a more cross-racial audience, a pattern repeated in other Black-oriented films such as *The Learning Tree* (1969) or *Sounder* (1972). This turn towards the universal ideas of family and familial love/bond omits the possibility of situating racism as the primary discursive issue.

REFIGURING THE CHILD-SIGNIFIER AND THE ACT OF WITNESSING

Several theorists argue that in adaptations of novels there is a tendency to convert a children's novel into a family film to target a family audience, along with simplifying the radical elements present in the novel. Anja Muller points out that this is accompanied by downsizing, oversimplifying or abridging cultural artifacts that impact the reception of such adaptations. During this process, there is a refiguring of the child-signifier in the film that is different from the novel and is situated within the cinematic codes and aesthetics of the time.

The film plays with the act of witnessing by focusing on the child's gaze and the points of view of Cassie and Stacey. The gaze of the child is important in this case as it enables the viewer to gain insight into the lived reality of the everyday life of Black children and people facing racism. The gaze looks not at the external and larger elements of racial oppression and struggle. It focuses on the inner private space of the home and traces the trauma-in-continuum experienced by different generations within their family and community. The beginning of the film shows the children looking out of the window; after that, the viewer follows the object of their gaze.

This first paratextual feature emphasizes the child's gaze, the act of witnessing, and subsequent learning by Cassie and her siblings. For instance, the four children are witnesses and party to the plans to boycott the Wallaces' store. They observe the trajectory of the boycott started by Mary, later taken over by David, with Mr. Jamison's support. Cassie and her siblings hear the conversation in the adjoining room and question further to understand more. Critics such as Michelle Martin and Jani Barker have noted how Cassie, in the novel, uses the interrogative stance to gain clarity and asks questions until she gains enough knowledge to be an agent. In this instance, Cassie learns that trying is enough sometimes.

Moreover, this privilege to interrogate is restricted to the private space rather than the public space, where it would render her vulnerable to racist attacks by whites. However, the film remains ambiguous in this depiction of Cassie. It allows Cassie to achieve this knowledge but only as a part of the family unit, highlighted in the visual positioning of the children together or with other family members.

The film opens with a voiceover by Cassie, who introduces the viewer to the family and gives an insight into their life. Cassie's narration, "We lived in Mississippi in 1933, on our own land bought by Grandpa long before we children were born. . . . I was eleven, and I did a lot of growing up that year" (Smight), situates the film both spatially and temporally, and establishes Cassie as the mediator through whose point of view the viewer can access the events. However, her viewpoint is structured within the power dynamics of the family on screen. Although the film represents Cassie and Stacey as primary child-signifiers who interrogate, and Christopher-John and Little Man as secondary child-signifiers who are still observing, the visual representation highlights the gendered dynamic within the screen family. In one of the opening scenes, while Mary and Big Ma tend to an injured David at home, the focus is on the family dealing with this problem. In the next scene, the camera places Stacey as the central figure and key witness, with Cassie questioning Stacey while Christopher-John and Little Man stand in the background. This scene replicates the patriarchal gender dynamic—Stacey's portrayal mirrors David's—or rather the stereotype of the man of the house in a family film genre. Unlike in the novel, in Stacey's and Cassie's gendered portrayal, the agency seems to shift to Stacey while Cassie remains a passive onlooker.

Bosmajian, in her discussion of the novel, explains the link between the family and the children, and its impact on their growth: "Mildred Taylor shows us Cassie's development not only in the context of growing up in a warm and nurturing family but also in the context of the middle-class values of life, liberty, and the pursuit of property (happiness). It is the Logans' landownership, threatened though it is by the difficulty of meeting tax payments, that is essential to their dignity, their life, and the liberty they claim" (144).

One of the significant problems the Logan family faces is paying off the mortgage on the land. The land is symbolic of their past trauma and their struggle for respect and freedom and is a crucial instrument to subvert or resist racial oppression. The importance of the land in the life of the Logan family is stressed throughout the film, with a focus on how this African American family's dignity is tied up with the land. The children participate in the family's struggle to own the land, even if the role is one of witnessing and understanding. This is emphasized in the film's depiction of one or all of the children in the adjoining room being privy to the conversation about the land and its mortgage or as witnesses to the problem and its eventual resolution. The film focuses on the act of witnessing and the gaze of the child during this act rather than after the fact. In doing so, it positions the children as onlookers and emphasizes their immediate responses using close-up shots and growing as agents rather than showing their introspection about the events. While the discussion of land ownership occurs between the adults in the dining room, the children are shown in the foreground.

While Cassie, Stacey, Christopher-John, and Little Man indulge in a few childish games, these acts of subversion are either only mentioned as having happened off-screen or are absent in the film. Stacey understands that he must not behave irresponsibly in his fight with T.J. However, Cassie needs her discussion with Mr. Morrison to understand that she must carefully orchestrate her revenge on Lillian Jean. Different adult family members make them realize the danger these acts can cause for their family, and these scenes centering adults become the film's primary focus. Childhood games and playground fights have more profound ramifications for Cassie and Stacey and other Black children than they do for white children, and this film focuses on the family helping the children become cognizant of their oppression and marginalized status.

Cassie and her siblings must engage with adult problems that permeate their lives. The four learn to confront racist attacks and racial trauma by witnessing the action of their family members. Observing and witnessing are intrinsic to their childhood. Cassie is cast as both witnessing and eavesdropping to understand the violence and the continuous threats they face. However, this act of witnessing and seeking information enables Cassie and her siblings to become subversive to object to their oppression while protecting themselves. It is not a mere ploy to be mischievous but a means to gain awareness. The film emphasizes the four children not as agents but as parts of a family unit, in resolving the major problems such as paying the mortgage or preventing T.J.'s lynching. However, due to the knowledge acquired from witnessing these incidents, the siblings can understand the need for resorting to subversion to facilitate change. Sarah Hardstaff observes of the novel: "Witnessing rather than acting appears to offer Cassie and the younger children protection from danger; the reader sees how Cassie is empowered by her victories, but simultaneously recognizes that Cassie's surroundings do not offer African American characters unlimited potential for developing agency" ("Papa Said" 10). For instance, the children are witnesses to their family's financial crisis despite their inability to help resolve it.

Moreover, "[a]dult agency in monetary matters is, by and large, presented as a model to children and young adults," even if they are not primary agents (Hardstaff, "Money and the Gift" 6). In the film, their personal and collective experiences, the unofficial and informal family history, and the communal history of racism enable—not just Cassie—but all her siblings to lean toward an interrogation of their marginalization. The act of witnessing is restrained by their roles as children in a family film where they can witness but not achieve the full potential of this act of witnessing present in the novel. The close-up shots of Cassie and her siblings capture the fear, anxiety, curiosity, and understanding. Still, Cassie and Stacey are repositioned as signifiers of hope in a patriarchal familial framework rather than as agents of subversion. The primary setting of the film where these scenes take place is the domestic family space. Therefore, it is interesting how, in the film, the perspective focuses on the private more than the public spaces the four children inhabit with their family, especially the home.

VISUALIZING SPATIAL DYNAMICS AND CHILDHOOD IN THE FILM

Through the interaction between the children and the common spaces inhabited by them, the film focuses on the function of the three ideological state apparatuses (Althusser's term) in the acculturation of the children: family, state, and church. Their experiences in these spaces enable them to move towards acquiring knowledge and a semblance of agency. These spaces form the microcosm where the children engage with their racial identity and seek the strength to resist and shelter from the racial trauma they encounter in the macrocosmic sphere. Children inhabit specific spaces such as the home, the school, the playground, the market, and the neighborhood that become sites where they negotiate with their world and identity. In a way, the dialogic function of these spaces enables children to experience problems oriented towards adults, imitate different subject positions, encounter oppression, learn to resist, and gain agency.

It is interesting to see how in the film, the children in the Logan family learn to construct their identity in relation to the land and through their encounters with race at school, home, market, and the neighborhood. The film depicts how differently racism infiltrates all spaces commonly occupied by children (school, home, market, and playground). The nature of racial discrimination is insidious at their school, where the focus is on suppressing their knowledge of African

American history and the difference in terms of their school infrastructure as well as the school calendar. However, the oppression becomes more dangerous and overt in the market and in their neighborhood, where they are subject to both verbal and violent racial attacks. In the adaptation, this is only evident in some of the montage-like sequences in the beginning or in events that happen off-screen. The focus in this version of the adaptation is more on the domestic space of the family rather than on the public space of the school. Of note is the space of the home, which works not only as a safe haven but also as a crucial space where the children can become cognizant of their shared, alternative history of slavery and racism in America. The film draws upon Taylor's usage of these spaces to show how the Logan family children are acculturated into society, become aware of racial politics, understand the history of their personal/collective trauma, and subsequently learn to subvert or resist.

The film, with its focus on a particular family and its members, uses the domestic space as a central space for socializing the children. The home, rather than the school, emerges as the leading site where the children are acculturated and educated. Most of the action in the film takes place within the family setup, either at home or occasionally in the public space, but surrounded by family. Following the generic setting, the film uses key spaces inhabited by children, especially the home, and depicts the children in the social spaces within the home: the dining room, the kitchen, the sitting room, and the porch. Here they learn about their shared history and the racial oppression their family and the community face. As Kelly McDowell argues in her analysis of the novel, "For the Logan children, history is represented through specific events that directly intersect with factors of race and class. It becomes transformative; knowing their history allows the Logan children greater freedom and agency" (216). There are a series of important scenes in the film in which an adult member from the Logan household in the home's communal spaces is sharing their experience with the children to teach them to think critically. It can be their grandmother's tale of their family's past or Mr. Morrison's fight to escape slavery. The film changes these scenes by positioning children on the sidelines or as part of a family unit sitting together at the dining table where the adults are talking to each other but not to the children. In other scenes that show either Stacey or Cassie being guided by their father and mother, respectively, the adults are visually represented in a position of power, made apparent by the lighting or a strategic focus on their facial expressions that show the adults talking down to the children.

The personal history that family members recount at home gives a glimpse into the continuous and shared trauma of the entire community. All five adults share their experience of racism, their experiences of the fight against slavery, the presence of racial oppression in their society, and their advice on ways to critically think it over and subvert/resist it. It facilitates a discussion so that racism can be questioned and the trauma of oppression can be brought to light and understood. It also educates the children into acquiring knowledge that can be instrumental in their empowerment. Bosmajian highlights the importance of discussions about justice and injustice explored within the Logan household as a family and the impact it has on the children. As she points out, "The values of personhood and community are instilled through the deep bonding among the members of the Logan family and their ability to 'talk things out'" (Bosmajian 147). Mary Logan's personal courage against injustice and David Logan's kind and disciplined nature provide the children with strong values.

Moreover, "David teaches his children separateness from whites as a means of survival" (Bosmajian 147). These conversations and acts of sharing experiences foster a strong bond in the family and reaffirm the value of kinship that is intrinsic to family films. This is reflected in the scene in which Mary consoles Cassie after she is subject to a racist attack in the market or when her grandmother and mother try to comfort her when she is scared after seeing the nightmen from her window. The film features similar examples, focusing on the entire family sitting together, either enjoying a meal or trying to resolve a problem. These scenes emphasize family bonding, where the family comes together as a unit and the adults prepare the children to face the realities of life. They offer reassurance and instill hope in the children, enhancing the socialization process of the children by providing alternative modes of learning about social injustice and the treatment of Black people, as well as their personal/communal traditions, beliefs, and customs.

The film stresses the importance of community and shared history in its constant depiction of the Logan family as a unified entity and through the representation of scenes from the church and the school. None of the Logan family members are portrayed in isolation in the film, except in the scenes where Cassie is alone in the bedroom and, even then, it is often followed in quick succession by either Big Ma or Mary checking in on her. This stresses the importance of the support system provided by the family and the larger community to combat racism. Mary Turner Harper explains the significance of the school and the church and argues, "In contrast, the 'weather-beaten' Great Faith Elementary and Secondary School and the Great Faith church are adjacent. That school and church are so situated and so named symbolizes the Black community's hope for the future, a place for both intellectual and spiritual sustenance. Each becomes an oasis amid seemingly unending struggles" (79).

The school and the church have a special place within the Black community, as seen in the film, where community values, the dissemination of alternative history, and a communal bond can be created and celebrated. The film heightens T.J.'s interruption of the church meeting with the Simms brothers, highlighting the danger faced by the Black community and the threat posed by

T.J.'s inability to understand this with the two white and much older brothers always in the foreground during the discussion. It allows the audience to see through the deception, manipulation, and the danger posed by the Simms brothers, highlighted through their smirks and exchange of glances, that T.J. is unwilling to recognize as antagonistic to him and his community. This is one of the few scenes where a crucial action in the film takes place during the church meeting, a public or community space, instead of the home or the domestic family space that remain the most dominant spaces in the film.

CHILDREN, FAMILY, AND ENTANGLED AGENCY IN THE FILMIC ADAPTATION

Family and domestic life conditions become determinants in the construction of childhood. In the film, the children tackle various personal and social problems as a family unit. The film represents how monetary and violent issues are the purview of the adults, while the problems the children deal with directly related to themselves or their peers are absent, off-screen, or simply mentioned to adults, unlike in the novel. The film conforms to the gendered power dynamics in the Hollywood family film genre. It represents gendered learning by the children, with the aid of a female adult figure in Cassie's experience and a male adult figure in Stacey's. The film incorporates the dominant patriarchal ideology and gendered typecasting prevalent in Hollywood films in these scenes, which departs from the novel. In another scene, Stacey is shown as a witness to the act of gaining complete ownership of the land when the mortgage money is paid at the bank. He is visually positioned between his uncle and father, while the camera shifts focus to David, Hammer, and the three of them as one unit. This matter concerning money is one where the children can only observe and learn. Since they have no means to acquire money, they are dependent on their parents to resolve this issue. It is interesting to note that Stacey's father and uncle take him to the bank, which positions Stacey as a young boy who has to share the burden of responsibility after he grows up. Elsewhere, Stacey receives guidance from his family, especially the male counterparts, to follow in his father's and uncle's footsteps. This is evident in the scene about the jacket Uncle Hammer gives Stacey, as well as the scene in which he tries to stop T.J.'s lynching. The film visually positions David as the central adult patriarch who is talking down to Stacey. At the same time, the director places Mary in the middle as an onlooker, and the rest of the family in the foreground.

Another area where the children cannot resolve the problem on their own is that of violence against the family. The threat of danger to one's life is equally palpable throughout the film with its use of foreboding music. The film uses typical music as cues to instill a feeling of suspense or danger. This is seen in the long tracking shot of the nightmen with their cars, the scene where David is injured, and the scene in which Mr. Morrison and the children have forgotten the shotgun at home. The music aims to hint at danger without emphasizing its immediacy, and minimizes the degree of harm by locating the danger off-screen. Staying firmly within the family film genre by adhering to these representational strategies and self-censorship, the film does not depict violent and gruesome scenes yet simultaneously depicts the threat of violence. The director achieves this by reworking violent scenes or by showing particular objects such as Kaleb's cars or the nightmen as harbingers of danger. The director also modifies the types of threats by changing the visual aspect of certain characters from the novel, such as Mr. Berry, in the film. In the novel, Mr. Berry is still alive but suffering from his severe burns, which the Logan children witness. The film depicts Mrs. Berry deranged and speaking to her dead husband, tempering the visual impact of the violence while still representing the level of brutality to which whites have subjected Black people. The director's choice to stay within the genre's constraints of what is deemed appropriate for a younger audience changes, but does not erase, the immediacy of the violence, the nature of oppression, and the radical call for resistance. The genre's aural and visual cinematic codes shift the focus from the danger of racism to a more simplified form of danger to family, undercuts the harsh reality discussed in the literary text, and limits its political message.

While the film chooses not to depict any violent or gruesome scenes, except the scene where David is injured and shot, keeping within the generic conventions and the suitability of such scenes for young viewers, some amount of violence against children is portrayed to emphasize the extent of racial oppression and the danger it poses to the lives of Black people, even children. One such incident is Cassie's treatment and her personal experience of a racist attack by Mr. Simms in Strawberry, and the other is a glimpse into the violent reaction of Mr. Wallace and other white people towards T.J. in the end when he is nearly lynched. Violence against children, of any degree, highlights the fissures in the social fabric of any community. The scene in which Mr. Simms pushes Cassie to the ground and publicly humiliates her while her peer, Lillian Jean, demands an apology, reflects the vulnerability of Cassie as a Black child during that time as well as the impact of intergenerational racism practiced by white adults and their children. Although Cassie does not understand why she is marginalized until her mother explains it to her, Lillian Jean is already aware of the power she can wield over Cassie as a white girl and delights in it. This scene foreshadows T.J.'s arrest at the end of the movie. Just as Cassie becomes a victim, so is T.J. victimized when he is blamed for the crime committed by the two white boys, the Simms brothers. The film highlights the differential treatment of children based on their race. In both cases, the Logan family as a unit intervenes. In the first case, Cassie's grandmother protects her at the market, and later her mother comforts Cassie while she explains the excuses used by whites to oppress them. In the second scenario, David burns his own cotton crop to prevent T.J. from being lynched by the white mob.

Bosmajian comments on the persistent threat of danger experienced by Black people and Taylor's handling of this ever-present violence in her novel for young readers. Bosmajian posits, "Taylor does keep within the conventions of literature for young readers by preserving Cassie from witnessing extreme acts of violence, but the threat of it permeates even the most intimate 'at home' moments" (147). The film adaptation conforms to the conventions and codes of the family film genre that value a positive message—a lack of violence that can cause potential harm and a more optimistic view of the world. The film relies on these aural and visual codes to reiterate the danger with the use of props such as the shotgun at home and the atmosphere of anxiety that permeates the home and both children and adults. The need to protect themselves after the accident is presented through the tense exchanges between the Logan family members. For instance, David is anxious when Mr. Morrison forgets the shotgun while the children go out with him. The circumstances are such that venturing out without a weapon could have grave consequences for them. The film depicts Cassie and Stacey as children aware of the danger, capturing their fear and anxiety through close-up shots of their faces, or by keeping them in the foreground as silent observers. For instance, Cassie has heard about the nightmen, is depicted looking at the row of headlights of their cars, her fear and anxiety are captured by a close-up of her expressions, and she has seen shotguns at home. It is only toward the end that she begins to understand the degree of violence Black people face. Even then, the film does not show Kaleb Wallace and others hitting, and the film undercuts Cassie's realization of the dangers of racial oppression by showing her secure in her bedroom at home, content with the thought that her family as a unit will be able to overcome similar incidents in the future.

The film highlights this aspect of the family's capability to resolve problems rather than showing the individual child's interior growth after witnessing or being subjected to racial discrimination. The unified image of the Logan family as an alternative resilient unit that grapples with the major and minor problems together ranges between hopeful and escapist, where the children are reassured that all issues can be resolved. A more positive message is apparent in the film adaptation than in the book. In resorting to such representational strategies and generic codes, especially the us (family) versus them (world) strategy, the film departs from the narrative of agency of the Logan children in the literary text.

UNDERMINING A RADICAL TEXT: FAULTY REPRESENTATIONAL STRATEGIES AND GENERIC CONSTRAINTS

According to Barbara Lupack, when novels with Black representation are adapted as a motion picture, they are often reworked or popularized for mainstream audiences so that much of their cultural and idiosyncratic importance is lost (xv). As can be seen in this filmic adaptation, there are various and problematic changes that reduce its potential as a radical text. Be it the gendered representation of children and adults in the film, or the limitation of the novel's political subtext, the adaptation is prone to oversimplification and a universalized narrative. The most noticeable and problematic change is the film's undermining of the centrality of the child-signifier, by aligning the emphasis on the family rather than the child-protagonist. It situates Cassie as the narrator in the present and seeks to incorporate the gaze of the child but mitigates the importance of Cassie as the primary child-signifier by restricting her within a generic framework of a child in a family film. Another way the film achieves this decentering is by alternating between Cassie and Stacy as central to scenes where Cassie is shown learning from her mother and grandmother, while Stacy is depicted as learning how to be a responsible adult patriarch from his father and other male adult characters. In several other scenes in the film, this gendered hierarchy among siblings is repeated, where Stacey appears to be more actively involved in the problems of the adult world, while Cassie tends to be introspective and interrogate events from within the domestic space. In the final scene featuring T.J.'s attempted lynching and the subsequent fire, Cassie can only be a witness from the house's porch and wait for information for her family's safety. In the film, there is a visible gendered demarcation in their learning and witnessing that can be attributed to the dominant patriarchal ideology prevalent in Hollywood.

This trend of problematic representation of women is repeated in the adaptation of Mary's character. Both Mary and Big Ma are secondary in relation to David, Hammer, and even Mr. Morrison in terms of the hierarchy within the family unit. Men often controlled women's stories and images, and in multiple mainstream Hollywood films, women characters' primary function was supportive rather than active (Kuhn). Their acts of agency are undercut in scenes where they are positioned as dependents to men. This regression in the representational strategies is influenced by the patriarchal heteronormative family setup in the family film genre and the typecasting of women and men in Hollywood film aesthetics.

A key instance in which the film's omissions undermine Mary's and its own radical potential are Mary's act of teaching the alternative history of slavery in America and her rebellious act of pasting paper over the county's record page inside the history books donated to the school. These acts of subversion in the novel enable Mary to facilitate the "unveiling of racist power structures. She continually attempts to teach her own children how power works against them" (McDowell 217). Her agency as a teacher and a working woman is either absent in the film or made invisible by being situated off-screen. Throughout the film, her subversive potential is hidden beneath the trappings of a mother figure in a family unit typical of a mainstream Hollywood family film narrative.

This is also evident in the visual representation of Mary's character, where she is shown in the majority of the scenes as a caring wife and mother who supports her husband's decisions and acts of defiance. She conforms to the stereotypical role of the wife and mother within the family film genre. It is most evident in the positioning of Mary in the domestic space of the family home rather than in the public space. Within the confines of the home, Mary is often seen as caring for David, greeting him, preparing food, or standing on the sidelines while David is teaching the children an important lesson. Another scene in the film that further suppresses women's agency is when David takes over the act of convincing the other families to boycott the Wallaces' store, something that Mary does in the novel. The film cannot channel the importance of Mary's resistance to racism, instead focusing more on her ability to provide comfort and support to her family rather than her ability to organize and resist racism. Interestingly, the adaptation and its edited version delete Mary's acts of subversion as a teacher, even though Janet MacLachlan, who plays Mary, had earlier famously played the role of a subversive teacher who chooses education and books to resist racism in *Sounder*. While in *Sounder*, the teacher is situated outside the domestic trappings of the family, in *Thunder*, Mary is a teacher but also a mother. This dual role is constrained by the limitations imposed on women within the domestic space within the Hollywood family film narrative. While in the book, Mary is a far more radical figure whose ability to resist racism is foregrounded, the film reduces her to a common one-dimensional stereotype of a dependent wife and mother figure who is devoid of agency.

In the final scene, David acknowledges and assuages Cassie's fears and worries, with the last shot on Cassie's smiling face as she goes off to sleep. Instead of crying herself to sleep, as seen in the novel, the film's stress to conform to a happy resolution undermines the subversive element in the text. The last image of Cassie, smiling and comforted at the thought that her parents have resolved the problem, highlights the film's tendency to use the child-signifier as a symbol of hope. Moreover, the attempt to provide a seemingly or fleetingly happy resolution at the end of this film is characteristic of most family films targeted at children. The film conforms to the generic architectonics of the American family film made in the 1970s rather than using the novel's potential as a text of resistance. Throughout the film, through the depiction of the problems and triumphs faced by the Logan family, Cassie and Stacey function as dual child-signifiers that become symbolic of social and individual transformation.

Moreover, their acquisition of agency is linked with and dependent on their family. The family and the home are major sites that empower, enable, and encourage the four children to understand the oppression of Black people, develop modes to subvert/resist, and overcome their marginalization. As Robin Wood suggests in "Images of Childhood," childhood is centrally linked to family, and the nature of childhood represented on screen has become varied where children can be portrayed as innocent and evil. This film's alternative image of childhood is constructed in tandem with the family. The focus has shifted from transforming the children, be it Cassie or her siblings, into agents to portraying them as representative figures, signifying the hope for social change for which adults have dreamed and fought.

CONCLUSION:
TRANSFORMING A TEXT OF RESISTANCE INTO AN UNPROBLEMATIC FAMILY FILM

Although these productions are limited by the censorship rules, and the conventions of the genre deemed suitable for children, the film adaptation shifts the perspective from the growth of a child protagonist as an agent to the collective trials and tribulations faced by a family. While the film is not unimportant in the larger discourse and conditions that enabled its production in the 1970s, it departs from the radical potential of the novel. Despite a minimum budget or a limited shooting schedule, the film's portrayal of an African American family in the late 1970s is in tandem with the proliferation of images of Black people on-screen in mainstream Hollywood films. This film is influenced by the literary text that it adapts and the intertextual relationship it shares with the other filmic texts prevalent at the time. While it is not effective as a counternarrative, unlike the literary text, its importance lies in its construction of a Black family, their history, their struggle, their hopes, and their strength that are contrary to stereotypical representations of Black people in American films.

The film has a tendency to transform the coming-of-age narrative of Cassie in the novel into a homogenized version restricted by the codes and conventions of the Hollywood family film genre. It transforms and undercuts the political orientation of the literary text using various aural and visual cinematic codes and representational strategies. This is evident in its entanglement of agency with family, in the emphasis on the family space, in the alternative and gendered portrayal of Cassie's and Stacey's acculturation, and in the gendered power dynamics within the family setup. The film's limited political orientation is situated within the hegemonic, dominant, patriarchal, heteronormative ideology prevalent in

Hollywood aesthetics and genre systems. In doing so, the positionality of Black people and its progressive elements are undermined by the trappings of the family film genre system, with its overtly optimistic and oversimplified narrative. Any future film adaptations of the novel will need to address the limitations of the genre system and avoid oversimplification, gendered demarcations, and reductive reading of the political messaging of the novel.

WORKS CITED

Althusser, Louis. "Ideology and Ideological State Apparatuses: Notes Towards an Investigation." *On Ideology*. 1971. Verso, 2008, pp. 1–60.

Booker, Keith M. "Conclusion: The Politics of Children's Film: What Hollywood Is Really Teaching Our Children." *Disney, Pixar, and the Hidden Messages of Children's Films*, ABC CLIO, 2010.

Bosmajian, Hamida. "Mildred Taylor's Story of Cassie Logan: A Search for Law and Justice in a Racist Society." *Children's Literature*, vol. 24, 1996, pp. 141–60. *Project MUSE*, https://doi.org/10.1353/chl.0.0330.

Brown, Noel. "Hollywood Children's Cinema and the Family Audience." *The Children's Film: Genre, Nation and Narrative*, Wallflower, 2017, pp. 35–60.

Brown, Noel. Introduction. *The Hollywood Film: A History from Shirley Temple to Harry Potter*, I. B. Tauris, 2012.

Brown, Noel, and Bruce Babington. "Introduction: Children's Films and Family Films." *Family Films in Global Cinema*, edited by Noel Brown and Bruce Babington, Kindle ed., I. B. Tauris, 2015.

Cartmell, Deborah. Introduction. *Adaptations: From Screen to Text, Text to Screen*, edited by Deborah Cartmell and Imelda Whelehan, Routledge, 1999.

Cripps, Thomas. *Making Movies Black*. Oxford UP, 1993.

Hall, Stuart. "Encoding/Decoding." *Culture, Media, Language: Working Papers in Cultural Studies: 1972–1979*, Routledge, 1980.

Hardstaff, Sarah (Layzell). "'Papa Said That One Day I Would Understand': Examining Child Agency and Character Development in *Roll of Thunder, Hear My Cry* Using Critical Corpus Linguistics." *Children's Literature in Education*, 2014, pp. 1–16. DOI 10.1007/s10583-014-9231-1.

Hardstaff, Sarah (Layzell). "Money and the Gift in the Novels of Mildred Taylor and Cynthia Voigt." *Barnboken: Journal of Children's Literature Research*, vol. 42, 2019, pp. 1–15. https://dx.doi.org/ 10.14811/clr.v42i0.417.

Harper, Mary Turner. "Merger and Metamorphosis in the Fiction of Mildred D. Taylor." *Children's Literature Association Quarterly*, vol. 13, no. 2, summer 1988, pp. 75–80. DOI: https://doi.org/10.1353/chq.0.0384.

Hutcheon, Linda. *A Theory of Adaptation*. Routledge, 2006.

Kirshner, Jonathan. "Before the Flood." *Hollywood's Last Golden Age*, Cornell UP, 2013, pp. 4–22. https://muse.jhu.edu/book/66730

Kuhn, Annette. *Women's Pictures: Feminism and Cinema*. 2nd ed., Verso, 1994.

Lawrence, Novotny. *Blaxploitation Films of the 1970s: Blackness and Genre*. Routledge, 2008.

Lupack, Barabra. Preface. *Literary Adaptations in Black American Cinema: From Micheaux to Morrison*, U of Rochester P, 2002.

Mazierska, Ewa. "Introduction: Marking Political Cinema." *Framework: The Journal of Cinema and Media*, vol. 55, no. 1, 2014, pp. 37. Project MUSE, muse.jhu.edu/article/556145.

McCallum, Robyn. "Introduction: 'Palimpsestuous Intertextuality' and the Cultural Politics of Childhood." *Screen Adaptations and the Politics of Childhood: Transforming Children's Literature into Film*, Palgrave Macmillan, 2018, pp. 1–32.

McDonagh, Maitland. "The Exploitation Generation: Or: How Marginal Movies Came in from the Cold." *The Last Great American Picture Show*, edited by Thomas Elsaesser et al., Amsterdam UP, 2004, https://www.jstor.org/stable/j.ctt46mxhc.8.

McDowell, Kelly. "*Roll of Thunder, Hear My Cry*: A Culturally Specific, Subversive Concept of Child Agency." *Children's Literature in Education* vol. 33, no. 3, Sept. 2002, pp.213–25.

Muller, Anja. "Introduction: Adapting Canonical Texts in and for Children's Literature." *Adapting Canonical Texts in Children's Literature*, edited by Anja Muller, Bloomsbury Academic, 2013.

Neale, Steve. *Genre and New Hollywood*. Routledge, 1999.

Pines, Jim. *Blacks in Films*. London: Studio Vista, 1974.

Reid, Mark. "Family Film: Black Writers in Hollywood." *Redefining Black Film*, U of California P, 1993.

Roll of Thunder, Hear My Cry. Dir. Jack Smight, Tomorrow Entertainment: 1978.

Russell, Margaret M. "Race and the Dominant Gaze: Narratives of Law and Inequality in Popular Film." *Legal Studies Forum*, vol. 15, no. 3, 1991, pp. 243–54.

Schatz, Thomas. "The New Hollywood." *Film Theory Goes to the Movies* edited by Jim Collins et al., Routledge, 1993.

Shohat, Ella, and Robert Stam. *Unthinking Eurocentrism: Multiculturalism and the Media*. Routledge, 1994.

Snead, James. *White Screen, Black Images*. 1994. Routledge, 2006.

Street, Douglas, editor. *Children's Novels and the Movies*. Frederick Ungar Publishing, 1983.

Taylor, Ella. "From the Nelsons to the Huxtables: Genre and Family Imagery in American eNtwork Nelevision." *Qualitative Sociololgy*, vol. 12, 1989, https://doi.org/10.1007/BF00989242,

Taylor, Ella. "Introduction: Cultural Analysis and Social Change." *Primetime Families: Television Culture in Post-war America*, U of California P, 1989.

Taylor, Mildred D. *Roll of Thunder, Hear My Cry*. 1976. New York: Puffin Books, 1991.

Whelehan, Imelda. "Adaptations: The Contemporary Dilemmas." *Adaptations: From Screen to Text, Text to Screen*, edited by Deborah Cartmell and Imelda Whelehan, Routledge, 1999.

Wojcik-Andrews, Ian. *Children's Films: History, Ideology, Pedagogy*. New York and London: Garland Publishing, 2000.

Wood, Robin. "Images of Childhood."*Personal Views: Explorations in Film*, Gordon Fraser, 1976, pp. 153–72.

How the Logans Travel to the East: Exploring the Persian Translations of *Roll of Thunder, Hear My Cry*, *The Friendship*, and *The Well*

Bahar Eshraq

INTRODUCTION

The influence of translated texts in different cultures has always been a critical issue in the translation of children's literature. Mildred D. Taylor's novels have been translated into several languages; however, these translations have not received critical attention. This chapter explores the influence of Taylor's works and their reception or, in other words, to see how they have been domesticated in Persian culture. It adopts Yuri Lotman's concepts of the Semiosphere and five-stage reception process as a tool for translation criticism of the Persian translations of *Roll of Thunder, Hear My Cry* (1976); *The Friendship* (1987); and *The Well* (1995). As cited in Kourdis, one of the implications of Lotman's semiotic approach is the study of sign systems in a culture regarding what they give to culture (149). Here, Taylor's literary texts work as a sign system conveying a message: resisting racism. This chapter focuses on how the language of resisting racism depicted in Taylor's books has been translated into Farsi. Even though slavery existed in Persian culture, the language of resisting racism was transferred into Persian culture in 1936 through the interlingual translation of American literature such as *Uncle Tom's Cabin* by Harriet Beecher Stowe (Rosenthal). In the first section of this chapter, extratextual analysis shows how this cultural act (the language of resisting racism) has been translated into Persian culture at a particular historical time. Moreover, since literary translation operates as a cross-cultural dialogue, the contrastive analysis of the semiotic features of the translated texts and sociocultural information decoded in the source texts shows how Taylor's literary texts have been domesticated. The second section of the chapter, using peritextual and textual analysis of the original and translated texts, describes spaces of translatability and untranslatability. Hence, this chapter discusses the texts in relation to the Semiospheres of the West (English source texts) and that of the East (Persian target texts), the dynamic processes conveyed in the social and cultural structures of these texts, and the reception of the translated texts.

By focusing on culture and cultural semiotics, this chapter also treats translation in a descriptive manner instead of in an evaluative way. It is not concerned with whether a translation is of "good" quality but instead focuses on translation as a cultural process, scrutinizing the semiospheric space of the translated texts to explore how the translated texts have been generated and received within the target culture. When translation scholar Gote Klingberg suggested the term "cultural context adaptation" for the translation procedure of replacing the source language's cultural elements with that of the target language (Klingberg et al. 86), he explained the real problem for the translator is to do something to retain "the degree of adaptation" and "to facilitate understanding or to make the text more interesting" when some "elements of cultural contexts" are not known to the readers of the target text (Klingberg 11–12). However, unlike Klingberg, most scholars of children's literature believe in "cultural adaptation," which means that the translated texts should be adapted to "cultural conditions depending on the concept of the child and childhood" in the reader's context (Nikolajeva 405). Therefore, domestication and foreignization techniques have become hotly debated issues in the translation of children's literature. First introduced by Lawrence Venuti (1995), these two techniques refer to how the translator can make the text conform to the target culture. Domestication is the technique of making the text closely conform to the culture of the translated text, while foreignization is preserving the source language values in the translated text. This has also been described as a tension between "dialogical versus equivalence" approaches (Nikolajeva 407). In the dialogical approach, the emphasis is on the reception of the text by the child reader. Hence, the translator pays attention to the target audience and does something to make the translated text function similarly to the way the original text functions. Therefore, by adopting the domestication technique, the translator "substitutes familiar phenomena and concepts for what may be perceived as strange and hard to understand," such as changing the spring season into the rainy season (Nikolajeva 409). In contrast, the aim of the equivalence approach is to preserve the strange concepts of the source text in the translated text and to make the target text approximately conform to the source text culture.

Klingberg believes translation aims to provide "international understanding and knowledge of a foreign country" (Klingberg et al. 86–87). This aim implies that translators should take an equivalence approach (in other words, translating like-for-like as much as possible). Therefore, foreignization occurs when the translator "decide[s] to keep some words untranslated to preserve the foreign flavor" and by doing this, the translator might create other effects far from the aim of the source text. For instance, Maria Nikolajeva gives the example of a Swedish cookie keeping its foreign name in an English translation (410). As Tiina Puutinen explains, the translation of children's literature is different from culture to culture because "the needs of the target audience, the status of the source text, and the special characteristics of the culture-specific norms" are significant elements that the translator should consider (qtd. in Jeong and Han 2).

Translated literature sometimes becomes an innovative force and takes a central position in the target culture (Even-Zohar), and the translation of good literary works aims to improve children's literature (Bamberger). As Wooseob Jeong and Hyejung Han emphasize, award-winning books are typically considered the best quality books worldwide. Hence, they are selected and translated into many languages to improve the children's literature of the target culture.

We can see this process at work for children's literature in Iran from the beginning of the twentieth century; after the Constitutional Revolution between 1905 and 1911, child-centric policies were formed. From then on, the translation of children's literature began, which led to the formation of modern children's literature (Qāeni and Mohammadi). Moreover, during the Pahlavi Dynasty (the 1960s), three significant children's institutions were established: The Children's Book Council (CBC, the Iranian section of IBBY) in 1962, the Educational Publishing Center of the Ministry of Education, and the Institute for Intellectual Development of Children and YA (IIDCY, better known as Kanoon) in 1965. The translation movement and the establishment of these children's institutions resulted in the transformation and improvement of children's literature and the (re)construction of the concept of childhood in Iran (Zowkāi). Parts of this transformation, improvement and (re)construction have happened through the translation of canonical children's literature from other countries because most of the experts working in these three institutions attempted to introduce canonical literary works, mainly the Western canon of children's literature, to children through translation.

Therefore, the selection of award-winning books for translation has been the intention of many educators, librarian-translators, writer-translators, and translators for many years. These books are thought to improve "children's cultural knowledge, literacy, and academic ability" (qtd. in Jeong and Han 3). They could also be a model for children's book writers to develop the children's literature of the target culture. Hence, from the 1950s and 1960s, the translation of canonical children's literature and award-winning books in Iran increased, introducing new writing models to writers of children's literature and promoting reading among children and young adults (Mohammadi and Qāeni).

Taylor's works have received international acclaim and won many awards, which made them the focus of attention of a few translators who were children's literature experts in children's institutions such as the CBC and IIDCYA or publishing houses. To find Taylor's works translated into Persian, I conducted an advanced search in the online public access catalog (OPAC) of the National Library of Iran and used OPAC of the Reference Library of the Institute for Intellectual Development of Children and Young Adults, along with various online bookstores. Of Taylor's works, three award-winning books, *Thunder*, *Friendship*, and *Well*, have been translated into Persian and reprinted at different times by different translators and publishing houses.

Jeong and Han propose that most studies conducted in the field of children's literature translation have focused on the modifications that happened in the content of the books to see how they have been domesticated in different languages. However, little research has been done on the materiality and physical structure of children's books in translation, such as the title, cover image, illustration, and so on.

This chapter adopts Lotman's semiotic approach to analyze the material form as well as the content of these three novels translated into Persian to offer a critical analysis of Taylor's works in translation. Since translation criticism is usually assumed to be an evaluative practice with a focus on "error identification" and "highly subjective appraisal" (Maier 238), this chapter also provides a model for descriptive translation criticism through a cultural semiotic perspective. The object of the study of cultural semiotics is the cultural reception of a text in different semiotic systems, which is the same as what Nikolajeva (405) calls "cross-cultural reception" because the texts are interwoven with culture.

The text, in Lotman's point of view, has a broader meaning and contains different codes. It extends to the body of literature, art, or even culture. DeBlasio and Epstein quote from Lotman that the text refers to the work itself while the code is the "system of rules" by which the text is produced by the author and understood by the reader. It shows a plurality of meaning in a text since it can be read according to different codes based on different cultural contexts. Kourdis also explains that "every cultural act that is a carrier of meaning is text and every text is a semiotic system" (150), so Taylor's literary texts can be signified as cultural acts in a semiotic approach and are the carriers of meaning, which is the language of resisting racism. As Torop asserts, this cultural act is always "something to be transferred from one locus to another, and this metaphoric act is at once an act of translation and an act of culture" (qtd. in Kourdis 150).

In the first phase of the chapter, I reveal how Taylor's language of resisting racism is transferred through Lotman's five stages of reception.

In his later works, Lotman defines the philosophically-oriented notion of semiosphere as a "semiotic space that precedes (exists prior to) any specific linguistic and cultural system or any specific system of signs" (DeBlasio and Epstein). As he explains, "[T]he unit of semiosis, the smallest functioning mechanism, is not a separate language but the whole semiotic space of the culture in question" (Lotman "Universe" 125). He calls this semiotic space "semiosphere" and describes it as a way of talking about culture both as a semiotic phenomenon and also as a text that generates meaning in the process of translation. This semiotic space has a core and periphery, and there always exists tension between the two because some texts take the core position inside the semiosphere while others live in the periphery. Every semiosphere (culture) divides the world into "its own internal space" and "their external space" (131), and the boundary or border of the semiosphere is the "hottest spot for semioticizing process" because it is a "mechanism for translating texts of an alien semiotics into 'our' language, it is the place where what is 'external' is transformed into what is 'internal'"; it works as a filter to make the new texts become part of the internal space of the semiosphere, and it has the ambivalent feature of separating and uniting (136–37). Hence, Lotman introduces translation as a crucial mechanism of meaning generation within a target culture because, through translation, a culture can receive and assimilate an alien semiotic system, text, or language to generate new texts. It is the "basic semiotic procedure that accompanies all acts of consciousness: to think means to translate from one language into another" (DeBlasio and Epstein). Therefore, he asserts that while the "elementary act of thinking is translation," the "elementary act of translating is dialogue" (Lotman 143). In a dialogic situation, we use different languages to communicate, and the participants in a dialogue change from the position of transmission to the position of reception. He explains that when this change of positions and dialogic situations happens, all cultures follow five reception stages to describe themselves.

In the first stage, the receiving culture receives new floods of texts (new ideas and codes) from other cultures. By receiving these new texts, the receiving culture considers its own texts as belonging to the past or tradition. So, the new texts are idealized and have high positions within the receiving culture because they "break with the past or tradition" (Lotman 146). But in the second stage, the "imported" texts and the "home culture" negotiate or "restructure" each other; "the translation, imitations, and adaptations multiply"; and the receiving culture tries to "look for roots" (146–47) and reestablish its links with the past or tradition. The new texts are understood as "an organic continuation of the old" (147).

In this "saturation" stage (145), tension ensues between the center and periphery of the semiosphere (culture) until the new texts take the core position in the receiving culture. In the third stage, there is a tendency to find high value in the new texts in the receiving culture, and the new texts find a place in the receiving culture. The new ideas and codes are considered acceptable to the receiving culture. In the fourth reception stage, the new imported texts are entirely "resolved" within the receiving culture, generating new texts in response (for example, academic essays and lesson plans). In the fifth stage, the dialogic situation occurs. The receiving culture becomes a transmitter culture, the generator of texts, and sends floods of texts to other cultures. It is a process of "changeover" between the center and periphery of culture (Lotman 145). For instance, according to Lotman, this cyclic process happened in Italy. From the fifth century, Italy was the text receiver from other cultures, such as Greco-Byzantine traditions. When a high degree of saturation happens, Italian culture becomes a "volcano" pouring out floods of texts to different cultures, becoming the transmitting culture, so the Renaissance and Baroque periods are called the "Italian period of European culture" (Lotman 145). As he explains, the emergence of the Enlightenment in French culture is a product of the same five-stage process.

Following Lotman, this chapter considers the three Taylor books in English (*Thunder, Friendship, Well*) and their Persian translations (one of *Thunder*, two of *Friendship*, and one of *Well*) related to their semiospheres. This allows us to describe how the texts have been translated and involved in a dialogic situation, identify the reception process, and decipher the role of the translator within the target culture. For instance, the motif of racism in these three source texts can not only act as a code or a cultural act to influence the American Semiosphere and help American society to participate in dialogue within the same semiosphere, but it can also influence other semiospheric spaces or cultural contexts if they are translated. To use Lotman's terminology, Taylor's works and their Persian translations consist of a border and dialogic mechanism, or a core and periphery. Taylor's works are translated into Persian; they metaphorically cross the border from external to internal space to take a core position in the target text's semiosphere. Since "the elementary mechanism of translating is dialogue" (Lotman 143), the translated Persian texts help the shift from "transmission" to "reception" (143) as well as being the reason for the dialogic mechanism to occur between the two Semiospheres. There is tension between the core and periphery of the source texts' semiosphere and that of the target texts' semiosphere. This tension continues until the five stages of reception occur in both semiospheres. Lotman also asserts that sometimes because of some historical causes, this five-stage process does not reach its final stage, and the dialogue between the cultures should be continued through the years so that a culture can progress through all the stages to become a transmitter. Like Lotman, this

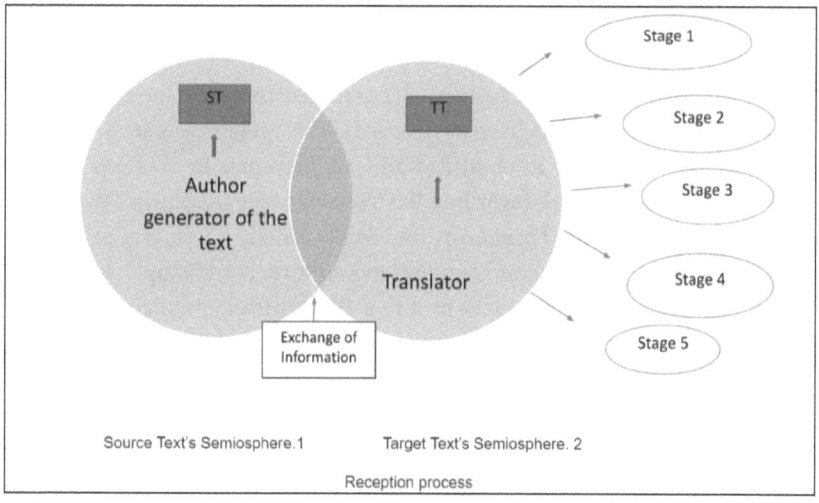

chapter acknowledges that all five stages do not always occur within every culture, and the texts entering a receiving culture, here the Persian semiosphere, cannot entirely complete the five stages of reception. In this case, the codes (such as racism) did not take the core position in this different cultural context or semiospheric space—Iran. Moreover, the producers of these texts (source texts and target texts), participating in the dialogic situation, are influenced by these two semiospheres. Hence, the agency of the transmitter, here the translators, is subject to the dominant semiotic sign system of the target text's semiosphere. The translators, as the receivers of the source texts, work in the periphery of the target text's semiosphere. They face five stages of reception that determine their role as staying in the periphery or moving to the core of the target text's semiosphere. This diagram demonstrates this dialogic situation and the reception process:

RECEPTION PROCESS

This chapter will answer these three questions:

1. How is the semiosphere reflected in *Thunder*, *Friendship*, and *Well* and their Persian translations?
2. If Lotman's five stages of reception do not always happen in every culture, in which stages of the reception process do the original and translated texts remain?
3. What is the role of the author and the translators in the dialogic situation of both semiospheres?

SEMIOSPHERE OF THE SOURCE TEXTS

Taylor's representation of the history of racism may be one of the most important reasons Taylor's books have won awards. This acclaim has secured a permanent place for Taylor in children's and YA literature in Western culture. Considering Taylor's work regarding the five-stage reception process, the language used in *Thunder*, *Friendship*, and *Well* initially signifies a peripheral position within the dominant language and culture. For example, in the first pages of *Thunder*, the characters find that Black history is silenced in their school books, signifying the peripheral position of Taylor's language within the American Semiosphere. Using literature, a symbolic system, to fight racism is a sign of the discrete language that Taylor uses to participate in a dialogue with the dominant language. In the second stage of reception, Taylor's texts negotiate with the dominant language of the American semiotic space, which leads to the third stage of the reception process. Through Taylor's texts, the American Semiosphere receives codes that signify the history of racism and resisting racism. These new codes are resolved in the American Semiosphere in the fourth stage. In the final stage, Taylor's literary texts move to the center of the American Semiosphere: they become mainstream, part of the transmitter culture, and generate new texts within the American semiotic space. Therefore, the source texts move from periphery to center, and the five reception stages have occurred within the source texts' semiosphere.

I will now explore how this process occurs in Taylor's case. Her early works were written ten years after the civil rights movement in the 1950s and 1960s, a time of discontent with racial discrimination and injustice. Inspired by her father's stories of the struggle of Black people to become landowners after the abolition of slavery, she started writing about racism. She decided to write about the unfair treatment of Black people, creating the Logan characters, "an African American family united in love and self-respect, with strong-sensitive parents trying to guide their children through a discriminatory society" (Peacock 119). Kenneth L. Donelson and Allen Pace Nilsen, in their 1985 *Children's Literature Review* article, quote Taylor's assertion that "it is my hope that to the children who read my books, the Logans will provide those heroes missing from the school books of my childhood—Black men, women, and children of whom they can be proud" (223). The dominant language of racism and injustice within the United States was increasingly challenged over the course of the civil rights movement; when Taylor published *Song of the Trees* in 1975 and *Thunder* in 1976, this social change allowed Taylor's texts to shift to the center of the American Semiosphere, where they acted as generators of secondary texts such as school companion guides and lesson plans (Collins 2000), scholarly book chapters (for example, Montgomery and

Watson 2009; Martin 2011; Brooks 2016) and articles (for example, Hardstaff 2015; Moussa 2018; Jacques 2020) on the Logan characters.

This quotation from Taylor depicts the reception process within the Semiosphere in which the author lives: "I get many letters from schools, including from those where the majority of students are white, and the children tell me they read *Roll of Thunder* along with other books about U.S. history" (qtd. in Peacock 123). When her books have won awards from different cultural associations, critics have noted that her works reflect an authentic vision of the Black experience, highlighting the positive reception of her literary works in the Western Semiosphere.

In a broader sense, the source texts wage war against injustice and racism and show survival within a racist American society. Although the source culture is still racist, Taylor's literary texts have been resolved within the Western Semiosphere and moved to the center. This is because they have met widespread acclaim through many critical essays, reviews, awards, and a large readership and have generated new coding systems within the Western Semiosphere that have inspired the next generation of writers, especially African American writers (Schafer 1998). Thus, Taylor's works have reached Lotman's fifth stage of the reception process. They are the generator of new texts in Western Semiosphere and have been centered as works of literature even though their calls for social action have not been fully realized.

But when these literary texts enter a new culture, in this case, Iran, they act differently, and the reception process is different. To see how Taylor's works have been reflected in the target texts' semiosphere, I analyze the Persian translations of *Thunder*, *Friendship*, and *Well*. To identify the semiospheric space of the books translated into Persian, this chapter focuses on the historical and sociocultural context in which the translations appeared.

Soryā Qezelayāq translated *Thunder* for Amirkabir publishing house in 1986. *Friendship* has been translated twice: first by Ali Ḵakbāzān for Hamšahri Press in 1997, then by Fahimeh Mehdizādeh for Naš-e no Publishing House in 2014. Qezelayāq's translation of *Thunder* was reprinted in 1998, and the translation of *Well* by Dāvud Š'abāni came out in 1999 and was reprinted in 2018 by Madreseh Publishing House.

SEMIOSPHERE OF THE TARGET TEXTS

The twentieth century marked a period of great upheaval in Iranian history due to the Constitutional Revolution (between 1905 and 1911), the Islamic Revolution (1979), and the Iran–Iraq War (1990). The Persian translation of *Thunder* emerged at the height of the Iran–Iraq War in 1986. During this year, Iran faced social, cultural, and economic stagnation due to the war. From 1984 to 1985, Iraqi soldiers invaded some parts of the country, and some Iranians had a zeal for fighting the enemy. But most of the attempts remained abortive, and Iran failed to recapture these areas. In 1986, the invaded areas were recaptured. Most of the Iraqi bloodshed and bombardment happened between 1985 and 1986; during this period, many civilians aged seventeen to twenty joined the army to defend the land.

Yusefi mentions most of the literature produced for children and young adults before the bombardment in Iran was didactically loaded ("Audience Analysis"; "Institutes of Children's Literature") and, as Zowkāi emphasizes, this didactic literature had been imbued with ideological, moral, and religious beliefs since the Islamic Revolution in 1979. The language of martyrdom and self-sacrifice included in children's literature continued during the Iran–Iraq War in 1980 and 1988 (Zowkāi; Yusefi; "Audience Analysis"; "Are Children the Appropriate Audience?"; "Institutes of Children's Literature"). In addition, even though various themes were added to children's literature during this period, people in Iran, particularly children and young adults, had little access to valuable books. It is believed due to "the monopolistic behavior [that] existed in the society" (Ḥejvāni 22–23; my trans.), cultural exchange decreased to a minimum; therefore, few options existed for translators in Iran's book market.

The Persian translation of *Thunder* appeared in 1986, loaded with the dominant language of martyrdom and self-sacrifice for the preservation of the frontiers. As the translator, Soryā Qezelayāq remembers, everyone around her reading or listening to the Persian translation of the novel felt it bolstered their courage to go on defending the land and forging ahead while they were facing the bombardment of their houses. She emphasizes that her translation of *Thunder* aimed to promote strong will and had an effective role in strengthening the fight for land and defense against the invasion (Qezelayāq, personal interview).

The language of resistance and survival in the semiospheric space of Iran is reflected in different episodes of the novel; one representative example from the translated target text can be read as exploring the situation of youth in a war-stricken society. The back-translation, translating the content of the target language sentence back to the source language in literal terms, can be a helpful way for readers to become familiar with the content of the representative example reflected in the Persian cultural context.

Example 1:

Roll of thunder ،غرش رعد
Hear my cry !فریاد مرا بشنو
Over the water از فراز آب

By and by ذره، ذره
Ole man comin'. او می آید.
Down the line از کناره،
Whip in hand to beat me down تازیانه در دست، تا مرا بکوبد.
But I ain't اما خیال ندارم
Gonna let him turn me 'round بگذارم تحقیرم کند.

Back translation: [Roll of thunder, hear my cry over the water, little by little; he is coming from the coast, whip in his hand to knock me down, but I don't want to let him **humiliate** me].

The theme of Taylor's poem and the substitution of the phrase "gonna let him turn me 'round" with the verb *tahqir kardan* ("to humiliate") signifies the negotiation between the new text and the dominant language of resistance, and survival in the Iranian Semiosphere in 1986.

However, the source text's dominant language of racial injustice and resistance to racism did not have obvious cultural parallels in the Persian semiotic space when *Thunder* emerged. The novel's main language is thus less effective and shunted away in the target semiosphere. Instead, the target text highlights other themes of the American and Iranian Semiospheres, such as the language of "survival" and of being "enraged by humiliation," as Mary Turner Harper puts it (qtd. in Peacock 124, 133); it also depicts themes such as bravery, and fighting to overcome invasion. According to Qezelayāq (personal interview), this led to the adaptation of the novel into a serial story broadcast from the national radio of Iran at the time of bombardment by Iraqi soldiers.

The translated novel of *Thunder* was the most notable book of the year in the CBC's annual booklist and received the CBC award in 1986. A few secondary texts were also generated, such as the publication of the two-volume book *Descriptive Anthology of the YA Characters* in 2002 by Aftābgardān Press, in which Cassie Logan is introduced as one of the most influential characters in YA literature. However, in a review article written on this two-volume book, Yusefi referred to Cassie as a less well-known character than Heidi, Sarah, or The Little Match Girl among Iranian children and young adults ("Dictionary"). In 2017, an academic article was written on the translation of *Thunder,* identifying "benevolence" as the element of spiritual intelligence in the novel and emphasizing that this spiritual element is reflected in the novel's themes and characters' thoughts (Rādmaneš). The article elides the language of racial injustice highlighted in the novel, and instead compares the benevolence of the Black characters to the philosophical thinking of Persian culture; in other words, the article focuses on the novel's cultural parallels in the target texts' semiosphere, not the cultural differences.

Even though Iran experienced the early "barda and barda-dāri" (slave and slavery) from the Achaemenid period (*Iranica*) and the slave trade was active in the nineteenth century, the language of resisting racism (Bāghoolizādeh, "The Color Black") or any kind of discrimination (Tālebi and Alizādeh, "Understanding") has rarely been discussed in the target culture and hardly ever reflected in local literature. Thus, I believe, since the target culture did not tend to focus on racism as reflected in the Persian translations of Taylor's work, the third, fourth, and fifth stages of reception did not happen in the target culture. The translated text did not move to the center; it stayed in the second reception stage in the Iranian Semiosphere. Hence, the translator and the translated text remained on the periphery instead of coming to the core.

The same reception process happened with the two translated versions of *Friendship* and one translation of *Well*, even though they appeared later. In the 1990s–2000s, these Persian-translated novels' historical and cultural contexts were changed entirely. Children's literature in Iran started to shift from didactic to nondidactic literature (Ḳowsronejād; Yusefi, "Audience Analysis"; Zowkāi). It became more developed in terms of theory and criticism and different approaches to writing for children such as "audience analysis" emerged (Ḳowsronežād; Yusefi, "Audience Analysis" 109). Therefore, the cultural contexts of children's literature in Iran flourished in the postwar periods. Still, the emergence of these two translated versions of *Friendship* and one translation of *Well* in these periods have not reached the fifth stage of reception and did not generate new texts in Persian culture.

Friendship was first translated by Ali Ḳākbāzān in 1997 for Hamšahri Press as an Aftābgardān newspaper supplement. It was retranslated seventeen years later in 2014 by Fahimeh Mehdizādeh for Našr-e No publishing house. *Well* was translated into Persian by Dāvud Š'abāni in 1999 and reprinted in 2018 by Madreseh publishing house. All these Persian translations occurred in a sociocultural context in which child-centered policies and children and young adults' issues were being promoted due to, as John Stephens asserts, some sort of "social liberalism" created after the presidential election of Mohammad Ḳātami in 1997 and the students' uprising movement in July 1999. In the 1990s, the influence of ideological and religious discourse decreased in children's literature; this was not only due to the "separation of social class" and "children's access to different media resources" [my translation], as Zowkāi (29) declares, but also due to the emergence of different translations of avant-garde Western children's literature. In this decade, new floods of books (even some controversial books by Roald Dahl) received permission from the Ministry of Culture and Islamic Guidance to be published in Iran. However, even though Taylor's universal messages of hope, altruism, equality, and the precious lessons she has given have always been in tune with the Iranian Semiosphere, no scholarly work has yet been produced about the two translated versions of *Friendship* and one translation of *Well* in Iran.

SPACES OF TRANSLATABILITY AND UNTRANSLATABILITY

As I mentioned earlier, Taylor's literary texts signified a cultural act, and this cultural act has been transferred to Persian culture through the interlingual translation of her texts. The peritextual and textual analysis of translational transformations can show how the translators attempted to domesticate the translated texts and reproduce the author's intent and the relevant information in the translated texts. This helps to "unravel the ways of sign transmission in translations" (Shapoval et al. 384) from a semiotic perspective.

In translation studies, translation criticism contrasts the target texts against the source texts to analyze and evaluate the differences. This section, using a semiotic approach, attempts to examine the sentences descriptively. Moreover, it will describe the physical structure of the texts semiotically. Since the translators have started a dialogue with the dominant language of the source texts' semiosphere, it is interesting to see the relationship between the Persian target texts and Taylor's source texts in terms of "variable degrees of translatability and spaces of untranslatability" (Lorusso 92). This section explores the degrees of translatability and untranslatability in the materiality and the content of these four Persian translations of Taylor's work through representative examples.

The Peritextual Analysis.

The peritextual analysis of the translated books indicates that some changes were made to the title and cover image of the Persian translations of *Thunder* and the first translated version of *Friendship*, but not that of *Well*. The second translated version of *Friendship* also underwent some changes to the cover image but not the title.

According to Donelson and Nilsen (226), the juxtaposition of the phrases "Roll of Thunder" and "Hear My Cry" has metaphorical significance and shows the resistance of humans' voice to thunder or nature. As the cover image of the Persian-translated version of *Thunder* shows, only the second part of the title has been translated into the translated text. The juxtaposition of the roll of thunder and the voice is not as effective in the target text's semiosphere, whereas "Hear My Cry" held broad metaphorical significance for Iran at that time, a war-stricken society in which a binary exists between the people of two countries. This emphasis on the conflict between people is reflected in the information provided on the hardship of the Black people and their resistance in the foreword, biographical information about Taylor, and a brief review of the book.

Even though the title of *Friendship* has an optimal equivalence in the Persian language, the title of the first translated version was changed to *Šelik be Tom Bee* [*Shooting Tom Bee*]. It was published in a paper-journal format with the series title "Monday Book," which appeared more prominently than the title *Shooting Tom Bee*. The change of title reveals the plot of the story, highlighting the shooting instead of the ironic meaning of the word "friendship." Instead of any information about the author and illustrator or an excerpt from the novel, the back cover features advertising for the Aftābgardān year book.

The title of the second translated version was *Refāqat* [*Friendship*], similar to the original. The Coretta Scott King award sticker on the book cover, some information about the author and the illustrator in the foreword, and a short passage about not calling a white person by his/her first name on the back cover have also been added.

The title of *Well* has been translated as *Čāh* [*The Well*], and no change has been made to the cover image. It shows a young David and Hammer standing by the well while the Simms brothers on the cart talk aggressively to them. However, instead of the original back cover's summary, the back cover features some quoted passages of the novel and a picture of Hammer.

In the case of *Thunder*, the semiotic aspects of the many different book covers of English-language editions in the US, UK, and beyond are indicative of the agency of the child characters and their concerns (see Onuora and Carnesi, this volume); they show Cassie alone or accompanying her brothers or her family. But the Persian book cover shows a girl and a man with his supporting hand on her shoulder, which could be interpreted as an adult giving hope to a child. The in-text picture of the original text shows Cassie with her family, but Cassie and her father are spotlighted in the translated text on the book cover. This father-daughter image highlights the father's agency which is similar to what Taylor specifies in the author's note by dedicating her novel to her father and talking about the similarity of David's character to her father. This shift from child-centered imagery to patriarchal imagery is relevant to the Iranian context of "parental power" (Wiesner-Hanks) because, men, particularly fathers, have been providers in Iranian culture and were considered the pillars of the family who support their children.

There is no sign of the African American family in the picture of the man and the girl. Their Black identity cannot be identified in the image, which might be interpreted in the Iranian context as a blue-collar worker reassuring a girl. The passage of text on the back cover narrating the historical life of African American people in the US informs readers of their identity:

This is the story of a family which has attempted to keep its **pride, independence, and integrity. They fight for their survival while they stick to ethical values**. It narrates the history of the US Black people when they lived with fear, torture, or being burned and lynched. This is the story of a girl named Cassie who has been humiliated merely for being Black. **This is the story of free will, love, and pride of the family resisting for their lives.** (My translation and emphasis)

Both translated versions of *Friendship* have also used in-text images for the book cover images, but the images are not as effective as the original text. The cover image of the original text signifies the Logans' concern about something. But the cover image of the first translated version shows the children wandering happily (on page 4 of the original text), contrasting with the title *Shooting Tom Bee*. The second translated version's cover image reflects the Logans' friendship with Jeremy (on page 23 of the original text). Some of the in-text images have also been omitted in both translations. For instance, the last influential image of Tom Bee being shot (on page 52) has been omitted in the second translation. Some in-text images have been carelessly moved between the text's passages in the first translated version. Even though Max Ginsburg's original illustrations are black and white, the producers of the first translated version have attempted to color some parts of the images.

Textual Analysis

Careful analysis of the translated texts indicates that some translational mistakes in text comprehension have occurred in all of these books. However, since this chapter's focus is descriptive, not evaluative, analysis, I will analyze the translation strategies used for different translation problems in this section. According to Peeter Torop, "[T]ranslational transformation" refers to the "linguistic or semiotic presentation" of translation strategies used for the description of the translation method (26). This translational transformation can be linguistic or cultural. For linguistic transformation, the translators might adopt "replacement, substitution, addition or deletion" whereas, for cultural transformation, they use "transcription or translation (neologism, substitution, indirect translation, contextual translation)" (26).

The textual analysis of the original texts and the target texts indicate they have domesticated the texts using the most frequently used substitution strategy, replacing the linguistic codes of the original text, items such as culture-specific terms, associations, and grammatical structures, with the most optimal Persian equivalences. In some cases, they have kept some words untranslated by transcription, so they have changed the linguistic code into a cultural code. The domestication technique is more prominent in *Thunder* [*Faryād Marā Bešno*], the first translated version of *Friendship* [*Šelik be Tom Bee*], and *Well* [*Čāh*]. In contrast, the second translated version of *Friendship* [*Refāqat*] includes some examples of the foreignization technique. The following representative examples will show the linguistic and cultural transformations in the four translated texts.

Torop explains that the translator might adopt a substitution strategy for linguistic transformation (26) or what Shapoval et al. call synonymous substitution of lexico-semantic transformation. Example 1 shows how the four translators have managed to create linguistic transformation, but for Example 2, the translator has offered a cultural transformation by the use of transcription or transcording translation strategies for the word "lynch":

Example 1:

—She flailed into R.W, crying "you **niggers** done killed Jim Lee! You done killed him!" (Taylor, *Thunder* 247).

خودش را به ار. دبلیو. اویزان می کند و با گریه می گوید: «شماها کاکاسیاها، جیم لی رو کشتین، شماها کشتینش» ص. 383.

Back translation: [Mrs. Barnett is coming close to R.W and crying, "you **Kākā-Siyāhs**, killed Jim Lee!, You killed him!" (My translation).

—Mr. Simms jumped up from the table. "John Wallace! You jus' gonna let this here old **nigger** talk t'ya this-a way? You gon' let him do that?" (Taylor, *Friendship* 47).

آقای سیمونز از جایش پرید: «جان والاس ! چطور اجازه می دهی این کاکاسیاه پیر با تو این طوری حرف بزند؟» ص. 28.

Back translation 1 (Kākbāzān): [John Wallace! How do you let this old **Kākā-Siyāh** talk like that way with you?]

«جان والس! تو می ذاری این کاکا سیای پیر، این جا، با تو این طوری حرف بزنه؟ تو به اون همچین اجازه ای می دی؟» ص. 49.

Back translation 2 (Mehdizādeh): [John Wallace! How do you let this old **Kākā-Siyāh** talk like that? Do you let him?].

—Don't ya go shamin' us like this front of **niggers**!" (Taylor, *Well* 90).

چارلی از روی زمین فریاد زد: «ما را این طوری جلوی این کاکاسیاه ها خوار و ذلیل نکن!» ص. 86.

Back Translation: [Don't be so scornful to us in front of these **Kaka-Siyahs**.]

All four translators have adopted a substitution strategy regarding the culture-specific item "nigger." Substituting the word with *Kākā-Siyāh* [Black brother] has created the same effect in target text readers. By the use of *Kākā-Siyāh*, the humiliating effect of the word has been reflected in the translations because, as Southgate explains, this word is used for "black slaves" with negative connotations in the Persian language (4). Even though Behrouzi believes *Kākā-Siyāh*, derived from the Shirazi dialect, refers to a brother who is closer in meaning to something like "uncle" as well as an enslaved Black person who has grown old in a house and is considered a "friend" (444), Southgate, Košneviss Ansāri, and Mirzāi refer to the negative depiction of enslaved Black people, mainly Africans, in Persian medieval literature and history ("African Presence in Iran"; "A History of Slavery"). Since the Indian Ocean Slave Trade began in the sixth century BCE, various ethnic groups captured by slave traders were sold over the centuries to the southern parts of Iran for commercial, political, and military purposes. But as Mirzāi ("African Presence in Iran") and Anthony Lee explain, in the nineteenth century, the highest number of enslaved Black people from Africa were enslaved for domestic slavery. Therefore, according to Southgate, many Persian words are used for "slaves of any race and sex," but *siyah* (black) is used for "black slaves of any sex, and, *kākā, kākā Sīāh*, and Zangi are used for male" enslaved persons (4). According to *Iranica, kākā Sīāh* is a Persian word commonly used to refer to an enslaved Black male person, not just African servants, from 1300–1800 in different dynasties such as the Il-Khanid, Timurid, Safavid, and Zand dynasties.

Example 2

—"These folks getting' so bad in here. Heard tell they **lynched** a boy a few days ago at Crosston." (Taylor, *Thunder* 40–41).

«باعث خجالته! اینا دیگه خیلی پررو شدن. شنیدم می گفتن که چند روز پیش توی کراستون یک پسری رو لینچ کردن.» ص. 68.

Back translation: ["Shame on them! They're gettin rude; I heard they lynched a boy in Crosston."]

The culture-specific word "lynch," primarily used in Black literature, could manifest untranslatability and cultural transformation. The *Oxford English Dictionary* defines lynching as "killing someone for an alleged offense without a legal trial, especially by hanging." The translator of *Thunder* has adopted the transcription/transcoding strategy (lynch) and the Persian infinitive form of the verb (make) to create the same effect for target text readers. In a footnote, she explains this word as "killing by torturing." The extrajudicial aspect of lynching has been lost in translation.

Representative examples extracted from the two translated versions of *Friendship* and the translation of *Well* indicate the change in the linguistic codes and the difficulties in translating the idiomatic language of Mildred Taylor's characters.

Example 3:

"Don't know nobody else to do, nobody colored I mean. Fact to business, don't know nobody colored call a white man straight to his face by his first name. (Taylor, *Friendship* 37).

Translation. 1 (Kākbāzān)

»هیچ کس جرئت ندارد سفیدپوستی را با نام کوچکش صدا بزند. منظورم از هیچ کس، سیاهپوست ها هستند.« ص. 23.

Back translation: [Nobody dares to call a white man by his first name. "Nobody" means the Black].

Translation. 2 (Mehdizādeh)

»هیچ کس دیگه ای چنین کاری نمی کنه؛ منظورم دورگه هان. در واقع، هیچ دورگه ای نمی تونه صاف تو روی یه سفیدپوست وایسته و اونو با اسم کوچیک صدا کنه.« ص. 39.

Back translation: [No one would do it anymore, I mean the mixed people. No mixed man could call a white man straight to his face by his first name].

The translational choices of the first translator of *Friendship* show more about racism and the derogatory situation; for example, in the translation of the word "colored," the first translator has used the Persian equivalence of *siāhpoost* [Black]. In contrast, the second has adopted *dorageh* [mixed race], which reflects different usages of the word in US and African history.

Example 4:

—"Boy, you disputin' my word? Just look at ya! Skin's black as dirt. Could put seeds on ya and have 'em growin' in no time!" (Taylor, *Friendship* 14).

Translation. 1 (Kākbāzān)

»بچه! مثل اینکه خیال داری با من یکی به دو کنی! به خودت نگاه کن! تو سیاهی! سیاه هم یعنی کثیف. دستهای تو آنقدر کثیفند که می شود رویشان سبزی کاشت!« ص. 6.

Back translation: [Boy, you talk back to me? Just look at you! You are black! Black means dirty. Your hands are so dirty that one could grow seeds on them!].

Translation. 2 (Mehdizādeh)

»پسر، تو حرف منو قبول نداری؟ درست به خودت نگاه کن! پوستت عین خاک سیاهه. اگه روش بذر بپاشی فوری سبز می شه!« ص. 15.

Back translation: [Boy, you do not believe in my words? Just look at you! Your skin is black as dirt. If you put seeds on them, they would be growing very quickly].

In this example, again, the first translator has changed the meaning of the sentence by the addition of the phrase "You are Black!" and the replacement of "skin's black as dirt" with the words "Black means dirty" to show the disrespectful behavior of the Wallaces.

Example 5:

—Mama waited, as still as a windless day. (Taylor, *Well* 41).

مامان مثل یک ظهر بدون نسیم تابستان، بی صدا منتظر ماند. ص. 38.

Back Translation: [Mama waited as the windless midday summer].

In this example, the linguistic transformation has occurred with the addition of "midday summer," while Caroline's expression has the same effect on the target text readers.

Examples 6 and 7 indicate linguistic transformation through deletion; they also go back to the point I make about the theme of racism being pushed to the side in the target culture's reception of the texts.

Example 6:

I, however, was not so restrained and as far as I was concerned, if T.J. **kept up with this coat business,** he could just **hit the dirt at the same time** as "Miss" Lillian Jean. (Taylor, *Thunder* 145).

اما من مثل او تحت تأثیر قرار نگرفته بودم. و تا آن جا که به من مربوط می‌شد اگه تی جی قضیه پالتو را بیشتر از این کش می داد خیال داشتم همان وقتی که خدمت لیلین جین می رسم پوزه ی او را هم به خاک بمالم. ص. 228.

Back translation: [But I was not much influenced and if **T.J. kept up the coat issue, I would** put the dirt on him as well **as Lillian Jean.**)

Qezelayāq (*Thunder*) could have kept the feeling of Cassie about "Miss" Lillian Jean, but she has merely transcribed the name of Lilian Jean by omitting the personal title. This example lessens the reader's awareness of a specific type of racism Cassie faces regarding expected terms of address when talking to white people.

Example 7:

"right now, I figure to stay here and give Ed-Rose and Charlie a hand with *our* water." (Taylor, *Well* 13)

«همین الان. می خواهم به اد-رُز و چارلی در بردن آب از چاه کمک کنم.» ص. 10.

Back Translation: ["right now, I want to give Ed-Rose and Charlie a hand with carrying water from the well."].

In *Well*, when Hammer is talking to his mother, the emphasis on the ownership of the well is shown in the italic form and by the pronoun "our," but the tension between the Black and white folks is lessened by the omission of "our" in the translation.

Example 8 shows the linguistic transformation by the replacement strategy, which has led to a change in the whole context.

Example 8:

— "It's one thing t' teach a nigger where he stand, but ya don't go destroyin' God's good earth t' do it!" (Taylor, *Well* 90).

»تو باید از یک کاکاسیاه که چاه خودش را در اختیار همه گذاشته، درس بگیری؛ ولی به جای این کار، تو این چاه آبِ گوارا را آلوده کردی.« ص. 85.

Back Translation: [You should learn from a Kaka-Siyah who has shared his well to all, but you spoiled the well].

In this example, instead of showing racial discrimination, the replacement sentence highlights the altruism of the Black family.

The peritextual and textual analysis helps us to explore how the translated texts have been domesticated: all four of these translators have attempted to reflect the author's intent and her cultural context even though in some cases a loss in translation has occurred. However, in some few cases mentioned, the depiction of the source's sociocultural values and African American identity have not been fully recognizable by some of the translational transformations. This contrastive analysis also shows how translation can be an act of meaning generation and exemplifies the "creative function of language and the text" (Lotman, "Universe of the Mind" 15). As Lotman explains, "[T]he combination of translatability-untranslatability determines the creative function" of a text (15). The publishers' choices of the material features of the books and the translators' translation strategies mirror what Lotman asserts as the three creative, meaning-generation, and memory functions of the text. These Persian translated texts have become the "generator of new meaning" as well as the "condenser of cultural memory" (18): "the act of translation that creates them [is] a creative act" (14).

CONCLUSION

This chapter demonstrates the reception of Taylor's books translated into the Iranian Semiosphere. The extratextual analysis shows that the source texts' semiosphere (the US/the West) has received Mildred Taylor's language of resistance to racism. In the tension between the center and the periphery, Taylor's language comes from the periphery to the center of the American Semiosphere (due to the awards and critical perspectives the texts have received, and the attention they get among readers). But the target texts' semiosphere (Iran) represents a crossroads of different types of languages. From 1980 to 1988 in Iran, the language of the center was martyrdom, self-sacrifice, and fighting against the invasion of the motherland. Therefore, the readers of *Thunder* and its Persian translation alike discover the theme of war against invasion. Black characters fight for personal land and survival in a racist society in the source text. In the target text, they fight for the maintenance of the motherland and survival in a war-stricken society.

Between 1991 and 2014, the dominant language of the target texts is in tune with all the minor themes of Taylor's works, such as "universal" human values (Schwartz). But in the translation process, the language of resistance to racism moves to the periphery. Since the translations and adaptation of the language of resistance to racism are not multiplied in the Persian Semiosphere, the saturation stage does not happen, and the translators and their translated texts also remain in the periphery. Their translated texts cannot be the generator of new texts about racism or Taylor's works in the Persian Semiosphere. Thus, the translated texts remain in the second stage of the reception process. Thus, if the translation of Taylor's books were repeated in the Iranian Semiosphere, the dialogue between the two semiospheres might continue to the point of allowing the five stages of reception to happen. Taylor's books translated into different languages can not only convey the voice of African Americans and their history on racism but also help other cultures with diverse ethnicities such as Iran to pay attention to cultural diversity and ethnic discrimination (Salehi and Sepehri, "Ethnic Challenges"). Taylor's books can encourage future generations to reach equal rights and resist discrimination.

The peritextual and textual analysis of Taylor's books and their Persian translated texts shows that by adopting a cultural translation strategy, the translators, mostly using the domestication technique, help the dialogue mechanism of both source texts and target texts. However, the impact of the translators is not so significant as to change the center of the target texts' semiosphere and generate other texts, notwithstanding some critical responses to the translation of *Thunder*. The translated texts have been overshadowed by the target texts' semiotic space (influenced by the Iran-Iraq War and social movements) and the dominant language (martyrdom, self-sacrifice, and universal human values) so that, so far, they have received no critical analysis in the target culture—until now. This chapter itself acts as an example of critical analysis of the target culture that will travel back from East to West, from Iran to American readers, and the original source culture of Taylor's novels.

APPENDIX

Fig. 7.2. Front cover from *Faryad Mara Beshno* (*Roll of Thunder, Hear My Cry*) by Mildred D. Taylor, translated by Soraya Ghezelayagh. Amir Kabir Publishing Corporation, published in 1365/1986 and reprinted in 1377/1998.

WORKS CITED

Bāghoolizādeh, Beetā. *The Color Black: Enslavement and Erasure in Iran*. Duke UP, 2024.

Bamberger, Richard. "The Influence of Translation on the Development of National Children's Literature." *Children's Books in Translation, the Situation and the Problems*, edited by Gote Klingberg, Mary Ørvig, The International Research Society for Children's Literature, 1978, pp. 19–27.

"Barda and Barda-Dāri, from the Mongols to the Abolition of Slavery," *Iranica*, https://iranicaonline.org/articles/barda-iv.

Behrouzi, Ali Naqi. *Širāzi and Kāzeruni Words and Proverbs*. Fars Art and Guidance publishing house, 1969.

Brooks, Wanda M. "Having Something of Their Own." *Critical Content Analysis of Children's and Young Adult Literature: Reframing Perspective*, edited by Holly Johnson et al., Routledge, 2016, pp. 77–91.

"Talif Dāstān—Qeirdāstān Tarjomeh." *Children's Book Council of Iran (CBC)*, https://cbc.ir/wp-content/uploads/2018/11/1365.pdf.

Collins, Mary B. *Roll of Thunder, Hear My Cry Lit Plan, A Novel Unit Teacher Guide With Daily Lesson Plans*. Teachers Pet Pubns Inc, 2000. https://www.teacherspayteachers.com/Product/LitPlan-Teacher-Guide-Roll-of-Thunder-Hear-My-Cry-Lesson-Plans-Questions-1774156.

"Colored." *Etymonline Dictionary*, https://www.etymonline.com/word/colored.

"Colored." *Oxford Lexico Dictionary*, https://www.lexico.com/definition/coloured.

DeBlasio, Alyssa, and Mikhail Epstein. "Yuri Lotman (1922–1993)." *Filosofia: An Encyclopedia of Russian Thought*, https://filosofia.dickinson.edu/encyclopedia/lotman-yuri/.

Donelson, Kenneth L., and Allen Pace Nilsen. "Literary Aspects of Young Adult Books." *Children's Literature Review*, vol. 12, edited by Gerard J. Senick and Melissa Reiff Hug, 1985, pp. 223–29.

Even-Zohar, Itamar. "The Making of Culture Repertoire and the Role of Transfer." *Target*, vol. 9, no. 2, 1997, pp. 355–63, https://doi:10.1075/target.9.2.09eve.

Hardstaff, Sarah (Layzell). "Papa Said That One Day I Would Understand: Examining Child Agency and Character Development in RTHMC Using Critical Corpus Linguistics," *Children's Literature in Education*, vol. 46, no.3, 2015, pp. 226–41, https://doi.org/10.1007/s10583-014-9231-1.

Ḥejvāni, Mehdi. "Seyri dar adabiyāt kudak va nojavān Iran pas az enqlāb, bakš 1" [A Look into Children's Literature of Iran after Islamic Revolution, part one], *Pažuheš Nāmeh The Research Quarterly of Children and Youth's Literature*, vol. 6, no. 20, 2000, pp. 19–38.

Jacques, Wesley S. "Reading Relational in Mildred D. Taylor: Toward a Black Feminist Care Ethics for Children's Literature," *Research on Diversity in Youth Literature*, vol. 2, no. 2, 2020, pp. 1–23, https://sophia.stkate.edu/rdyl/vol2/iss2/6.

Jeong, Wooseob, and Hyejung Han. "Transformation of Newbery Award Books in Chinese, Japanese and Korean Translation." *Proceedings of the American Society for Information Science and Technology*, vol. 51, no. 1, 2015, pp. 1–4, https://doi.org/10.1002/meet.2014.14505101135.

Kākbāzān, Ali, translator. *Šelik be Tom Bee* [Shooting Tom Bee]. By Mildred D. Taylor, Aftābgardān newspaper-Hamshahri Press, 1375 [1997].

Kowsronejād, Morteza. *Masumiyat va tajrobeh: Darāmadi bar falsafeyeh adabiyāt-e kudak* [Innocence and Experience: An Introduction to the Philosophy of Children's Literature]. Našr-e Markaz Publishing, 2003.

Khošneviss Ansāri, Royā. "Representing Positive Image of African Slaves in Persian Literature", *2nd International Conference on Humanities, Historical and Social Sciences IPEDR*, vol. 17, 2011, pp. 327–29. https://www.ipedr.com/vol17/63-CHHSS%202011-H10113.pdf.

Klingberg, Gote. *Children's Fiction in the Hands of Translators*. Bloms Boktrycheri AB, 1986.

Klingberg, Gote, et al. *Children's Books in Translation: The Situation and the Problems*. Almqvist and Wiksell International for the Swedish Institute for Children's Books, 1978.

Kourdis, Evangelos. "The Semiotic School of Tartu-Moscow. The Cultural Circuit of Translation." *Going East: Discovering New and Alternative Traditions in Translation Studies*, edited by Larisa Schippel and Cornelia Zwischenberger, Frank and Timme GmbH, 2017, pp. 149–68.

Lathey, Gillian. *Translating Children's Literature*. Routledge: 2016.

Lee, Anthony A. "Enslaved African Women in Nineteenth-Century Iran: The Life of Fezzeh Khanom of Shiraz." *Iranian Studies*, vol. 45, no. 3, 2012, pp. 417–37. *JSTOR*, https://www.jstor.org/stable/41445217.

Lewanska, Izabela Maria. "Problems in Connection with the Adaptation of the Classics in Poland." *Children's Literature in Translation: The Situation and the Problems*, edited by Gote Klingberg et al., Almiqvist and Wiksell International, 1978, pp. 90–96.

Lotman, Yuri M. "On the Semiosphere." *Sign Systems Studies*, vol. 33, no. 1, 2005, pp. 205–29.

Lotman, Yuri M. *Universe of the Mind: A Semiotic Theory of Culture*. Tauris, 1990.

Lorusso, Anna Maria. *Cultural Semiotics for a Cultural Perspective Semiotics*. Palgrave Macmillan, 2015.

Maier, Carol. "Reviewing and Criticism." *Routledge Encyclopedia of Translation Studies*, edited by Mona Baker and Gabriela Saldanha, Routledge, 2009, pp. 236–40.

Martin, Michelle H. "Let Freedom Ring: Land, Liberty, Literacy, and Lore in Mildred Taylor's Logan Family Novels." *The Oxford Handbook of Children's Literature*, edited by Julia L. Mickenberg and Lynne Vallone, Oxford UP, 2011, pp. 371–88.

Mehdizādeh, Fahimeh, translator. *Refāqat* [Friendship]. By Mildred D. Taylor, Našre- no publishing house,1393 [2014].

Mirzāi, Behnāz A. "African Presence in Iran: Identity and its Reconstruction." *Outre-mers*, vol. 89, no. 336–37, 2002, pp. 229–46, https://www.persee.fr/doc/outre_1631-0438_2002_num_89_336_3991.

Mirzāi, Behnāz A. *A History of Slavery and Emancipation in Iran, 1800/1929*. U of Texas P, 2017.

Mohammadi, Mohammad H. and Zohreh Qāeni. *Tārik̲-e adabiyāt-e kudak, Asr-e mašruteh* [*The History of Children's Literature of Iran*], vol. 3 Constitutional Era (1847–1921). Chista Publishing, 2002.

Mohammadi, Mohammad H. and Zohreh Qāeni. *The History of Children's Literature in Iran*, vol. 6 Modern Era (1920–1960). Chista Publishing, 2003.

Montgomery, Heather and Watson, Nicola J. *Children's Literature: Classic Texts and Contemporary Trends*. Palgrave McMillian, 2009.

Moussa, Maher Ben, "Empowerment and Collaborative Agency in *Roll of Thunder, Hear My Cry*." *International Journal of Applied Linguistics and English Literature*, vol. 7, no. 4, 2018, pp. 219–24.

Nikolajeva, Maria. *Children's Literature Comes of Age: Toward a New Aesthetic*. Routledge, 1996.

Nikolajeva, Maria. "Translation and Cross-cultural Reception." *Handbook of Research on Children's and Young Adult Literature*, edited by Shelby Wolf and Karen Coats, Routledge, 2011, 404–16, Doi: 10.4324/9780203843543.ch29.

Oittinen, Riita. *I Am Me, I Am Other: On the Dialogics of Translating for Children*. U of Tampere, 1993.

Oittinen, Riita. *Translating for Children*, Garland Publishing, 2000.

O'Sullivan, Emer. *Comparative Children's Literature*. Translated by Anthea Bell, Routledge, 2005.

Qezelayāq, Sorayā, translator. *Faryād Marā Bešno* [Hear My Cry]. By Mildred D. Tayor, Amirkabir, 1365 [1984].

Qezelayāq, Sorayā, translator. *Faryād Marā Bešno* [Hear My Cry]. By Mildred D. Taylor, Amirkabir, 1377 [1998].
Qezelayāq, Sorayā, translator. Personal interview. Jan. 20, 2019.
Peacock, Scott. "Mildred D. Taylor." *Children's Literature Review*, vol. 90, edited by Scott Peacock, 2004, pp. 119–49.
Rādmaneš, Šahrzād. "Moqāyeseye Mo'alefehāy Huš-e Manavi dar Do Romān-e Faryād Marā Bešno va Saḵtoon" [The Comparative Analysis of Spritual Intelligence in Two Novels Hear My Cry and Sakhtoon], *Comparative Literature*, vol. 9, no. 17, 2017, pp. 81–105, https://ensani.ir/file/download/article/1538384003-9814-170.pdf.
Rosenthal, Debra J. "Staging Uncle Tom's Cabin in Tehran." *2018 Faculty Bibliography*, vol. 9, 2018.
Š'abāni, Dāvud, translator. *Čāh* [The Well]. By Mildred D. Taylor, Madreseh publishing house, 1378 [1999].
Š'abāni, Dāvud, translator. *Čāh* [The Well]. By Mildred D. Taylor, Madreseh publishing house, 1397 [2018].
Salehi, Mansour, and Mohammad Bagher Sepehri. "Ethnic Challenges in Iran: A Case Study of Ardabil," *Canadian Social Science*, vol. 9, no. 3, 2013, pp. 1–10, https://dx.doi.org/10.3968/j.css.1923669720130903.3291.
Schafer, Elizabeth. "'I'm Gonna Glory in Learnin': Academic Aspirations of African American Characters in Children's Literature." *African American Review*, vol. 32, no. 1, 1998, pp. 57–66, https://doi.org/10.2307/3042268.
Shapoval, Mariana, et al. "The Semiotic Approach to Translation." *Postmodern Openings*, vol. 13, no. 1, 2022, 377–94, https://doi.org/10.18662/po/13.1Sup1/432.
Schwartz, Shalom H. "Are There Universal Aspects in the Structure and Contents of Human Values." *Journal of Social Issues*, vol. 50, no. 4, 1994, pp. 19–45, https://doi.org/10.1111/j.1540-4560.1994.tb01196.x.
Senick, Gerard J. and Melissa Reiff Hug. "Mildred D(elois) Taylor." *Children's Literature Review*, vol. 9, edited by Senick and Hug, 1985, pp. 223–29.
Southgate, Minoo. "The Negative Images of Blacks in Some Medieval Iranian Writings", *Iranian Studies*, vol. 17, no. 1, 1984, pp. 3–36, https://www.jstor.org/stable/4310424.
Stephens, John. "Iranian Cinema and a World through the Eyes of a Child." in the author's possession, Oxford UP, 2021.
Tabbert, Reinbert. "Approaches to the Translation of Children's Literature, A Review of Critical Studies since 1960." *Target: International Journal of Translation Studies*, vol.14, no. 2, 2002, pp. 303–51, https://doi.org/10.1075/target.14.2.06tab.
Tālebi, Abotorāb and Sajād Alizādeh. "Understanding the Ethnic Discrimination and Inequality in Iranian Universities: Case Study of the Turks and Kurds." *Quarterly Journal of Social Sciences*, vol. 26, no. 87, 2020, pp. 59–91, https://doi.org/10.22054/qjss.2020.44699.2135.
Taylor, Mildred D. *The Friendship*. Puffin Books, 1987.
Taylor, Mildred D. *Roll of Thunder, Hear My Cry*. Dial Press, 1977.
Taylor, Mildred D. *The Well*. Puffin Books, 1995.
Torop, Peeter, "The Book as/in Culture." *The Book Phenomenon in Cultural Space*, edited by Katalin Kroo, Eotvos Lorand U, U of Tartu, 2019, pp. 18–32. *Academia*, doi: https://www.academia.edu/38629767/P.Torop._The_Book_as-in_Culture._2019.
Venuti, Lawrence. *The Translator's Invisibility: A History of Translation*. Routledge, 1995.

Wiesner-Hanks, Merry E. "Patriarchy." *Encyclopedia.com*, https://www.encyclopedia.com/social-sciences-and-law/anthropology-and-archaeology/anthropology-terms-and-concepts/patriarchy.

Yusefi, Mehdi. "Farhangnāmeh yā majmo-e maghālāt?" [Dictionary or a Collection of Articles?] *Ketāb-e Māh Koodak o Nojavān* [Monthly Book of Children and YA], vol. 6, no. 68, 2003, pp. 42–45.

Yusefi, Mehdi. "Tārik̲-e yek mahfom: Mok̲ātabšenāsi va adabiyāt-e kudak dar Iran" [The History of the Concept "Audience Analysis" and Children's Literature of Iran.] *Rošanān*, vol. 14, 2012, pp. 108–219.

Yusefi, Mehdi. "Āyā kudak mok̲ātab-e monāsebi baray-e qessehāy-e Soleimāni hast" [Are Children the Appropriate Audience for Soleymani's Stories?] *Pažohešnāmeh Adabiyāt Kudak va Nojavān* [Research Quarterly for Children and Young Adult Literature], no. 64, 2014, pp. 48–65.

Yusefi, Mehdi. "Tamāyozyābi nahādhāy-e adabiyāt kudak dar daheye 1340" [Chapter 2. Institutes of Children's Literature in the 1960s]. *Darāmadi bar motāleāt-e kudaki dar Iran* [An introduction to childhood studies in Iran]. Āgāh, 2016, pp. 49–88.

Zowkāi, Mohammad Said. "Motāleāt-e kudaki: Taārif va roykardhā" [Chapter 1. Childhood Studies: Definitions and approaches]. *Darāmadi bar motāleāt-e kudaki dar Iran* [An Introduction to Childhood Studies in Iran]. Āgāh, 2016, pp. 1–19.

Part 3

The World Outside:
White Supremacy, Justice, and the Land

White Supremacy and the Black Storyteller's Narrative Unveiling

Susan Browne and Wanda Brooks

Scholars possessing expertise in African American children's literature study the distinctive textual features that create rich and authentic narratives, such as their recurring themes and motifs, linguistic patterns, imagery, aesthetics, values, cultural practices or markers, and more. (Bishop; Harris; Martin; McNair). Authors within this literary tradition are contemporary storytellers who carry out African oral traditions and indicate that literature must not stand apart from culture. Mildred D. Taylor represents one such author (among an impressive cadre of others) who authentically and convincingly writes about African American life for young readers.

The telling of family stories was a regular feature of Taylor's childhood. Family storytellers told about the struggles relatives and friends faced, which inspired Taylor as an author. Taylor's storytelling has "provided entertainment, passed on messages, communicated fears, hopes, dreams, fantasies, explanations of the world, visions of reality and a sense of truth" (Feelings 48). In her novels, Taylor invites us to witness the past. As she said in her 1997 ALAN Award acceptance speech, "In the writing of my books I have tried to present not only a history of my family, but the effects of racism, not only to the victims of racism but also to the racists themselves." In this way, Taylor's works assert the same argument made by Zeus Leonardo that "[w]hite privilege, or the analysis of white racial hegemony, must be complemented by an equally rigorous examination of white supremacy, or the analysis of white racial domination" (137).

Although often based on tragic and traumatic events crafted from volatile racial encounters, at their core Taylor's books are about strength and self-love within characters who work towards the future despite being confronted with antiblack racism. Her body of work is also about "movement building" that goes beyond identifying problems to provide deeper understandings of the existence of these problems within historical, sociocultural, and political contexts that explain the meanings and persistence of such problems (Taliaferro Baszile 210). Taylor's books resonate with Denise Taliaferro Baszile's perspectives on movement building as they offer a context for examining the history of African Americans in the United States while promoting opportunities for critical inquiry. This analysis explores the construction of whiteness, particularly white supremacy, in three of her stories: *Roll of Thunder, Hear My Cry* (*Thunder*), *The Friendship* (*Friendship*), and *The Well* (*Well*). As composite counterstories, each text recounts a racialized past through charters representing experiences inherent to the segregated South. The books unveil truths, as Taylor understands them, about the ways Black folks made sense of and reacted to the illogical nature of white supremacy during those time periods and how antiblack beliefs and racism get passed down across generations in white families.

THE LOGAN FAMILY SAGA

In Taylor's Newbery Medal novel, *Thunder*, Cassie is the novel's first-person narrator. As the story unfolds, Cassie becomes increasingly aware of the racial injustice that surrounds her and the importance of owning and holding onto acres of land for her family. Cassie narrates an impactful event from the same time period in Taylor's novella, *Friendship*. Cassie and her brothers witness the unprovoked shooting of Mr. Tom Bee, an elderly Black male, because he chose not to utter the word "Mister" before addressing his white male counterpart. White supremacist attitudes that question the humanity of Black folks and institutionalize racial hierarchies powerfully emerge in this short story. Taylor's novella, *Well*, tells the boyhood story of David Logan (Cassie's father). The story takes place in the early 1900s when all of the wells in the area have gone dry because of drought except for the Logans'. White neighbors travel for miles for water from the Logan well, frequently bringing with them their white supremacist attitudes and behaviors.

ANTIBLACKNESS AND AFRICAN AMERICAN LITERARY TRADITIONS

Thunder, *Friendship*, and *Well* are historically nuanced in the portrayal of Southern racial segregation as an oppressive force to keep Black people as subordinates. As each story unfolds, white supremacist disregard and disgust for Blackness emerges. Although it is an overt form of racism, antiblackness, according to Michael Dumas, has no singular theory, list of principles, or tenets. However, antiblackness is central to Afro-pessimist theoretical perspectives that articulate inherent oppositional relationships between Blackness and humanity. Afro-pessimism situates antiblackness as a distinct form of racism. "Afro-pessimist scholars contend that the Black is socially and culturally positioned as slave, dispossessed of human agency, desire, and freedom" (Dumas, "Against the Dark" 13). Each text is framed by what Ralph Ellison refers to as a "concord of sensibilities" (113) shared by group members who work to define their identity. In the case of these three Taylor novels, those sensibilities are derived from enslavement and its vestiges.

Afro-pessimism acknowledges that despite manumission, African Americans continue to be impacted generations later by slavery. It represents a historically based position and gives way to interrogations of white supremacist manifestations such as the murder in 2015 of nine worshipers at Emanuel African Methodist Episcopal Church in Charleston, South Carolina; the 2017 murder of Heather Heyer in Charlottesville, Virginia; the mass shooting at an El Paso, Texas, Walmart in 2019, where twenty-two people were murdered and twenty-four people were injured; the 2020 killings of Ahmaud Arbery, Daniel Prude, Breonna Taylor, George Floyd, and Walter Wallace Jr.; the 2021 murder of Daunte Wright and police shooting of Jacob Blake. Literature by Black authors such as the works of Mildred Taylor has illuminated the ways in which antiblackness exists as a form of violence against Black people not only in the past but currently.

Similar to Afro-pessimism, critical race theory (CRT) in education insists "that we cannot truly assess, respond to, and promote educational research and praxis devoid of the deep and entrenched nature of white supremacy in U.S. Society" (Ledesma and Calderón 208). As indicated similarly elsewhere in the volume, we understand CRT as a methodological, conceptual, and theoretical construct that examines and redefines "fairness, meritocracy, colorblindness, and neutrality" (Howard and Navarro 258). Racism's permanent nature is both alleged and defined as structural in critical race theorizing. As advanced in this body of scholarship, the progress made by Black people seldom occurs institutionally unless white people receive some sort of equal benefit (Howard and Navarro 260). We situate our discussion of Taylor's novels through CRT and pay particular attention to the call for documenting the lived experiences of oppressed groups through the concept of composite counternarratives.

Taliaferro Baszile insists that CRT is not more or less about storytelling than other paradigms; however, it differs in its level of transparency regarding the politics of counterstorytelling. She asserts that critical race counterstorytelling embraces thinking and feeling human beings who are raced, gendered, and embody other subjectivities, in ways that storytelling shaped by dehumanization and racial domination does not. Counterstories or narratives oppose majoritarian stories and the concept of race neutrality. As a type of counter-narrative, composite stories depict the lives of many across time and space through single representations, and the stories are not conceived of as isolated or irregular tellings. Further, the characters in composite counterstories represent and stand in for the multitude of others for whom they speak. According to Daniel Solórzano and Tara Yosso: "Composite stories and narratives draw on various forms of "data" to recount the racialized . . . experiences of people of color. Such counter-stories may offer both biographical and autobiographical analyses because the authors create composite characters and place them in social, historical, and political situations to discuss racism . . . and other forms of subordination" (33).

Our texts represent composite counterstories that challenge the veracity of white supremacy by bearing witness to and exposing its flawed logic and violent enactment through the voices of four generations of the Logan family in segregated Mississippi.

METHODOLOGY

We approached the novels using a critical content analysis method that includes a deductive and inductive, two-step process of inquiry (Johnson et al. 11). Through the deductive phase, we brought a set of a priori concepts to the readings of the texts rooted in antiblackness and critical race theoretical frames (i.e., white supremacy, racism, trauma, dehumanization, transparency, and counterstories). At the same time, new thematic discoveries were made possible with the more traditional inductive approach wherein we created an initial round of codes that we then merged into broader conceptual themes (Willig 185). We carried out a prolonged engagement with the novels as they were read and reread multiple times by both authors. Last, we provide thick descriptions from the novels as an approach to ensuring trustworthiness.

Through carrying out this close analysis of the texts individually and collectively as a text set, three themes emerged that exemplify Taylor's construction of white supremacy in the novels:

1. "Boundaries and Place": The Nature of Inscribing White Dominance
2. Antiblackness Undermining the Struggle for Humanity, and
3. Acts of Subjugation and Brutality.

"BOUNDARIES AND PLACE": THE NATURE OF INSCRIBING WHITE DOMINANCE

Taylor's narratives create a racial landscape of the segregated South that has implications for examining the past and understanding the present. It is important to note, as in other Taylor writings, the three texts present supremacist ideologies that unveil the persistence of whiteness and power and African American characters resisting and challenging these threats. "In order for white racial hegemony to saturate everyday life, it has to be secured by a process of domination, or those acts, decisions, and policies that white subjects perpetrate on people of color" (Leonardo 137). Taylor depicts white characters made from the racist ideologies of the South. Readers are able to see the characters' insistence upon securing dominance and the insidious nature of these dispositions on a regional ethos.

In *Friendship*, siblings Stacey, Cassie, Christopher-John, and Little Man experience the racial injustices common to 1933 Mississippi. The book's focus on kinship and respect for the elderly are linked to a white supremacist culture of oppression that can be examined through explicit intergenerational teachings on segregation, discrimination, and understanding boundaries and one's place. In the early moments of the novella, the Logan children express palpable experiences derived from racial dominance. Although the text's main characters are Stacey, Cassie, Christopher-John, Little Man, and Mr. Tom Bee, their stories exist among a multitude of experiences lived by many living in the South and emerging from racial subordination.

The theme of knowing one's "boundaries and place" (which Taylor depicts both metaphorically and literally) becomes apparent early in the novel when the Logan children's parents warn them never to go into the Wallace store because "[t]hey said the Wallaces didn't treat our folks right and it was best to stay clear of them" (10). The Logan parents explicitly teach their children about race to help them identify boundaries and to avoid crossing them. For Black children, then and now, life comes with warnings/talks meant to keep them safe and alive. In *Breathe: A Letter to My Sons*, Imani Perry writes, "Eyes watch you. The world is filled with watchmen, poised for your error meriting correction or punishment" (53). The understanding of watchfulness related to place becomes clear when the siblings step onto the porch of the Wallace store and Stacey warns, "Now don't y'all go touchin' nothin.'" And to Cassie, he adds, "Don't you say nothin" (9). The children naively go into the Wallace store anyway and cross boundaries to get their neighbor and fictive kin, Aunt Callie, headache medicine. As the narrative progresses, this simple act of kindness and respect has major ramifications for the children. Cassie narrates, "We stood in the entrance a moment, somewhat hesitant now about being here"

(10). The existence of boundaries take shape in this narrative through the strict admonishments of parents to keep their children safe, an older brother responsible for the welfare of his younger siblings, a feeling of hesitancy evoked from a place where one does not feel welcomed, and the eventual confirmation that an unsafe border has been crossed. The delineation of boundaries speaks pointedly to the Logan children and their evolving definition of what it means to be Black in the segregated South.

In *Well*, one might hope that those coming from miles away to the closest well in a community would do so with graciousness and gratitude. However, this is not the case in the novella's postslavery Mississippi setting. The white Simms family have a long history with the Logans that is characterized by class- and race-based hatred and contempt. The Simms are tenant farmers on forty-five acres of land, while the Logans own two hundred acres of land, orchards, and livestock. Sarah Hardstaff, who identifies family economics as an under-explored topic in literature for young readers, writes that "Taylor presents money as a social tool, used to acquire things of value (rather than having inherent value)" (11). As such, the Logans provide readers with a composite counterstory that represents Black people who have worked for and fought to acquire wealth. Their worldly possessions are social markers that would garner respect and recognition in the wider community if they were not Black. However, as David points out in *Well*, "[T]he Simmses didn't like it—that we had and they didn't. They didn't like it one bit" (10).

In *Caste: The Origins of Our Discontent*, Isabel Wilkerson describes race as the basis of a caste system built on human division. According to her, the American caste system is what has allowed racism and white supremacy to endure. The caste system primes the dominant caste to experience discomfort, unfairness, at the sight of a lower-caste person in a position above their perceived station and more particularly above them, and they may feel the need to restore equilibrium by putting the lower-caste person in their place (272). In *Well*, a common basic need for humans and livestock to have access to water is thwarted by racial dominance. As a young boy, narrator David points out that economic prosperity could not prevent the prevalence of white dominance and control:

> Now back then white folks ruled everything. A white man said jump, and most black folks did. White man said move out the way, and most black folks did. White folks could say and do what they wanted, just because they ruled things; because just one word out of them against a black person—man or woman, or even a child—and that black man or that black woman or that child could be hanging from a tree just for mouthing off. (12)

Throughout the novel, David at age ten and his older brother Hammer find their very existence threatened by the Simms brothers, who are nearly the same age they are. When the Simms brothers come to the Logan farm for water, Hammer is disturbed by the lack of respect they give him and his brother by not responding to Hammer's question about the purpose of the visit. Instead, the Simms brothers ask for the whereabouts of the Logan parents. To espouse his own significance, Hammer says, "Don't you worry 'bout where they are. I'm the one standing here" (11). Hammer displays what Wanda Brooks describes as an "engrained sense of entitlement" that "propelled the audaciousness with which the protagonist negotiated with white men" (41). In response to Hammer's reaction, Ed Rose asks, "You gettin' smart with me, boy?" (11). Charlie Simms retorts, "Look-a-here, you smart talkin' nigger—" (12). The words were meant to remind a self-assured Hammer that he had better remember his "place."

The idea of boundaries and place continues to unfold convincingly as positions to be understood literally and figuratively in the text. The Logans' older cousin Halton cautions, "Them Simmses ain't never been nothin' but trouble. Y'all little scounds stay clear of 'em" (19). Halton makes it clear that the Simmses will persist to maintain place, and confrontation is an effective way to do so. Other examples of place are present as we see attempts to exert power over David and Hammer when they take livestock to a watering hole where they encounter Charlie and Ed Rose, accompanied by their friends Dewberry and George, and Joe McCalister, who is Black. When the white boys see that the Logans have more livestock than the Simmses, this evokes a series of angry rants to display their dominance.

> Dewberry orders, "Hold it right there! There ain't water 'nough here for all them, cows!"
> Charlie laughed, "Don't tell me y'all niggers gotta come to the creek now t' water your animals. Thought y'all had a pond t' water from." . . . Charlie spoke again, "Y'all Logans some mighty uppity niggers, ya know that? Think y'all good's white folks 'cause you got a little land and some livestock."
> . . . Dewberry continues, "Y'all ain't waterin' no nigger cows down here t'day!"
> Ed Rose chimes in, "go on and water em from that pond of y'alls!" (24–25)

The systematic confrontation from multiple people reveals that having more livestock not only fails to change the Logan's "place" in society; it also opens them up to increased threats. At the same time, Dewberry's words, "Hold it right there," create an imposed physical boundary to prevent the Logan children from accessing a watering hole that is presumably shared and an unowned space vital to the wellbeing of the Logans' livestock.

Similar to the previous novellas, in *Thunder*, Cassie is confronted with navigating boundaries and place while attending her first trip into Strawberry to shop with Big Ma. Soon after arriving, Cassie must hastily leave the mercantile because she questions the white store owner's refusal to wait on her family. As she is ushered out of the store, Cassie reflects on why Mr. Barnett behaves in such a manner. Cassie's lack of awareness is due in part to the sheltering and love received at home. Pondering the events and feeling distracted, she carelessly bumps into Lillian Jean Simms, a white girl, near her same age on the sidewalk. The events described next serve to instruct Cassie about her geographic and psychological place:

> "You bumped into me. Now you apologize." I did not feel like messing with Lillian Jean. I had other things on my mind. "Okay," I said, starting past, "I'm sorry." Lillian Jean sidestepped in front of me. "That ain't enough. Get down in the road." I looked up at her. "You crazy?" "You can't watch where you going, you get in the road. Maybe that way you won't be bumping into decent white folks with your little nasty self." (113–14)

Regrettably, this event escalates, and adults get involved. Feeling that an egregious boundary has been crossed, Lillian Jean's father aggressively shoves Cassie off the sidewalk and commands, "When my gal Lillian Jean says for you to get yo'self off the sidewalk, you get, you hear?" (114). Eventually, Big Ma demands that Cassie apologize again, fearing the growing threat around them. Later on, Cassie muses that "[n]o day in my life had ever been as cruel as this one" (116). Describing how Mary Logan explains white supremacy to Cassie following this event, Hjun-Joo Yoo writes:

> Mary Logan helps Cassie recognize that the reason she must call Lillian Jean "Miz" is not out of sincere respect, but due to white coercion and sociocultural brainwashing. She kindly, but seriously, explains to Cassie that Mr. Simms needs to adhere to the belief that whites are superior to blacks and to hold on to that belief, which is materialized and buttressed through honorific words. In this exchange, Mary Logan reveals to Cassie the very process of the construction and cementation of white supremacy and authority. (343)

Yoo's explanation aligns with CRT's assertion of the endemic and permanent nature of racism and white supremacy (Ledesma and Calderón 208). The Wallace store, the Logan well, and Mr. Barnett's mercantile and outside sidewalk all metaphorically represent places where boundaries must be known and followed by the Black families. These geographical places serve as sites where inscriptions of white supremacy occur. Taylor allows readers to witness how a white code in the segregated South positioned Black bodies in racialized ways and held consequences for crossing. Being Black meant learning the margins in which you were to exist in relationship to white authority. Wilkerson asserts that Blackness is an affront to racial caste and its system of marginalization that pushes against its borders (292). The three texts unveil the oppressive nature of such borders for generations of the Logans and, as composite counternarratives, open the way for a historical examination of resistance to racial boundaries.

ANTIBLACKNESS UNDERMINING THE STRUGGLE FOR HUMANITY

Although the Logan children (as depicted in *Friendship*) are mindful of staying in their place when entering the Wallace store, this does not prevent them from encountering inhumane antiblackness (our second theme). Little Man, the youngest Logan sibling, known to be a particularly fastidious child, was certain to have looked tidy and clean that day. However, when he places his young hands on a glass counter, an adult Dewberry Wallace hurls insults and threats at Little Man:

> Dewberry, a full-grown man, stared down at Little Man. Little Man, only six, looked up. "Now I'm gonna hafta clean the glass again," snapped Dewberry, "seeing you done put them dirty hands of yours all over it."
> "My hands ain't dirty," Little Man calmly informed him. He seemed happy that he could set Dewberry's mind to rest if that was all that was bothering him. Little Man pulled his hands from behind his back and inspected them. He turned his hands inward. He turned his hands outward. Then he held them up for Dewberry to see. "They clean!" he said. "They ain't dirty! They clean!" (14)

Little Man's examination of his own hands that he already knew to be clean indicates his resistance to being defined by how Dewberry has described him. An infuriated Dewberry comes from around the counter to make his point: "'Boy, you disputin' my word? Just look at ya! Skin's black as dirt. Could put seeds on ya and have 'em growin' in no time!' Thurston Wallace laughed and tossed his brother an ax from one of the shelves. 'Best chop them hands off Dew, they that filthy!'" (14).

Along with being terrified that they actually intend to chop his hands off, Little Man, who always seems to know exactly who he is, now struggles with the hurt of Dewberry's actions and words and his sense of self. After leaving the store, Christopher-John tries to console his brother by telling him not to worry because, "We knows you ain't dirty!" (17). His oldest brother, Stacey, tells him to pay them no mind. Little Man responds, "But St-Stacey! They said they could plant seeds on me!" (20). Stacey reassures his brother that although they can do plenty, they cannot plant seeds on him. Little Man puts more stock in Dewberry's words than his own brother's. "But-but Stacey, th-they s-said they was g-gonna c-cut off my hands. They done s-said they gonna do that c-cause they ... they dirty!" (20). Stacey continues to try and comfort Little Man and tells him that the Wallaces were just joking. Little Man settles down, but after a while he reaches down and places his hand on the dirt. Although it is doubtful that Dewberry Wallace would actually cut off Little Man's hands, the psychological impact of his words and actions are embedded in a master narrative of antiblackness designed to inscribe self-doubt and self-loathing. In describing Little Man as dirt, Dewberry challenges his humanity and causes Little Man to question what he knows to be true about himself. Cecily Cobb suggests that "[f]or Taylor, this problem of double-consciousness is a key element of her overall mode of social realism. In other words, Taylor, in each of her novels, attempts not only to connect her stories to particular historical events and tensions but also to show how those tensions influence the psyches of African Americans" (73). Although difficult to comfort in that moment, Little Man will soon return to himself by maintaining his sense of identity while also carrying with him the ways in which antiblackness challenges one's humanity.

In *Well*, Hammer and Charlie Simms ultimately have the fight we anticipate will occur when Charlie gives David a backhand across the jaw. Hammer punches Charlie with his "iron fist" leaving him sprawled out and thought to be dead, causing Hammer to run to the woods for safety and from the consequences of false accusations.

Fortunately, Charlie is alive but, unable to accept the results of a fair fight, he accuses David and Hammer of hitting him with a log. When Old Man McCalister Simms comes to the Logan property, he spews a series of antiblack insults and threats while demanding that David and Hammer be punished. In his dialogue below, he further dehumanizes David and Hammer with his repeated use of racial epithets:

> Where's them niggers 'at done hit my Charlie? ... I want 'em and I wants 'em now! Ain't gonna 'low them niggers getting' away with this! ... Them niggers done jumped my boy, ain't they? I had my way, I'd do more'n lay a strap to 'em. I 'member the time we would've done already took these two little niggers to a tree for what they done. Can still do it! ... One nigger get away with hittin' a white man, what you think come

next? I got a good mind to deal with this my own way, me and mine. I get finished with 'em, I guarantee ya they won't be raisin' their fists again t' 'nother white man! (47, 50–51)

In her author's note for *All The Days Past, All the Days to Come*, Taylor explains that she often heard the word "nigger" growing up and that she uses painful language in her novels to authentically portray the time periods about which she writes. In the perspective of many white folks living in the segregated South, the frequent use of this word designates David and Hammer as a problem and positions them as things rather than as young men struggling for humanity in the face of antiblackness. Unwilling to believe that Hammer could have beaten Charlie in a fair fight, Old Man McCalister Simms demands that Hammer and David's mother whip both boys, giving no consideration to the fact that David is on crutches. In her husband's absence, Caroline Logan whips her two sons in front of the Old Man Simms, his laughing sons, the sheriff, and Clinton Melbourne, who happens to be there getting water and does not seem to enjoy the experience. However, the delight displayed by the Simms boys speaks to the struggle for humanity that David and Hammer face because their white male peers view them unworthy of fairness and empathy.

This family's racial trauma is intergenerational. Ma Rachel, the grandmother of David and Hammer (the great-grandmother of Stacey, Cassie, Christopher-John, and Little Man) had been enslaved. In carrying some of the physical and emotional scars of slavery, Ma Rachel has dementia and is often viewed as "kinda touched in the head . . . 'specially when it comes to white folks" (20). Multiple times in the text, Ma Rachel murmurs, "They done took my name!" (17). "They jus' takes everything. They takes the water and don't think nothin' 'bout it, takes it and still treat us like we ain't got no feelings. Like we don't hurt none. They takes the water jus' like they done took my name" (60). She pleads for Caroline not to beat David and Hammer and relates it to the beating of her own mother during slavery.

After the humiliating whipping, David sits down beside Ma Rachel and listens to her tell the story of how her name was taken even though he had heard this family history before. She explains that she could not have the name Rachel because the mistress on the plantation had a baby at the time she was born and named her daughter Rachel and "she ain't wantin' no Negroes on her place carryin' the same name as her child" (61). Ma Rachel goes on to tell David that her mother was told to call her Daisy or Pansy or another name after a flower. So they called her Pansy, but her mother called her Daughter in front of other folks and Rachel when no one else was around. However, on one occasion the mistress heard her mother call her Rachel, for which she was tied to a post and whipped. "She done kept on callin' me Daughter in front of white folks, but at night when she tucked me in, when nobody but me and her and God could hear, she called me Rachel, 'cause that's my name. She said don't never forget it" (62).

Listening to Ma Rachel's story following the whipping in front of the Simmses represents the point where Ma Rachel, David, and Hammer share the devastation of antiblackness that crosses generations. Taylor shows us how each of them loses some of their personhood at the hands of white dominance. In light of what the Logan boys experience from a humiliating whipping based on lies and the demand to work at the Simms place, Ma Rachel's story that had been heard so many times before now manifests the realization of what it means to have a part of you taken away by an oppressor. Taylor provides readers with composite counterstories able to transcend the story worlds of the characters in her books to become symbols of humanity that resist against antiblackness. Cobb points out that "Taylor uses a mix of public and private discourse; her characters publicly encounter and acknowledge problems of race relations and then reflect on their implications at a personal level" (70). David has come to see his grandmother beyond family ties; he sees her now with the humanity of an African American young man forced to grapple with his own humanity. He has come to understand the parallel nature of Ma Rachel's experiences and his own. He realizes that the gaze of the world or his Mississippi community and how he views himself will differ, yet like Ma Rachel and the Logan family in general he ultimately knows who he is.

In *Thunder*, two noteworthy examples of antiblackness stand out among the many depicted in the novel. These incidents occur in the opening pages and impact the youngest member of the Logan household, Little Man. One takes place as a school bus carrying white children drives by the Logan children and their friends while they walk to school. Dehumanizing the Black children while providing enjoyment and laughter for those on the bus, the driver deliberately speeds by the Logans on their hour-long trek to Great Faith School. In doing so, the bus splatters mud on the children, ruining their clothes, and forcing them to run up the side banks in fear. An incredulous Little Man asks his older brother Stacey to explain why the bus driver would do such a thing. Trying to downplay his anger, Stacey answers matter-of-factly that "they like to see us run and it ain't our bus" (13). Stacey then explains to his brother, who wonders where their bus is, "We ain't got one" (14).

Not providing the Black children with a bus is one example of the inequitable distribution of resources found in the school system. This macro level dehumanization serves to institutionalize an antiblack ethos. In many ways the bus (and lack thereof) symbolizes the ways macro- and microsystems converge to humiliate the children day in and day out while providing barriers to their own educational advancement. There are several other examples of this type in the novel.

On the first day, for instance, the schoolbooks given to the Logan children were "badly worn" (21), and the characters depicted "girls with blond braids and boys with blue eyes" (22). The inside cover graphic in the text reveals that the books initially belonged to white students for twelve years—and lists their condition in 1922 as "very poor" for the "nigra'" children (25). Here the display of antiblackness is deeply felt by Little Man, who will not accept his book and stomps on it. Cassie, likewise, defends Little Man and does not accept her book either. About this incident, Leona Fisher writes, "We hear and experience the pain in Cassie's voice, but we also rejoice that she does understand" (132). Their understanding and staunch refusal allows them to both maintain a sense of self while defying the presumed lack of agency available in that situation (Campt 34).

This incident also sets in motion the refusal of Mary Logan, who later pastes over the inside cover of the books. These sorts of educational inequities are institutionally sanctioned and still occur in various ways today. Dumas observes, "We have countless examples of the dehumanization of Black bodies, from the long legacy of federal, state, and district policies and practices designed to deprive Black communities and children of educational resources" (418). Through Taylor's story, we can trace these actions as rooted in systematic practices of antiblackness. At the same time, in this composite counterstory, Taylor's characters manage to avoid hopelessness and despair by coming to awareness and resisting in small but not insignificant ways. These practices permit them to counter antiblackness while deepening their own feelings of self-worth.

ACTS OF SUBJUGATION AND BRUTALITY

In each novel, menacing acts of white supremacy appear thematically through subjugation and brutality that instantiate the enduring reality that Black bodies do suffer violence at the hands of white oppressors. In *Friendship*, Little Man faces the threat of violence while in the Wallace store, and the threat develops into action when Mr. Tom Bee enters the store. When Mr. Tom Bee repeatedly takes the liberty of calling the store owner by his first name, this infuriates Dewberry and Thurston, the sons of store owner, John Wallace. Reluctantly eating candy from the Wallace store that Mr. Tom Bee shares, a puzzled Stacey respectfully asks him how he came to call John Wallace by his first name. Mr. Tom Bee explains that he has known John Wallace since he was fifteen years old, when he saved him from sinking in the swamp and how at that time, John declared that Tom could always call John by his first name. "And he told me things wasn't never gonna be that way. He says to me, I'm John t' you now, gonna always be John t' ya, cause you been like a daddy t' me an' I couldn't never 'spect my daddy to go callin' me mister" (39). Mr. Tom Bee goes on to explain that he aims to make him keep his word: "I'm close 'nough to meetin' my Maker, it don't much matter if he likes it or not" (42). Tom resists the defeat of being lied to and pushes back against the white supremacist tradition of saying what is convenient to a Black person deemed unworthy of a real promise. He is disrupting "a majoritarian story that distorts and silences the experiences of people of color" (Solórzano and Yosso 29). Tom Bee risks his life to force a white man to keep his word to a Black man.

When the Logan children and Mr. Tom Bee pass the Wallace store again on the way home from delivering Aunt Callie her headache medicine, Tom Bee stops in the store for some tobacco. "'Ey there, John!' he called, 'Give me some-a that chewin' tobaccie! Forgot to get it when I was in before'" (46). There are people at the gas pump, and the Simmes are at the store along with the Wallace boys. John Wallace tells Mr. Tom Bee that he best be getting out of the store. Tom Bee continues to call him John and ask for his tobacco. A nervous Stacey beckons for Mr. Tom Bee to come along. There is rage in the store, and many watchful white eyes are fixed on Mr. Tom Bee. John Wallace gives Tom the tobacco, and Tom again uses his first name to thank him and again when he tells him to put it on his charges. "He got as far as the steps. The boys and I turned to go. Then we heard the click. The explosion of a shotgun followed and Mr. Tom Bee tumbled down the steps, his right leg ripped open by the blast" (50). The presence of an angry audience and the ultimate need to demonstrate power over Black bodies leads to the brutal shooting of Mr. Tom Bee. Seeing himself as completely justified, John Wallace points out:

> You made me do that, Tom. I coulda killed ya, but I ain't wantin' to kill ya 'cause ya done saved my life an' I'm a Christian man so I ain't forgetting that. But this here disrespectin' me gotta stop and I mean stop now. You gotta keep in mind you ain't nothin' but a nigger. You gonna learn to watch yo' mouth. You gonna learn to address me proper. (51)

For John Wallace, saving face has to do with demonstrating his power over Tom Bee in front of his white peers and affirming that he is more indebted to his white counterparts than the man who saved his life and nurtured him back to health. John feels no sense of loyalty or moral obligation to Tom. In shooting Tom Bee, he makes it evident that violence is a resource for achieving white dominance. Further, white men can kill Black men without punishment or fear of the law. For the Logan children, their parents' warnings to steer clear of the Wallace store are painfully put into perspective. The children bear witness to the subjugation and brutality from which their parents have tried to protect them. They are spectators like the readers to the unthinkable events that take place in and outside of the Wallace store. Together we see Mr. Tom Bee linked to an unexpected event in which he becomes an unlikely hero able to educate, inform and engender racial pride (Harris 551). He does not waver in his conviction for what is right while also reminding readers of the historic brutality put upon Black bodies in the heinous name of white supremacy.

The theme of subjugation and brutality presents itself in *Well* when David and Hammer work at the Simms place. While at the chopping place, Charlie tells Hammer to open a burlap bag hanging from a tree and look inside. Hammer tells Charlie that he does not need to open the bag because he can smell the animal moving inside. The Simmses provoke Hammer's disgust and then turn that disgust back on him through their violent conflation of Hammer and the animal. Below Dewberry Wallace uses the opportunity to violently threaten Hammer.

> "Best you look on in there," said Dewberry Wallace. "Could be you'll find yourself hanging from a tree like that one day."
> "You do hang, said Charlie, ain't gonna be no cuttin' you down. We gonna make sure you hang there 'til you rot and stink, jus' like what's ever in that bag. Go on boy! That's an order! Cut that sack down, open it up, and let's see what we got!" (65)

Although Hammer tells the Simms boys that he takes orders from their daddy and not them, he reaches into the bag and pulls out a skunk. "'Now, how'd ya like t' find that floatin' in that fine well of y'alls?' laughed Ed-Rose" (66). The Simms boys make good on their threat and poison the Logan well with animal parts from a possum, raccoon, and skunk, destroying the only well in the community. Hammer and David know who is responsible, and McCalister Simms must accept the fact that his sons are responsible when he learns that they have been hunting for the very animals found in the well. Interestingly, Old Man McCalister is angered by the actions of his sons and their lies when all of the evidence undoubtedly points to them: "'Don't you go lyin' t' me boy!' said Mr. McCalister Simms and with one mighty fist knocked Charlie to the ground. 'It's one thing t' teach a nigger where he stand, but ya don't go destroyin' God's good earth t' do it!' He reached inside his wagon. He pulled out a bullwhip" (90).

Charlie Simms begs his father not to whip them in front of "niggers." Instead, Mr. Simms makes each boy take turns going down into the well to retrieve the animal parts. The cruel act of contaminating the well is an attempt at conquest for Charlie and Ed-Rose and brings to fruition generational racism. They want to do harm to the boys and their family without regard to the impact on the larger community. Their father has to accept that his sons are responsible because of the overwhelming evidence against them. He too clearly bears the responsibility of his sons and their destruction of the well. By his example, they have been taught that Black people in general and the Logans in particular are deserving of acts of subjugation and brutality. The question comes to mind: How would McCalister Simms react to the contamination of the well if he had not been forced to rely on it?

Taylor's inscriptions of the subjugation and brutality of white supremacy in *Thunder* occur within the first several pages. These acts are repeatedly and vividly depicted throughout the novel. Creating composite counterstories, Taylor resists "a revisionist history that supports dangerous majoritarian stories that disappear whites from a history of racial dominance, rape, mutilation, brutality, and murder" (Dumas and ross 431). Below, Taylor includes a dialogue with remarkable imagery between T.J. (a friend of Stacey Logan) and the Logan children about a "burning" of three Black men: "'He's low sick all right—'cause he got burnt near to death. Him and his two nephews. And you know who done it?' . . . Finally T.J. said, 'Okay. See, them Berry's burnin' wasn't no accident. Some white men took a match to 'em.' 'Y-you mean just lit 'em up like a piece of wood?' stammered Christopher John, his eyes growing big with disbelief" (9–10).

Readers learn from these opening pages that Mr. Berry's wife has summoned the children's grandmother, Big Ma, to their home for medical assistance. Big Ma chooses not to tell the children why she goes or what happens. We eventually find out that Mr. Berry and his two nephews were dragged out of their house (namely by the Wallaces who likewise own the store) and they "lit him afire with them boys" (40). These actions happen simply because a white person said, "That's the nigger Sallie Ann said was flirtin' with her" (39).

Because Cassie narrates, the rationale for the violence in the minds of the white characters isn't revealed, and Taylor rarely shares inner thoughts through their dialogue. Further, the complex and volatile history of sexual attraction and engagement (real or imagined) between Black men and white women is not explained or known to the younger Logan children. On a number of occasions, however, the children ask about why the violence across races happens, and each child gradually hears and learns messages about white supremacy. For example, one night Cassie overhears Mama's talk with Mr. Avery about the night riders: "'But why? Why are they riding? What's happened?' 'I don't rightly know,' said Mr. Avery. 'But y'all know how they is. Anytime they thinks we steppin' outa our place, they feels like they gotta stop us'" (62).

This presumed lynching involves a group of seven cars (a caravan) of Ku Klux Klan night riders who approach the driveway of Cassie's home. It stops, two men step out and turn around upon realizing they are at the wrong house. Cassie's description of how she feels speaks for itself: "Feeling sick, I crawled onto the porch and crept trembling toward the door. . . . I leaned against the latch while the waves of terror swept over me. . . . I lay very still for a while, not allowing myself to think. But, soon, against my will, the vision of ghostly headlights soaked into my mind and an uncontrollable trembling racked my body" (68).

Instilling this sort of terror in Black families derives from a collective action taken by white men in the community who feel the need for vengeance. The creation of terror through acts of subjugation and brutality are established as potential reactions able to show up at any time and in any place. Whether victim or witness, this kind of physical, psychological, and/or emotional abuse characterizes the type of white supremacy that historically leads to death for Black people. These acts are instrumental in establishing the permanence of racism and the quest for white domination. And while Cassie and her siblings experience the intended terror and are likely too young to respond otherwise, a compelling counterstory is evidenced through Big Ma, Mary Logan, and Mr. Morrison who stay up all night, with shotguns and rifles in hand, to protect their land, property, and each other.

FALSE NARRATIVES AND COMPOSITE TRUTHS

In Taylor's historical fiction, readers are able to merge the present with the past and examine how these points in history dialogically exist (Moller and Allen 148). The books are pieces of wisdom passed from Taylor's father and "representations of the love extended to her from family members across generations" (Brooks 36). The counternarratives in *Thunder*, *Friendship*, and *Well* "respond to racism and its dominant ideology" (Brooks 36) as Taylor constructs whiteness, particularly white supremacy in each of the books. She chronicles the white perpetrators of antiblackness as she chronicles her own family. Taylor's narratives come to life to tell stories of race in America. In each of the texts, white supremacy manifests through the themes of (1) boundaries and place, (2) antiblackness and (3) subjugation and brutality. Each theme emerges powerfully by way of Taylor's storytelling.

Like other chapters in the volume, we highlight past realities still occurring as argued in the Black Lives Matter movement. Our exploration of the themes in these texts works to illuminate the narratives in a historical context and documents the prevalence of white supremacist attitudes as a response to Black lives. Each book on its own or considered together has the ability to construct and influence understandings of race and racism. Read as composite counternarratives, however, the books represent larger stories embedded in what the storyteller provides. As Leonardo explains of composite counterstories: "they are based on real trends through composite stories that capture a more complete portrayal of race relations. . . . Their aggregated appearance dispels notions that racism is happening locally to this or that person or group, but is pervasive and affects an entire society, from micro- to macroaggressions" (605).

With each novel, Taylor's imagination unveils a simultaneous story that represents composite truths. Her portrayals allow readers to challenge anti-blackness and disrupt the myth of white superiority. As the streets of our nation and world call for Black Lives to Matter, Taylor reminds us of how long similar calls have existed through her characters' lives and composite renderings. She has presented herself as writing on behalf of her community (Davis-Undiano 12). Together these three books provide openings for discourse around the racialized experiences of Black people in the South, giving readers windows into the historical underpinnings of racism in America and the structures leading to its rootedness in present day society.

WORKS CITED

Bell, Derrick. *Faces at the Bottom of the Well: The Permanence of Racism*. Basic Books, 1992.
Bishop, Rudine Sims. *Free within Ourselves: The Development of African American Children's Literature*. Heinemann, 2007.
Bishop, Rudine Sims. "Reflections of the Development of African American Children's Literature." *Journal of Children's Literature*, vol. 38, no. 2, 2012, pp. 5–13.
Brooks, Wanda. "An Author as a Counter-Storyteller: Applying Critical Race Theory to a Coretta Scott King Award Book." *Children's Literature in Education*, vol. 40, no. 1, 2009, pp. 33–45.
Campt, T. M. *Listening to Images*. Duke UP, 2017.
Cobb, Cicely Denean. "The Day That Daddy's Baby Girl Is Forced to Grow Up: The Development of Adolescent Female Subjectivity in Mildred D. Taylor's *The Gold Cadillac*." *ALAN Review*, vol. 34, no. 3, 2007, pp. 67–76.
Davis-Undiano, Robert. "Mildred D. Taylor and the Art of Making a Difference." *World Literature Today*, vol. 78, no. 2, 2004, pp. 11–13.
Dixson, Adrienne, and Celia Rousseau Anderson. "Where are We? Critical Race Theory in Education 20 Years Later." *Peabody Journal of Education*, vol. 93, no. 1, 2018, pp. 121–31.
Dumas, Michael J. "Against the Dark: Antiblackness in Education Policy and Discourse." *Theory into Practice*, vol. 55, no. 1, 2016, pp. 11–19.
Dumas, Michael J. and kihana miraya ross. "'Be Real Black for Me': Imagining Blackcrit in Education." *Urban Education*, vol. 51, no. 4, 2016, pp. 415–42.
Ellison, Ralph. *Shadow and Act*. Vintage Books, 1964.
Feelings, Tom. "Illustration is My Form, The Black-Experience My Story and My Content Illustrated Works." *Advocate*, vol. 4, no. 2, 1985, pp. 73–82.
Fisher, Leona. "'Bridge' Texts: The Rhetoric of Persuasion in American Children's Realist and Historical Fiction." *Children's Literature Association Quarterly*, vol. 27, no. 3, 2002, pp. 129–35.
Harris, Violet J. "African American Children's Literature: The First One Hundred Years." *The Journal of Negro Education*, vol. 59, no. 4, 1990, pp. 540–55.
Hardstaff, Sarah (Layzell). "Money and the Gift in the Novels of Mildred Taylor and Cynthia Voigt." *Barnboken: Journal of Children's Literature Research*, vol. 42, 2019, pp. 1–15.

Howard, Tyrone C., and Oscar Navarro. "Critical Race Theory 20 Years Later: Where Do We Go From Here?" *Urban Education*, vol. 51, no. 3, 2016, pp. 253–73.

Johnson, Dianne. "A Tribute to Mildred D. Taylor." *World Literature Today*, vol. 78, no. 2, 2004, pp. 4.

Johnson, Holly, et al. *Critical Content Analysis of Children's and Young Adult Literature: Reframing Perspective*. Routledge, 2017.

Ledesma, María C., and Dolores Calderón. "Critical Race Theory in Education: A Review of Past Literature and a Look to the Future." *Qualitative Inquiry*, vol. 21, no. 3, Mar. 2015, pp. 206–22.

Leonardo, Zeus. "The Color of Supremacy: Beyond the Discourse of 'White Privilege.'" *Educational Philosophy and Theory*, vol. 36, no. 2, 2004, pp. 137–52.

Martin, Michelle. *Brown Gold: Milestones of African American Children's Picture Books, 1845–2002*. Routledge, 2004.

McNair, Jonda C. "A Comparative Analysis of The Brownies' Book and Contemporary African American Children's Literature Written by Patricia C. McKissack." *Embracing, Evaluating, and Examining African American Children's and Young Adult Literature*, edited by Wanda Brooks and Jonda McNair, Scarecrow/Rowman and Littlefield Press, 2008, pp. 3–29.

Moller, Karla, and JoBeth Allen. "Connecting, Resisting, and Searching for Safer Places: Students Respond to Mildred Taylor's *The Friendship*." *Journal of Literacy Research*, vol. 32, 2000, pp. 145–86.

Perry, Imani. *Breathe: A Letter to My Sons*. Beacon Press, 2019.

Solórzano, Daniel G., and Tara J. Yosso. "Critical Race Methodology: Counter-Storytelling as an Analytical Framework for Education Research." *Qualitative Inquiry*, vol. 8, no. 1, 2002, pp. 23–44.

Solórzano, Daniel. "Images and Words that Wound: Critical Race Theory, Racial Stereotyping, and Teacher Education." *Teacher Education Quarterly*, vol. 24, no. 3, 1997, pp. 5–19.

Taliaferro Baszile, Denise. "In Pursuit of the Revolutionary-Not-Yet: Some Thoughts on Education Work, Movement Building, and Praxis." *Educational Studies*, vol. 53, no. 3, 2017, pp. 205–17.

Taylor, Mildred. "Acceptance Speech for the 1997 Alan Award." *The ALAN Review*, vol. 25, no. 3, 1998.

Taylor, Mildred. *All the Days Past, All the Days to Come*. Viking, 2020.

Taylor, Mildred. *The Friendship*. Puffin, 1987.

Taylor, Mildred. *Roll of Thunder, Hear My Cry*. Puffin, 1976.

Taylor, Mildred. *The Well: David's Story*. Puffin, 1998.

Wilkerson, Isabel. *Caste: The Origins of Our Discontents*. Random House, 2020.

Willig, Carla. *Introducing Qualitative Research in Psychology*. Open UP, 2013.

Yoo, Hyun-Joo. "Rewriting American History in *Roll of Thunder, Hear My Cry*: Metahistoricity, the Postcolonial Subject, and the Return of the Repressed." *Children's Literature in Education*, vol. 50, no. 3, 2019, pp. 333–46.

"Don't Speak for the Trees—Listen"
Mildred D. Taylor's *Song of the Trees* for Environmental Justice

Lauren Rizzuto

> How can narrative embody life in words and at the same time respect what we cannot know? How does one listen for the groans and the cries, the undecipherable songs, the crackle of fire in the cane fields, the laments for the dead, and the shouts of victory, and then assign words to all of it?
> —SAIDIYA HARTMAN, "VENUS IN TWO ACTS" (3)

I begin with this epigraph to attune us—writers, teachers, scholars, and gatekeepers of children's literature—to the formidable task that Saidiya Hartman names and Mildred D. Taylor undertakes: to make legible a history of inexpressible pain. In "Venus in Two Acts," a reflective essay on the writing of her memoir *Lose Your Mother*, Hartman deliberates whether it is possible to know, let alone convey in words, the pain that Black bodies have endured since slavery without compromising black[1] people's humanity. She decides that the existing verbal narrative is insufficient to represent either the violence of slavery or the subjectivity of enslaved individuals. With *Lose Your Mother*, she attempted to fill in the gaps but found that "the limits of the sayable," the vast and excruciatingly painful historical records detailed in ledgers, ships' logs, and the like of what did actually happen during slavery, stopped her. Other writers face this problem, too, she notes; evidence of their attempts often surfaces in moments of narrative restraint, a visible "refusal to fill in the gaps and provide closure," as well as "the imperative to respect black noise—the shrieks, the moans, the nonsense, and the opacity, which are always in excess of legibility . . ." (12). Leaving the gaps open, rather than writing an alternative history in the form of a story, draws attention to the ongoing presence of violence instead of unwittingly papering over unsayable pain.

But what happens when a narrative is not solely verbal but visual?

Can we perceive the sonic excess of black noise despite the confines of the white page?
Can the noise ever become a song?
These are the questions that ground my analysis of Mildred Taylor's first book, *Song of the Trees* (1975), illustrated by Jerry Pinkney. Set in Depression-era rural Mississippi, *Song* is an illustrated work of historical fiction for children that questions the authority of a stable, predominantly white-authored historical record. Based on an event from Taylor's father's life, *Song* relates how the Logans, a close-knit, African American family, defend themselves and the trees on their land from racist white lumbermen who try to cut down the trees for profit without the Logans' permission.

Stories of African Americans' everyday resistance and resilience in the Jim Crow era do not appear as often as they should in historical fiction for children. By taking inspiration from her family's (then-unwritten) biography, Taylor subjectifies and diversifies accounts of Black experience in *Song*. Further, by grounding this account in an illustrated book, one that intertwines the Logans' survival with that of the trees on their land, *Song* invites readers to understand history differently—not only in regard to what happened but also in terms of *how* it is recorded, in relation to the earth. For, in addition to being a work of historical fiction, *Song* is a text for environmental justice. As a practice, reading for environmental justice retrains us as literary critics to delve into long-held reserves of sensory knowledge. *Song* alerts readers to the presence of what Hartman calls the "black noise" that persists "in excess of legibility"—what is (not) said, what is (not) seen, what is (not) heard. Using visual and ecocritical analysis, my essay illuminates the role that multimodal dialogue (that is, the give-and-take between words and images, book and reader, as well as human being and tree) plays in creating space for black noise, which in this case has been transposed into a *Song of the Trees*. While it is not within the scope of this essay to examine in-depth Taylor's entire Logan sequence, I hope that my analysis makes room for future ecocritical readings of Taylor's work and that of other African American and Black authors, whose efforts go unrecognized in a white-centric environmentalist movement.

WHY READ FOR ENVIRONMENTAL JUSTICE?

Published in 1975—only five years after the first formal celebration of Earth Day in the United States—*Song of the Trees* has not yet been read as an environmental justice text. More often, critics hail Taylor's oeuvre for its singular voice and "authentic portrayal of racism" in children's historical fiction (Crowe and Brown 77).[2] However, *Song* and other titles from the Logan sequence (e.g., *The*

Land; The Well: David's Story; Roll of Thunder, Hear My Cry; and most recently *All the Days Past, All the Days to Come*) draw an emphatic connection between human rights, the Logans' mistreatment at the hands of their white neighbors, and misuse of natural resources. Possibly, scholars' reluctance to read Taylor's work as overtly environmentalist stems from the whitewashed perception of "environmentalism" in the United States' public consciousness to date.[3] Thus, Taylor's linking of Black lives to earth matters advances an important corrective to the dominant paradigm: she redraws our attention to the fact that people of color have played a vital role in the global environmentalist movement for a long, long time. Moreover, Taylor's participation in the genre of children's historical fiction disturbs the presumed stability of the past, thus expanding readers' notions of Blackness and what counts as an "*authentic* portrayal of racism" (Crowe and Brown 77; emphasis added). Not only a historical novella but also an environmental justice text, *Song* actually interrogates the legibility of the historical record and makes plain the need to reimagine slavery and its afterlives as crimes against people *and* the earth we all call home.

Taylor is not the first African American writer to make the connection between justice for African Americans, environmental justice, and racial justice. In his short story "Po' Sandy," published in 1888, Charles Chesnutt reveals whites' cruelty towards enslaved peoples to be symptomatic of whites' desire to conquer all of earth's other inhabitants, human and other-than-human alike. Even the popularizing of the term "environmental justice" is largely due to African Americans' activism (though, certainly, Indigenous peoples and other people of color occupy a central place as well). In 1991, at the People of Color Environmental Leadership Summit in Washington, DC, the Environmental Justice Movement was officially launched in the United States, inspired by the research of African American activists such as Dr. Benjamin Chavis, who coined the term *environmental racism* in 1986, and Dr. Robert Bullard, frequently called the "father of environmental justice." Thus, reading *Song* as an environmental justice text is not so much a reframing as a return, and a recentering, of African American thinking and literature in the environmentalist movement.

The first of the Principles of Environmental Justice issued by the 1991 Summit is this: "Environmental justice affirms the sacredness of Mother-Earth, ecological unity and the interdependence of all species, and the right to be free from ecological destruction" (People of Color Environmental Leadership Summit, henceforth PoCELS). Historically, ecological destruction has been and continues to be more of a threat for African Americans than for whites. Chesnutt expresses this truth through his fiction, which testifies to the ways "enslaved people [were] forced to live in terrible conditions, endure separation from those they love, and labor as unpaid workers" according to whites' law (Ammons and Roy 61). In "Po' Sandy," Chesnutt tells of an enslaved man named Sandy whose wife Tenie conjures him into a tree so that they may stay together on the same plantation instead of being sold or loaned out at the enslavers' whims. When Sandy is cut down in his tree-state and gruesomely sawed into lumber, his fate symbolically indicates a material reality. Under white, anthropocentric law, black bodies and trees are one and the same: expendable.

Like Chesnutt, Taylor uses her fiction to reveal how environmental injustices against nature and African Americans have been historically institutionalized, that is, *naturalized*, by whites. Set in the Depression, *Song* does not take place during slavery but, as a single episode in the Logan sequence that retells a single family's history from slavery through civil rights, it persuasively demonstrates that slavery's crimes did not end with abolition. The callous attitude of the supervising lumberman, the white Mr. Andersen, replicates that of the master Marrabo and his wife from Chesnutt's tale. With no regard for anyone but himself, Andersen decides to cut down the trees on the Logan family's land without their consent and sell them for his own profit. His rationalization of the theft bespeaks his racist worldview: "These folks ain't got no call for them," he tells Tom, another white man. "I do. I got me a good contract for these trees and I aim to fulfill it" (*Song* 23). That Andersen has not asked the Logans whether he may buy the trees, let alone cut them down, before pursuing a business opportunity matters not; under the law, all the earth is his for the taking. But Andersen does feel somewhat uneasy about confronting David Logan, who staunchly refuses to obey the laws of a legal institution that denies him his humanity. Andersen cowardly waits to make his move until David is away laying railroad tracks in Louisiana for extra money so that his ill wife Mary can afford to buy medicine. Andersen offers David's mother a mere sixty-five dollars—a "good price," he says (27)—for all the trees on their land and threatens to harm her son if she does not comply.

As the first of Taylor's works to be published, *Song* sets a precedent for future books to intertwine and restore future Logan generations' relationship with the earth and other-than-human beings. In *The Land* (2001), which chronologically comes first in the sequence, David's father, Paul-Edward, has no greater wish than to acquire land. Descended from white enslavers on his father's side and African and Native peoples on his mother's, Paul-Edward hungers for a piece of land to care for, farm, and protect in the way that his mother's ancestors did.[4] After much hardship, he finally achieves his goal, and it is this piece of land that grounds the trees Andersen desires in *Song*. As the Logans know and Andersen does not, cultivating an interdependent relationship with one's environment, equally sharing the benefits of ecological protection and the burdens of ecological costs, is the only way to ensure equitable, mutual survival. David Logan learns this lesson in his childhood, chronicled in *The Well*, when their town goes through a drought. Graciously, the Logans make their well water, the only water supply that has not dried up, freely accessible to everyone, regardless of race. The community survives together until Charlie and Ed-Rose Simms, two white boys who are resentful that the Logans have more land and more water than they do, poison the well.[5]

The stakes are high when disregard for the earth and its inhabitants persists to the degree that individual profit is more important than human lives. In *Song*, Taylor enacts this critique by deploying the unconventional narrative perspective of an innocent, eight-year-old African American girl, Cassie Logan, David's daughter. As Noel Sturgeon observes, most environmentalist media for children only confer agency upon white male characters, like Captain Planet or Zak from *Ferngully: The Last Rainforest* (1992), or more recently Obe Devlin in Amy Sarig King's *Me and Marvin Gardens* (2017). When female people of color are present, they often appear as brown-skinned earth goddesses (Gaia from *Captain Planet and the Planeteers* being one example) and have comparatively little power to effect real change (Sturgeon 264).[6] Cassie Logan is exceptional in that her environmental advocacy is informed by her lived experiences: she is a young African American girl who loves the outdoors and is only beginning to confront whites' racism directly. She is surprised and outraged to learn that, even if all she and her family want is the right to enjoy a self-sustaining, rural existence, the consequences they face for doing so are grave. Simply put, for Cassie the personal can't help but be political.

Like her father and grandfather, Cassie focuses her attention on the land, particularly on the trees. When she awakes in the morning, she looks out the window to receive "a song of morning greeting" as a breeze moves past them (*Song* 7). Cassie's worldview is biocentric. To her mind, both humans and trees have agency. That is, they act—though their actions may be imperceptible to those who would deny their self-worth. She regards the trees as her friends, and as such, she feels kinship with them. Though she endures teasing from her brothers for it, she insists that the trees sing to her, and during morning chores, she greets them as one would a neighbor:

> "Good morning, Mr. Trees," I shouted. They answered me with a soft, swooshing sound. "Hear 'em, Stacey? Hear 'em singing?"
>
> "Ah, cut that out, Cassie. Them trees ain't singing. How many times I gotta tell you that's just the wind?" He stopped at a sweet alligator gum, pulled out his knife and scraped off a glob of gum that had seeped through its cracked bark. He handed me half. (13)

Stacey's disinterest in the trees' personalities does not stop him from appreciating their goods. But Cassie recognizes that the gum is a gift, and despite her older brother's irritation, she thanks the giver respectfully: "'Thank you, Mr. Gum Tree'" (13). Cassie's acknowledgment is more than a simple thank-you for an unanticipated treat; it signifies her family's dependence upon the trees for their survival as well as the interdependent relationship the Logans have with the land. For, despite the name, sweet gum is not sweet. While it is satisfying to chew, historically its uses are medicinal: when chewed, the bitter-tasting gum helps with digestion, and when applied topically, the anti-inflammatory properties in the sap help to soothe insect bites.[7] As Cassie and Stacey chew the trees' resin, they are fortifying their health when food is scarce; in turn, their good health will help them to protect the trees from those who would harm them for capital gain.

Environmental justice works to bring out the stories that those in power either ignore or actively suppress. Acknowledging the impossibility of a complete historical record invites contemplation of the ways we recognize authority, and how it, too, may be limited by top-down, anthropocentric values—values that, it should be said, are not exclusive to white people or adults. Taylor brings nuance to a discussion of race because she refuses to equate environmental advocacy with ethnic identity or age. Indeed, by drawing a stark contrast between Cassie and Stacey's worldviews, she rejects universalizing, problematic discourse that would suggest that all African Americans are "closer to nature" by showing how even in a single biological family there will be varying perspectives. In contrast to Stacey's skepticism, Cassie's kinship with the trees aligns with the thinking of indigenous writers, like Winona LaDuke (Anishinaabe/Ojibwe) and George Tinker (Osage), who also regard the earth and its inhabitants as family.[8]

As the children continue their morning route to pick blackberries for supper, Cassie identifies each tree by name. She spots "a giant old pine" and gives its "warm trunk" a hug (16), a meaningful gesture that gained global attention with the Chipko (i.e., tree-hugging) movement of the 1970s and 1980s in India.[9] Cassie even includes the trees in a game of tag. The facing illustration for this passage depicts her hiding amongst the foliage: "As I waited for [Christopher-John] to get closer, I glanced up into the boughs of my wintry-smelling hiding tree expecting a song of laughter. But the old pine only tapped me gently with one of its long, low branches. I turned from the tree and dashed away" (16). Laughing, she reveals her hiding place, taunting her brother—or is she teasing the pine that's tagged her?—chanting, "'You can't, you can't, you can't catch me.'" As she runs, she names and describes the trees she encounters, "shaggy-bark hickories and sharp-needled pines . . .

blue-gray beeches and sturdy black walnuts," intimating that each is as familiar as one of her own family.

In the foreword to *Song*, Taylor writes, "I often listened to my father recount his adventures growing up in rural Mississippi during the Depression. His vivid description of the giant trees, the coming of the lumbermen, and the events that followed made me feel that I too was present" (3). As the multitude of awards Taylor has received illustrate, readers of her work have long felt as if they are also in the presence of a master storyteller. Yet, humbly, Taylor has described her role as that of a historian, a diligent scribe. In contrast to her father, grandparents, and other relatives, Taylor says, "I have only been the one who held the pen, the one tapped on the shoulder to write down the stories" ("Tapped on the Shoulder" 61). Leaving modesty aside for the moment, it is worth noting that Taylor's self-description positions her as a listener—a role she models through the text itself. When the old pine "tap[s her] gently," Cassie embodies the role that Taylor herself assumes: the historian, "the one tapped on the shoulder" to bear witness, in this case to the trees, who themselves have become Cassie's family, an "ancient forest" of ancestors whose song, though silent to some, is nonetheless sung (*Song* 16).

Just as Andersen's stubborn disavowal of the Logans' rights does not rob the family of their humanity, Stacey's unwillingness to hear the trees sing does not erase the existence of their song. Moreover, by transposing her family's history into a "*song* of the trees," a song that only willing listeners can hear, Taylor indicates that there are other songs, other (hi)stories in circulation that remain "in excess of legibility" (Hartman 12). In an original and insightful analysis of Taylor's novella, Osayimwense Osa observes that Cassie's perspective evinces a spiritual relationship with the natural world, practiced by her African ancestors but ignored by the academic majority: "While one does not expect a complete undiluted African spiritualism among African Americans three hundred years after their ancestors got to America, its survival is evident in African American social institutions which scholars have not really paid enough attention to. Frankly, literary scholars have not taken spiritual matters, and the entirely different way of knowing they posit very seriously" (91).

One need not speculate on the reasons academia has excluded and continues to exclude spiritual knowledge on claims of illegitimacy; scholars' refusal to acknowledge other ways of knowing is yet another symptom of institutionalized racism that privileges the authority of the white page. Yet *Song* challenges this notion through genre: as a work of historical fiction, it nonetheless requires the reader to take elements of *this* family's history, and by extension the history of African American people, on faith, not fact.

SEEING SILENCE

As I have been attempting to show, it would be a mistake to classify Taylor's characterization of the trees as pathetic fallacy and leave it at that. Taylor's decision to have Cassie attribute human traits to the trees, even if the trees themselves do not necessarily respond to *her*, requires closer scrutiny. We should ask: Why is it that the trees do *not* articulate their intentions or emotions in human language, especially since other works of children's literature commonly (and often indiscriminately) personify other-than-human nature? Leaving open this gap productively emphasizes our gaps in knowledge, not only in regards to the earth but also about each Other, even (or especially) when our lived experiences differ. For me, a white reader, the major takeaway from *Song* is not an answer to the question of whether trees can actually sing but what Cassie's hearing them reveals about the lived experience of African Americans, and how this experience might intersect with environmental racism. It is no coincidence that Andersen's denying the trees their right to live is analogous to his denying the Logans their humanity because, for Taylor, the lives of the trees and the lives of the Logans are intertwined, familial, and interdependent. But to make sense of this relationship, one needs an ecocritical reading, a practice that retrains us to rely on sensory knowledge. In this case, examining not only what is said but the traces of what is left *un*said redirects our attention to the presence of narrative restraint. As she and Stacey continue their morning walk, Cassie pauses:

> I stared at the trees, aware of an eerie silence descending over the forest. Stacey walked toward me. "What's the matter with you, Cassie?" he asked.
> "The trees, Stacey," I said softly, "they ain't singing no more."
> "Is that all?" He looked up at the sky. . . . "The wind just stopped blowing, that's all," said Stacey. "Now stop fooling around and come on." (18–19)

Despite her brother's scoffing, Cassie correctly interprets the trees' silence as a warning. Suddenly, the children observe that they are surrounded by trees all painted with an ominous "X." Panicked at the sound of two white men's voices approaching, Cassie and her siblings quickly hide. Like the trees, the children keep quiet, which enables them to detect wrongdoing by eavesdropping and then relate it to someone who is willing to listen—namely, the reader.

Osa suggests that the text's emphasis on silence is culturally located: "Cassie Logan has to resolve the conflict between her African/aural roots and her American/visual orientation—between James Baldwin's declaration that 'it is only in his music that the Negro has been able to tell his story' and Ralph Waldo Emerson's assumption that 'the eye is final; what it tells us is the last stroke of nature; beyond color we cannot go'" (92–93). I agree, and yet I would also suggest that *Song* troubles the absolutes of Baldwin's "only" and Emerson's "last" ways of knowing through its form, an *illustrated* book for children. Just as Taylor's words dispel the assumption that there can be one, authoritative version of history, Jerry Pinkney's art textures the notion of "Black experience." Pinkney, too, is an African American artist; he does not simply draw without bias or subjectivity but offers yet another translation of the story's events, which in turn multiplies the number of possible interpretations of the same story.

Notably, Pinkney's art presents a distinct narrative perspective, that of third-person omniscient narrator, which might be described as a counterpoint to Taylor's text, which is told from Cassie's limited first-person perspective. Like a sketch artist in a courtroom who draws a witness at the stand, Pinkney does not literally retell the story's events from Cassie's point of view but recasts her as an actor in the Logan family drama. Further, Pinkney's illustration effects the hindsight of adult experience—something that Cassie's characterization as a child, still innocent of the consequences of whites' racism, cannot believably summon.[10] "'I won't let him cut them,'" Cassie threatens in the presence of Mr. Andersen. Fearless, she says, "'The trees are my friends and ain't no mean ole white man gonna touch my trees.'" Her mother then steers her away from the evident, yet unspoken, danger of a young black girl insulting a grown white man (Taylor, *Song* 27). Whereas for Cassie the trees' destruction is devastating and personal, Pinkney's art symbolically reveals its wider, historical, and varied political impact.

In 1976, Barbara Bader would claim that the picturebook is best conceived as a dynamic art form that "hinges on the interdependence of pictures and words, on the simultaneous display of two facing pages, and on the drama of the turning of the page" (1). As its composite name indicates—it is *picturebook*, not picture book—the verbal and the visual are in constant dialogue. Often, figures will appear in the pictures that go unnamed in the text, and vice versa. Thus, contrary to Emerson's dictum that "'the eye is final'" (qtd. in Osa 92–93), pictures in children's books dispel the notion of any final, stable interpretation. Meaning is made through the reader's negotiation of a number of possible interpretations from page to page, image to text, color, shape, scale, medium, and composition—all of which affect one's overall perception of the story's events. Granted, an illustrated book like *Song* is not a picturebook per se because the text can operate independently of the pictures and thereby influence our reading of them. However, even if Pinkney's art would seem to be of secondary importance to readers who privilege word over image, I maintain that his contributions are not merely decorative. Pinkney *is* a celebrated picturebook creator, and he approaches all illustration with the mindset of one who lets the pictures speak, albeit silently, for themselves. Of his own process, Pinkney has noted that words and images work together to create a cohesive "marriage, or the possibility of a marriage, between drawing and design" ("The Artist at Work"). One must not overpower the other, he insists—a statement that not only signifies his illustrations' complementary weight to the text but also indicates that the visual does something markedly *distinct* from the verbal, even as they harmonize to compose a whole *Song*.

Pinkney demands that readers interact with *Song* differently than one would with a purely verbal text by deploying direct address. He explains, "I . . . try to make the viewer and the characters become one. Often you'll see characters in a book looking out at you" ("The Artist at Work").[11] Whereas direct address in a novel has the effect of distancing the reader from the fictionalized character (e.g., "[You should] Call me Ishmael," or "Reader, I [not you] married him"), breaking the fourth wall in an illustration manageably shortens the distance between them. The cover image of *Song*, for instance, features Cassie looking directly out toward the viewer while leaning back against a tree (see fig. 1). Her half-smile and relaxed posture suggest friendliness and beckon the reader to open the book. On the back cover, however, there's a different scene where Little Man, Christopher-John, and Stacey amble in and amongst the trees. None are smiling, and Stacey in particular appears restless: he locks eyes with the viewer in mid-stride, indicating impatience or even a sense of warning. "Don't get too comfortable," he seems to be saying. "There is more of this story to come."

The visual counterpoint between Cassie and Stacey's expressions on the book's jacket thereby alludes to the turmoil inside the pages, which Pinkney stresses through his book design. Critic Susan Gannon has observed, "One of the most important choices an illustrator can make is the selection of scenes to be shown. . . . [I]n the design of an illustrated book there are some illustrations which hold positions of special rhetorical force" (91). In *Song*, there are twelve illustrations over the span of forty-eight pages, two of which are double spreads. In contrast to the single-page illustrations, both of the double spreads occur at especially tense moments in Taylor's text. The first spread occurs in the aforementioned scene where Cassie notices the trees' "uneasy silence," and she and her brothers, suddenly hearing the encroaching voices of strangers on their family's land, hide in the brush: "Two white men emerged. We looked at each other. We knew to be silent" (19). The enlarged format of the illustration, which stretches across two pages, invites pause; the reader's page turning halts; the absence of text visually effects quiet (see fig. 2).

But Pinkney's decision to devote a full double spread to the Logan children's hiding in the forest deserves a closer look—or, to put it another way, a harder listen. To begin, Pinkney organizes his composition so that the Logan children occupy the most space on the page. Stacey, Christopher-John, Little Man, and Cassie exchange glances with one another while the white men, Mr. Andersen and Tom, conspire above them in the middle ground of the page, oblivious to the children's presence below them. Pinkney's arrangement of space silently communicates what remains unsaid: this is not a white person's story. Though the whites' higher position on the page alludes to their superior social status, by making them the focal point instead of the focalizers, Pinkney ensures that they remain objects of the reader's and the Logans' silent but steady gaze. The men's jowly faces are nearly physically indistinct from one another. Their bodies are only partially visible, from their upper waists up, and what is visible appears small and cramped. These details, along with their off-centered placement and the fact that the men are permitted less visual space on the page, all imply a relative lack of narrative authority to the children who lay in wait, fully figured, below. Ironically, though Andersen and Tom have painted the letter X on each of the tree trunks to mark them as future lumber, it is *their* "trunks," or upper bodies, in this image that have been truncated.

And, yet, even if the illustration literally foregrounds the Logan children's perspectives, it also accentuates their vulnerability. Pinkney's style here is scratchy, sketchy, and full of movement. Though he will later become known for his sweeping watercolor adaptations of folktales like *John Henry* (1994) and *The Lion and the Mouse* (2009), which garnered a Caldecott Honor and a Caldecott Medal, respectively, in this earlier work, he relies more (though not exclusively) on the simple pencil, which he uses to effect tension and confusion in an otherwise still moment. Notably, when taking in the whole of the composition, the viewer observes that not all of the exes on the trees in fact depict an "X"—the one to the far right appears to be an "N." The fine pencil lines that signify painter's strokes do not crisscross in the middle, as would an X; instead, Tom seems to have used *three* swipes of his painter's brush. It's a radical, and I would say subversive, artistic choice to allude to the N-word (for it is only an *N* here) in an illustrated book for children. Yet, as Taylor indicates through the whites' dialogue, it's a mistake to think that even children are safe from racists' cruelty:

> "You mark them all down here?" one of the men asked.
> "Not the younger ones, Mr. Andersen."
> "We might need them, too," said Mr. Andersen, counting the X's. "But don't worry 'bout marking them now, Tom. We'll get them later. . . ." (*Song* 19–22)

In Andersen's view, it is not enough to cut down trees that have grown to maturity; he decides that, regardless of whether or not they will turn a profit, he "might need" even the saplings. However, his callous attitude is not exclusive to profiteers; it is common among all who see life on earth in terms of hierarchy. The counterpoint between words and image makes it uncommon, and disturbing, as it exposes the children and the trees' mutual danger. Though "the younger ones" in Taylor's text refer to saplings, Pinkney's art emphasizes the younger ones who lay hiding in the forest.

Whereas the first double spread depicts the children hiding in the foreground, the second reveals that, with the trees cut down, there is no place left for them to hide. In place of where the Logan children lay in the earlier image, there now appears a graveyard of jagged stumps (see fig. 3). Again, Pinkney plays with spatial composition and perspective to increase the viewer's discomfort. Cassie and her mother Mary stare blankly out over the scene of destruction. Their bodies are small, taking up less than an eighth of a single page. Previously, Andersen and Tom seemed crammed into the picture; now, the Logans are the ones who are closed in. Diagonally leaning trees frame their figures, signifying the danger their family faces. If, as picturebook artist Molly Bang determines, diagonal lines in an illustration create tension (7), the Logans are in a precarious situation indeed. Their faces are too far away, however, to determine whether their expressions are exacting sympathy from the reader or assigning blame; I would venture to say they are accomplishing both. Cassie's wrists, crossed so that her entire body assumes the posture of an X, remind the reader that she could be next—but, as it did for Malcolm X, the crisscrossed signifier may also indicate defiance, a refusal to acquiesce to whites' demands despite evident, overwhelming danger.

"THE USES OF ANGER"

In a keynote address delivered at the National Women's Studies Association Conference in 1981, Audre Lorde declared, "Any discussion among women about racism must include the recognition and the use of anger" (8). In contrast to guilt, which she calls "just another name for impotence ... a device to protect ignorance," or hatred, whose "object is death and destruction," anger serves a practical purpose. "Anger is a grief of distortions between peers," Lorde writes, "and its object is change" (8). I see this dialectic at work in *Song*. It is a spare text, often overshadowed by Taylor's vast oeuvre, but at its heart it is also an *angry* text, a tale of grief, a hymn for change. With the rise of the Black Lives Matter movement, *Song* reminds me, a white reader, to recognize how that anger manifests in conspicuously silent ways, particularly in children's literature, to act as a catalyst for racial and environmental justice.

Ecocriticism works to complicate, enervate, or otherwise question the authority of a predominantly verbal text. *Song* invites this questioning through form—that is, it is a book intended to appeal to children. Just as Pinkney makes clear the stakes of the Logans' situation through visual cues, Taylor reveals her anger in telling language that draws readers' attention to what is *not* being said. Taylor is writing for not one but at least two intended audiences. As historical fiction for children, *Song* appeals to a younger audience who are theoretically less experienced with racism and American history, but it also indirectly addresses adults who will evaluate literature for its truthfulness before distributing it to child readers. Taylor's choice to narrate the story through the eyes of an eight-year-old, speaking in a reflective past tense, evinces this dual address quite clearly. Cassie Logan is a child character; therefore, her indignant, then heartbroken, reaction to the trees' destruction reflects her protectiveness of her friends and her regard for their feelings, rather than the sole fear of being threatened by a white man. Adult readers, on the other hand, will recognize the threatening subtext. Nowhere does *Song* use the word "lynched," but it emphatically gestures toward this reality several times through the character of Andersen. Although Andersen does not ever state explicitly that he will lynch David, he insinuates as much when he tells the Logan women, his mother Big Ma and his wife Mary, that if David refuses his offer, he "'could possibly have . . . an accident,'" to which Mary replies: "'In Mississippi, black men do not have accidents'" (25; ellipsis in original). Taylor's deployment of ellipses and the subjunctive ("*could possibly*") evinces narrative restraint: the specifics of Andersen's threat are left off the page but nonetheless heard. Yet the ellipsis also makes room for the interruption of what Hartman calls "black noise" (12), the cries of pain and fury that silently disrupt and in *Song* eventually usurp the dominant white narrative of black subjection.

As the body count of black lives, young and old, wasted by police in the United States continues to rise, so does our culture's need to recognize and utilize anger in art. In the Black Arts Movement of the 1960s, anger was a fundamental quality of African American literature, and, as Michelle H. Martin determines in her timely study of African American picturebooks, *Brown Gold*, anger persists in children's literature today where it continues to serve "the underlying purpose of radicalizing or destroying the Western aesthetic" (73). Not unlike the song "Strange Fruit," *Song of the Trees* works to deconstruct the "[p]astoral scene of the gallant South."[12] The historical setting of the novella, rural Mississippi, and its centering of African American children's experience serves as a painful reminder of at least one tragedy to come, the murder of fourteen-year-old Emmett Till, who is explicitly mentioned in Taylor's final novel, *All the Days Past, All the Days to Come*. In this earlier work, Cassie's crossing her arms, almost in solidarity with the fallen trees, visually reminds readers that Till died in the woods in the tiny town of Money, Mississippi, in 1955 at the hands of two white men who tortured him before throwing his body, weighed down by a cotton gin fan that they tied around his neck with barbed wire, into the Tallahatchie River. These are facts of which Pinkney (who was born in 1939 and who can remember[13] encountering the horrifying news story while living in segregated Philadelphia) and Taylor (who was born in Jackson, Mississippi, in 1943 but whose family moved to Toledo, Ohio, to escape racial violence shortly after her birth) would most assuredly be aware. It is therefore unsurprising that Till's murder would seep into *Song* as a subtext—even if it is not apparent to readers more familiar with the all-white pastoral scenes depicted in children's books like Frances Hodgson Burnett's *The Secret Garden* (1911) or E. B. White's *Charlotte's Web* (1952).

Nature, or more specifically the pastoral (i.e., the depiction of wooded areas, tranquil spaces away from urban centers, hiking trails and swimming holes, green parks, and overgrown gardens) in children's literature commonly signifies the presence of healing and goodness. Yet the open enjoyment of the outdoors remains the special province of white people, both in terms of literary representation and material reality.[14] Although we may not commonly think of Emmett Till's murder, let alone the 581 lynchings on record[15] in Mississippi from 1882–1968, as environmental injustices, the commonplace practice of whites "stringing up" human beings from trees are indeed crimes that took place *in nature* and have continually functioned as a threat to people of color. In her autobiographical essay "Black Women and the Wilderness," Evelyn C. White confesses how her fear of the outdoors has prevented her from moving outside the city:

> Each house-hunting trip I have made to the countryside has been fraught with emotions: elation at the prospect of living closer to nature and a sense of absolute doom about what might befall me in the backwoods. My genetic memory of ancestors hunted down and preyed upon in rural settings counters my fervent hopes of finding peace in the wilderness. Instead of the solace and comfort I seek, I imagine myself in the country as my forebears were—exposed, vulnerable, and unprotected—a target of cruelty and hate. (284)

With great resolve, White does eventually become less fearful of enjoying the outdoors (286). Even so, it is necessary that we read *Song* in the terrifying historical context that White first identifies if we are to feel the force of Taylor's work. The loss of the trees on the Logans' land is symptomatic of the long, violent history of whites' cruelty towards African Americans. As an environmental justice text, *Song* summons intervention: it reveals slavery and its afterlives as ongoing forms of environmental racism, and it revises the all-white pastoral narrative through its depiction of the Logans, who take great pleasure in nature and, in the case of Cassie and David, see their lives as interdependent with the trees on their land.

Still, Taylor neither ignores the real dangers an African American family might face when challenging whites' authority nor consoles readers with wish fulfillment by ending her story with the Logans triumphing over Andersen and the lumbermen without consequence. Despite the Biblical significance of David Logan's name, *Song* is no David-and-Goliath tale, and Cassie's observation of the forest's devastation indicates as much: "On the ground lay countless trees. Trees that had once been such strong, tall things. So strong that I could fling my arms partially around one of them and feel safe and secure" (31). Cassie's mourning certainly reflects her sadness at having lost her companions, but her personification of the trees extends her grief to those who lived, and died at whites' hands, before her. She says that the trees are "old":

> So old that Indians had once built fires at their feet and had sung happy songs of happy days. So old, they had hidden fleeing black men in the night and listened to their sad tales of a foreign land.
> ...
> Those trees that remained standing were like defeated warriors mourning their fallen dead. But soon they, too, would fall, for the white X's had been placed on nearly every one. (31–34)

White environmentalism unwittingly reaffirms environmental racism whenever it exclusively mourns the loss of wilderness, animals, and land without mentioning how human beings are also affected. *Song* reroots readers' sympathies so that we understand how Andersen's decision to cut down the trees emblematizes white disregard for brown and black people's survival. The repetition of "old" in this passage impresses upon the reader the scale of Andersen's destruction. With each white X, he annihilates a being that has stood witness to generations of human life.

Cassie listens to the trees because she understands them as her friends. David goes a step further in that he risks his life to save theirs. Yet it is important to note that David's reaction to Andersen's callousness, while justified, is still somewhat anthropocentric. When David returns home from Louisiana, he and Stacey set dynamite throughout the forest. Then, when Andersen and the lumbermen arrive, David—thinking he is alone—greets them with his hands on the detonator. The lumbermen are horrified:

"You're bluffing, David," [Andersen] said. "You ain't gonna push that plunger."
"One thing you can't seem to understand, Andersen," Papa said, "is that a black man's always gotta be ready to die. And it don't make me any difference if I die today or tomorrow. Just as long as I die right." (Taylor, *Song* 43–44)

In planting the dynamite and confronting Andersen, David determines that his life and the trees' are equal. If they die, he dies with them. Yet, on the other hand, this suicide pact does not afford all of earth's species "the right to be free from ecological destruction" (PoCELS). The trees have not agreed to this bargain, and there may be other unintended consequences since Cassie and siblings lay hiding nearby, unbeknownst to David. And, as Pinkney's final illustration shows (see fig. 4), David's decision comes at an unbearably high cost—total annihilation. Though one may at first suppose that the visual association between the X on the tree's trunk and the X on Tom's overalls jointly mark them, and only them, as the casualties of this scene, Pinkney's use of scale communicates that the trees' destruction will affect them all, together. The figure that occupies the most space here is an enormous tree that stretches out of the frame. The tree dwarfs the human beings to its right, who are stacked one on top of the other to demonstrate their respective power over each other. At the top stands David, his hands on the plunger, then Andersen and Tom, and at the very bottom one of the lumbermen, an African American presumably hired to do the white man's dirty work. Pinkney's use of scale makes this visible hierarchy null and void. For, despite their number and comparative social status, the tree is larger than all of them put together; its gigantic presence emphasizes that the loss of its life will mark the loss of *all* of theirs.

CONCLUSION

Song of the Trees makes it clear that those burdened with environmental injustices must often make impossible choices. It is unconscionable that David must risk his, Andersen's, and his children's lives so that his adversary will finally listen. It is cruelly ironic that David jeopardizes the lives of the very trees he seeks to protect in order to save them both. And it is no wonder that Taylor refuses to end this *Song* on a consolatory note. "'Dear, dear old trees,'" David calls, "'will you ever sing again?'" (48). Cassie, like readers, listens hard for what the trees have to say: "I waited. But the trees gave no answer." But perhaps

Cassie is mistaken. Perhaps, as it was before, the trees' silence *is* the only answer they can muster. Or perhaps we still are not listening hard enough.

Taylor's text, when coupled with the effects of Pinkney's remarkable illustrations, compel readers to pay closer attention to the ways we demarcate boundaries between human and nature, subject and Other. What can we learn from a history that demarcates some human beings as more human, and therefore more deserving of land rights, than Others? If we rethink the boundaries between humans and other-than-human nature on a global scale, might we arrive at more equitable solutions in the face of climate change? And how might storytelling, in particular an illustrated book for children, help us to imagine and make space for the subjectivity of those who have not been heard?

There are no easy answers here. Yet, as a way to keep thinking, I offer this final comparison between *Song* and its more famous contemporary, *The Lorax* by Theodor Geisel (popularly known as Dr. Seuss), to provide a small example of the global, environmental costs of speaking for someone else. Putting Taylor's novella in conversation with Geisel's picturebook not only confirms their difference of perspective, but also how this difference (the former, an African American *Song* for environmental justice; the latter, a white cautionary tale for conservation) comes to bear on cultural understandings of environmentalism, and what counts as environmental action.

Geisel was first inspired to write *The Lorax* in 1969 while mournfully surveying the loss of the California coastline from his highrise art studio in La Jolla. Later, moved by the celebration of Earth Day in 1970, Geisel yearned to contribute something that would express his anger: "Everything God took years to put there, they are tearing down in a week-and-a-half," he said (qtd. in Jones 355). However, it wasn't until he and his wife took a safari trip to Kenya, and he was surveying a herd of elephants from the particular vantage point of their resort's swimming pool, that the book took shape. The narrative Geisel crafted was that of a repentant entrepreneur, the Onceler, who chops down Truffula trees for profit until he realizes, much too late, that he has done irreparable damage.

I recount the backstory of *The Lorax* here to emphasize the differences in Geisel and Taylor's environmentalism. Geisel, working in his studio, relaxing in a swimming pool in Kenya, is not unlike the enterprising Onceler of the tale who stands a good distance apart from the wreckage—they are affected, surely, but not threatened. And, as the Onceler's cautionary refrain at the end of *The Lorax* implies, neither of them desires to get any closer, instead pushing responsibility onto the (default) white boy in the text: "UNLESS someone like you / cares a whole awful lot, / nothing is going to get better. / It's not" (Geisel; emphasis in original). In the early twenty-first century, when the United States is beginning to recognize the effects of climate change (which have been felt elsewhere in poorer nations for quite some time), it is time to reevaluate who this "you" is; and the individual responsibility you—or, more accurately, I— bear as we evaluate and distribute environmentalist messages for the young, those who will inherit the earth in the state we leave it.

To that end, it is also time to reevaluate what environmental writing for children looks and sounds like. Although the Onceler's dictum is not wrong, per se, it betrays the top-down colonialist viewpoint that pervades and, I would argue, inspired the story. In contrast, *Song* retells a story of displacement from the point of view of those who were and are actually displaced (the Logan family, specifically Cassie and David Logan, and by extension Mildred Taylor, her father, and their family), first through the slave trade, then Jim Crow laws, and today with zoning laws and discriminatory housing practices. Whereas the Onceler dictates orders to a nameless "you"—"You're in charge of the last of the Truffula Seeds," he says, tossing the seed down from his highrise Lerkim to the open arms of a white boy—together Cassie and David occupy the "you" and transform it into an "we," two people who can and in fact have effected change. They take up this environmental responsibility, however imperfectly, when they regard the trees' lives as important, in and of themselves. Still, perhaps the most significant difference between *The Lorax* and *Song* is their individual use of narrative authority. It is no surprise that in Geisel's text, the Onceler gets the last word, for he has been lecturing the listener for nearly the entire book. But in Taylor's novella, which troubles the ways we perceive knowledge, the last word (or, more accurately, the lack thereof) goes to the trees, who remain silent in Cassie's narration of events: "I waited. But the trees gave no answer" (48). Indeed, their quiet compels us to reevaluate who speaks for whom.

In *Days*, the final installment of the Logan sequence, an adult Cassie returns to Mississippi after her father's death to continue fighting for civil rights, even though it would be much easier to return north with her brothers. While Cassie sits, watching the trees' branches "swaying like giant green fingers strumming at a guitar," she quietly reflects upon the work she's done, and the work still to be done: "and I murmured, 'Dear, dear old trees . . . dear old trees. . . .' There was so much, so much I wanted to say, and that's all I could think to say" (481). With these words, Taylor concludes her final novel as she did with *Song*, published nearly fifty years earlier: on a discordant note, or what Hartman calls the productive tension that "embod[ies] life in words and at the same time respect[s] what we cannot know" (Hartman 3). There are other silences that compel us to listen. Even if we never hear them, it is only by listening for them that we will attain the connection and stability so desperately needed to survive together.

APPENDIX

Fig. 9.1. Back and front cover from *Song of the Trees* by Mildred Taylor, illustrated by Jerry Pinkney. Dial Press, 1975.

Fig. 9.2. "We knew to be silent." *Song of the Trees* by Mildred Taylor, illustrated by Jerry Pinkney. Dial Press, 1975, pp. 20–21.

Fig. 9.3. "On the ground lay countless trees." *Song of the Trees* by Mildred Taylor, illustrated by Jerry Pinkney. Dial Press, 1975, pp. 32–33.

Fig. 9.4. "The black box was now set." *Song of the Trees* by Mildred Taylor, illustrated by Jerry Pinkney. Dial Press, 1975, p. 47.

NOTES

1. Given that there is much debate over whether to capitalize the word black when referring to people and culture, my choice is to follow the lead of the authors I cite so as not to misrepresent their views. Hartman uses the lowercase, as does Taylor in *Song of the Trees*. However, Taylor has elsewhere referred to the Logans as an African American family, so I defer to this descriptor when discussing the Logans specifically (even though the family has Native American ancestors as well). I capitalize Blackness to emphasize shared (though diverse) experience amongst one group of people of color or to refer to specific political movements (e.g., Black Lives Matter). As a white person, I feel comfortable using the lowercase (white) as an adjective and the capital (Whiteness) for the noun.

2. Michelle Martin rightly concludes that Chris Crowe's assessment of Taylor's work might be representative, but it is not authoritative. His book-length study *Presenting Mildred Taylor* is only surface level, potentially useful for readers who have little familiarity with her work or its historical context, but offers "little of value" for those looking for a deeper understanding (Martin, "*Presenting Mildred Taylor*" 56–57).

3. Jebediah Purdy observes that whites hold the vast majority of leadership positions in national environmental organizations, and most major environmental regulations, like the Clean Air Act and the Clean Water Act, were penned with white priorities in mind "with no attention to the unequal vulnerability of poor and minority groups."

4. Paul-Edward's maternal grandfather, named Kanati, belonged to the Nation. At one point in a private conversation between him and his father, Paul-Edward remarks that his father's land "'belonged to his [Kanati's] people first,'" to which his father replies, "'Maybe that's where you get part of your love for the land'" (Taylor, *Land* 42).

5. The two white boys, Ed-Rose and Charlie Simms, throw the dismembered corpses of a possum, a raccoon, and a skunk down the Logans' well, illustrating their utter disregard for any life, human or other-than-human, besides their own. Their father, Old Man McCalister, forces them to retrieve the parts while the Logans and several other community members watch. David (then a child and the narrator of *Well*) remarks, "Seeing those parts, all of us standing there knew that Ed-Rose and Charlie hadn't taken any chances about spoiling our well. They hadn't just thrown dead animals down there in the night; they'd hacked them up before they did" (Taylor, *Well* 92).

6. See also Susan Jaye Dauer's essay, "Cartoons and Contamination: How the Multinational Kids Help Captain Planet Save Gaia" from *Wild Things* (254–66).

7. The medicinal uses of the sap from the sweet gum tree have been commonly known for thousands of years. When researching this article, I found numerous popular sources that confirmed what my grandfather (who farmed in Gum Pond, Mississippi, an area named for its preponderance of gum trees) had told me on our walks through the woods. However, I was unaware of the current medical applications of the tree, which include inhibiting the H1N1 virus (swine flu) by extracting shikimic acid from the seed pods. See the 2015 study performed by Lingbeck et al.

8. See LaDuke's *All Our Relations: Native Struggles for Land and Life* and Tinker's article "The Stones Shall Cry Out: Consciousness, Rocks, and Indians," published in the *Wicazo Sa Review*, vol. 19, no. 2, 2004, pp. 105–25.

9. The Hindi word *chipko* means "to hug" or "to cling to." In the first Chipko protest in 1973, the villagers of Mandal quite literally deployed tree-hugging to prevent a sports manufacturing

company from industrial logging on their land—a practice that, in addition to depleting the village of local resources and threatening a self-sustaining agroecological system, weakens naturally occurring protection against monsoon flooding. When the villagers (mostly women) refused to leave the forest after several days of protests, the loggers were forced to retreat.

10. My analysis of how Taylor's text works in relation to illustrations is perhaps unique to *Song* since her characterization as a narrator alters as she ages in the Logan Family Saga. While Cassie's narration here illustrates her inexperience with racism, her narration in *Thunder* is that of an adult looking back and is therefore more worldly and retrospective. In any case, Taylor's depiction of Cassie as naïve in *Song of the Trees* is not a shortcoming but a vital component of the dialogic nature of the text. For further discussion of how youthful narration works in Taylor's work and others, see Jani Barker's articles, "Racial Identification and Audience in *Roll of Thunder, Hear My Cry* and *The Watsons Go to Birmingham–1963*" (2010) and "Naive Narrators and Double Narratives of Racially Motivated Violence in the Fiction of Christopher Paul Curtis" (2013).

11. See also Anthony L. Manna's study, "Reading Jerry Pinkney Reading" (1991), in which Manna elaborates upon the theatrical qualities of Pinkney's illustration.

12. The song *Strange Fruit* juxtaposes images of a rustic pastoral with poplar trees, magnolia, and a "southern breeze" with the gruesome scene of a lynching: "Southern trees bear a strange fruit / Blood on the leaves and blood at the root . . . Pastoral scene of the gallant South / The bulging eyes and the twisted mouth." The song, made famous by Billie Holiday and Nina Simone, was written by a Jewish man, Aber Meeropol. A lover of trees and of people, Meeropol published the song under the pseudonym Lewis Allan (the names of his two stillborn sons) after seeing a photograph of a lynching. Incidentally, he would later adopt Robert and Michael Rosenberg, the children of Ethel and Julius Rosenberg, who were executed under McCarthyism, after meeting the boys at W. E. B. Du Bois's house. See Blair.

13. See Pinkney, "My Father's Unknowing Gift" (2016).

14. Using examples as varied as James Fenimore Cooper's Leatherstocking novels to the murder of Emmett Till, Mei Mei Evans determines that "heterosexual white manhood" has been constructed as the American social identity that "naturally" belongs in and is lord over nature (183). Michelle Martin and J. Elizabeth Mills also find that there is a dominant white presence in children's picturebooks about enjoying the outdoors. In a paper for 2019 Children's Literature Association Conference, Martin and Mills were only able to locate four picturebooks that included "positive representations of Black children experiencing wildness in wooded and curated wild spaces" (9).

15. See NAACP, "History of Lynchings," recounted at www.naacp.org/history-of-lynchings/.

WORKS CITED

Ammons, Elizabeth, and Modhumita Roy, editors. *Sharing the Earth: An International Environmental Justice Reader*. U Georgia P, 2015.

Bang, Molly. *Picture This: Perception and Composition*. Little, Brown, 1991.

Barker, Jani. "Naive Narrators and Double Narratives of Racially Motivated Violence in the Historical Fiction of Christopher Paul Curtis." *Children's Literature*, vol. 41, 2013, pp. 172–203.

Barker, Jani. "Racial Identification and Audience in *Roll of Thunder, Hear My Cry* and *The Watsons Go to Birmingham—1963.*" *Children's Literature in Education*, vol. 41, no. 2, 2010, pp. 118–45.

Blair, Elizabeth. "The Strange Story of the Man Behind 'Strange Fruit.'" *Morning Edition* from NPR, Sept. 5, 2012. https://www.npr.org/2012/09/05/158933012/the-strange-story-of-the-man-behind-strange-fruit.

Bullard, Robert D., editor. *Confronting Environmental Racism: Voices from the Grassroots*. South End Press, 1993.

Chesnutt, Charles. "Po' Sandy." *Sharing the Earth: An International Environmental Justice Reader*. Ammons and Roy, pp. 61–68.

Crowe, Chris, and Jace Brown. "*Roll of Thunder, Hear My Cry*: Disrupting the 'All-White World of Children's Books.'" *Critical Explorations of Young Adult Literature: Identifying and Critiquing the Canon*, edited by Victor Malo-Juvera and Crag Hill, e-book, Routledge, 2019.

Dauer, Susan Jane. "Cartoons and Contamination: How the Multinational Kids Help Captain Planet Save Gaia." *Wild Things: Children's Culture and Ecocriticism*, edited by Sidney I. Dobrin and Kenneth B. Kidd, Wayne State UP, 2004, pp. 254–66.

Evans, Mei Mei. "Nature and Environmental Justice." *The Environmental Justice Reader: Politics, Poetics, and Pedagogy*, edited by Joni Adamson et al., U Arizona P, 2002, pp. 181–93.

Gannon, Susan R. "The Illustrator as Interpreter: N. C. Wyeth's Illustrations for the Adventure Novels of Robert Louis Stevenson." *Children's Literature*, vol. 19, 1991, pp. 90–106. Project MUSE, doi:10.1353/chl.0.0243.

Geisel, Theodor. *The Lorax*. Random House, 1971.

Hartman, Saidiya. "Venus in Two Acts." *small axe*, vol. 12, no. 2, 2008, pp. 1–14. Project MUSE, https://muse.jhu.edu/article/241115.

Jones, Brian Jay. *Becoming Dr. Seuss: Theodor Geisel and the Making of an American Imagination*. Dutton, 2019.

LaDuke, Winona. *All Our Relatives: Native Struggles for Land and Life*. South End Press, 1999.

Lingbeck, Jody M., et al. "Sweetgum: An Ancient Source of Beneficial Compounds with Modern Benefits." *Pharmacognosy Review*, vol. 9, no. 17, 2015, pp. 1–11. PubMed, https://www.ncbi.nlm.nih.gov/pmc/articles/PMC4441155/?fbclid=IwAR1YHqZfVGAQMK6EZ9w53B6DqxoKcdnESXuY2Ug6jchWHfNz9knl74hD010.

Lorde, Audrey. "The Uses of Anger." *Women's Studies Quarterly*, vol. 9, no. 3, 1981, pp. 7–10, https://academicworks.cuny.edu/wsq/509.

Manna, Anthony L. "Reading Jerry Pinkney Reading." *Children's Literature Association Quarterly*, vol. 16, no. 4, 1991, pp. 269–75.

Martin, Michelle. *Brown Gold: Milestones of African-American Children's Picture Books, 1845–2002*. Routledge, 2004.

Martin, Michelle. "*Presenting Mildred Taylor*." Review of *Presenting Mildred Taylor* by Chris Crowe. *Children's Literature Association Quarterly*, vol. 26, no. 1, 2001, pp. 55–57.

Martin, Michelle, and J. Elizabeth Mills. "Welcoming Black Children into Literary Wildscapes: Wildness in African American Children's Picture Books." Children's Literature Association Conference, June 13–15, 2019, The Westin Indianapolis, Indianapolis, IN. Conference paper.

NAACP. "History of Lynchings." *NAACP*, www.naacp.org/history-of-lynchings.

Osa, Osayimwense. "Africanism in African American Children's Literature: Mildred Taylor's *Song of the Trees* and *The Friendship*, and Eleanora Tate's *The Secret of Gumbo Grove*."

Obsidian III, vol. 3, no. 1, 2001, pp. 89–99. *Gale Literature Resource Center*, https://link.gale.com/apps/doc/A205734631/LitRC?u=mlin_m_tufts&sid=LitRC&xid=58f02bb7.

People of Color Environmental Leadership Summit. "Principles of Environmental Justice." Ammons and Roy, pp. 279–80.

Pinkney, Jerry. "The Artist at Work: Characters Interacting with the Viewer." *The Horn Book Magazine*, vol. 67, no. 2, Mar./Apr. 1991, pp. 171–79.

Pinkney, Jerry. "My Father's Unknowing Gift: A Safe Place for a Budding Artist." *Safe Kids Stories*, July 13, 2016. https://safekidsstories.com/my-fathers-unknowing-gift-ae1248698179#.pgwo5swze.

Purdy, Jebediah. "Environmentalism's Racist History." *The New Yorker*, Aug. 13, 2015, https://www.newyorker.com/news/news-desk/environmentalisms-racist-history.

Sturgeon, Noël. "'The Power is Yours, Planeteers!' Race, Gender, and Sexuality in Children's Environmental Popular Culture." *New Perspectives on Environmental Justice: Gender, Sexuality, and Activism*, edited by Rachel Stein. Rutgers UP, 2004, pp. 262–76.

Taylor, Mildred D. *All the Days Past, All the Days to Come*. Viking, 2020.

Taylor, Mildred D. *The Land*. Phyllis Fogelman Books, 2001.

Taylor, Mildred D. *Song of the Trees*. Illus. Jerry Pinkney. Dial Press, 1975.

Taylor, Mildred D. "Tapped on the Shoulder." *World Literature Today*, vol. 88, no. 5, Sept. 1, 2014, pp. 60–61. *Gale Academic Onefile*, https://link.gale.com/apps/doc/A381147987/AONE?u=mlin_m_tufts&sid=AONE&xid=acaead86.

Taylor, Mildred D. *The Well: David's Story*. Dial Press, 1995.

Tinker, George "Tink." "The Stones Shall Cry Out: Consciousness, Rocks, and Indians." *Wicazo Sa Review*, vol. 19, no. 2, 2004, pp. 105–25.

White, Evelyn C. "Black Women and the Wilderness." *Names We Call Home: Autobiography on Racial Identity*, edited by Becky W. Thompson and Sangeeta Tyagi, Routledge, 1996, pp. 283–86.

Contested Space
The Black Agrarian Tradition in Mildred D. Taylor's *The Land*

Emily Cardinali Cormier

Mildred D. Taylor's novel *The Land* (2001) offers readers a glimpse into the complicated world of farming and land ownership for Black families during Reconstruction. It also gives voice to the great quietness that characterizes writing on Black Agrarianism in ecocriticism, despite ecocritical attention to other forms of agrarianism. Taylor's consistent and detailed interest in agrarian community should have become a natural choice for New Agrarian scholarship since the publication date of *Land* coincided with the increased interest in agriculture represented in literature, yet scholarship has been slow to emerge. While New Agrarians have not written about the novel, Karen Chandler offers a meaningful analysis of *Land* in *Tending to the Past: Selfhood and Culture in Children's Narratives about Slavery and Freedom* (2024), where she argues that Paul-Edward can be read as a Black Adam whose relationship with the land is deeply connected to his community and the broader economies of the South (Mississippi, specifically) during Reconstruction; she also identifies Paul-Edward as a protagonist who can facilitate readers' understanding of the problematic nature of Jeffersonian agrarianism and the cultural mythology around agrarian ideals (180, 182). Chandler's detailed reading offers insight into the interplay of the business relationships Paul-Edward Logan forms (as carpenter, laborer, and landowner) and personal relationships, such as his friendship with Mitchell and his marriage to Caroline. Importantly, Chandler elucidates how these relationships are affected by racism and white supremacy. As Chandler closes her argument, she notes that Paul-Edward mixes a reverence for the land with a ready willingness to log, farm, and otherwise use land resources to provide for and protect their family and community (191). While Chandler acknowledges that there is no "sustainable farming" plan set forth in the novel, she emphasizes the "caretaker" role of the Logan family (191). I suggest that one way of conceptualizing this role is to consider Paul-Edward as not only Black Adam, but also Black Agrarian.

Black Agrarianism has rarely been broached by scholars of New Agrarianism, but the novel is important and calls for more critical discourse in this area. Much of the scholarship on New Agrarianism in the early 2000s acknowledged the manifesto published in 1930 titled *I'll Take My Stand: The South and the Agrarian Tradition*. The twelve authors of the collection of essays were reacting to attacks on Southern culture; however, their nostalgic reaction embraced and romanticized the Old South, ignoring slavery, among other things. While New Agrarianism tries to distance itself from the manifesto, it ignores the underlying racism implicit in that collection, rather than taking up a true examination of Black Agrarian contributions to the culture and farming of the South, or to even recognize that Black Agrarianism existed at all. As Janet Fiskio aptly points out, "The New Agrarianism . . . has tended to elide racialized disparities in its analysis of the problems of contemporary agriculture" (304). In this chapter, I read *Land* as a text that offers readers an opportunity to understand the "racialized disparities" to which Fiskio refers.

New Agrarians are scholars, critics, writers, and sometimes farmers who promote the notion that the relationship between humans and the soil forms the basis for societal, community, and even interpersonal relationships. They embrace the idea that agriculture—what humans do to make the land productive—to some extent dictates culture. While there are many types of agrarianism, all tackle the question of how farming influences culture, politics, community, and individual character. All lay some claim to Thomas Jefferson's notion that farming and farm labor breed virtue, character, and health—the ideal making of a good citizen. But, whose labor? Whose character? Indeed, whose farm and on whose land? And, who was protected and supported by local and federal governments and agencies in their endeavor for centuries of American farming, and in the present moment? How these questions are answered in a large way determines how one situates oneself within agrarianism. And, as one might imagine, a highly racialized picture emerges.

Black Agrarianism typically distinguishes itself from other forms of agrarianism because of its link to civil rights and a more collective approach to the economic health and stability of a community. Katrina Quisumbing King et al.'s article "Black Agrarianism: The Significance of African American Landownership in the Rural South" recognizes that Black Agrarianism's "distinctive positive feature is an emancipatory thrust, born out of the history of subjugation experienced by Black people" (691). As such, the authors note that "Black agrarianism is a vision of racialized freedom, not 'liberty' predicated on the exploitation of others, as in aristocratic agrarianism, nor on individual freedom from wage labor, as in democratic agrarianism. It is an assertion of civil and political rights, derived from opposition to white supremacy" (696). This doesn't mean that there are no shared agrarian ideals between agrarians in a predominantly white tradition and Black Agrarians, but white supremacy has influenced and continues to influence land ownership so Black Agrarianism must be predicated on civil rights and equality, which have not been guaranteed. Thus, "while democratic agrarianism focuses on individual freedom, the Black tradition emphasizes the legal, political, and economic *collective* conditions required for having a relationship to the land" (King et al. 695). Mildred Taylor's novels offer a comprehensive literary expression of this Black Agrarian tradition.

Black Agrarianism has received only a scant mention in the literature on agrarianism. It seems that when Black labor is mentioned in the context of many agrarianisms, it is to acknowledge (and sometimes very cursorily) some debt to the millions of enslaved Black Americans who built this country and worked for landowning (and/or slaveholding) white farmers. Little attention is paid to Black Agrarians—landowning, farming families who see land ownership as a critical part of their security and survival. But, writing on Black Agrarians is emerging, and I argue that the stories of Black landowning farmers—particularly for children and young adults—are critical to the conversation on African American history, literature, and identity formation of young people. As Debra A. Reid points out in her introduction to *Beyond Forty Acres and a Mule: African American Landowning Families since Reconstruction*: "Relatively few black farmers became landowners, but if scholars assume that all black farmers were sharecroppers then they accept 'the basic logic/assumption of the postbellum white power structure'—that all blacks had been slaves; that all blacks were laborers—and scholars will continue to 'see the landowners as anomalies'" (7). Reid then calls for increased attention to "black landowning farm families" so that scholarship is "no longer anomalous" but "mainstream" (7). While Reid, as a historian, has a slightly different project, as a scholar of literature, I take up this invitation to increase the visibility of Black landowning families in my discipline where there have been similar gaps. I suggest, though, that scholars of children's and young adult literature may be slightly ahead of the curve due to their familiarity with the Logan family from Mildred Taylor's (now canonical) *Roll of Thunder, Hear my Cry* (1976).[1] And while this book has received the most attention by readers and critics alike, Taylor's *Land* offers the crucial backstory to how the Logan family became landowners decades earlier.

What follows is my effort to bring attention to the important ecocritical and political value of *Land*, and to bring more attention to the importance of Black Agrarianism as a distinct and meaningful kind of agrarianism. As Sonya Postmentier writes in her introduction to *Cultivation and Catastrophe: The Lyric Ecology of Modern Black Literature*: "the imperative to account for environmental experience, far from being a curious nostalgic throwback to the plantation, forms one basis for black modernity in the twentieth century" (3). In *Land*, Taylor crafts a meaningful relationship between her protagonist, Paul, and the land he loves, while showing that Paul's biracial identity complicates his attitudes toward the land. It is important to recognize that this is an intentionally fostered relationship that also has a spiritual basis; this underscores the idea that a genuine relationship with the soil is possible, despite a vexed history with agriculture. Taylor shows farming to be a choice for Paul, not a default. I argue that it is critically important for readers to consider that nostalgia, so heavily used in children's farm novels, is not a driving force in Taylor's representation of early Black Agrarianism. Instead, Taylor asks us to question a single-minded understanding of the very word "nostalgia" since she selectively employs aspects of longing associated with nostalgia, which is a way of fomenting a renewed interest in a place for, in Taylor's own words, "future generations" (375). Using Svetlana Boym's framework of "restorative" and "reflective" nostalgia, I argue that Taylor works against a nostalgia that presents an idealized version of the agrarian past, but nevertheless employs a kind of nostalgia when giving renewed attention to the figure of the Black Agrarian in the collective memory to remind readers of the breadth of experience that is a part of African American history.

CONNECTING WITH THE LAND

While *The Land* is one of the most recent of Taylor's works, its setting is chronologically the oldest, taking place shortly after the US Civil War. This novel not only sets the stage for understanding the history of the Logan family land, but it also does important work in terms of shaping model members of agrarian communities and showing that there is a mutually constitutive relationship between members of the Logan family and the land they own. Early on, we are given details about Paul's deep connection with his father's land: "I loved my daddy's land. In the beginning I always thought of it as my land, too. I knew every bit of the place. I knew every rise and knoll, every cave and watering place, every kind of plant and tree" (*Land* 35). The meditative gaze in this passage seems to foreshadow Paul's later experience when he first sees the land he would later own: "Gazing from the slope where I sat beside the rock, I felt I was sitting where God Himself must have once sat and been pleased with Himself" (159). Taylor uses the extended gaze to highlight Paul's spiritual connection with the land. It is not love alone that ties Paul to the land, but also a sense that there is something beyond the scope of human understanding pulling him to the land. It is no coincidence that this spot later becomes the "praying rock" (350) where Mitchell is buried, and Paul and Caroline decide to get married. While early in the narrative, the reader doesn't get a sense of Paul Logan as a man who works the land, the reader certainly understands his intimate knowledge of the land and his sense of ownership. Early in his childhood, there is "love" expressed for the land, in addition to a sense of entitlement ("my land") even though Paul as adult narrator knows that the land was not and never would be his own. Paul's love for the land is also clearly tied to his love for his father, which was uncomplicated from early in his childhood: "when I was a small boy, there seemed no one like him to me. I'm not ashamed to admit it. In those early days I adored my Daddy" (41). But, Paul's mother is African American, formerly enslaved by his white, landowning father, and while his father offered some level of support for Paul's mother and their children, Paul does not inherit family land from his father. But that first uncomplicated connection with the landscape is vital to our understanding of Paul; it is as if Taylor suggests that love of the land and desire for connection with the land come first, while the practicalities of land ownership follow. In other words, if one foments the desire for land and connectedness first, then figuring out how to bring that somewhat romanticized vision down to earth through acquiring and working the land will eventually follow.

In terms of an ecocritical reading of this novel, the landscape that the child Paul loves is a working landscape, "dotted with cows and horses grazing" (35). Paul is not especially drawn to pristine, untouched nature, although the image he calls up is admittedly romanticized. He's enamored of domesticated nature and the signs of domesticity, albeit a domesticity from which his race excludes him, noting to himself that his favorite view includes "a hillside that overlooked the pasture and my daddy's house." He is drawn to an agrarian landscape. Later, when Paul happens upon the land he would later buy, it is tempting to read it as Edenic, or at least undomesticated. However, in the midst of the more high-flying descriptors of this parcel of land, Paul walks "into the forest along a cow trail laden with dung" (159), signaling that this land holds potential as farmland. Certainly, Paul longs to connect with the earth, and the connections he seeks are both spiritual and agricultural. Through these avenues, he uses the land to replicate the original relationship he had with his father, before he more fully understands that race divides his family in irrecoverable ways.

Paul wants to connect with the land, his family, and also his wider community. Strong agrarian community requires not only a tie to the land but also positive relationships with community members. This is complicated for Paul, whose natural intellectual bent has been given fodder for growth, since his father's race and class privilege afforded Paul an education denied to other members of his community. Despite the racism that Paul himself faces, his peers view him as a privileged outsider. When we first meet the novel's protagonist, he is "reading beside a creek on [his] daddy's land" (3), showing the reader his fervent desire to read. Paul mentions that he "was always reading anything [he] could get [his] hands on," noting, too, that his reading got him "into more trouble with some of the colored boys" (35). Earlier, we learn how Paul starts to build community with Mitchell, the son of a sharecropper who works on Paul's father's land, by sharing his ability to "read and write and figure" (16). Despite the fact that this novel takes place after emancipation (thus making the teaching legal), when Paul offers to share these skills with the wider group of sharecropping children, he faces the complexities of building community and teaching literacy skills in a racially charged situation. The children turn down Paul's offer with good reason; by using his father's power as a white landowner and his brothers' power as white children of a landowner, Paul has previously threatened the safety of the same children he offers to teach (10). In other words, Paul might represent some version of white supremacy to his peers because he has benefitted from a society in which adequate education is offered to white children but often denied to Black children. One can understand why the children would not trust him as a teacher: "We got our own schools now, and we wanted t' learn any of that stuff, we'd be goin' there. We'd hardly be takin' any teachin' from the likes of you. You with yo' white daddy" (36). If we understand agrarian community as something fostered by strong ties both to the land and within the community working the land, it is easy to see how difficult it is to forge such relationships when the power dynamics are so radically perverted by race, the history of slavery, and class-based privilege.

Paul cannot hope to create meaningful and trusting bonds within a community that allows some members to own hundreds or thousands of acres while preventing others from even owning the quarter acre around their home; and landowning is unambiguously tied to educational access. This is an excellent example of how the thrust of Black Agrarianism expands beyond the New Agrarian notion that people must forge meaningful relationships with the land they inhabit. While of course Black Agrarians are focused on creating a sustainable relationship with their soil, they have a more urgent need that is tied to the ability to own and cultivate land: access to equal education. Civil rights and agrarian ideology must go hand-in-hand for those who can't assume that they will be provided with appropriate educational opportunities. In interviews with Black landowners, King et al. report that "respondents said that land provides educational and political opportunities for their children" (691). As is evidenced in the interaction between Paul and his sharecropping peers, differences in educational opportunities exist for children based on race and landowning. Early on in *Land*, Taylor clearly acknowledges that a Black Agrarianism is inherently different from an agrarianism rooted in white supremacy.

Because of his father, Paul is implicated in the power of whiteness. However, it is not only Paul's father's whiteness that causes problems for Paul, but his status as a landowner compounds the problem, both with his peers and within himself. Essentially, his love for his father is so strongly tied to his love for the land that the two become inextricable. He sees firsthand that there is power in whiteness but also power in landownership. One is out of his control; the other he feels compelled to obtain. Paul longs for an uncomplicated relationship with the land he loves, and the white side of his family that he also loves. This is suggested in a passage early in the text in which Paul's father talks to him about the land:

> "You're much like me," he told me once. "When I was a boy, I loved to read and I loved horses. I loved this land too. My granddaddy had gotten it before I was born, back before the turn of the century, when there were plenty of Indians settled around here. There still were some here when I was a boy, and I got to know a few and they taught me a lot." (41)

This passage positions Edward Logan as seeing himself like his son, nearly placing Paul in the lineage of male inheritors but falling just short of doing so. Paul responds by pointing out that the land was not only stolen from Native Americans but stolen directly from his Native American grandfather: "This land ... it belonged to [Kanati] first" (42). Without even a nod to the unjust assumption of white ascendancy, Edward says "That's a fact. . . . Maybe that's where you get part of your love for the land" (42). Land ownership and inheritance happen in this community within a system that is thoroughly racist, sexist, and colonialist. Edward, being privileged in terms of both, simply says, "That's a fact." The ease of this statement and the ease with which Edward lays out such "fact[s]" to Paul points to the world of power to which Paul will never have access, and this is the world upon which most American agrarianisms are built. On the heels of this conversation, Paul comes to the full realization of how the racist social system in which the agrarian South is rooted will never allow him the entitlement to the land that he sees in his father. Paul's exclusion from inheritance and privilege with regards to the land are also exclusions from one side of his family, and one side of himself. Since Paul is just shy of twelve, his mother won't allow him to sit with his father's family at the table when guests are visiting. In anger, he storms out of the house, out of the kitchen where his mother has given him his meal and looks at the land: "I . . . leaned against a post and looked out across the backyard to my daddy's forest. I stared at that forest, the forest that had always seemed to be a part of me, and felt alienated from it, from it and everything that was my daddy's" (51). Here Paul feels "alienated from" something that "had always seemed to be a part" of himself. If Paul's relationship with the land is coupled with his relationship with his father's family, then his later longing to buy land can also be read as a longing for a time in his childhood before he fully grasped what it meant to have a fractured identity. In his relentless pursuit to buy land, we see Paul urgently attempting to sew together an identity rent by racism.

Private land ownership is one of the basic tenets of New Agrarianism, but as we see in *Land*, most pathways to land ownership are opened by status, privilege, and financial means. This circumstance happens to be one of the most confounding challenges for African Americans in a time and place where the humanity and dignity of Black people was held in such low regard as to make their signatures on a legal document worthless unless accompanied by the signature of a white male with some social status. The very concept of land ownership is a legal one, and Black people had no protection or status under the law during Reconstruction. Watching Paul work against nearly insurmountable odds, from his childhood desire to own land, to his ultimate status as a landowner, is like watching an agrarian everyman figure grow from child to adult. While the circumstances of his birth and family prevented him from easily obtaining land, the same circumstances provided him with some advantage when compared with other sharecroppers on his father's land. To wit, the money that ultimately allows Paul to buy the land comes from his mother, who perhaps because of her relationship with a white man (and despite the coercive circumstances that gave her no choice in the matter), had more money than her peers. Paul embodies all the characteristics (except for not being white) of the ideal agrarian man in a system where living up to the expectations of one's gender role translates to security and stability for one's family and community.

Paul Logan's brand of masculinity also challenges, or even collapses, binary gender roles that have long been a point of discussion for New Agrarian thinkers. Agrarianism has been criticized by feminists and ecofeminists for its adherence to traditional family roles and gendered divisions of labor by which women have been oppressed. Wendell Berry responds to critics of New Agrarianism, proposing that the modern economic system has created oppression for all people, not just women.[1] Berry points out that the modern "man" is tied into systems that render him unable to operate outside of an economy of money, modern infrastructure, and the conventional gender norms that put him in power (*Unsettling* 21). But, as William Major points out, if an ideal agrarian male exists for Berry, he would not simply embody the "rough-and-ready individual who makes his own way in this world" but would also act as a nurturer (163), and this is what we see in Paul Logan, who is both "rough-and-ready" and nurturing. Paul's nurturing is apparent in his innate ability to connect with one particular wild horse, who he carefully trains not by force, but by "talking softly" and "giving him apple wedges" (23). It is this kind of nurturing Black male figure that bell hooks lauds as the type who created a safe space for her as a child growing up in Kentucky: "Men who would never think of hurting any living thing" (42). She characterizes these men as "gentle and full of hope," words that could easily apply to Paul as well (42).

But Paul is also of the "rough-and-ready" sort. Long after the scene in which he gentles the Appaloosa, the reader learns exactly what Paul would do if all outside systems of support failed him. The rhetorical question Berry poses suggests that the modern man cannot function outside of the modern economy—a circumstance that creates a person dependent on systems that degrade the earth and humanity. But what if, in order to survive, a man could not rely on the infrastructure Berry faults? Taylor answers that question in Paul Logan, whose race excludes him from integrating into such systems to a far greater extent than any of his white "agrarian" peers who benefit from being included in "society." Indeed, Paul loses his livelihood when he chooses to ride another gambler's horse against his father's will; the economy, such as it was in the South at the time, has indeed failed; the police do not protect the Black community; the infrastructure that is in place for white business owners and farmers is often inaccessible for Black people; the woman Paul hopes to marry is in love with his best friend. Again and again, Paul demonstrates he is "rough-and-ready" by building a life for himself even when he lacks nearly every kind of support.

While there is strong support within the African American community once Paul has moved to Mississippi, it is clear that the smooth functioning of a true agrarian community requires both infrastructure and community partnership. Eric Freyfogle offers a definition of the meaning of community for agrarians: "Despite their strong sense of individual responsibility, agrarians view humans chiefly as social beings. . . . People thrive best when knitted into responsible community structures" (xxix). But, Freyfogle writes chiefly of communities that have benefitted from a society built on white supremacy. King et al. express this in different terms: "Black property owners articulate a unique vision of agrarianism, one that prizes independence—indeed, liberation—from the white power structure along many social dimensions: psychological, economic, political, cultural, and local community life" (691). Because of his race, Paul is often an outsider in the modern economy, but not entirely. Paul develops business relationships with storekeepers by building furniture and landowners by logging; he also becomes "knitted into responsible community structures" with the interracial community he builds as he works toward owning his land. Ultimately, the two hundred acres that Paul buys results from enduring family ties. Paul's white brother, Robert, hand-delivers the necessary money for the purchase (money from Paul's mother who sold back her own ten acres to Paul's father, as well as money from his older sister Cassie). To avoid "play[ing] the fool" again and trusting a contract with a white man, Paul enlists the help of a trustworthy white lawyer, Charles Jamison (father of Wade Jamison, the lawyer who appears in the other Logan books), who works on Paul's behalf to ensure his legal right to the land will "hold" (356–57). In moments like this, we see Paul working toward an agrarian community, despite color lines that have created a profoundly dysfunctional agrarian system.

Paul doesn't fall into farming because he has no other choices. In fact, compared with any other African Americans in *Land*, Paul holds a position of privilege unavailable to his peers because he is the multiracial son of a white landowner who chose to support and educate his multiracial children. Because his father apprenticed him to a carpenter, it is clear that Paul would have been able to live as an expert wood craftsman. A woman for whom Paul works as a young man also encourages him to go into the professions, which were open to him largely due to the education he received at home as a child from his father and white siblings: "Why, you could go to one of the colored schools here in Mississippi or even north to study. You could become one of the great educators to your people, or even a lawyer or doctor to them.... You've already got the foundation and you're certainly bright enough. You could do it easy" (142). Perhaps the key word here is "easy." For although it certainly wouldn't be easy by most measures for an African American to become a professional in the late 1800s, to buy a large and desirable tract of land from a white landowner would be an equal, if not greater, challenge. Nevertheless, many African Americans did become landowners, suggesting that while Paul may be exemplary, people with ambition to own land were sometimes able to find a way to do so. Kimberly K. Smith explains that:

> Most freedmen focused on acquiring land in the South. By 1910, southern blacks had acquired about 15 million acres of land, and nearly 17% of southern farm owners were black.... Freedmen typically had little capital to begin with and limited access to legal services or credit. White landowners were often reluctant to sell to blacks. Faced with legal disabilities and a social climate infused with racism, buying and holding property was a constant challenge. (*African* 72)

Smith is writing about a time in US history, before the Great Migration started in 1916, when land ownership and farming land were thought of as perhaps the most admirable and attainable dream for rural southern African Americans. Frederick Douglass encourages this calling as well: "Go to farming. Be tillers of the soil.... Our cities are overrun with menial laborers, while the country is eloquently pleading the hand of industry to till her soil and reap the reward of honest labor" (212; ellipsis original). Perhaps Paul is written as a response to this, as a Black Agrarian archetype—a symbol of the vision for solidarity among those seeking their security through land ownership. While Taylor's chronologically later books take readers through the persecution of

Jim Crow and the Great Migration, here we see an earlier vision for African Americans, one which was so widely accepted and promoted that both Booker T. Washington and W. E. B. Du Bois saw value in it.

In choosing to pursue land ownership over a trade or profession, Paul is also choosing a rural life over an urban life, a pattern that was reversed once the Great Migration began. Here, Taylor is showing us something important about Black Agrarian culture: that it could be an active choice, not always a default. Land ownership, despite the problematic relationship between agriculture and slavery, was keenly sought after, suggesting that a relationship with the soil does not have to be rejected de facto based on a fraught history. But the majority of the farming families in Taylor's novels are sharecroppers, whose relationship to farming was deeply scarred by class and race, whose economic position prevented them from being able to practice true agrarianism, and whose scant educational opportunities typically prevented them from being able to enter other trades or professions. For although Black Agrarianism was not a default, sharecropping certainly was. Paul decisively rejects any path that doesn't lead him to land ownership:

> What I wanted was land. I wanted land like my daddy's. In a way, I suppose, I was driven by the thought of having land of my own. In my early years, before I truly realized my two worlds, I had figured that I'd always live on my daddy's land, that my daddy's land would be mine and I would always be a part of it. When I discovered that wouldn't be, I created my own land in my mind. I knew that land was what I had to have. (142)

It is notable to see how Taylor uses language to construct the relationship between Paul and the land. As a youngster, Paul thought he would always be "part of" the land, and as he grows and realizes that wouldn't be so, he "created [his] own land in [his] mind." In both instances the phrasing is intimate and all-encompassing; the land and the person are of a piece. It is as if Paul sees himself as embedded in the land, or the land embedded in him. Indeed, Paul continues to associate land ownership with his father and the ease with which his father was able to move in the community. His dream for land is tied to trying to reunite his "two worlds," and entering the professions would not have satisfied that longing. When Paul rejects the suggestion that he should become a doctor, lawyer, or educator, he again echoes Frederick Douglass's imperative to turn to the land (212) and avoid a situation in which African Americans are "universally and completely dependent upon white men for the necessaries of life" (212). Berry's agrarianism echoes this point about dependence as well. The notion that a landowner could provide the basic sustenance for his family if all other systems fail is not simply a worst-case scenario. The political disempowerment and lack of the most basic legal and civil rights in the late 1800s gave African Americans good reason to question the reliability of any opportunity that was part of the oppressive political structure at the time.

When Paul finally happens upon the land that he wants for his own, he not only feels it viscerally but spiritually as well: "A fallen tree lay beside the pond, and I sat upon it as the morning light slit through the trees and shone everything golden. For the first time since I'd left my daddy's land, my heart soared, higher than any mountain I'd ever imagined, up to God's own perfect clouds, and I felt a peace come over me" (159).

This intimacy with the land is perhaps the most defining characteristic of the true agrarian, who sees the land as an extension of personal, spiritual, and communal health. In Paul's case, I would argue that it is also an extension of the agrarian imperative to care for land that will be in the family for generations. While Paul is not legally allowed to be the heir to his father's property, obtaining property to pass on to his future children shows his agrarian longing to pass on something of his "daddy's land" (even if it is just a spiritual connection, or a commitment) to his children. bell hooks, in *Belonging: A Culture of Place*, writes about the great agrarian and educator George Washington Carver, pointing out that his relationship with the land was spiritual: "To Carver, maintaining a caring relationship to the earth, to nature, was a means to have union with the divine.... Indeed, experiencing the divine through union with nature was a way to transcend the imposed belief that skin color and race was the most important aspect of one's identity" (62).

In Paul's moment when his "heart soared . . . up to God's own perfect clouds" and he "felt a peace come over" him, we glimpse for a moment Paul transcending the world in which he feels divided by his multiracial identity. As hooks suggests, an intense relationship with the earth can create a "counterhegemon[y]" (8). In the case of Paul, this could mean that instead of allowing the dominant white supremacist culture to define and limit him, he instead allows a primal bond with the earth to supersede the power structures created by humans. Paul's fervent desire for land and for a long-term, multigenerational relationship with that land reverses many of the attempts by the white supremacist culture to take land away from him.

NOSTALGIA AND CHILDREN'S FARM NOVELS

While Taylor's novels do not sugarcoat the past, there is a tangible strain of longing to reconnect readers with an overlooked landowning agricultural history. Taylor evocatively sheds light on the value of farming, land ownership, and community; these come across as both forward looking and tenderly written aspects of the Logan family story. The cultural value of landowning in Paul-Edward's story is not limited to *Land*, but continues through the last book in the Logan family novels. Taylor writes about the beginnings of this landowning project with admiration and an apparent desire to reclaim the narrative about the experience of working the land during Reconstruction. One may even be tempted to use the word nostalgia, which would be well within the scope of the larger world of American farming novels for young people (and agrarian writing in general), but certainly outside the expectations of children's novels about Black experience in the United States.

Furthermore, the charge of nostalgia is often levied against both agrarians and children's literature authors. William Major notes that "[t]oday, farmers, farming, and rural life enjoy something of an ideological echo which says that they are intrinsically moral, simple, and good—fertilizer for a vibrant republic. We find ourselves squarely within the realms of myth and nostalgia" (19). The very same words, "moral, simple, and good," have been used to refer to (or dismiss) children's literature. With only a few word changes, Major's observation about nostalgia over farms, farming, and rural life sounds remarkably like what one might say about childhood and children's literature. Nostalgia can be productive; it can provide insights into both the author's own time period and the earlier time period about which she has written. Nostalgia also contributes to our cultural colonization of childhood as a time of "innocence" and ingenuousness.

Writing about nostalgia for farm life, Major explains that "Nostalgia is the enemy of history, for it blinds us . . . from understanding and appreciating the material conditions of life—never the land of milk and honey of our imaginings" (20). Naturally, this line of reasoning leads directly to a discussion of the oppression of African Americans in the United States, which poses a significant challenge to anyone nostalgic for the agrarian past in our country. Major wonders whether bell hooks is "waxing nostalgic" (21) when she suggests that "[l]iving close to nature, black folks were able to cultivate a spirit of wonder and reverence for life. Growing food to sustain life and flowers to please the soul, they were able to make a connection with the earth that was ongoing and life-affirming" (qtd. in Major 21).

Major goes on, pointing out that despite many African Americans having a close relationship with the earth, it is clear that many "understood that it was worth giving up. That there might be other costs when people left the land (land they often did not own) can only be calculated in retrospect" (21). The question Major raises in this passage, whether one can be nostalgic for an agrarian past if you, your family, or your people were oppressed during that time, like the Logan family, is a pertinent one. Certainly, any writer can wax nostalgic about any era of history, since memory is not a recorder of indisputable fact. It is notable, though, that Taylor's books about children and farming are fairly unnostalgic, and it is this relative lack of nostalgia for the past that sets her novels apart from some other farm novels for children. If nostalgia asks one to look back longingly at a lost past, Taylor's books do the opposite: they look at the past as a time of terror and oppression. While they do, at times, suggest that the way out of the oppression is through an authentic relationship with the land, they fall short of being nostalgic for that relationship because the land itself is a contested space on both a literal and figurative level. Literally, the question of legal ownership arises repeatedly because the land is a space shaped by white supremacy and figuratively because the land of the American South has been both stolen from Native people and labored on by enslaved people, and as such is haunted by a past that precludes an idealized relationship with the land. Taylor is unambiguous about the past being a place of loss and brutal inequality, and yet, there are moments when there *is* a longing for what has been lost. Here we see a kind of cognitive dissonance play out in *Land* itself—the brutality of the past coexists with an attempt at an authentic and fulfilling relationship with the land—the reader is invited to experience this ambivalence.

Part of this ambivalence is the ability to toy with the idea of nostalgia, not as an attempt to obviate the present or future but as a way of valuing and validating elements of family history and connectedness to place, such as we see play out in the Logan family novels. Perhaps it is the term nostalgia that is problematic in this context. Is nostalgia a fixed concept? Or might the concept of nostalgia play with the elusive natures of memory, yearning, and historical fact? Indeed, nostalgia theorist Svetlana Boym rejects a simplistic approach to the term nostalgia; her nuanced approach explores (among other things) two different types of nostalgia: restorative and reflective, which have different functions in the formation of culture. Boym writes, "Restorative nostalgia stresses *nostos* and attempts a transhistorical reconstruction of the lost home. Reflective nostalgia thrives in *algia*, the longing itself, and delays the homecoming—wistfully, ironically, desperately" (xviii).

While restorative nostalgia thinks of itself as "truth and tradition," Boym articulates that "reflective nostalgia dwells on the ambivalences of human longing and belonging and does not shy away from the contradictions of modernity" (xviii). Reflective nostalgia explores the possibilities of "doubt" within memory, while restorative nostalgia precludes any ambiguity in favor of a "truth" (xviii).

The two kinds of nostalgia are here treated as separate concepts: one about restoring a time that has passed, and one about exploring the heteroglossia implicit in history and narrative. Taylor's works recognize that which is undesirable about the "reconstruction of the lost home" associated with restorative nostalgia (xviii). Thus, when William Major calls into question whether bell hooks could be waxing nostalgic in her writings about agrarianism, and when earlier I declared that Taylor's works are "decidedly un-nostalgic," I believe I am writing about "restorative nostalgia." Undoubtedly, in common usage, the term encompasses "a return to the original stasis, to the prelapsarian moment" and "is not supposed to reveal any signs of decay" while remaining "eternally young" (Boym 49). This is what I reject when I write about the near impossibility of nostalgia for a time of oppression, as is the case with much of African American children's literature.

Yet Boym's concept of "reflective nostalgia" allows one to revel in the pleasures of nostalgia, without being mired in regression. Reflective nostalgia admits to its own selectivity in memories and does not attempt to pin memory and history to a board like a butterfly under glass. Importantly, reflective nostalgia is about "individual and cultural memory" (49). Taylor's dedication in *Land* reads, "To my family, past, present, and future, and to the memory of my beloved father, the storyteller, for without his words, my words would not have been," alerting the reader to the personal nature of the novel to follow. In the author's note at the end of the novel, Taylor rounds out her dedication by offering some detail both about her family's past stories about the land they held (and continue to hold) in Mississippi, as well as the land Taylor herself has purchased in Colorado (371–75). Taylor attributes her dedication to land owning both in Colorado and Mississippi to "family values and teachings passed on from generation to generation" (375). Importantly, she connects this land ethic to generations before and after her own, writing: "It was my great-grandparents who left my family this legacy, and my grandparents, my father, aunts and uncles, and other family members who passed it on to my generation. Now my generation is passing it on to the next, and they in turn will do the same" (375). By pointing out these intergenerational ties, Taylor investigates the past and envisions the future. Nostalgia is often considered a one-way longing, but this is not the case for Taylor. Boym explains: "Nostalgia is not always about the past; it can be retrospective but also prospective. Fantasies of the past determined by needs of the present have a direct impact on realities of the future" (xvi). This concept is fantastically important when considering the role of nostalgia in Black Agrarian literature. The moments of nostalgia in Taylor's book suggest an alternative to the notion that African Americans' relationship with the earth is "moot and mute" (Ruffin 53). Nostalgia acts proscriptively in this context to assert that the stories of the past can help shape cultural identity of the future, particularly when such stories have not been voiced in dominant culture.

Thus, it is too dismissive of the term "nostalgia" to say that Taylor's work is not nostalgic—that seems to oversimplify. So, too, it is not entirely accurate to say that Taylor works only in "reflective nostalgia." In some of her moments of nostalgia, Taylor earnestly attempts to recreate the archetypal Black Agrarian family before the Great Migration. This is not "prelapsarian," nor could it be, considering its historical situation, yet, as "restorative nostalgia," it "takes itself dead seriously" (Boym 49). This calls for continued examination of how children's literature scholars have used the term nostalgic as if works "are" or "are not," perhaps without confronting the complexity of the word itself. Because of its multivalent meanings, such as we see in a book like *Land*, Boym is right to assert that "[n]ostalgia tantalizes us with its fundamental ambivalence" (xvii). *Land* and some of Taylor's other novels do the work of nostalgia, which is "about the relationship between individual biography and the biography of groups or nations, between personal and collective memory" (Boym xvi).

In writing the stories of her family, Taylor recreates her own past while creating a cultural artifact that contributes meaningfully to both the ecoliterary landscape and the world of children's literature. This is not only true of *Land*, because in all the Logan family novels, land is a central, constant element that unites the family itself and the community around them. What her works point to is perhaps a time when New Agrarians understand more deeply the debt they owe to Black Agrarians—whose intimate understanding of the complexities of race, class, privilege, and civil rights inform their practice of sustainability and commitment to community. Outside the world of literature and criticism, there is tremendous cultural and agricultural work being done at places like Soul Fire Farm—where Leah Penniman (and others) provide opportunities for people to connect with Afro Indigenous farming practices, end land-based oppression and food racism, and enact a culture of "radical community care" (soulfirefarm.org). It is my hope that if more scholars engage with the ecoliterary aspects of Taylor's work, we can add to the active culture of people who are examining the problematic nature of a land and food system predicated on white supremacy. As New Agrarianism and Black Agrarianism evolve as theoretical frameworks, continued opportunities will emerge to expand our understanding of its roots and its future growth. *The Land* works in both directions.

NOTES

1. Both sexes, Berry argues, are oppressed by the "specialization, degradation, trivialization, and tyrannization" of the modern economy both by how it treats humanity and how it degrades the earth (*What* 184). His main point is crystallized when he writes, "The problem is not just the exploitation of women by men. A greater problem is that women and men alike are consenting to an economy that is exploiting women and men and everything else" (185). Berry defines all that a modern nonagrarian man lacks: "He does not know what he would do if he lost his job, if the economy failed, if the utility companies failed, if the police went on strike, if the truckers went on strike, if his wife left him, if his children ran away, if he should be found incurably ill" (*Unsettling* 21).

WORKS CITED

Berry, Wendell. *The Art of the Commonplace: The Agrarian Essays of Wendell Berry*, edited by Norman Wirzba, Shoemaker and Hoard, 2002.
Berry, Wendell. *The Art of Loading Brush: New Agrarian Writings*. Counterpoint, 2017.
Berry, Wendell. *The Unsettling of America: Culture and Agriculture*. Sierra Club Books, 1977.
Berry, Wendell. *What are People For?: Essays*. Counterpoint, 1990.
Boym, Svetlana. *The Future of Nostalgia*. Basic Books, 2001.
Carlson, Allan. *The New Agrarian Mind: The Movement Toward Decentralist Thought in Twentieth-Century America*. Transaction Publishers, 2000.
Douglass, Frederick. "An Address to the Colored People of the United States" [1848]. *African-American Social and Political Thought*, edited by Howard Brotz, Transaction, 1992, pp. 208–12.
Fiskio, Janet. "Unsettling Ecocriticism: Rethinking Agrarianism, Place, and Citizenship." *American Literature*, vol. 84, no. 2, 2012, pp. 301–25.
Freyfogle, Eric T. *The New Agrarianism: Land, Culture, and the Community of Life*. Island Press, 2001.
hooks, bell. *Belonging: A Culture of Place*. Routledge, 2009.
Jefferson, Thomas. *Notes on the State of Virginia*. 1787. *The Norton Anthology of American Literature*, edited by Nina Baym, 6th ed., vol. A, Norton, 2003.
King, Katrina Quisumbing, et al. "Black Agrarianism: The Significance of African American Landownership in the Rural South." *Rural Sociology*, vol. 83, no. 3, 2018, pp. 677–99.
Major, William H. *Grounded Vision: New Agrarianism and the Academy*. U of Alabama P, 2011.
Martin, Michelle H. "Let Freedom Ring: Land, Liberty, Literacy, and Lore in Mildred Taylor's Logan Family Novels." *The Oxford Handbook of Children's Literature*, edited by Julia L. Mickenberg and Lynne Vallone, Oxford UP, 2011, pp. 371–88.
Nel, Philip. "Breaking Up with Your Favorite Racist Childhood Classic Books." *Washington Post*, May 16, 2021, https://www.washingtonpost.com/education/2021/05/16/breaking-up-with-racist-childrens-books/.
Ruffin, Kimberly N. *Black on Earth: African American Ecoliterary Traditions*. U of Georgia P, 2010.
Smith, Kimberly K. *African American Environmental Thought: Foundations*. UP of Kansas, 2007.
Smith, Kimberly K. *Wendell Berry and the Agrarian Tradition: A Common Grace*. UP of Kansas, 2003.
Soul Fire Farm. soulfirefarm.org. Jan. 26, 2022.
Taylor, Mildred. *The Land*. Penguin, 2001.
Taylor, Mildred. *Roll of Thunder, Hear my Cry*. Puffin Books, 1976.
Twelve Southerners. *I'll Take My Stand*. Harper, 1930.

Her Bandage Hides Two Festering Sores That Once Perhaps Were Eyes

"Justice" in the Logan Family Saga and *To Kill a Mockingbird*

Catharine Kane

That Justice is a blind goddess
Is a thing to which we black are wise:
Her bandage hides two festering sores
That once perhaps were eyes

—"JUSTICE" BY LANGSTON HUGHES

In the wake of George Floyd's murder in May 2020, American libraries and bookstores saw a spike in requests for books about antiracism and the history of race in the United States, as reported in, for example, the *Washington Post, Guardian, Star Tribune, USA Today*, and *LA Times*. This spike indicated a desire, especially among white people, to better understand racism in the United States, because Americans began to realize Floyd's death was not an aberration but the latest in a pattern of officially sanctioned violence against Black Americans. (Whether this recognition of the system's flaws will catalyze real change remains to be seen). The officer who murdered Floyd was only a small piece of a much larger system ingrained in the building blocks of American democracy. From Article I of the US Constitution, which declared that only three out of every five enslaved individuals counted as people; to the National Housing Act of 1934, which legalized and even encouraged redlining (the practice of defining the riskiness of mortgages based on the racial makeup of neighborhoods; areas with sizable Black populations were marked in red ink on maps as a warning to mortgage lenders); to the government-sanctioned assassination of activists like Fred Hampton under COINTELPRO (1956–1971); to modern Stop and Frisk police practices, discrimination against Black Americans is embedded in America's legal system.

MADE FOR THE WHITE FOLKS

In one of *To Kill a Mockingbird*'s best-known passages, Atticus Finch tells his children, "[T]he one place a man ought to get a square deal is in a courtroom, be he any color of the rainbow, but people have a way of carrying their resentments right into a jury box" (Lee 250). Through Atticus, Harper Lee suggests racist individuals are the reason Black people are treated unfairly in the court system. But while *Mockingbird* certainly deserves credit for awakening many to the injustice of racism, its narrative of one white man standing firm in his belief that all people are equal in the eyes of the law is an incomplete portrait of race in America. Too many American institutions, from schools to local and state governments, fail to recognize racism in the United States' economic, social, and legal infrastructure. Instead, the focus is on punishing individuals and private groups whose racist acts are illegal, like cross burnings or church bombings. The United States government should, of course, prosecute people like Dylann Roof, who in 2015 shot and killed nine Black people at Mother Emanuel AME Church in Charleston, South Carolina, or white nationalists inciting violence like at the 2017 Unite the Right rally in Charlottesville, Virginia, and the January 6, 2021, attack on the US Capitol. Just as important, however, is recognizing the role American institutions played in shaping and sanctioning Roof's and others' behavior. Americans'—particularly white Americans'—determination to see racism as isolated incidents, instead of as part of a system, impedes antiracism efforts. Dean Spade, a legal scholar whose work focuses on "the shortcomings of equality approaches and the 'limits of law'" (Oswin), explains the dangers of seeing racism as individual and even intentional:

> The focus on "discrimination" as the way to understand racism in the U.S. has meant that racism is considered a question of discriminatory intentions—whether or not somebody intentionally left someone out or did something harmful because of their biased feelings about a person's race. This focus on individual racists with bad ideas hides the reality that racism exists wherever conditions of radicalized maldistribution exist. Law reforms in the U.S., ostensibly enacted to prohibit racism, have

proven ineffective because they focus on bad intentions of individuals and fail to comprehend population-level conditions. (qtd. in Oswin)

For instance, while we are willing to condemn a single white person for calling the police on a Black person barbequing, or shopping, or selling lemonade, we are less willing to consider the larger framework of the situation: that calling the police on a Black person is a threat. Too often when police confront a Black person, it ends in the Black person's death, and there are numerous laws and policies in place to protect police from facing prosecution. It is far easier to point at an individual and call them racist than to acknowledge the laws and power structures that enable and protect them.

"[The] law like jus' 'bout everything else in this country is made for the white folks" (35), David Logan says in Mildred D. Taylor's *Let the Circle Be Unbroken*. *Circle* talks back to texts like *Mockingbird* that maintain that the law is just, and the way to end racism is to change individuals' minds, not to dismantle or restructure the American legal system. *Mockingbird*'s continued popularity is one example of how the American education system often ignores or misrepresents the government's role in sanctioning and perpetuating racist laws and practices. Students learn about Franklin D. Roosevelt's New Deal but not that it favored developers who created segregated neighborhoods (Rothstein 70); they learn about the 1941 bombing of Pearl Harbor but not about the Port Chicago Fifty, a group of Black sailors at a government-run munitions plant in California who were jailed for protesting unsafe working conditions in 1944 after an explosion killed 320 people, two-thirds of them African-Americans (Sheinkin 10). Teaching antiracism—and arguably, American history—is only possible when there is a critical understanding of how the US government has perpetuated racism. Enid Lee, author of *Beyond Heroes and Holidays: A Practical Guide to K–12 Anti-Racist, Multicultural Education and Staff Development*, identifies the goal of antiracist education as "equipping students, parents, and teachers with the tools needed to combat racism and ethnic discrimination, and to find ways to build a society that includes all people on equal footing" (Lee). One of those tools is providing students with examples of people—both real and fictional—who embody antiracist ideals. An essential part of embodying antiracism, however, is recognizing racism as a system of communal laws, beliefs, and practices, not just the words or actions of an individual.

When David Logan tells his children "the law ... is made for white folks," he is explaining why their friend T.J. Avery, a sixteen-year-old Black boy, will not receive a fair trial. Cassie Logan, Taylor's eleven-year-old protagonist, experiences "a surging feeling of panic" (*Circle* 35), as she realizes that she or her brother could face prosecution if white people knew they had helped T.J. the night of his arrest. Through witnessing T.J.'s trial, as well as local efforts to organize a union, and helping a Black woman who attempts to register to vote, Cassie (and the reader) sees the social forces of her world laid bare. Taylor's work is important, even essential, because it not only documents how national, state, and local governments oppressed Black people, but it also shows the potential for American citizens, even children, to challenge and deconstruct racist laws and political structures. *Mockingbird* and *Circle* both contain trial scenes in which a young Black man is found guilty of a crime he did not commit, but while Scout Finch's father tells her "in [the United States] our courts are the great levelers, and in our courts all men are created equal" (Lee 233), an older Black man watching T.J.'s trial tells Cassie, "trial or lynching, it always be's the same" (Taylor 85). The Logan Family Saga presents a far more complete—and complex—portrait of race in America than *Mockingbird*, because unlike Lee, Taylor forces readers to acknowledge the truth of Hughes's claim that Justice "[has] two festering sores / That once perhaps were eyes."

THE MYTH OF THE MOCKINGBIRD

According to Marla Harris, in the twentieth century "the burden of rewriting U.S. history, at least for children and young adults . . . shifted from textbooks to historical fiction" (112); but the questions of who is doing the rewriting, and how that history is presented, need to be addressed, particularly in light of the legalized killings of too many Black Americans. *Mockingbird* is "America's best loved book" (Knight), according to a 2018 PBS poll with over four million participants; not only did *Mockingbird* win this honor, but it also held the lead during the entire five-month voting period. *Mockingbird*'s supporters claim that the novel teaches children essential lessons about tolerance and inequality, awakening children to the realities of what it means to be Black in the United States: "It is a book that helps us grow and move towards becoming a more understanding and tolerant society, which is ultimately what we would all like to have happen . . . It is [read at] a time in which students are starting to question and consider the perspectives of others, as Atticus says, 'to climb in someone's skin and walk around in it.'" (Seale qtd. in Crum).

Mockingbird is focalized through Scout Finch as she begins to recognize the inequality inherent in her society: she is angry when classmates judge her father for defending a Black man (Lee 85), shocked when Tom Robinson is found guilty (241), and unable to understand why her teacher opposes the oppression of Jews in Germany but not Black people in America (282). An increasingly vocal number of critics, however, have challenged *Mockingbird*'s status as *the* novel used to teach American children about racism and social justice. While that criticism is directed in part at the novel's content, it is also aimed at the embedded assumption that a novel with a white focalization is the best tool for teaching antiracism. Autumn Allen writes, "*To Kill a Mockingbird* pushed several generations of white readers to examine racial injustice in American society," but while "Atticus's views were progressive for his time and environment [they] fall short of advocating true equality" (18, 19). Allen does not believe *Mockingbird* should be banned from classrooms, rather that the myth of *Mockingbird* as the perfect text for teaching antiracism needs to be dispelled.

Allen questions *Mockingbird*'s ability to teach tolerance and understanding: "throughout the text, readers are only given access to White characters' points of view" with "limited characterization of Black characters" (12). Allen's article is a case study of a small group of students reading and analyzing *Mockingbird*, and her conclusions about the text's shortcomings are drawn directly from the students' responses. One student, a white girl, "could not fathom why Tom [Robinson] would escape from jail if he were innocent" (10), and Allen concludes: "she could [not] imagine the desperation of a Black man in 1930s America imprisoned for raping a White woman, and the text does not help her to develop it by portraying Tom as a human with emotions" (13). Allen's experience teaching the text proves Jani Barker's claim that racism "is imperceptible to most members of the dominant society except in its most blatant forms but all too perceptible to members of less privileged groups" (Barker 122). In *Mockingbird*, Atticus Finch leads his children to believe that the courts treat everyone fairly, suggesting that the American legal system is not flawed in and of itself, only that some of the individual actors—jurors, judges, lawyers, police—are flawed in their refusal to uphold the law. In *Mockingbird*, Judge Taylor, Sheriff Heck Tate, and even the prosecutor all recognize the unfairness of Tom Robinson's plight but are unable (or unwilling) to do anything that steps outside the boundaries of the law. Yet Heck Tate also refuses to arrest Boo Radley or Jem Finch for killing Bob Ewell, suggesting he values justice and even compassion more than the letter of the law—at least when it comes to white people (Lee 317). Thus, in Scout's world, the justice system can and should be trusted, because even when unjust events occur, police and courts will do their best to right the wrongs within the confines of the law. Critical race theory, which "centers race as a key to understanding power, legal and property rights, economics and labor, and ideology" (Barker 121), disputes this notion, putting the onus not on the individual's failure to respect the law, but on Americans' deliberate construction of the law as a tool to oppress and control. To claim *Mockingbird* is still essential reading in the twenty-first century is to assert that white voices are the authority on racism in the United States, and doing so ignores both the rich body of work from Black authors and the lived experiences of Black Americans—in the 1930s and today.

In *Shadow and Substance: Afro-American Experience in Contemporary Children's Fiction*, Rudine Sims writes that "concern about the potential of children's literature to influence readers' attitudes ... and to increase social awareness" (2) is at the center of the debate about the portrayal of Black characters in children's literature. Sims splits children's books about Black characters into three categories: social conscience books, melting pot books, and culturally conscious books. *Mockingbird* is paradigmatic of social conscience books:

1. "Whites writing about Blacks for a white audience" (6); Harper Lee was white, and she focalizes the story through Scout Finch, who is also white.
2. *Mockingbird* has often been described by white teachers as a "'universal' stor[y], with which Any Child (read 'white middle-class child') can identify" (7) (see also Crum; Hatch; Pengelly).
3. "Black culture, as reflected in such books, is a monolithic 'culture of poverty'" (9); Scout describes the Black church as "unceiled and unpainted ... there was no sign of piano, organ, hymn books, church-programs" (Lee 136).
4. "The stock villain is ... a [white] male ... of low socioeconomic status, as indicated by his nonstandard speech" (Sims 22); when Bob Ewell is introduced Scout notes his family lives in extreme poverty, and when asked to confirm his name, Ewell answers "that's m'name cap'n" (Lee 195).
5. "Afro-American [characters] appear quaint or exotic. This quasi-foreignness then becomes an excuse for paternalism or patronizing on the part of the non-Afro-American characters, or the narrator, or, by implication, the author" (Sims 27). During Tom Robinson's trial, the emotional heart of Lee's novel, the African American characters are a Greek Chorus: largely indistinguishable as they stand off to the side so the audience can watch a white man argue with another white man about the actions of a Black man, presided over by a white man and a panel of white men.

In her examination of Martha Finley's Elsie Dinsmore novels, critic Marla Harris writes, "[H]er inability to conceive of an African American subjectivity is at odds with, or independent of, her white desires that limited what she could understand and write about the period, despite her good intentions" (113), a sentiment that also describes Harper Lee. Sims specifies that texts by Black authors about Black characters are not "closed to whites" (8), but texts by white authors about Black characters are too often "closed" to Black readers because the Black characters are plot devices to show the heroism of the white characters. Sims concludes that "while they might have been a step in the right direction and served some useful purpose at the time of their writing, the social conscience books deserve a long and relatively undisturbed rest on the library shelves" (31). Per Sims, books such as *To Kill a Mockingbird* should be recognized as instruments of social change; however, it is a disservice to pretend that the same text that shifted white attitudes more than fifty years ago will have the same impact on today's white students, while simultaneously alienating today's Black students through its homogenous and stereotypical portrayal of Black characters.

A viable alternative to the social conscience books, according to Sims, is culturally conscious fiction, books that show "the social and cultural traditions associated with growing up Black in the United States. In contrast to the social conscience books, they are not primarily addressed to non-Blacks, nor are they focused on desegregating neighborhoods or schools. . . . [T]hey recognize, sometimes even celebrate, the distinctiveness of the experience of growing up simultaneously Black and American" (Sims 49).

While all of Taylor's books interrogate the American justice system, *Roll of Thunder, Hear My Cry* and especially *Let the Circle Be Unbroken* serve as counternarratives to books like *Mockingbird*, that treat the law as sacrosanct. This counternarrative is focalized through a young Black protagonist, a character who because of her embodied identity personally experiences injustice both in the form of those ignoring the law, and of unjust laws themselves. Cassie's Blackness is important because it gives Black children a chance to see themselves, and just as essential, it forces white children (and teachers) to follow Atticus Finch's oft-quoted lesson that "you never really understand a person until you consider things from his point of view" (Lee 33). Those who wish to preserve the legacy of *Mockingbird* are actually going against Atticus's advice when they fail to recognize the importance of Black voices telling Black stories.

"FOLKS ARE JUST FOLKS" VS. SYSTEMIC RACISM

Atticus insists that men such as Walter Cunningham, a man who is part of the mob that comes to lynch Tom Robinson, are simply ignorant, not inherently bad or wrong. He differentiates between men like Bob Ewell and Cunningham because he claims the former openly hates Black people while the latter is simply misguided (Lee 254). This notion of people being blameless for their racism if it's simply the reality of their society is dangerous, because it assumes a white positionality when reading *Mockingbird*, and gaslights nonwhite readers in its insistence that ostensibly good white people like Atticus and Heck Tate are in the majority and not part of the problem. To Lee, the law is a set of near-infallible principles that would ensure a just world if only individual actors like Bob Ewell or the jury members would respect its inherent power. The courtroom scene is *Mockingbird*'s most iconic because the law and its foundations—logic and reason—are weapons Atticus wields to overcome human prejudice and convince both the characters and readers of Tom Robinson's innocence. This scene suggests that men are fallible, but the law is not, and every American is equal in the eyes of the law. In contrast, while Taylor, through Cassie Logan, demonstrates a respect and appreciation for the law, she also recognizes that men created the law and it is therefore inherently biased and imperfect. *Circle* makes this clear with the introduction of Suzella, a relative of the Logans who has a Black father and a white mother. South African comedian Trevor Noah recounts, in his 2016 memoir *Born a Crime*, his experience growing up under Apartheid with a Black mother and a white father. Like Noah, Suzella was "born a crime," her very existence a violation of the law, and irrefutable proof that everyone is not treated equally in the eyes of the law. *Mockingbird* allows Americans to cling to the fiction that the problem is not with the very foundations of their country but instead with ignorant and/or racist individuals. The Logan Family Saga shows how oppression is a system embedded in every aspect of American law and society, and it will take a paradigm shift, not passionate speeches from lawyers, to move toward true, fair, just, and equal treatment for all.

Taylor's work, with its Black focalization and interrogation of the American legal system, has the potential to push this and future generations to examine racial injustice in American society. Barker maintains that "when white readers read only books reflecting the experiences of the dominant group, both they and society suffer," but "well-written, authentic multiethnic children's literature can provide healing from the damages of living in a racist society" (122). Critics such as Michelle H. Martin, Hamida Bosmajian, Barker, and Harris have identified Taylor's Logan Family Saga as a source of detailed, nuanced, and engaging stories about Black Americans—and specifically Black children—observing and wrestling with the realities of racism. Like those of Harper Lee, Taylor's stories are focalized through the perspective of a young girl in the 1930s Deep South, and like Scout Finch, Cassie Logan observes the inner workings of the American justice system. The key difference is that Cassie, a Black girl, sees the flaw in the system itself—the laws were written by and for white men—while Scout, a white girl, sees the trial system and its insistence that all men are innocent until proven guilty as proof of the law's stability and fairness. As Scout learns from Atticus, it is only individuals' decisions to ignore the rules that result in the unfair treatment of Black Americans. Through Cassie's eyes, Taylor explores how race intersects with other identities, including gender, education, income level, and legal status.

Bosmajian describes Taylor's early works as "Cassie's ongoing education in and growing consciousness of the liberating power of just laws" (141), through which Taylor upholds "the values of constitutionally guaranteed rights, no matter how these rights are violated in temporal local statutes" (145). In this way, while Scout's story teaches the evils of racism, Cassie's story teaches "the intertwining of racism and power in economics, law, and daily life," (Barker 127) an understanding of which is essential to the work of antiracism. Fighting racism is not (or not only) a matter of changing individual people's minds but of acknowledging and dismantling racism in America's legal, social, and financial building blocks. Atticus Finch says "there's nothing more sickening to me than a low-grade white *man* who'll take advantage of a Negro's ignorance" (Lee 252; emphasis added) but Mary Logan explains that T.J. Avery's trial is pointless because racism is embedded in American law and society: "You [Stacey] think *these people* are going to believe anything you have to say? T.J.'s going to trial before an all-white jury and a white judge *in a town and a state and a country ruled by white folks*" (Taylor, Circle 34–35; emphasis added). When focalized through a Black character, that character disabuses readers of the illusion that racism is one person mistreating another person. While white people have the privilege of seeing this discrimination as isolated incidents, Black people understand it is a constant and persistent threat. Unlike Scout, Cassie sees racism embedded in every aspect of her society.

Marla Harris believes Taylor is at the forefront of "late twentieth-century authors of historical fiction for children and young adults" who "have broadened the notion of who and what U.S. history is about" (114). Of the aborted lynching in *Mockingbird*, Autumn Allen notes that "readers do not share Tom's perspective when he is inside the jail and the white mob is outside. ... [R]eaders share Scout's perspective as she worries for Atticus, who stands guard" (12). In a similar scene in *Thunder*, a white mob captures T.J. Avery, and a white lawyer tries to protect him from physical harm. Also similar is the removed perspective as we watch the scene through Cassie's eyes, not T.J.'s or Jamison's. The key difference, however, lies not only in Cassie's race but in the level of danger the mob poses to her own safety, and to that of her family. Scout's encounter with a mob has the potential for violence—"'I'll send him [Scout's brother Jem] home,' a burly man said, and grabbed Jem roughly by the collar" (Lee 173)—but she is unaware of any real danger, thinking Jem wants to stay with Atticus because he fears punishment at home, not because Atticus (or Tom) might be hurt or killed. Scout and Cassie are almost the same age (Scout is eight [Lee 179]), and Cassie is nine [Taylor, *Thunder* 181]), but Scout's biggest fear is parental punishment, while Cassie fears the mob hurting or even killing her family. Cassie worries that her brother Stacey will try to stop the mob, and only when the mob suggests lynching Mr. Morrison and her father (Taylor,

Thunder 256) does she leave Stacey to go warn the rest of her family. Cassie is forced to decide between warning her father and protecting her brother, aware that either way, she is risking the lives of people she loves.

CASSIE LOGAN'S SEARCH FOR JUSTICE

George Floyd's death in May 2020 brought the narrative of police as part of a racist justice system to the forefront of American discourse, but in Taylor's work, Black children in the 1930s are well aware that the police as an institution will not protect them. While observing T.J.'s trial, Cassie narrates, "Sheriff Hank Dobbs testified that the gun . . . had been found by Clyde Persons, a citizen of the town deputized to apprehend the thieves. 'Deputy my foot!' I grumbled. 'Ole Clyde Persons was one of them lynchmen'" (Taylor, *Circle* 69). Cassie's reaction demonstrates that to her, someone who is violent and/or racist should not be a deputy. Barker says Taylor's work "provides an analytical dissection of racism that lays bare its structures and workings in 1930s Mississippi" (120). Key to Cassie's development is identifying the unspoken and unwritten laws that, due in part to their ill-defined nature, take precedence over actual laws. Cassie admires others who believe the laws can help achieve justice: Mr. Jamison's passionate defense of T.J. at his trial, Dubé's work with the union organizers, and Russell's use of logic and reason to challenge Granger's scare tactics. Cassie learns, however, that doing the right or just thing is never clear-cut or easy. In the Logan Family Saga, there are no clean resolutions like in *Mockingbird*, which ends with Sheriff Tate claiming Bob Ewell fell on his knife, a solution that neatly protects the Finches, Boo Radley, and even, indirectly, Helen Robinson and Mayella Ewell. Lee positions Sheriff Tate and Atticus's cover-up of Bob Ewell's murder as an act of kindness to Boo Radley. Bob Ewell is a bad man, and his death is justice; Boo Radley is a good man, and prosecuting him would therefore be unjust (arguably, Boo Radley would also meet the legal definition of diminished capacity). Meanwhile, *Thunder* also ends with the main character's father lying (by omission) to cover up a crime but at great personal cost not only to himself but to his family as well. It has been established that the Logans, like all their neighbors, have had a lackluster harvest season and can ill afford to lose any crops, let alone acres and acres. Whether or not it is legal for David Logan to burn his own land is never made explicitly clear; however, if he were honest and identified himself as the fire starter, he would undoubtedly be jailed and likely lynched—again showing the law is not an infallible institution. Cassie's father is essentially burning money his family cannot spare, in a gamble where success is far from guaranteed, all to prevent T.J.'s lynching—for now. As Martin has said, the Logan Family Saga is not a morality tale where villains are punished and heroes never face any lasting consequences for doing the right thing (12). It is a complex portrait of a family and a community fighting for survival and identity in the face of extreme and often unjust difficulties.

In all her novels but particularly in *Circle*, Taylor shows how the law provides little protection to Black people, who are subject to multiple and sometimes contradictory social forces. Throughout the book, Cassie studies the Mississippi State Constitution with her mother and Mrs. Lee Annie Lees. She is surprised at her own interest in the law as she begins to recognize the power the law possesses. In the law, she sees the potential for a more equitable future for herself and others and hopes that future will come sooner than her mother predicts: "one day equal rights will be for everyone, but as far as [Cassie's mother] could see, that day was still a ways off" (*Circle* 198).

Concurrent with Cassie's education in the written law is her recognition of the unwritten laws that govern her world. Cassie observes a group of white boys interacting with Jacey, a fifteen-year-old Black girl. The first time, Cassie picks up on the anger of Stacey and his friends but doesn't understand the source (*Circle* 110), and later she senses Jacey's discomfort but does not understand why her Uncle Hammer is so angry about the white boys talking to Jacey (145). Cassie does not make the connection between the shared positionalities of herself and Jacey, and she is angry when Stacey tells her "when a white boy's 'round a colored girl, they's up to no good.... You jus' remember that" (147). Cassie understands that the boys present a danger to Jacey because they are white and she is Black, but she does not yet understand the danger the boys present because they are male and Jacey is female, or how the intersections of those identities put Jacey, let alone Cassie herself, at risk.

POLICING BLACK BODIES, THEN AND NOW

Cassie begins to put the pieces together when she finds out Jacey is pregnant by one of the white boys: "had the [baby's] father been black, [Jacey's father] could have seen to it that the boy married Jacey and Jacey's future could have been saved, but . . . all the shotguns in the world gave [Jacey's father] no power where a white boy was concerned" (*Circle* 262). Jacey's pregnancy gives Cassie context for Stacey's anger, even if she does not yet recognize that Jacey's consent is questionable at best. Cassie realizes that Stuart, the white boy, has no intention of helping Jacey or the baby, and no Black person could, or white person would, force him to take responsibility. Bosmajian notes: "as Cassie gets older, she becomes aware that the physical violence of whites against black men expresses itself as a sexual threat against black women" (146). Cassie understands that an unspoken law of her community, that Black women in particular must avoid interactions with white men, exists to counteract the unspoken law of white society, that white men can use Black women's bodies as they please.

Cassie's understanding deepens when the same white boys flirt with her cousin Suzella, mistaking Cassie's cousin for a white girl. Cassie understands the danger of Suzella's passing because the boys will be angry that Suzella lied by omission, but she also senses the danger is more acute because the boys clearly find Suzella attractive (*Circle* 246). After Stuart learns Suzella is Black, he lashes out at her father Bud, not Suzella herself. Bud has wronged Stuart (in Stuart's mind) because he "tricked" Stuart into being attracted to a Black girl. Stuart is unaware of the irony: he himself is the father of a mixed-race child, the very "crime" of which he accuses Bud. Stuart and his friends seek casual fun in how they approach Jacey and Suzella, but the threat of Jacey's and Suzella's fathers asserting dominance over the white boys, even unintentionally, challenges white supremacy, although the Black men are much older than the teenage boys.

Taylor uses Bud and Stuart to show how the written and unwritten laws treat Black and white men differently: in Mississippi, Bud could be prosecuted for marrying a white woman he loves, while white boys like Stuart face no repercussions for taking advantage of Black girls. Like too many encounters between police and Black men, the white boys do not actually care that Bud has broken the law; they care that Bud does not immediately give in to their unreasonable demands. Their anger comes from their belief that the Black men are disrespecting their "authority." Similarly, the white crowd in the courtroom reacts with anger when Tom Robinson says he "felt right sorry" (Lee 224) for a white woman. Though Atticus has established Tom was physically incapable of causing Mayella's injuries, Tom's inadvertent suggestion that he is in some way better than Mayella is enough to condemn him. In his closing argument, Atticus also perpetuates the harmful myth of Black men as dangerous to white women, saying Mayella Ewell's "offense" is not lying about her interactions with Tom Robinson, but flirting with him. Atticus says, "[S]he was white and she tempted a Negro. . . . Not an old Uncle, but a strong young Negro man" (Lee 231), thus suggesting both that if Tom had attacked Mayella it would have been her fault, and worse, that Black men experience uncontrollable sexual urges and are therefore dangerous to white women. The oppressors are less concerned with the breaking of any written laws and more concerned with the perceived upending of the unwritten laws of how society dictates Black men should behave around white men, particularly white men in positions of authority.

THE LAW—WRITTEN AND UNWRITTEN

The written and unwritten laws violently collide in *Circle* when Cassie accompanies Mrs. Lee Annie Lees to Strawberry so she can register to vote. Again, Taylor demonstrates that laws themselves, not just the people charged with enforcing them, can be oppressive and racist. Mrs. Lee Annie must pass a test administered by the registrar; the sole purpose of the test, and the law requiring the test, is to keep Black people from registering to vote. A neighbor tells Mrs. Lee Annie, "I recalls the time colored folks gone to take that there test and the ole registrar, he puts out a jar of jelly beans and says for 'em to tell him how many there is in the jar, and that there was yo' test" (*Circle* 328), pointing out that even though Mrs. Lee Annie can recite Mississippi laws from memory, she may still be found unqualified to vote. Mrs. Lee Annie recalls how her father voted "in the time of Reconstruction . . . didn't hafta take no test back then" (114). A group of "night men" (the Ku Klux Klan) nearly beat her father to death, yet the law was eventually used to suppress the Black vote more effectively than vigilante terrorism. In 1899 approximately 9 percent of Black men in Mississippi were registered to vote; in 1940 approximately 0.4 percent of Black men and women in Mississippi were registered to vote (McMillen 36). Mrs. Lee Annie goes forward with her plan, knowing it may prove dangerous to her family as well as herself, though not even Mary Logan anticipates the massive repercussions of Mrs. Lee Annie's decision.

Mrs. Lee Annie's registration attempt coincides with a protest/riot of Black and white sharecroppers who are being kicked off their land. Taylor again shows how the written law can be a tool of oppression as well as a tool for positive change, as the sheriff tells the crowd "now y'all wanna speak y'alls piece, y'all jus gonna hafta go through the proper channels. Y'all present y'alls' complaints in a civilized manner in the proper way and at the proper time" (*Circle* 368). Throughout the novel, Dubé and others work hard to convince local sharecroppers that everyone will benefit if white and Black farmers band together. The focus is on a specific issue in a specific space: Morris Wheeler, the white union organizer, says the union doesn't support Blacks and whites "schooling together, socializing together, and certainly not marrying together" (370–71). His pitch to the farmers is instead based on the shared problems of poverty and the argument that they will be more likely to affect change if their numbers are larger.

Dubé and Wheeler's work is undermined when Harlan Granger, the property owner who is leaving the families destitute, uses Mrs. Lee Annie as an object lesson in what happens when white people give Black people any sort of power. Harlan Granger quells the protest by turning the white people against their Black neighbors, using the fear of lawlessness and societal breakdown to convince the white sharecroppers they are making a mistake. "Anxiety makes the oppressor permanently vigilant against the slightest signs of insubordination, signs that nearly always trigger an excessive response" (Bosmajian 146). Taylor exposes the multiple systems that perpetuate oppression, including class warfare. Cassie even observes that "most of the people ... were white, but there were some black faces too" (*Circle* 364). Granger disperses the crowd by making them feel powerless and divided, even though the white protestors are likely numerous enough on their own to force Granger to meet their demands.

According to Barker, many poor white people "were also locked into the exploitative system but still considered themselves superior to all blacks" (127); Taylor understands that the feeling of superiority is itself born of poverty and desperation: "The poor white farmers ... [had] little more to hold onto than the belief that they were better than black people" (*Circle* 371–72). According to Barker, Taylor demonstrates that racism "is not a matter of individual feelings, but institutionalized power structures that create deep-rooted cultural norms highly resistant to change" (132). While this scene shows Cassie how the law can be a tool of oppression, it also shows her that the law is not set in stone. People can push for change, and though the protest does not work, Granger's difficulty in quelling the crowd demonstrates for Cassie that people can recognize laws are unjust, and enough dissenting voices have the potential to topple oppressive systems and change the law. At the same time, Harlan Granger demonstrates how the suggestion of Black empowerment is an effective scare tactic to convince white people to maintain the status quo. A justice system that favors white people and vilifies Black people, particularly Black men, is central to that status quo. As Cassie witnesses the demonstration in Strawberry, she begins to understand the entanglement of racial prejudice and the American justice system—an understanding that leads to Cassie's decision to attend law school in *All the Days Past, All the Days to Come*.

In *Circle*, Stacey and his friend Moe seek work on sugar cane plantations and find themselves trapped in a labor contract similar to sharecropping. The workers share small shacks and must pay the plantation store for blankets, clothes, and even the machetes needed to harvest the sugar cane (389). Eventually, Stacey and Moe flee with three other boys. Stacey chooses to leave without his pay, not arguing when the plantation owner denies him every cent he has earned. When Stacey learns one of the other boys has stolen their wages from the plantation owner, he demands they split up and refuses to take his share, correctly anticipating that doing so would prove a major risk to his ability to return home, not to mention to his life. Underlying Stacey's caution is the presumption that as a young Black man, he will be assumed guilty by white people—a presumption that, depressingly, would not be out of place even if the novel were set in 2020 instead of 1935. In response to the deaths of Trayvon Martin, Michael Brown, and Stephon Clark, people quickly brought up Martin's school suspensions, Brown's (nonviolent) juvenile record, and Clark's past robbery convictions, as if those (unrelated) incidents justified their deaths. In the court of public opinion, if Black men and boys are innocent of the crime for which they were arrested or tried, they must be guilty of something: "[American] society considers young black men to be dangerous, interchangeable, expendable" (Robinson). Taylor shows that for Black people, wariness of white people is a more important survival skill than being polite or even law-abiding. Stacey is intelligent, compassionate, and fair throughout the Logan Family Saga, yet when he runs away from home, his survival is dependent less on his intelligence or goodness and more on the skills his parents have taught him to keep himself safe when dealing with white people.

CONCLUSION: *ALL THE DAYS PAST, ALL THE DAYS TO COME*

In 2013, George Zimmerman was acquitted of the murder of seventeen-year-old Trayvon Martin. Zimmerman himself does not dispute the basic facts of the case: he was out patrolling his neighborhood when he observed Martin and decided to follow him. Ignoring a 9-1-1 operator's orders to stay away, Zimmerman pursued Martin and confronted him. Zimmerman was found Not Guilty under Florida's "Stand Your Ground" law, which defense attorneys used to argue that Trayvon Martin, a Black teenager carrying a bag of Skittles, posed a serious threat to the life of George Zimmerman, who was following Martin with a loaded gun. Eugene Robinson wrote, "Trayvon Martin was fighting more than George Zimmerman that night. He was up against prejudices as old as American history, and he never had a chance." Robinson references George Zimmerman's profiling of Martin as suspicious because he was a Black male wearing a hoodie, as well as the failure of the police or prosecutor to investigate Martin's death as a murder until pressured by the public; six weeks passed between Martin's death and any attempt to gather evidence. His death proves that while the United States likes "to think of itself as colorblind" (Allen 13), serious work still needs to be done.

American children must learn the true history of race in America, a history that is systemic and deeply embedded in society. *To Kill a Mockingbird* has been an important tool, but using a narrative from and focalized through the oppressive culture to teach about the oppressed culture is simply another, subtler way of perpetuating systemic racism in the United States. Unlike in *Mockingbird*, in the Logan Family Saga readers see the dangers of racial injustice through a Black positionality. At the end of *Mockingbird*, Atticus tucks Scout into bed, and Scout falls asleep, comfortable in the knowledge that her father will watch over her all night (Lee 323). Meanwhile, in *Thunder* Cassie awakens alone in the aftermath of a barely-averted lynching that comes at the cost of her family's crops, and the knowledge that the lynching has likely only been delayed, not prevented: "I cried for T.J. For T.J. and the land" (Taylor 276). Mildred D. Taylor's work is more important than ever, not only because it gives voice to Black stories, but because it asks readers to join Cassie's exploration of American law as a dynamic and evolving institution, one that has been used to persecute Americans but also one that can be used to shape a more just and equitable future.

WORKS CITED

Allen, Autumn. "'Whose Side Are You On?' Moral Consequences of Young Readers' Responses to *To Kill a Mockingbird*." *Research on Diversity in Youth Literature*, vol. 2, no. 2, Jan 2020, pp. 1–22, https://sophia.stkate.edu/rdyl/vol2/iss2/5.

Barker, Jani L. "Racial Identification and Audience in *Roll of Thunder, Hear My Cry* and *The Watsons Go to Birmingham—1963*." *Children's Literature in Education*, vol. 41, 2010, pp. 118–45, https://doi.org/10.1007/s10583-010-9101-4.

Bosmajian, Hamida. "Mildred Taylor's Story of Cassie Logan: A Search for Law and Justice in a Racist Society." *Children's Literature*, vol. 24, 1996, pp. 141–60. *Project MUSE*, https://muse.jhu.edu/article/246344/pdf.

Crum, Maddie. "High School English Teachers On Why Harper Lee's *To Kill a Mockingbird* Endures." *Huffington Post*, July 13, 2015. https://www.huffpost.com/entry/high-school-english-teachers-on-why-to-kill-a-mockingbird-endures_n_55a02146e4b0ecec71bc269f.

Flood, Alison. "Anti-Racist Book Sales Surge in U.S. and Britain after George Floyd Killing." *The Guardian*, June 3, 2020. https://www.theguardian.com/books/2020/jun/03/anti-racist-book-sales-surge-us-uk-george-floyd-killing-robin-diangelo-white-fragility.

Harris, Marla. "A History Not Then Taught in History Books": (Re)Writing Reconstruction in Historical Fiction for Children and Young Adults." *The Lion and the Unicorn*, vol. 30, no. 1, 2006, pp. 104–14. *Project MUSE*, https://muse.jhu.edu/article/192838.

Hatch, Adam. "Why Schools Removing *To Kill a Mockingbird* Has Everyone Outraged." *Bored Teachers*, Oct. 14, 2017. https://www.boredteachers.com/trending/schools-removing-to-kill-a-mockingbird.

Hernandez, Daniel. "Nonracist to Antiracist: Seven Rapid Culture Shifts Since the Killing of George Floyd." *Los Angeles Times*, June 12, 2020. https://www.latimes.com/entertainment-arts/story/2020-06-12/antiracist-shift-cultural-trends-black-lives-matter.

Hughes, Langston. "Justice." *Scottsboro Limited; Four Poems and a Play in Verse By Langston Hughes; With Illustrations By Prentiss Taylor*. The Golden Stair Press, 1932, unpaged. Public domain (https://poets.org/poem/justice).

Knight, Christina. "*To Kill a Mockingbird* Wins the Great American's Read Vote." *THIRTEEN*, Oct. 24, 2018. https://www.thirteen.org/blog-post/to-kill-a-mocking-bird-wins-great-american-read-vote/.

Lee, Enid. "Taking Multicultural, Anti-racist Education Seriously." Interview by Barbara Miner. *Philadelphia Public Schools' TheNotebook*, Sept. 25, 2002. https://thenotebook.org/articles/2002/09/25/taking-multicultural-anti-racist-education-seriously/.

Lee, Harper. *To Kill a Mockingbird*. Hachette Book Group USA, 1960.

Martin, Michelle H. "Exploring the Works of Mildred Taylor: An Approach to Teaching the Logan Family Novels." *Teaching and Learning Literature with Children and Young Adults*, vol. 7, no. 3, 1998, pp. 5–13.

Mayes, Brittany Renee, et al. "Demand for Antiracist Literature is Up. These Black Bookstore Owners Hope it Lasts." *Washington Post*, July 2, 2020. https://www.washingtonpost.com/graphics/2020/business/black-owned-bookstores-anti-racist-literature/.

McMillen, Neil R. *Dark Journeys: Black Mississippians in the Age of Jim Crow*. U of Illinois P, 1990, pp. 36.

Noah, Trevor. *Born a Crime*. Spiegel and Grau, 2016.

Oswin, Natalie. "On Normal Life: Dean Spade, Interviewed by Natalie Oswin." *Society + Space*, Jan. 15, 2014. https://www.societyandspace.org/articles/on-normal-life.

Pengelly, Martin. "Mississippi Students Allowed to Read *To Kill a Mockingbird*—With a Parent's Note." *The Guardian*, Oct. 28, 2017. https://www.theguardian.com/us-news/2017/oct/28/mississippi-to-kill-a-mockingbird-harper-lee.

Robinson, Eugene. "Trayvon Martin Never Had a Chance." *Washington Post*, July 15, 2013. https://www.washingtonpost.com/opinions/eugene-robinson-black-boys-denied-the-right-to-be-young/2013/07/15/d3f603d8-ed69-11e2-9008-61e94a7ea20d_story.html.

Ross, Jenna. "After George Floyd, Minnesota Fights Racism with Free Books and Films." *The Minnesota Star Tribune*, June 20, 2020. https://www.startribune.com/after-george-floyd-minnesota-fights-racism-with-free-books-and-films/571366502/.

Rothstein, Richard. *The Color of Law: A Forgotten History of How Our Government Segregated America*. Liveright, 2017, p. 70.

Sheinkin, Steve. *The Port Chicago 50: Disaster, Mutiny, and the Fight for Civil Rights*. Roaring Brook Press, 2014, p. 61.

Sims, Rudine. *Shadow and Substance: Afro-American Experience in Contemporary Children's Fiction*. National Council of Teachers of English, 1982.

Taylor, Mildred D. *Let the Circle Be Unbroken*. Penguin Group, 1981.

Taylor, Mildred D. *Roll of Thunder, Hear My Cry*. Dial Press, 1976.

VanDenburgh, Barbara. "Anti-Racist Book Dethrones 'Hunger Games' Prequel on Best-Seller List Amid Mass Protests." *USA Today*, June 10, 2020, https://www.usatoday.com/story/entertainment/books/2020/06/10/anti-racist-books-dominate-best-seller-list-white-fragility-how-to-be-an-antiracist-ta-nehisi-coates/5331188002/.

Part 4

The World Beyond:
Legacy, Activism, and Education

Disrupting Mavericks
Roll of Thunder, Hear My Cry, The Hate U Give, and Critical Race Theory

Annette Wannamaker

On US President Joe Biden's first day in office, hours after he had been sworn in, he disbanded the "1776 Commission," which had been established just months earlier by former President Donald Trump. The Commission's report, released in January 2021, is a concise and chilling document that lays out the right's long-term efforts to create a patriotic, whitewashed, and nationalistic school curriculum as it advocates for "a restoration of American education" (1). Universities, its authors claim, teach future educators a "revisionist history" that "shames Americans by highlighting only the sins of their ancestors, and teaches claims of systemic racism that can only be eliminated by more discrimination" (18). The authors imply that teaching about the complex and fraught history of race in the US is a threat to patriotic unity: "states and school districts should reject any curriculum that promotes one-sided partisan opinions, activist propaganda, or factional ideologies that demean America's heritage, dishonor our heroes, or deny our principles" (17). The language is purposely vague because it allows the authors of the report to label any antiracist teaching as "partisan" or "factional." Even though the commission was shut down, the arguments described in its report serve as the foundation for battles that have been breaking out around the nation throughout the early 2020s as multiple states have passed laws censoring discussions of race and racism in schools and as school boards and teachers have been besieged by angry parents demanding that "critical race theory" no longer be taught to their children.[1]

It is as if the US is witnessing, on a national level, the scene in *Roll of Thunder, Hear My Cry* when members of the school board converge on Mary Logan's classroom just as she is teaching the children of sharecroppers a history of slavery that is not included in their textbooks:

But Mama did not flinch: she always started her history class the first thing in the morning when the students were most alert, and I knew that the hour was not yet up. To make matters worse, her lesson for the day was slavery. She spoke on the cruelty of it; of the rich economic cycle it generated as slaves produced the raw products for the factories of the North and Europe; how the country profited and grew from the free labor of a people still not free. (Taylor 183)

Before he fires her for this and other acts of civil disobedience, Mr. Granger admonishes her, saying teachers must teach only the state-sanctioned material in the textbook. Mrs. Logan responds: "I can't do that. . . . Because all that's in that book isn't true" (184). She is a threat to the county's plantation owners, who profit from systems—sharecropping, Jim Crow laws, peonage—they would rather not have examined, especially since teaching young people to question such systems might lead the next generation of sharecroppers to resist exploitation.

Even though the contemporary term "critical race theory" is, of course, nowhere in a novel set in the 1930s and written in the mid 1970s, that is indeed what Mrs. Logan is teaching to her students, her children, and her community. For readers of this children's book, when Mrs. Logan is fired for teaching about systemic racism, it serves as yet another example, among many, of the systemic racism that pervades the Logans' community. We, through Cassie's narration, are able to see the patterns that make up the system. And, when she proudly tells us that "Mama did not flinch" (183), we also learn that teaching young people about those patterns and oppressive systems is a dangerous, necessary, and important act of civil disobedience.

In this chapter, I make the case that Mildred D. Taylor's *Thunder*, along with one of its major contemporary successors, Angie Thomas's *The Hate U Give*,[2] are works of fiction that double as works of critical theory, addressing the causes and effects of systemic racism in the United States.[3] After all, if one purpose of critical theory is to provide frameworks that help us to think about difficult-to-decipher social, political, and economic systems, then carefully crafted works of fiction, even children's fiction, can serve a similar purpose. As Kenneth Kidd notes, "[A] good amount of European and American children's literature is bound up with philosophy and theory as well as with progressive politics" and that, as a result, "contemporary children's literature often models and invites critical engagement" (12). Both novels I discuss here—in their content and their narrative structure—depict and theorize intersectional maps of communities, families, histories, and social, legal, and economic systems. They are also books that make the workings of these intricate systems accessible and concrete to a wide range of readers, both adult and child. Furthermore, when these two books are considered in dialogue with one another, they create myriad opportunities to examine our own contemporary communities and systems. They also invite us to view history, not as linear or deterministic but as a contested and constantly evolving construct that deeply informs and can be strategically used to frame contemporary debates at national and local levels, in public and private spaces, and even in our most intimate relationships.

Since this chapter is part of a collection about the works of Mildred Taylor, I assume most readers are familiar with *Thunder* but may not have read Thomas's work. I am placing more emphasis on Thomas's novel and am including a summary for readers unfamiliar with her work.

THE HATE U GIVE AS ADAPTATION AND HOMAGE

The Hate U Give is set in a US city left purposefully vague because the events in the novel can and do occur in places like Philadelphia, Chicago, St. Louis, Atlanta, Jackson, Minneapolis, and Detroit. The protagonist, sixteen-year-old Starr Carter, feels out of place as she tries to navigate between the Black community where she and her family live and the mostly white suburban school she attends. Starr speaks to us through first-person narration but, unlike Cassie Logan, her story unfolds in the moment instead of as a reflection on past events. A childhood friend gives Starr a ride home from a party, and he is stopped by a police officer who shoots and kills him. After witnessing the murder, a shocked Starr explains, "They finally put a sheet over Khalil. He can't breathe under it. I can't breathe. I can't. *Breathe*" (26; emphasis in the original). Her internal monologue, with its repetition of the word "breathe," is a direct reference to the 2014 killing of Eric Garner, who died after being choked by a New York City police officer. Video of his violent arrest posted on the internet and on news programs clearly shows Garner being choked while saying, over and over again, "I can't breathe," a phrase that has since been repeated on signs and in chants at multiple Black Lives Matter protests against police brutality toward Black people. In the wake of the 2020 murder of George Floyd, which led to mass protests around the world, it is a phrase that triggers: for many, it ignites memories and feelings of trauma, helplessness, rage, and fear, but for a growing number of people on the American right, phrases such as this now fall under the umbrella of "critical race theory," subject matter they do not want shared with young readers.

Thomas's popular novel, which, like *Thunder*, doubles as a work of critical theory, draws from such varied influences as the Black Lives Matter movement, the Harry Potter series, the 1990s television comedy *The Fresh Prince of Bel-Air*, and Tupac Shakur's song lyrics. But a less obvious influence on the novel is the work of Mildred Taylor. In an interview with Goodreads, Thomas said:

One of my favorite book families comes from one of my favorite books of all time—the Logan family in *Roll of Thunder, Hear My Cry*. Throughout the novel, the family faces struggles, but they always face them as a unit. That was a huge inspiration for me as I wrote Starr's family in *The Hate U Give*. I kind of wanted them to be a contemporary version of the Logans. ("A Life in Books")

Starr Carter's family—through the events that happen to them, the communities in which they live and work, the school and housing segregation that defines those communities, and the racialized violence and trauma that infuse the characters' everyday lives—is indeed "a contemporary version of the Logans." The connections between these two novels run so deep because they are both intently focused on grounding current social justice issues within the larger historical context they share. Both novels portray American history as a continuum, as an on-going series of actions in which each new generation must play a part. Because both novels share a commitment that social activism be informed by an intimate understanding of oneself as an heir to history, education and a respect for one's elders are central themes as well.

Thomas does not simply allude to Taylor's work; she honors it and her literary elder in the most respectful and meaningful way possible by carrying its ideals forward into a new context and for a new generation. For example, Thomas names Starr Carter's father Maverick because Mary Logan is called "a disrupting maverick" (*Thunder* 30) by a fellow teacher.[4] These two parental figures parallel one another in the ways they model community activism and teach their children about histories not being taught in educational institutions. Just as Mary Logan teaches her students and her own children the history of slavery and Reconstruction, Maverick Carter teaches his children about the Black Panthers and the civil rights movement. The result of this informal education[5] is that the young protagonists in both books come of age by learning that the present world depicted in each novel is a direct result of and a continuation of our nation's history of slavery, segregation, racialized violence, socioeconomic inequality, corrupt laws, and systems of justice, as well as the various movements that have worked to call attention to, reform, and address these injustices.

What follows is a consideration of the stakes involved in teaching books such as these two at a time when "critical race theory," the Black Lives Matter movement, and other movements for civil rights, including basic voting rights, are now seen as existential threats by many conservative Americans, factors that have created an environment in which many teachers are fearful that simply teaching our nation's history, or books like these two, may put them at risk of losing their jobs. While we don't know yet what long-term effects these recent events will have, they will most certainly have a chilling effect, especially on untenured teachers and faculty with little job security, many of whom are BIPOC (Black Indigenous and People of Color). I am a white, tenured, full professor at a university with a strong union; my position of relative privilege allows me, at least for the time being, to teach and write about systemic racism, white privilege, and all manner of critical theory without fear of losing my job. Teachers having to confront angry parents and school boards do not have this privilege, nor do untenured or contingent college and university faculty who are sometimes evaluated based primarily or even solely on evaluations from students.

HISTORICAL CONTEXTS AND WHAT IS AT STAKE IN TEACHING IN AND ABOUT THEM

Significantly and not coincidentally, recent coordinated attacks on antiracist teaching come at a time when we are under other truly existential threats to our democracy: a rise in white supremacist domestic terrorist groups, an aggressive assault on voting rights, a proliferation of destructive lies and conspiracy theories meant to weaken democratic norms, and an unwillingness to reckon with, work to remedy, or even to acknowledge the flaws inherent in our existing institutions, which have foundations built by enslaved people on land stolen from Indigenous people. Some claim that the right's recent obsession with "cancel culture" and the teaching of "critical race theory" is simply a distraction, a way to divert our attention away from more important matters, but it is not; it is a carefully crafted narrative meant to frighten and incense certain groups of white Americans and meant to depict teachers and intellectuals as enemies of the state. In other words, recent efforts in the US to silence discussions about systemic racism are examples of systemic racism.

The fog is deliberate too, meant to veil the fact that such efforts are not new and have been an important part of the right's game plan for decades. These efforts are deliberate and coordinated, coming from well-funded think tanks and organizations, and not from grassroots movements.[6] For example, The Heritage Foundation released a handy guide for parents titled "How to Identify Critical Race Theory: Knowing Critical Race Theory When You See It and Fighting It When You Can," which alerts parents to look out for terms like "white privilege," "systemic racism," and "equity" that may seem benign but all fall under the umbrella of dreaded "critical race theory" (Heritage). Well-funded and well-educated folks, who know exactly what "critical race theory" actually is and is not, are redefining the phrase as a way to teach their followers to reject any kind of antiracist teaching.

There is a wide gap between what scholars in various fields mean by "critical race theory"[7] and what right-wing leaders and pundits are trying to make the phrase mean in popular discourse. The phrase has been appropriated, mimicked, and redefined by the right as a convenient portmanteau to thinly disguise what is actually anti-intellectualism and racism. Indeed, *not* understanding the phrase's precise meaning is precisely the point: in our contemporary media environment, it has become a catchall phrase into which opponents can pour white grievance while claiming to protect the innocence of children.[8] It is a cynical misappropriation that works best in a closed right-wing media ecosystem where fear-filled consumers have also already been convinced that Black Lives Matter is a terrorist organization, that our nation's cities are on fire, and that liberals are intent on turning the US into a communist nation. The three individual words in the phrase "critical race theory" trigger the perfect combination of fear, anger, and resentment already simmering among many white Americans: someone is being "critical" of me, I'm tired of people talking about "race," and "theory" is something the intellectual elites talk about to make everyone else feel stupid, to baffle us all with bullshit, to manipulate us. Exasperated teachers and scholars have tried to explain that, "No, that's not what that phrase means" or "Don't be silly. We don't teach critical race theory to children," but I'd like to suggest a different strategy, which is, essentially, that we have a responsibility to teach "critical race theory" to young people because race is central to our nation's history, laws, social practices, and identity. Works of fiction are one way to approach this complex, difficult subject.

LITERATURE AS THEORY; PEDAGOGY AS ACTIVISM

Works of children's and young adult literature teach adults as well as children: they feature adult characters who are role models for how to (or how not to) be a mentor, teachers who demonstrate how to (or how not to) effectively teach, and parents who model (or don't) loving ways to teach resilience and strength. Most teachers in US schools are white, middle-class women, many of whom don't have training in antiracist teaching or a background in critical theories about race. These two novels are instructive for readers of all ages, including teachers. They are as much about adult mentors as they are about their young protagonists in need of mentorship, and they depict adult characters able to educate young people about our fraught history, while also allowing young people enough agency to find their own way in a complicated world.

Set almost a century apart, both novels feature a young, African American female protagonist struggling to get an education while also combating economic disparity, state-sanctioned racialized violence, and widespread discrimination. The books function as works of critical theory accessible to younger readers in the ways they describe, through an accretion of detail, the effects of the systemic racism their protagonists encounter in every part of their everyday lives. The Logan children walk an hour through red Mississippi dust to attend Great Faith Elementary School, while the Carter family's children make a daily forty-five-minute freeway commute to the Riverton Hills suburb, where they attend high school. Cassie contends with faux-friend Lillian Jean just as Starr contends with faux-friend Hailey, two racist white girls in different eras who are profoundly oblivious about the harm they cause. At home, both protagonists are supported by families with long histories of activism and community engagement. As the elders in both families struggle to maintain a balance between protecting their children from harm while also teaching them to be activists, they work to instill cultural pride but must also teach their children that there are times when pride has to give way to survival so that one can live to fight another day. Cassie is devastated when Big Ma cannot protect her from a "growing crowd" of white people in Strawberry and forces her to apologize to "Miz Lillian Jean" (115). Similarly, Starr, who has just witnessed her friend's murder by a police officer, must stand by, helpless, while police harass her father and make him lie face down on the sidewalk outside of the very store he owns. She explains, "Daddy looks at us. His expression apologizes for the fact that we have to see this" (193). In both cases, young protagonists see older family members in situations where they are just as vulnerable to state-sanctioned violence and abuses of power as younger family members. Because of the systemic racism woven into the fabric of their lives, the process of coming of age and learning to take on adult responsibilities necessarily involves understanding that attaining adulthood does not ensure moving into a position of power, control, or safety, privileges that many white people assume automatically accompany adulthood.

Starr, like Cassie, learns about history at home from her family and community, but her parents, unlike the Logans, are depicted as imperfect role models more akin to the flawed and damaged adults who populate more contemporary children's and young adult literature. Starr's father, Maverick, was imprisoned after becoming involved with a gang. He owns a store and is a community leader, but because of his personal history, he's not universally respected within his community in the ways that the Logans are. His past failures do not make him less of a role model. Instead, they complicate Starr's, and the reader's, understanding of the idea of progress. Maverick has taught his children to memorize each item from the Black Panthers's Ten-Point Program, "the same way other kids learn the Pledge of Allegiance" (320). When violence erupts and threatens the Carter family the night before Starr is supposed to testify about Khalil's murder, she shouts at her parents, "I'm not going!" and explains that, "I thought they were gonna kill you. . . . Because of me" (320). In this moment of doubt and fear, her father kneels in front of her, lifts up her chin, and demands she recite points:

"Point seven."

"We want an immediate end to police brutality," I say, "and the murder of black people, other people of color, and oppressed people."

"Again."

. . .

"And what did Brother Malcolm say is our objective?"

Seven and I could recite Malcolm X quotes by the time we were thirteen. (320–21)

Starr has knowledge and a family history of activism upon which to draw, yet she does not do so uncritically. Indeed, her knowledge about the failures of the civil rights movement to secure a present free from the problems of the past, adds to her doubt and inertia: "By any means necessary didn't keep Brother Malcolm from dying, possibly at the hands of his own people," Starr tells her readers, though not her father. "The reality is, I may not make it to the courthouse in the morning" (321). Her understanding of her legacy is more nuanced than Cassie's because she is older, because her parents have educated her about the complexities of civil rights movements, and because she lives in a time that gives her a broader historical perspective.

Both texts are told in first-person by a Black girl whose coming-of-age narrative involves coming to terms with racial violence and trauma, but the girls are different ages, and the novels target readers of different ages. Readers witness the racialized violence in Starr's world almost immediately when a police officer murders her friend and "[t]hey leave Khalil's body in the street like it's an exhibit" (25). *Thunder*, aimed at a middle grade audience, seems to reveal the violence threatening the Logans' community in more gradual ways, but it is there, all around the Logan children, from the very beginning of the narrative, as the children pass by plantations on their way to school, when they are preyed upon by a monstrous yellow school bus, when they encounter the "emaciated" (8) bodies of their friends who are the children of sharecroppers, and as they discuss rumors about three men burned when "some white men took a match to 'em" (10). Indeed, just a few pages into the novel, six-year-old Little Man is asking, "What does death look like?" (10), a question that is met with derision from an already world-weary T.J.

Just as *Thunder* ends with Cassie mourning for T.J., the land, and her community, *The Hate U Give* ends with Starr mourning for Khalil. Thomas is more explicit and direct in explaining how Starr's mourning is compounded by the weight of an historical trauma that extends far beyond her personal, familial, or community relations: "It would be easy to quit if it was just about me, Khalil, that night, and that cop," she explains. "It's about way more than that though" (443). And then Starr recites a long, familiar, and continuously growing list of names that has become a litany: "Aiyana/Trayvon/Rekia/Michael/Eric/Tamir.... It's even about that little boy in 1955 who nobody recognized at first—Emmett. The messed up part? There are so many more" (443). Thomas makes concrete the historical weight of Khalil's death by showing us how traumas compound and multiply: his murder is one of many, part of a pattern of state-sanctioned racist violence embedded so deeply in our nation's history that it is inseparable from who we are as a nation. In these ways, Starr's final tribute to Khalil helps us to better understand the last lines of *Thunder*, "I cried for T.J. For T.J. and the land" (276), as extending far beyond the Logan land or her falsely accused neighbor.

There are multiple instances in *The Hate U Give* that work to enrich our reading of *Thunder*, which is set in the 1930s but was written after the civil rights movement so that it is subtly infused with nods to events that happened long after the events in the novel. The 1955 murder of Emmett Till is directly referenced, explained, and discussed several times in *The Hate U Give* in ways that educate readers about the historic and cultural significance of his murder. Even though *Thunder* is set twenty-five years before Till's murder by vigilante white supremacists, Taylor subtly alludes to these events when we read that Mr. Berry and his nephews were burned because a white woman said one of them "was flirtin' with her" (39), when we learn that a group of people "lynched a boy a few days ago at Crosston" (40), and when Mary Logan takes her children to visit a badly burned and disfigured Mr. Berry (97–101). After the visit, she explains to them that the assault on Mr. Berry is part of a pattern of violence and that they are organizing a boycott of the Wallace store, which is owned by people who commit these violent acts. After reading *The Hate U Give*, readers can find these connections on their own and can see that, while Emmett Till's murder made racialized violence and trauma visible to the nation as a whole, these dangers were already well known among members of the Black community who experienced them as part of their everyday lives.

RACE AND CHILDHOOD INNOCENCE

While both novels portray whole communities of morally complex and varied characters, which means there is never one individual made to represent an entire culture, both also center Black boys as the most vulnerable members of their communities. Much in the way that Toni Morrison's Pecola Breedlove serves as an allegorical embodiment of the trauma systemic racism, sexism, and colorism inflict on the most powerless, T.J. and Khalil come to bear the brunt, the full weight of white supremacist violence and the corrupt institutions that enable it—a literary device that risks turning individuals into symbols. Althea Tait, who describes *The Hate U Give* as one of several recent "protest novels" written in response to the "cyclical violence Black youth endure within this nation" (217), cautions readers against fixating on the body of the Black child as a symbol of racist violence: "The challenge before us is to give consideration to this body of literature as a theory for empathy without rendering the Black child's body as a site for reified history for the mutually engaged and entangled: in this way, the child becomes a peculiar mammy—mother to us all" (219). Tait asks us to find ways to learn to empathize while also acknowledging that being able to imagine oneself "climb[ing] in and out of the marginalized political locations" is itself a form of privilege (222). After all, the amount of knowledge about trauma and violence that we adults choose to reveal or not to reveal to children is intricately connected to various positions of privilege or oppression. Many Jewish children, for example, learn about the Holocaust and antisemitism far earlier than non-Jewish children, just as many Black children must learn about our racist history earlier than most white children. Brigitte Fielder explains that, "African American children have never been fully shielded from experiences of or knowledge about anti-Black racism, and this fact is reflected in the ways they have been positioned and understood as readers by those who have attended to them" (160).

Differences in how we conceive of childhood innocence affect the kinds of stories we choose to share with young people and the ways authors of texts for children and young adults construct their imagined child readers. Just as all children's literature addresses a dual audience of adult and child, books like *Thunder* or *The Hate U Give* address yet another dual audience of readers: those who are part of the Black community and those who are not.[9] While many white parents, educators, authors, and publishers prioritize maintaining childhood innocence over educating children about potentially traumatizing subjects, parents of children in marginalized groups don't always have this same choice. Robin Bernstein explains that, "Different trajectories of white and black childhood during the second half of the nineteenth century resulted, by the turn of the twentieth, in sharply bifurcated visions of American childhood" (63). White children were associated with innocence while Black children were viewed as insensate, rendering them as unsympathetic: "Innocence had become the exclusive property of the vulnerable white child, while the pain-free pickaninny was exiled from innocence and with it, from childhood—and humanity" (68). These different views of childhood, a direct result of systemic racism, create an environment in which a twelve-year-old Black boy is viewed as a threat by police and Black girls as young as six years old are dragged out of schools in handcuffs for "misbehavior."[10]

White teachers who grew up reading all or mostly books by white authors and about white children, and who were educated in white-dominated institutions, may have internalized these race-based ideologies about what "normal" or "innocent" American childhood should be. Furthermore, because we've all been taught to assume that childhood innocence is natural—just the way things are, just common sense—many have difficulty recognizing these assumptions as a cultural construct. In their 2002 study "Centering the Margins: White Preservice Teachers' Responses to *Roll of Thunder*," Wendy Saul and Kendra Wallace note that many of their white students majoring in education worried that *Thunder* might not be "appropriate" to teach in a classroom because of its use of racist language and its depictions of white characters as "mean or stupid" (46). Based on their analysis of four years of student responses to the book, Saul and Wallace concluded that the white preservice teachers in their classrooms "approach a critical classroom discussion about race as a highly contentious and threatening venture—one they would prefer to avoid altogether" (50). Their study, though twenty years old, is still applicable today because these same preservice teachers are still in classrooms and because their discomfort with even discussing race is most certainly compounded by current attacks on antiracist teaching. Many teachers who were already reluctant to discuss systemic racism may be even more so now when faced with coordinated efforts, backed by well-financed, powerful conservative institutions, whose goal is, indeed, to distort and disrupt antiracist teaching.

DECENTERING WHITENESS IN THE CLASSROOM

One reason I chose to teach and write about these novels in dialogue with one another is because doing so has taught me, as a white woman, to reexamine my own place within the systems, institutions, and power relationships that shape my discipline, scholarship, teaching, and activism. I've learned that, because the institutions and systems I was learning and teaching in were, in and of themselves, white-dominated spaces that catered to mostly white student bodies, the well-intentioned antiracist teaching I had been doing for decades ultimately worked to center whiteness. When I first started teaching about systemic racism in the 1990s, I used the texts that had taught me that African American history *is* American history and that my whiteness was constructed as part of a destructive binary that defined Blackness as Other. For example, I taught texts like Beah Richards' 1950 piece "A Black Woman Speaks" and Peggy McIntosh's 1988 work "White Privilege: Unpacking the Invisible Knapsack" to almost all-white student populations in Ohio and Oregon because these were texts that had taught me to see how moving through the world in a raced body affects even the most mundane-seeming of everyday encounters and experiences, often in ways white people are oblivious to. I had hoped these texts would affect my students in the same ways.

When I started teaching at Eastern Michigan University (EMU), however, I learned that teaching white students about white privilege, while necessary and important, wasn't addressing the needs of all of the students in this far more diverse population.[11] While teaching white students antiracist thinking might have helped my BIPOC students in some abstract, incremental way, it did nothing to help them to survive and succeed. Conversations with my EMU students over the years taught me that I needed to teach children's books about Black joy, not just ones focused on oppression, and contemporary stories, not just historical ones. Teaching *The Hate U Give* alongside *Thunder* was an attempt to decenter myself, both as a white person and as a teacher. On some levels it worked because, instead of simply listening to me lecture about the histories of Jim Crow, lynching, sharecropping, and other events that students need to know about in order to understand *Thunder*, my students were able to educate me about their contemporary communities and cultures in ways that put us on more equal footing and established the classroom as a space where we could all be comfortable with not knowing and with asking questions so that we could work toward constructing knowledge collaboratively. Teaching the two novels in dialogue with one another was a messy weeks-long process of working together to map and remap a historical timeline in which the present informed and revised our understanding of the past. Our growing knowledge of both historical and contemporary contexts came to create a foundation to help us understand the weight and the urgency of this particular historical moment in which we find ourselves.

In a nation where many of us are segregated by age into grades, schools, jobs, and nursing homes or into arbitrary generational categories that pit Zoomers against Boomers, novels such as these depict intergenerational conversations that may not be occurring in the everyday lives of many of our students. Teaching these two books together, then, not only highlights the historical parallels between the narratives but also makes visible the long-term effects and the ebbs and flows of social activism, which may not always be immediately visible over the short term or even over the course of one lifetime. By weaving in historical facts and stories from previous generations, the two novels work in tandem to depict the same series of events and movements but from different points on a lengthy yet connected, multigenerational timeline. Both books depict inspiring young protagonists who are guided by loving families and grounded by their heritage. In this way, they carefully situate their characters and readers within multi-faceted, multigenerational communities where readers are able to learn different temporal, generational perspectives, and strategies for resistance and resilience.[12]

bell hooks writes that "[g]enerations of black Americans living in a white-supremacist country have known what it means to see education as the practice of freedom, have known what it means to educate for critical consciousness"

(63). We see this practice, "educat[ing] for critical consciousness," in both *The Hate U Give* and *Thunder*, books that provide us with role models of adult teachers and mentors; characters who use their knowledge and wisdom to empower themselves, one another, and the next generation. Both books employ a narrative structure that educates readers of all ages about the workings, causes, and effects of systemic racism across generations, while also showing us ways to survive and combat it. Works such as these two novels are powerful tools that can help this generation of educators to develop tactics for antiracist teaching in an environment that is hostile to such work. They are especially important at a time when teachers in many US states are being called upon to practice civil disobedience in their classrooms. The Zinn Education Project posted a petition in June 2021 supporting antiracist teaching practices, which are coming under attack by the right wing: thousands of educators signed their pledge, which states simply, "We, the undersigned educators, refuse to lie to young people about U.S. history and current events—regardless of the law" (Zinn). Mary Logan's explanation to the school board member about to fire her—"I can't do that. . . . Because all that's in that book isn't true" (184)—is a model for principled resistance in the 1930s, 1970s, and again today.

NOTES

1. By 2022, the number of states to have passed laws to restrict education on racism expanded to twenty-eight. The restrictions vary in specificity and severity: "Many of these efforts have attempted to ban critical race theory, the academic framework that examines how policies and the law perpetuate systemic racism. In other states, lawmakers have tried to restrict specific kinds of antiracism training or the teaching of 'divisive' concepts" (Stout and LaMarr LaMee). According to a *New York Times* article, challenges and book bans, especially of titles promoting diversity, have been on the rise: "Parents, activists, school board officials and lawmakers around the country are challenging books at a pace not seen in decades. In early 2022, The American Library Association said in a preliminary report that it received an 'unprecedented' 330 reports of book challenges, each of which can include multiple books, last fall" (Harris and Alter).

2. I want to thank Montgomery Jones, my former student and Eastern Michigan University alum, whose infectious excitement about *The Hate U Give* (which I'm pretty certain she read the day it was released) inspired me to read the novel and include it in future courses.

3. Children's literature scholars have long analyzed works of literature for younger readers using the same critical lenses we employ to study literature for adults. Over the past decade or so, some are shifting from using theory to explicate fiction to putting fiction on equal footing with theory, even using fiction to explicate, challenge, or complicate theory. The introduction to Kenneth Kidd's 2020 book, *Theory for Beginners: Children's Literature as Critical Thought*, includes a thorough summary of these recent conversations. It also explains what interdisciplinary humanities scholars mean by the phrase "critical theory."

4. "[Thomas] also said that, although she didn't see herself in many books growing up, she *did* recognize herself in Cassie Logan of Mildred D. Taylor's *Roll of Thunder, Hear My Cry*" (Flax).

5. Kelly McDowell's essay "*Roll of Thunder, Hear My Cry*: A Culturally Specific, Subversive Concept of Child Agency" distinguishes between the formal and informal education that children in the novel receive from the adults in their community and the important role education plays in the novel.

6. Nancy MacLean's 2017 book *Democracy in Chains: The Deep History of the Radical Right's Stealth Plan for America* documents, among other patterns, the ways that the right has continuously used schools as a battleground to incite their base. In the mid-twentieth century, segregation was framed by them as a "states' rights" issue, and in the early 2000s, they worked to weaken our public school systems by creating the concept of "school choice." Think tanks and even whole university programs funded by wealthy conservative libertarians like Charles Koch have strategized for decades about how to use words and concepts like "freedom" to enlist and motivate conservative citizens. "It was never really about freedom as most people would define it," MacLean explains in her book's conclusion. "It was about the promotion of crippling division among the people. . . . Its leaders had no scruples about enlisting white supremacy to achieve capital supremacy. And today, knowing that the majority does not share their goals and would stop them if they understood their endgame, the team of paid operatives seeks to win by stealth" (254). These same teams of paid operatives are the ones behind current debates about the teaching of "critical race theory." In other words, it is a debate they created and which, for the moment at least, they have successfully weaponized.

7. A concise description of the origins, meaning, and purpose of "critical race theory" is included in the 2017 essay "Race to the Bottom: How the Post-racial Revolution Became a Whitewash," written by one of the theory's early founders, legal scholar Kimberlé Williams Crenshaw.

8. Childhood and childhood innocence are often used as rhetorical devices or as symbols that carry the weight of adult anxieties. Because childhood innocence intersects with factors like race and class, it can be used as a tool to promote racist ideologies under the guise of "protecting the children." Scholars like Kate Capshaw and Robin Bernstein make a compelling case that innocence is often denied to Black children, which means that the "innocent child" being protected from "critical race theory" is a white child.

9. Jani Barker, analyzing responses of Black and white readers to Taylor's novel, explains that Taylor's construction of broad communities of individuals creates spaces for all readers: "The novel refuses a simple binary of black as good and white as evil. Racism itself is presented as evil, but black and white characters within the evil system demonstrate that no race has a monopoly on virtue or vice" (129). She continues, explaining that "[a] second strategy for targeting racism, not the white race, as antagonist of the novel is the depiction of sympathetic antiracist white characters with whom readers can identify, thus rejecting identification with racists" (130). *The Hate U Give* employs a similar strategy by depicting a range of characters, both enemies and allies, in both the white and Black communities inhabiting the novel.

10. In a *New York Times* column titled "Let Black Kids Just Be Kids," Robin Bernstein writes, "People of all races see black children as less innocent, more adultlike and more responsible for their actions than their white peers. In turn, normal childhood behavior, like disobedience, tantrums and back talk, is seen as a criminal threat when black kids do it."

11. Roughly, our student population at EMU is usually around 60 percent white, 20 percent African American, and 20 percent students who are Latinx, international, Native American, Asian American, and Arab American. Michigan, sadly, has one of the most segregated K–12 school systems in the nation (Chambers and MacDonald). Therefore, when they come to our campus, students who went to mostly African American and Latinx schools in the Detroit area interact, often for the first time, with white students from rural and suburban Michigan, who attended mostly white schools, and with students from nearby Dearborn, which has the largest Arab American population in the United States.

12. While I am not citing her work directly here, Ebony Elizabeth Thomas's tweets and posts over the years have strongly influenced my thinking about the ways we construct generations and relationships among generations.

WORKS CITED

"A Life in Books: Angie Thomas - Goodreads News and Interviews." *Goodreads*, Feb. 20, 2017, www.goodreads.com/interviews/show/1226.Angie_Thomas.

Adams, Char, et al. "Map: See Which States Have Passed Critical Race Theory Bills." June 17, 2021. Nbcnews.com.

Barker, Jani L. "Racial Identification and Audience in *Roll of Thunder, Hear My Cry* and *the Watsons Go to Birmingham—1963*," *Children's Literature in Education*, vol. 41, no. 2, 2010, pp. 118–45.

Bernstein, Robin. "Let Black Kids Just Be Kids." *The New York Times*. July 26, 2017. https://www.nytimes.com/2017/07/26/opinion/black-kids-discrimination.html.

Bernstein, Robin. *Racial Innocence: Performing American Childhood from Slavery to Civil Rights*. NYU Press, 2011.

Stout, Cathryn, and Gabrielle LaMarr LeMee. "Efforts to Restrict Teaching About Racism and Bias Have Multiplied Across the U.S." *Chalkbeat*. July 22, 2021. https://www.chalkbeat.org/.

Chambers, Jennifer, and Christine MacDonald. "Despite Gains, Mich. Schools among Most Segregated." *Detroit News*, The Detroit News, Dec. 5, 2017, www.detroitnews.com/story/news/education/2017/12/04/michigan-schools-education-segregated/108295160/.

Crenshaw, Kimberlé Williams. "Race to the Bottom: How the Post-racial Revolution Became a Whitewash." https://thebaffler.com/salvos/race-to-bottom-crenshaw.

Crowley, Michael. "Trump Calls for 'Patriotic Education' to Defend American History from the Left." *The New York Times*. Sept. 17, 2020, https://www.nytimes.com/2020/09/17/us/politics/trump-patriotic-education.html?smid=url-share.

Fielder, Brigitte. "Before *The Brownies' Book*." *The Lion and the Unicorn*, vol. 43, no. 2, 2019, pp. 159–71. Project MUSE, doi:10.1353/uni.2019.0016.

Flax, Shoshana. "Out of the Box: Recap: Angie Thomas at First Parish Church in Cambridge, MA." *The Horn Book* website, 2018, www.hbook.com/?detailStory=recap-angie-thomas-first-parish-church-cambridge-ma.

Harris, Elizabeth and Alexandra Alter. "Book Ban Efforts Spread Across the U.S." *The New York Times*. Jan. 30, 2022. https://www.nytimes.com/2022/01/30/books/book-ban-us-schools.html.

Heritage Foundation. "How to Identify Critical Race Theory: Knowing Critical Race Theory When You See It and Fighting It When You Can." https://www.heritage.org/civil-society/heritage-explains/how-identify-critical-race-theory. June 24, 2020.

hooks, bell. *Talking Back: Thinking Feminist, Thinking Black*. South End Press, 1989.

Kidd, Kenneth. *Theory for Beginners: Children's Literature as Critical Thought*. Fordham UP, 2020.

MacLean, Nancy. *Democracy in Chains: The Deep History of the Radical Right's Stealth Plan for America*. Viking, 2017.

McDowell, Kelly. "*Roll of Thunder, Hear My Cry*: A Culturally Specific, Subversive Concept of Child Agency." *Children's Literature in Education*, vol. 33, no. 3, Sept. 2002, pp. 213–25.

President's Advisory 1776 Commission. "The 1776 Report." Jan. 2021. https://en.wikisource.org/wiki/The_1776_Report.

Saul, Wendy, and Kendra Wallace. "Centering the Margins: White Preservice Teachers' Responses to *Roll of Thunder*." *Teaching Education*, vol. 13, no. 1, Apr. 2002, pp. 41–53.

Stout, Cathryn and Gabrielle LaMarr LaMee "Efforts to restrict teaching about racism and bias have multiplied across the U.S." *Chalkbeat*. July 22, 2021. https://www.chalkbeat.org/22525983/map-critical-race-theory-legislation-teaching-racism.

Tait, Althea. "Empathy: 'The [Probing] Problem We All Live With.'" *The Lion and the Unicorn*, vol. 43, no. 2, 2019, pp. 215–35. *Project MUSE*, doi:10.1353/uni.2019.0020.

Taylor, Mildred. *Roll of Thunder, Hear My Cry*. Random House, 2001.

Thomas, Angie. *The Hate U Give*. Balzer and Bray, 2017.

Zinn Education Project. "Pledge to Speak the Truth." Aug. 11, 2021. https://www.zinnedproject.org/news/pledge-to-teach-truth.

Care Ethics and Activism in Mildred D. Taylor's Roll of Thunder, Hear My Cry and Angie Thomas's The Hate U Give

Bryanna Somers

Antiracist protests—many organized by young BIPOC—surged across the United States following the deaths of George Floyd and Breonna Taylor. Youth activist Mari Chiles calls this kairotic moment "[her] generation's Civil Rights Movement" (qtd. in Strauss), emphasizing the connections between current and historical violence against Black folks. Organizers across the country call for "an end to police brutality, an end to the institutionalized remnants of slavery and the reform of American law enforcement" (Strauss) with many specifically insisting on defunding the police. These protests also grow from the work done by the Black Lives Matter movement, which rose in prominence following the 2013 acquittal of George Zimmerman for the fatal shooting of Trayvon Martin and the 2014 killings of Michael Brown and Eric Garner by police officers. Such conditions and activist responses shape the experiences of young people and inform the construction of youth literature.

Angie Thomas's *The Hate U Give* (2017) was published during this time of heightened awareness regarding police brutality, entering into a multigenerational conversation about how we work to dismantle systemic racism. *The Hate U Give* centers on sixteen-year-old Starr Carter, who lives in the economically disenfranchised neighborhood of Garden Heights while attending the wealthy, predominantly white, Williamson High Preparatory School. Starr's family is modeled after Mildred D. Taylor's Logan family, and—as also discussed by

Annette Wannamaker in her chapter in this volume—the book draws inspiration from *Roll of Thunder, Hear My Cry*. In numerous interviews, Thomas names Taylor's *Roll of Thunder, Hear My Cry* (1976) as her favorite book and a huge influence on her own work, saying, "Though Cassie Logan's story is set decades before I was born, she, like me, was a black girl living in poverty in Mississippi. She was the hero I aspired to be, and as a reader, this was the first time I read a book and saw myself on its pages" (qtd. in Haber). After watching her friend's death at the hands of police, Starr—like the Logans—must work to balance care for her own safety while caring for others in her community. Starr struggles to determine the best way to work toward creating institutional change as she debates sharing her story with the media and navigates what role she wants to have in the public uprising that follows.

Set in 1933 rural Mississippi during the Great Depression, *Thunder* follows nine-year-old Cassie Logan and her family—one of the few Black families to be landowners at this time. The Logans work to improve conditions in their community through organizing a boycott against the oppressive white-owned stores that maintain the disenfranchisement of Black people in their community. For the Logans, caring relationships within their family and their community inform their activist practices. Winner of the 1977 Newbery Medal, *Thunder* has had a lasting impact on generations of readers, and the larger Logan Family Saga has been crucial in educating young readers on how racism has impacted multiple generations of Black families. In both *Thunder* and *The Hate U Give*, the characters engage in activism relative to their specific cultural, historical moments. The activist practices of both families are rooted in the caring relationships built with their family and their community, as well as by the regulating institutions and systemic racism that impact these relationships.

Thunder lays the groundwork for representations of activism in children's literature that centers a feminist ethic of care. *The Hate U Give* then extends Taylor's emphasis on the interconnectedness of caring relationships to modern activist movements such as Black Lives Matter. I will use feminist care ethics to examine the rich intertextuality between these texts, looking closely at how relational care informs the activist practices in each book. In this chapter, I will focus specifically on *Thunder* as opposed to the entire Logan Family Saga—because of its direct influence on Thomas's work, and because it is the most widely taught of Taylor's books—though I will make brief reference to other Logan texts when needed. Ultimately, I argue that both Taylor and Thomas model ethical ways of enacting care within ourselves, our families, and our communities, demonstrating how important a feminist ethic of care—situated within cultural historical contexts—is to activist practices.

APPLYING A BLACK FEMINIST ETHIC OF CARE

Like others, I trace the roots of feminist care ethics to Carol Gilligan's *In a Different Voice* (1982) and Nel Noddings's *Caring: A Feminine Approach to Ethics and Moral Education* (1984), both of which established the framework as a relational ethic grounded in the experiences of women. Gilligan challenges Lawrence Kohlberg's theory of moral development, claiming that existing conversations about moral reasoning are biased against women and insisting that we need to listen to the experiences of women in our approach to understanding moral reasoning. Gilligan also sought to reposition how we think about care; because caring duties fall to women in a patriarchal society, care is too often undervalued. Yet for Gilligan, an ethic of care helps us to see the self and the other coming together to inform one another's development of morality.

Noddings builds on this framework, arguing for the importance of reception and engrossment. With reception, for a relationship to be ethical, the cared-for—who is the object of the care—must somehow receive the care given by the one-caring (Noddings 178). A potential one-caring—that is, someone who wants to care for another person—cannot just decide what is best for the cared-for; they must situate themselves within the needs of the other. When applying this to activist practices, I add that activists must situate themselves within the needs of the community in which they are trying to make a difference. Additionally, when forming relationships with other people and communities, we in turn develop a view of ourselves in relation to them. Noddings writes:

> When I reflect on the way I am in genuine caring relationships and caring situations—the natural quality of my engrossment, the shift of my energies toward the other and his projects—I form a picture of myself. ... I see that when I am as I need the other to be toward me, I am the way I want to be—that is, I am closest to goodness when I accept and affirm the internal "I must." (35)

For Noddings, this picture of ourselves as our best cared-for and one-caring selves in relation to others—which involves engaging in reception and engrossment—makes up our ethical ideal.

Much work has been done in examining the limitations of Noddings's and Gilligan's early works—namely, that Gilligan and Noddings are writing from a particular white, Western subjectivity, one that values individualism over collectivism, so the focus tends to be on women and family units rather than on local or global communities. While Gilligan and Noddings have laid significant groundwork, feminist ethics of care have since been taken up by others such as Joan Tronto, Fiona Robinson, and Virginia Held, who extend these conversations to a more global application in thinking about how to shape more equitable and just communities. According to Fiona Robinson, "Care ethicists argue that people experience their moral lives in the context of webs of relationships with individuals and groups of particular others" (30). It is not just about the parent/child or teacher/student relationships explored in Gilligan and Noddings; today, most care theorists consider all people to be in relation with numerous others. The ways in which people and communities are connected can be referred to as relationality. Further, because of how systemic oppression informs relationality, "one of the main tasks of moral inquiry is to think about how care and responsibilities for care are distributed both within and across societies" (Robinson 30). Virginia Held adds that feminist care ethics "appreciates as well the value of care between persons of unequal power in unchosen relations such as those between parents and children, and between members of social groups of various kinds" (*The Ethics of Care* 46). These unequal power relationships are present in our dominant institutions—such as between teacher and student, doctor and patient, lawmaker and resident. Ideally, the more powerful party is meant to serve the less powerful, but these relationships often serve to further oppress marginalized people. To cultivate ethical caring relationships within these regulating institutions, we have a responsibility to use feminist care ethics to redefine who cares, what caring is, what value we place on caring, and how caring extends to our institutions and our various communities of belonging.

Part of this work requires decentering whiteness in conversations about caring. Scholars such as Audrey Thompson have critiqued feminist care ethics for centering the experiences of white women in private spaces, thus extending the conversation to how care theory can be applied to larger conversations about equity and inclusion. In "Not the Color Purple: Black Feminist Lessons for Educational Caring," Thompson argues that while feminist ethics of care are important to any society, they must be critiqued for their colorblind roots and taken up in new ways (528). In his 2020 article "Reading Relational in Mildred Taylor: Toward a Black Feminist Care Ethics for Children's Literature," Wesley S. Jacques takes up feminist care ethics by advocating for a dual framework of Black feminist thought and feminist care ethics in children's literature scholarship.

Applications of feminist care ethics to the study of children's literature are rare; Mary Jeanette Moran's 2014 article "Making a Difference: Ethical Recognition Through Otherness in Madeleine L'Engle's Fiction" exemplifies how feminist ethics of care can be a valuable framework for examining relationality and othering in children's literature. In her book *Twenty-First-Century Feminisms in Children's and Young Adult Literature* (2018), Roberta Seelinger Trites includes a helpful overview of Moran's contributions to the application of feminist care ethics to children's literature. She notes: "Moran demonstrates an ethics of care in which female characters in children's and YA novels can 'unite the personal satisfaction of intellectual achievement with the communal goal of caring for others,' while still avoiding 'the expectation that they must sacrifice themselves in the service of their relationships'" (qtd. in Trites 158).

In her own analysis of feminism, disability studies, and narrativity, Trites draws from Moran's application of feminist care ethics to children's literature (159). Similarly, Jacques's article draws inspiration from Moran's application of feminist care ethics, especially regarding relationality. In particular, Jacques focuses on how Moran "argues for connection and empathy through apparent difference" (6). Ultimately, he affirms that feminist care ethics "offers an undeniably generative vocabulary for equitable readings of children's literature" while insisting that "considerations of alternate standpoints—not simply adult, white women—add significantly to politically-attuned ethical praxis" (2).

Informed by the work of Patricia Hill Collins and Jennifer Nash, Jacques applies this dual framework to Taylor's *Thunder* specifically. He claims *Thunder* "thoughtfully illustrates, and effectively theorizes, in its own right, a Black feminist care ethic that is simultaneously critical of how we, as a plurality of peoples, care for one another while reifying the radical potential of care" (2-3). In light of Taylor's important theoretical contributions, Jacques goes on to insist that "Taylor's work, as well as the tradition of Black feminist thought that it emerges from, should be positioned in history and in praxis to (in turn) inform our understanding of a feminist ethics of care" (7). Based on Jacques's work, a Black feminist care ethic centers the experiences of marginalized voices; considers the impact our various subjectivities have on our caring relationships; is critical of how we care for one another "while reifying the radial potential of care" (3); remains "critical of our relationships to power" (5); and considers the situational and contextual factors, as well as the vulnerability of others (8).

Jacques makes the case for Black feminist care ethics in children's literature scholarship and insists that *Thunder* is itself a theoretical text. I extend this conversation to activist practices specifically, considering how Taylor's work, as theory, informs representations of activism in contemporary youth literature. Because contemporary texts such as *The Hate U Give* are informed by both Taylor's work and the cultural context of the Black Lives Matter movement, their relationships and activist practices are also shaped by Black feminist care ethics.

INSTITUTIONS AND CARE DYNAMICS

How people enact care might look different when that care takes place in a public versus a private sphere. I consider private care to involve caring work being done within oneself, between two individuals, or within a family unit. Public care involves caring for some level of community, whether that be local, national, or global. Delineating between the two helps us consider how power dynamics and subjectivity shape the way people care for others, themselves, and their communities. That being said, public and private care are fluid and do not serve as binaries, and the ways we care—publicly and privately—are interrelated. Together, *Thunder* and *The Hate U Give* make visible the persistent interconnected nature of care and activism. Throughout the books, characters choose how to engage in activism based on their relationships, the institutions that regulate them, and the cultural moment in which they live.

Because activists work within a web of relationships, they must often consider competing needs for public and private care. In *The Hate U Give*, after Starr witnesses her friend Khalil's death at the hands of a white police officer, she struggles between her sense of responsibility to come forward as a witness and her desire to protect both herself and her family members. Refraining from giving her story could be an act of individual care, protecting her from engaging in a possibly retraumatizing event. Meanwhile, telling the truth about the events of the shooting is an act of public care; after all, Khalil can't tell his side of the story, and a narrative controlled by only the accused officer and the institution of the police has the potential to cause harm to the community of Garden Heights, perpetuating negative stereotypes about victims of police brutality in the larger cultural conversation. Both choices are ethical, but Starr must decide whether to act in a way that prioritizes care for her family or care for her community.

The ethical caring relationships in *The Hate U Give* have clear roots in Taylor's Logan Family Saga. Cassie and the Logans reveal how public and private care overlap and work to shape one another. Perhaps the most evident example of this influence comes from the nuances found within caring relationships between parents and children in these texts. In *Thunder*—as well as other Logan family books such as *The Land* (2001), *Song of the Trees* (1975), and *The Well* (1995)—parents balance the need to reveal information to their children with their desire to protect them, deciding how much the children need to know and when.

Often, these decisions are informed by the injustice the children experience and their need to learn how to navigate and subvert racist systems. When Mary and Caroline Logan educate the children about inequities in the bussing system, they are each serving as one-caring in a caring relationship that occupies a private space. When the youngest Logan, Little Man, is frustrated by the inequities in the bussing system, they inform him about how racism impacts economics and institutions in their community. Cassie narrates:

> Although he had asked Mama after the first day of school why Jefferson Davis had two buses and Great Faith had none, he had never been fully satisfied with her answer. She had explained to him, as she had explained to Christopher-John the year before and to me two years before that, that the county did not provide buses for its black students. In fact, she said, the county provided very little and much of the money which supported the black schools came from the black churches. (44)

Here, the parents inform Little Man about how racism shapes institutions—as well as how the community members care for one another to help address racial and economic disparities. The Black church, an institution in its own right, works to fund the schools because of how thoroughly this racist society—and the racist education institution—have failed to care for Black children. In this way, care is a means of working towards equity. The adult Logans emphasize how the Black community works together to respond to the injustice enacted by a white supremacist culture.

These acts of care between parents and children are shaped by the structural racism of American culture; multiple generations of Logan parents work to empower their children, but they also have to prepare them for the violence they will face. According to Thompson, "In a hostile, racist society, Black families cannot risk having their children caught unaware by racism. One of the tasks of the Black family, therefore, is to prepare children to cope: to face racism with resilience" (535). As a result, parents often take into consideration a child's relationality in both public and private spaces when deciding how to care for them. Because systemic racism informs these caring relationships, the parents cannot always care for children in the way the child wants to be cared for. Yet the caring relationships remain ethical nonetheless, which we can see when applying Noddings's principles of reception and engrossment. The parents remain engrossed in the needs and wants of the children, even if they can't always give them what they need. When Little Man insists that the treatment he is experiencing from the bus driver—as well as the lack of bussing for Black students—just isn't fair, Big Ma (Caroline, their grandmother) replies with empathy that is rooted in the realities of their social conditions. Cassie narrates: "Big Ma was not one for coddling any of us, but now she turned from the stove and, wiping her hands on her long white apron, sat down on the bench and put her arm around Little Man. 'Now, look here, baby, it ain't the end of the world. Lord, child, don't you know one day the sun'll shine again and you won't get muddy no more?'" (*Thunder* 45). When Little Man says things would be different if the white bus driver would slow down or if Black children had a bus to take them to school, Big Ma says, "Well he don't and you don't. . . . So no use frettin' 'bout it. One day you'll have a plenty of clothes and maybe even a car of yo' own to ride 'round in, so don't you pay no mind to them ignorant white folks. You jus' keep on studyin' and get yo'self a good education and you'll be alright" (45). Here, Big Ma emphasizes the need to understand the way things work now, while also insisting that education is a tool for systemic change and a source of hope.

Systemic racism informs the ways these two women care for the Logan children. Little Man's reception—like care itself—is socially situated. Little Man wants care from the bus driver and the education system, but he doesn't get it. Mary and Big Ma cannot do anything to relieve Little Man of the abuse from the bus driver, and they can't solve the issue of bussing in their community. However, they can teach him about how systemic racism is reinforced and emphasize the role education can play in creating a better, safer future—and this constitutes a caring relationship. We see Little Man's reception of the care through how he and the other Logan children use this knowledge to navigate the world around them and to inform their ethical ideal.

The Logan children often want to know more—or, such as in their conversations about the bussing system, want immediate action—and therefore might not immediately receive or understand how the adults are caring. Likewise, because the adults are focused on long-term goals of survival and liberation, they may not seem fully engrossed in the immediate needs or wants of the children. This is due to the power dynamics in a parent-child relationship; the parents have power over the child and have more experience operating under structural racism. They use that power and experience to give the children the knowledge and skills they need to make their own decisions about how to enact care within themselves and their communities.

This influence from the Logan parents, and the ethical ideal we see developing throughout *Thunder*, impacts the decisions characters make in later books as well. In *All the Days Past, All the Days to Come* (2020), which occurs eleven years later, Little Man (now just Man) decides to step off the bus when the driver tells him and Cassie to move back to make room for white passengers—a decision informed by the formation of his ethical ideal. He cannot care for himself by following the bus driver's orders, and he cannot care for himself or his family, including Cassie, who accompanies him, by lashing out at the bus driver—but he can, and does, remove himself from the situation. Events and relationships in *Thunder* shape his ethical ideal and inform how he engages in activist practices moving forward. The reception for the caring relationship between Little Man and his parents is: Little Man lives, Little Man bears witness, and Little Man joins with his family to work towards liberation. He weighs his options on the bus and chooses the action that best aligns with his ethical ideal.

Stacey's friend T.J. serves as a stark contrast to the Logan children. He fails to care for himself, his family, or his community, letting Stacey take the blame when he has cheated; revealing that Mrs. Logan started the boycott, thus resulting in the school board firing her; and allying with the Simms boys to steal from the store, refusing to acknowledge the ways he is being manipulated by the Simmses and ultimately resulting in his being blamed for the Simmses' murder of Mr. Barnett, the shop owner. In *Thunder*, failing to care puts the characters, their family, and their community in danger.

The conversations that the children have with Mary, Big Ma, and David in *Thunder* are precursors to "the talk"; that is, the hard conversations Black parents have with children about how to protect themselves when faced with instances of racial violence. Because Cassie is older than Little Man, we see the talk play out more fully in her interactions with Big Ma and her parents. When Cassie leaves Logan land to go to the market in Strawberry with Big Ma, she accidentally bumps into Lillian Jean, a white thirteen-year-old who attends the neighboring school. Lillian Jean and her father intimidate Cassie until she is forced—under the guidance of Big Ma—to apologize. Cassie resents Big Ma for this, which Mary challenges: "Big Ma didn't want you to be hurt. . . . That was the only thing on her mind . . . making sure Mr. Simms didn't hurt you" (*Thunder* 126). The threat of violence causes Big Ma to care first for Cassie's physical safety, which means she cannot show Cassie care in the way that Cassie herself wants. Systemic racism and institutionalized white supremacy inhibit reception here because Cassie does not actively receive Big Ma's care. Like Little Man earlier, Cassie insists that this is not fair; indignant, she asks why Mr. Simms pushed her into the road. Mary is direct, explaining that Mr. Simms thinks Lillian Jean is better than they are because she's white (*Thunder* 126–7). We've seen Cassie experience institutional oppression and hear stories about her family's experiences with racism, yet this still comes as a shock to her.

As others have noted, Cassie's awakening to the racism in her community serves as a pedagogical device, helping to educate young readers about the historical context through Cassie's experiences. But this lack of awareness is also the result of how her parents have effectively cared for her and her siblings. In "Let Freedom Ring: Land, Liberty, Literacy, and Lore in Mildred Taylor's Logan Family Novels," Michelle H. Martin writes:

> Cassie does not understand even as a nine-year-old that white people consider her and all black people inferior, suggesting that Mary and David have insulated Cassie from racism—perhaps to a fault. What functioned as sheltering at home becomes a handicap in the racially

mixed environment of Strawberry—a handicap that feels like entrapment to Cassie, who now glimpses how little she knows about the social systems to which she is subject. (381)

This sheltering doesn't come from a desire to protect innocence, though; according to Thompson, "Far from trying to protect childish innocence, caring African American adults are intent on alerting young people to the various threats to their survival and flourishing, to help them to cope with racism (and sexism) without loss of integrity" (535). The Logan parents have worked to empower their children while also trying to make sure they have the tools they need to survive—and thrive. According to Noddings, when someone is used to receiving care, they may be "already strong, receptive, expecting to be cared for ... meet[ing] others with the expectation of genuine encounter" (76). Cassie has been well-cared for by her parents, so she—rightly—expects to be cared for when she goes out into the world. While protection puts Cassie at risk, it also empowers her to know her worth and to learn how to fight for social justice in effective ways.

Just as the Logan parents work to educate their children on the effects of structural racism in their historical context, *The Hate U Give* shows how "the talk" plays out for contemporary Black families living under a changed, yet persisting, structural police violence. We see this in conversations between Starr and her father, Maverick, who explains how structural racism negatively impacts their community of Garden Heights:

> Now, think 'bout this. . . . How did the drugs even get in our neighborhood? This is a multibillion-dollar industry we talking 'bout, baby. That shit is flown into our communities, but I don't know anybody with a private jet. Do you? . . . Drugs come from somewhere, and they're destroying our community. . . . That's the hate they're giving us, baby, a system designed against us. That's Thug Life. (Thomas 170)

Much like how Taylor educates young people about historical constructions of racism, Thomas illuminates how these racist systems have persisted and continue to work today. This moment between Maverick and Starr captures a caring relationship dynamic that has always existed in the US: the conversations Black caregivers have with their children to keep them safe. Behind the death of Khalil is a history of police violence and economic oppression of poor communities—that is, of a lack of ethical caring practices. Debating giving her statement, Starr says, "I wish I could say yes, but I don't know. On one hand, it's the cops. . . . On the other hand, it's the cops" (55). For Starr, and many BIPOC, the police cannot be a source of protection, justice, or care because the police have been the aggressors in her community, even long before Khalil's death.

Taylor herself depicts historical police violence in *The Gold Cadillac* (1987), which takes place in the 1950s. In this novella, the narrator, 'lois, witnesses her father get pulled over by police and accused of stealing the car he is driving—a car he owns. He survives, but the police arrest him, fine him, and follow him as he drives out of town, creating a very real threat to the family's safety. When 'lois asks her father about the arrest as well as Jim Crow laws, he explains that this violence descends from slavery (*Gold Cadillac* 36–37). Taylor's Logan family series traces the continuity of racial violence from slavery to Reconstruction to Jim Crow, and *The Hate U Give* reveals how this violence persists into the twenty-first century.

As they did with 'lois sixty years before, the police present a very real threat to Starr, and this threat must inform her relationality; after all, the officer points his gun at Starr after killing Khalil, and his fellow police officers later shake down her father, Maverick, in retaliation for Starr's having given her statement. In providing her statement to the very police who are responsible for Khalil's death, Starr puts herself—and her family—at further risk. Like the Logans, though, Starr feels responsible for sharing her experience; being alive is itself a form of privilege when others like Khalil can't tell their own story. The police, as a regulating institution, and the violence against Black bodies in this cultural landscape shape Starr's decision about how to engage in activism. Starr ultimately decides to share her experience with the police and to tell her story on television—two decisions that are informed by her caring relationships with others. Her need to speak against violence exemplifies the internal "I must" that comes with engrossment (Noddings 35); to attain her ethical ideal, Starr must use her voice to care for others as well as for herself: to protect the memory of Khalil, to hold police accountable, and to invest in systemic racial justice that Garden Heights—and the entire country—needs.

GENERATIONAL CARE THROUGH INCLUSION AND SUBVERSION

People, communities, and institutions operate within a web of relationships, and this relationality helps us understand how intersecting systems of oppression inform care practices. In Taylor's and Thomas's books, any work towards liberation involves considering both the needs of the individual and those of the community within the context of the systems and institutions that regulate them. The Logans make careful, deliberate decisions about how they will work towards the larger goal of justice and institutional change, and some of these methods involve subversive work within regulating institutions. According to Martin,

"African Americans in general and the Logan family in particular obtain true freedom only through owning land; actively fighting injustice, even as children; pursuing an education, which includes acquiring literacy; and understanding their own history through family oral traditions" (372). The Logans accomplish each of these approaches to liberation over multiple generations, and such liberation is cultivated by caring relationships. David inherits the Logan land that Paul-Edward and Caroline struggled and succeeded in procuring, thanks in no small part to Paul-Edward's education. Owning their own land means they can't lose housing when they boycott white business owners, and it means they have the potential to open up a line of credit for other Black families if they need to (albeit at great risk). Land ownership functions as a kind of protective institution; the system of land ownership is structured to prevent a Black person from owning land, with most being sharecroppers, through which white landowners and shopkeepers kept Black people in a perpetual state of debt.

One way the Logans work to enact care is through inclusion and subversion within such dominant institutions, often made possible by access to education. Perhaps the most visible act of care through subversion, though, surfaces in Mary Logan, who works as a school teacher. This position gives her the opportunity to actively shape the education of Black children in their community. It's later revealed that Mary has been deviating from the prescribed curriculum and textbooks in order to give the children a quality education—one that isn't shaped by white ideologies and whitewashed histories. Inadvertently, a lack of care from the government and the education institution comes with a lack of oversight on the part of white stakeholders in education, which allows Mary for a time to structure her curriculum in the way she sees fit.

Mary's methods for enacting change in the school are informed by her relationships with the students, including her own children. Her activist practices become more overt when she becomes engrossed in their needs as well as the needs of others in the community. When Mary hears that Little Man and Cassie have refused their textbook copies, she empathizes with them and knows that what they are resisting is the system that denies them access to new textbooks with accurate, ethical contents. In solidarity with them, she pastes over the racist ledger on the inside cover of each book. Miss Crocker, another school teacher, challenges Mary, saying the children need to be made aware of the way things are (Taylor, *Thunder* 30). Mary replies, "Maybe so . . . but that doesn't mean they have to accept them . . . and maybe we don't either" (30). This moment portrays a key act of care as Mary supports her children and the other students, and it marks Mary's move away from subversion and towards a more direct form of action: a plan to organize a mass boycott of white-owned stores. Her subversive teaching practices only come to the attention of the white community when Harlan Granger and Kaleb Wallace seek retribution for the boycott, which results in her firing. Even though inclusion in these institutions gives the Logans power to subvert norms and work toward systemic change from inside the system, there are still risks in that work. The Logans must constantly negotiate the balance between the challenges and affordances of these caring opportunities.

Set seventy-seven years after the events in *Thunder*, Thomas's *The Hate U Give* demonstrates how racism and relationality continue to inform care within individuals, families, and communities. Similar to the Logans, the Carters work within institutions to care for their community while also achieving economic mobility for their family. Here, liberation through property is extended to business ownership. Black-owned businesses are important to the Garden Heights community; indeed, Mav's convenience store plays an essential role in Garden Heights, which is otherwise a food desert. It also allows him to hire Khalil and DeVante at different times to help them turn their lives around and support their families. Instead of putting their money back into the hands of white business owners, people in Garden Heights can invest in Black businesses and therefore in the economic growth of their community. Similar to Mary Logan's role in caring for her community as a teacher, Starr's mother, Lisa Carter, provides care as a nurse, working within the health care system—an institution that often fails to provide adequate care to Black patients—to provide access to care for vulnerable people in Garden Heights. The Carters work within institutions to care for their community while also achieving economic mobility for their family.

Yet even with this in mind, in *The Hate U Give*, the Carters must balance their desire to protect their family and care for their community; a central conflict between Maverick and Lisa Carter is whether to continue living in Garden Heights or to move to a safer community. Lisa insists they move to protect their children, while Maverick wants to stay and help others in their community. Still, no strict divide exists between public and private care. By the end of the book, the Carters decide to move to a safer neighborhood while continuing to enact care in Garden Heights. They visit friends, Maverick keeps the shop running, and Lisa continues to work at the community health care clinic outside her new, higher-paying position at the hospital. Maverick, Lisa, and Starr come to see themselves as having a shared identity with this larger community. Only through this shared identity and solidarity can they create change within themselves, their family unit, and Garden Heights.

Such relationality is modeled in *Thunder* when characters disagree about the best way to work toward fighting acts of racism, particularly when the Logan parents are deciding what to do about the Wallace store and the violence done to Mr. Tatum and the Berrys. These acts of injustice present two different kinds of racial violence: physical violence and structural economic violence. Mr. Tatum was tarred and feathered after having challenged a white shop owner, who had added items he hadn't ordered to his tab. The Wallaces lynched John Henry, Beacon Berry, and Samuel Berry after John Henry and Beacon were accused of flirting with a white woman. Only Samuel survived, though he was badly burned. The Wallaces also work to bring Black youth to their shop, giving them alcohol and cigarettes to inflate their families' tabs at the Wallace store and chip away at the moral fabric of the Black community. Mary advocates for a nonviolent approach: a boycott of the Wallace store. In contrast, Uncle Hammer wants to deal with these injustices through violent retaliation, saying, "I'd rather burn them out myself. . . . Ain't gonna have nothing noway. . . . You think by shopping up at Vicksburg you gonna drive them Wallaces out, then you got no idea of how things work down there" (Taylor, *Thunder* 151). The boycott puts the Logans in jeopardy in several ways; they risk physical violence by the night men—that is, the Ku Klux Klan—but they also risk losing their land as Harlan Granger uses his bank connections to make the full mortgage due. The Logans, in owning land and being free from sharecropping, have more privilege than others in their community, and they leverage that privilege to advocate for the rights and protection of others. Ultimately, the boycott doesn't last, as many families face the prospect of losing their jobs and housing if they continue. Still, the act of going through with the boycott represents a stand against injustice while reinforcing the relational care of the community members. David says, "I want these children to know we tried, and what we can't do now, maybe one day they will" (164–5). The boycott initiates collective action, chips away at a larger systemic problem, and models ethical caring practices for the next generation of Logan activists.

While the Logans experience multiple forms of oppression, they also hold more power and privilege than other Black folks in their community because they own land and therefore aren't subjugated and regulated by white landowners. The Logans work to leverage that power and privilege on behalf of those who have less. Within their caring practices, both the Logans and the Carters prioritize the care of future generations as much as they do their children or their respective communities, which aligns with Black feminist care ethics. According to Thompson, "The Black feminist tradition of caring requires helping all African Americans to survive racism without loss of integrity; in part, this means helping to make society more just for generations as yet unborn" (533). One way both books work toward generational change is by modeling different approaches via adult characters and unpacking how these approaches influence the ethical ideal of young people. Referring to the Lillian Jean encounter in Strawberry, Martin notes that each adult's different response to racial injustice "offers Cassie different perspectives on prejudice and power, and each helps her settle into her own ethos concerning the balance between self-respect and self-preservation" (382). Extending this to the boycott, each perspective shows a deliberation and relational care that isn't present in the children's decision-making earlier in the book, when the Logan children decide to act on their frustrations with the bussing system without first considering the potential consequences this could have for their family and their community.

Stacey, Cassie, Christopher-John, and Little Man dig a ditch in hopes of stopping the bus on its route home. The plan works, albeit more successfully than they had planned; the ditch widens in the rain, and the bus gets stuck for at least a week. Their decision to take this action is understandable; they want to do something to feel empowered, and they want to take a stand against the inequities in the bussing system. However, their approach is not relational; they don't think of how this might jeopardize the safety of others—which their mother points out—and they don't consider the repercussions that could result. That night, the night men ride, and the children fear that it's because of their actions. While they later learn that the night men are out for different reasons, the terror of that night has a lasting impact on their ethical decision-making. Activism without relational care is flat-out dangerous. The threat of violence that night greatly impacts Cassie's approach to activism, as she becomes more aware of the ways racism and white supremacy impact her ability to create change.

Further shaping Cassie's ethos is her father's advice about whether, and in what way, to take action in response to racial injustice:

> Cassie, there'll be a whole lot of things you ain't gonna wanna do but you'll have to do in this life just so you can survive. Now, I don't like the idea of what Charlie Simms did to you no more than your Uncle Hammer, but I had to weigh the hurt of what happened to you to what could've happened if I went after him. If I'd've gone after Charlie Simms and given him a good thrashing like I felt like doing, the hurt to all of us would've been a whole lot more than the hurt you received, so I let it be. I don't like letting it be, but I can live with that decision.
>
> But there are other things, Cassie, that if I'd let be, they'd eat away at me and destroy me in the end. And it's the same with you, baby. There are things you can't back down on, things you gotta take a stand on. But it's up to you to decide what them things are. (Taylor, *Thunder* 175–6)

According to Jacques, David "speaks also to how inequality is anathema to care, and how, in the context of the narrative and the racial history of the United States, all care and relationships are simply not created equal" (20). Further, Jacques adds, "A Black feminist care ethics sheds meaningful light on these realities, while also providing language to realities that remain difficult to describe" (20). The debate about the boycott, as well as the Black feminist ethic of care embodied in her father's advice, inform Cassie's decision to confront

Lillian Jean. After deciding it is something worth acting on, she heeds her father's advice, taking time to calm down and plan a strategy that will hopefully avoid repercussions for her family.

ANGER AS CARE AND ACTIVISM

Both Taylor and Thomas legitimize anger, pushing back on stereotypes such as that of the angry Black woman. In doing so, they reveal how anger—and even violence—can serve as both care and activism. In "The Uses of Anger," Audre Lorde writes:

> Every woman has a well-stocked arsenal of anger potentially useful against those oppressions, personal and institutional, which brought that anger into being. Focused with precision it can become a powerful source of energy serving progress and change. And when I speak of change, I do not mean a simple switch of positions or a temporary lessening of tensions, nor the ability to smile or feel good. I am speaking of a basic and radical alteration in all those assumptions underlining. (280)

For Lorde, anger is a tool in an activist's toolbox, and it can be used to dismantle the very injustice that caused it.

Building on Lorde's work, in "Not the Color Purple," Thompson examines the relationship between women and anger in care ethics. She discusses the way adolescent girls in Brown's *Meeting at the Crossroads* and Gilligan's *Between Voice and Silence* feel "that, to be loved by adults, they must repress any signs of conflict, anger, disagreement, or disapproval that they might feel. They have to be *nice*" (Thompson 537). Feeling rage, then, is itself an act of resistance. When the Logan and Carter families experience injustice, their anger and their caring relationships shape their activism.

In Taylor's Logan Family Saga, anger is an ethical response to a historical lack of care and justice, and such anger operates in relation to others. In *Thunder*, the Logan parents honor the anger that their children feel even as they warn about the dangers of acting on it. This is evident in the aforementioned moments when Cassie and Little Man express frustration about how they are treated and how their parents direct that anger into constructive action or reflection. We also see rage keenly in the character of Uncle Hammer, who wants retribution for the violence done to Cassie and to others in the community.

While both examples of anger align with care ethics, Hammer's actions fail to use anger as a tool for social change. Hammer's rage leads to his desire to enact violence. The other Logans also worry about his safety, even going so far as to send Mr. Morrison to stop him from enacting violence. However, Hammer's rage is very much in relation to his family and others in his community. In *The Ethics of Care: Personal, Political, Global*, Virginia Held writes: "Those who conscientiously care for others are not seeking primarily to further their own individual interests; their interests are intertwined with the persons they care for. Neither are they acting for the sake of all others or humanity in general; they seek instead to preserve or promote an actual human relation between themselves and particular others" (12). Hammer's care for himself, his family, and his community are intertwined. He empathizes with Cassie, connecting her experience to his own and to the hurt and rage others feel who have experienced racial injustice. Still, Hammer is presented as reckless. While his rage is legitimate, and his actions align with Held's claim about caring relationships, his actions further endanger his own life, as well as the rest of the Logans, while achieving little or no long-term gain.

In contrast to Hammer, Cassie wields her rage as a tool for change, demonstrating how acting on anger can align with caring relationships and long-term racial justice. Reflecting on her parents' warnings, Cassie weighs whether—and how—to act on her rage towards Lillian Jean. She chooses to confront Lillian Jean using violence—a choice that is intentional and strategic, unlike her immediate response in town. This decision is an act of both care and activism: Cassie cares for *herself* by demanding respect and working to prevent Lillian Jean from harming her in the future. This, too, is an act of relational care; Cassie protects the Logan family from the Simmses' retribution by blackmailing Lillian Jean and refraining from leaving marks on her face. Ultimately, Cassie uses her anger as a tool to care for both herself and her family.

Like Cassie, Starr must navigate how to express her anger while protecting herself and others. In *The Hate U Give*, Starr describes how she resists expressing anger for fear of being stereotyped: "I cannot go angry Black girl on her" (Thomas 340). This stereotype silences Starr for much of the book. However, Thompson argues that anger can be one way Black women enact an ethic of care. Referencing Audre Lorde, she writes:

> Refusing to consider her anger as misbehavior, not-niceness, or a failure of relationship, Lorde insists that it is because she is in relationship with the White women whom she addresses that she is willing to act on and express her anger. Her anger expects a response, expects responsibility. It is, in fact, an expression of love and of trust in the relationship. Interestingly enough, Lorde seems to represent a model from whom women of color and White women alike might profit. (Thompson 537)

Expressing anger, then, is an act of trust. It asks the receiver of the anger—whether that be Starr's friend Hailey or the police within the community—to consider their own behavior and/or ideology and to reciprocate in a way that aligns with an ethic of care. Starr can eventually express her anger publicly because of how others, such as her parents and Ms. Ofrah, have cared for her and encouraged her. In sharing her anger with the police during the protest or with the public during her interview, Starr is challenging the police and the viewers to help create a more caring society.

Significantly, neither Taylor's nor Thomas's representations of activism and care lack violence. When we see acts of violence by the Logans in the Logan Family Saga, it is violence informed by relational care. In *Song of the Trees*, Mr. Andersen attempts to intimidate the Logans into selling their lumber for less than it's worth, while also plotting to take more than he paid for. David confronts him, threatening to blow himself and Mr. Andersen and his men up with dynamite that he and Stacey have planted in the grove of trees. David's threat is violent, but it's still an act of care; he sets aside his own safety and immediate financial needs to protect the land for future generations. This extends to *Thunder* as well; Cassie takes particular pleasure in beating up Lillian Jean, and David starts the fire to protect his family and stop the lynching of T.J.

The fire in particular emphasizes how a violent act can serve as relational care. When the Simms brothers frame T.J. for murder, he is in danger of being lynched—and the Logans are in danger, too, should the violence escalate. To protect T.J. and his family, David sets fire to his own crops, losing a third of them in the process. This act is grounded in the Logans' class privilege; in addition to showing their children care, the Logan parents model community care and ethical activism by risking their lives, land, and status to advocate for others. Concerned that the fire will spread to other land nearby, the town comes together to put it out: "Moving across the field, slowly, mechanically, as if sleepwalking, was a flood of men and women dumping shovels of dirt on fire patches which refused to die. They wore wide handkerchiefs over their faces and many wore hats, making it difficult to identify who was who" (Taylor, *Thunder* 267). For David, who places so much emphasis on the value of his land and his desire to protect his family's legacy, this act of care involves being fully engrossed in the needs of others, setting aside his own wants to foster community care. David's is also an ethical response to the violence enacted on Black folks within a white supremacist culture.

For Cassie, the question is which battles to fight and how to do so while considering her relationships with others. For Starr, it's whether and how to use her voice to enact care for others. Like Cassie, how Starr has been cared for by others—particularly her father and her attorney, Ms. Ofrah—informs her ethical ideal. This leads Starr to consider how using her voice can be a way of caring for her community. She says, "Ms. Ofrah says this interview is the way I fight. When you fight, you put yourself out there, not caring who you hurt or if you'll get hurt" (Thomas 290). Starr's words signify a displacement of her own motivation to enact care for Khalil's legacy and for the larger Black community, aligning with Noddings's requirement of engrossment. Furthermore, Thomas employs fighting language to describe the impact one's voice can have in fighting against injustice. During her televised interview, Starr says, "I don't understand how everyone can make it seem like it's okay he got killed if he was a drug dealer and a gangbanger," then tells the reader that this line is "a hook straight to the jaw" and, later, "[t]he moment I say it, it's my jab to the mouth" (288). While speaking up is an act of nonviolence, the language Starr uses serves to legitimize her rage and emphasize how different forms of activism respond to the violence enacted on people of color. Whether it's Starr's words on national television or the protests in the streets of Garden Heights, all means of protest here are ethical responses.

Starr's ability to express her anger is fed by her involvement in two very different protests in town: one that features looting and violence, and a separate, nonviolent protest led by the nonprofit Just Us for Justice. At the former, the crowd sings to N.W.A.'s "Fuck tha Police." Starr empathizes with their anger and stands in solidarity with them: "I yell it out too. Part of me is like, 'What about Uncle Carlos the Cop?' But this isn't about him or his coworkers who do their jobs right. This is about One-Fifteen, those detectives with their bullshit questions, and those cops who made Daddy lie on the ground. Fuck them" (Thomas 394). Here, Thomas is further legitimizing the rage that people feel in the face of injustice, presenting these actions as an act of collective care.

Despite her empathy with the crowd, Starr removes herself once looting starts taking place. She says, "I'm just as pissed as anybody, but this . . . this isn't it. Not for me" (Thomas 395). The focus isn't on judging those who participate in the looting; it's on how Starr is deciding what kind of activism is right for her. Instead, Starr joins Just Us for Justice at the location where Khalil was killed. There, she ends up on top of a car, speaking through a bullhorn. Describing the bullhorn as "heavy as a gun" (411), Starr further reinforces the theme that one's voice is the most powerful tool for enacting care. She shouts, "I'm sick of this! Just like y'all think all of us are bad because of some people, we think the same about y'all. Until you give us a reason to think otherwise, we'll keep protesting" (412). She acknowledges that the crowd and police are relational, emphasizing the fact that the crowd's actions are in response to the systemic, historical, unending violence enacted on their community.

ARRIVING AT AN ETHICAL IDEAL

While the ethical decision-making of the parents influences the children's approach to care and activism, the activist practices of the children in turn encourage the parents to do more as well. Thus, the development of an ethical ideal for each individual and the family as a unit is itself relational. According to Jacques, "Even as the story presents formal educators, business owners, community leaders, and friends as morally compromised by Jim Crow-era white supremacy, Taylor's novel suggests that young people remain indispensable to ethical work, both in theory and in praxis" (1). Further, the significance of the activist practices of the Logans and the Carters isn't that they create immediate change; Starr admits more work must be done to improve conditions for people of color (Thomas 432). Activist practices, too, are relational; as care informs activist practices, the activism in turn informs caring relationships. The Logans mobilizing the boycott empowers others in their community, and their activist practices and care influence the ethical ideals of their children, who continue working toward systemic change. Moreover, Starr and Maverick inspire others in their community to act in alignment with care ethics—particularly DeVante, who turns witness against the oppressive drug lord King to protect the Garden Heights community (Thomas 430). Once individuals begin enacting a community-centered ethic of care, others are encouraged to do the same. By the end of the novel, both Starr and Maverick come to see themselves as having a shared identity with this larger community. Only through this shared identity and solidarity can they create change within themselves, their family unit, and Garden Heights.

CONCLUSION

I have juxtaposed Mildred Taylor's *Thunder* with Angie Thomas's *The Hate U Give*, arguing that Taylor's work grounds activism in feminist care ethics. Taylor, in turn, influences modern texts such as *The Hate U Give*, which apply feminist care ethics to representing contemporary protest movements. Both Taylor and Thomas are informed by and inform the cultural landscape of their times.

Audrey Thompson has critiqued feminist care ethics for its colorblind roots and argued for it to be taken up in new ways. Wesley Jacques has answered that call, proposing a dual framework of Black feminist care ethics that situates feminist care ethics within the tradition of Black feminist thought. He applies Black feminist care ethics to the study of children's literature, arguing that Taylor's work serves as theory about care. I've taken up this framework in examining how care shapes activism in Taylor's *Thunder* and how this influences contemporary texts such as *The Hate U Give*. However, I am a white woman entering into a discourse about care that has been dominated by the voices of white women. It is important that the voices of Black scholars, writers, and activists be centered in these conversations.

This essay itself emerges out of the context of two major historical events: the global COVID-19 pandemic, which has disproportionately impacted BIPOC, as well as the protests rising across the country in response to the incessant violence done to Black bodies, made more visible by the deaths of Breonna Taylor, Ahmaud Arbery, and George Floyd. This particular historical moment emphasizes the continued relevance and interconnectedness of the works of Taylor and Thomas. Written in the context of the Black Lives Matter movement, *The Hate U Give* continues Taylor's efforts of making institutional violence visible while demonstrating the role caring relationships can have in mobilizing communities and creating systemic change. Understanding how care shapes activism does two things: one, it disrupts dominant narratives about activist movements, revealing the way care informs both nonviolent and violent action while considering how systemic oppression impacts the ability to care and how people care; and two, it leaves a roadmap for future generations. Without Cassie, we would have no Starr. These stories both represent and help shape the lived experiences of young people, and they position different methods of activism as ways of enacting care within our various communities of belonging. Looking ahead, more work needs to be done in examining representations of activist movements in youth literature within their respective cultural contexts, perhaps with more consideration of how activist movements serve as texts in conversation with youth literature.

WORKS CITED

Collins, Patricia. *Black Feminist Thought: Knowledge, Consciousness, and the Politics of Empowerment*. Routledge, 2008.

Gilligan, Carol. *In a Different Voice: Psychological Theory and Women's Development*. Harvard UP, 1982.

Gilligan, Carol. "Looking Back to Look Forward: Revisiting *In a Different Voice*." "Defense Mechanisms," special issue of *Classics@*, vol. 9, 2011, https://classics-at.chs.harvard.edu/volume/classics9-defense-mechanisms/.

Goodreads. "A Life in Books: Angie Thomas." *Goodreads*, 2017.

Haber, Leigh. "10 Books *The Hate U Give* Author Angie Thomas Thinks Everyone Should Read." *O: The Oprah Magazine*, 2019.

Held, Virginia. *The Ethics of Care: Personal, Political, Global*. Oxford UP, 2006.

Held, Virginia. "Morality, Care, and International Law." *Ethics and Global Politics*, vol. 4, no. 3, 2011, pp. 173–94., doi:10.3402/egp.v4i3.8405.

Jacques, Wesley S. "Reading Relational in Mildred D. Taylor: Toward a Black Feminist Care Ethics for Children's Literature," *Research on Diversity in Youth Literature*, vol. 2, no. 2, 2020, pp. 1–23.

Lorde, Audre. "The Uses of Anger." *Women's Studies Quarterly*, vol. 9, no. 3, 1981, pp. 7–10. *JSTOR*, www.jstor.org/stable/40003905.

Martin, Michelle H. "Let Freedom Ring: Land, Liberty, Literacy, and Lore in Mildred Taylor's Logan Family Novels." *The Oxford Handbook of Children's Literature*, edited by Julia Mickenberg and Lynne Vallone, Oxford UP, 2011. 371–88.

Moran, Mary Jeanette. *Caring: A Feminine Approach to Ethics and Moral Education*. 2nd ed., U of California P, 2003.

Moran, Mary Jeanette. "Making a Difference: Ethical Recognition Through Otherness in Madeleine L'Engle's Fiction." *Ethics and Children's Literature*, edited by Claudia Mills, Routledge, 2016, pp. 89–102.

Noddings, Nel. "Caring in Education." Infed.org, Apr. 4, 2013, infed.org/mobi/caring-in-education/.

Robinson, Fiona. *The Ethics of Care: A Feminist Approach to Human Security*. Temple UP, 2011.

Strauss, Valerie. "This is My Generation's Civil Rights Movement." *Washington Post*, June 6, 2020.

Taylor, Mildred D. *All the Days Past, All the Days to Come*. Viking Books for Young Readers, 2020.

Taylor, Mildred D. *The Gold Cadillac*. Puffin Books, 1998.

Taylor, Mildred D. *The Land*. Puffin Books, 2001.

Taylor, Mildred D. *Roll of Thunder, Hear My Cry*. Puffin Books, 1976.

Taylor, Mildred D. *Song of the Trees*. Dial, 1975.

Taylor, Mildred D. *The Well: David's Story*. Puffin Books, 1998.

Thomas, Angie. *The Hate U Give*. Walker Books, 2018.

Thompson, Audrey. "Not the Color Purple: Black Feminist Lessons for Educational Caring." *Harvard Educational Review*, vol. 68, no. 4, 1998, pp. 522–55, doi:10.17763/haer.68.4.nm436v83214n5016.

Trites, Roberta Seelinger. "Caring, Disability Studies, and Narrative Structure." *Twenty-First-Century Feminisms in Children's and Adolescent Literature*. UP of Mississippi, 2018, pp. 156–86.

Blending Fact and Fiction
All the Days Past, All the Days to Come as a Novel of Black Resistance

Jennifer Ansbach

My first images of Mississippi came from Mildred D. Taylor's *Roll of Thunder, Hear My Cry* as Cassie described the red dust sifting onto her brother's shoes as they walked to school. Reading the novel in elementary school, I found myself transported to another time and place, discovering literature's power to show me the world through the eyes of someone whose lived experience differed so greatly from my own. A few years ago, through funding from the National Endowment for the Humanities Landmarks program, I spent a week studying the Mississippi Delta at The Delta Center for Culture and Learning at Delta State University, immersed in the history and culture of the area. That experience inspired me to understand the ways in which the civil rights movement has been co-opted for other purposes, often erasing the truth of the people and the movement. Taylor's novel reflects various sites of Black resistance to white dominant narratives about Black history, experiences, and culture; embodies Black resistance; and, through documenting past resistance, urges readers to continue to resist.

The Logan Family Saga, grounded in personal and family history, offers readers a window into the historical realities of life in rural Mississippi. In 1976, Mildred D. Taylor published *Roll of Thunder, Hear My Cry* (*Thunder*), inspired by her family's stories of growing up in the Mississippi Delta in the 1930s. The highly lauded second book in the Logan family series, *Thunder* focuses on the plight of Great Depression–era Black Americans in the Jim Crow South, touching on education, sharecropping, arson, and lynching of Black families, and the inequality of the justice system, among other issues. Jim Crow laws enforced a system of institutional and systemic power that codified white privilege, and Taylor demonstrates how this shaped daily life.

Nine-year-old Cassie Logan narrates the story of her family and the injustices they and their neighbors face. In 2020, Taylor declared the series complete with the publication of the final book in the series, *All the Days Past, All the Days to Come* (*Days*). The book follows a now-adult Cassie to Toledo after World War II as part of the Great Migration, exploring the country from California to Boston and in-between, and ultimately back to the Delta for the Freedom Rides and civil rights work of the early 1960s. Key moments of the civil rights movement, including the kidnapping and lynching of Emmett Till, the NAACP's advocacy of Medgar Evers, and James Meredith's challenge to the University of Mississippi for his enrollment, take place alongside the violence of white supremacy and Cassie's work as a lawyer volunteering to register voters in Mississippi.

OFFERING TESTIMONY AND BLACK KNOWLEDGE PRODUCTION

Mildred Taylor's work offers readers access to the knowledge production of her family and herself. Storytelling, while often dismissed by white-dominated institutions as less valuable or truthful than other forms of knowledge, provides an important link back to Black cultural knowing. Scholar Stephanie Toliver draws upon existing frameworks of Endarkened epistemologies, Indigenous storywork, and Afrofuturism to craft her framework of Endarkened storywork, which "allows space for storytelling through fiction, honoring the ways of griots who were the scholars of their African nations" (xv) and is a response to research methods that resist "Black cultural ways of being and knowing" (xvi). Toliver's Endarkened storywork allows for the analysis of storytelling in a way that recognizes African-rooted knowledge and knowledge production. Taylor's storytelling, which often employs characters in conversation telling stories to each other, embraces alternative and subversive ways of knowing. Perhaps most germane to Taylor's work is that Endarkened storywork "refuses objectivity by acknowledging that the basic belief system guiding people's worldviews are different based on one's background as well as their social and cultural heritage" (xviii). In this way, Taylor honors the knowledge of the family members who shared their stories with her, and through her fiction of the Logan family, generalizes this to the larger power and persistence of Black storytelling. Shari Stone-Mediatore notes that "stories of marginalized experiences tend to conflict with 'common-sense' knowledge and to enter public discussion explicitly as stories" (6). Taylor's entire oeuvre is an act of resistance and the embodiment of her own role as griot in American culture, telling stories to youth and, if they pay attention, to the adults who open her books.

EMBRACING BLACK GRASSROOTS ACTIVISM AND RESISTANCE

Throughout *Days*, Taylor shows the resistance to the laws that restricted and endangered Black lives, both invisible and through grassroots activism. Cassie becomes a lawyer, resisting gender and race expectations. The culmination of her work is returning to Mississippi to work on the Mississippi Delta registration drives. Taylor's decision to frame the work through the local residents, rather than framing it through the use of figureheads often credited with the movement, resists simplistic narratives of the history and returns agency to the people. While Taylor foregrounds this local activism against a variety of civil rights movement actions, including the lunch counter sit-ins of 1960, student-led demonstrations around the South, and the Freedom Riders, in which Clayton takes part and for which he serves time in Parchman Prison in the novel, the inclusion of the community schools and voter registration drives, she resists the dominant civil rights narrative of key people such as Rosa Parks driving the movement in favor of showing grassroots organizing. Cassie returns home to Mississippi to teach classes to help residents pass the literacy test for voter registration. In *I've Got the Light of Freedom*, historian Charles Payne states that "nearly ten thousand people would be trained as teachers, and as many as two hundred schools would be in operation at one time" (75). This shifts the focus from charismatic leaders to people like Septima Clark, who helped organize the Citizenship Schools that offered voting and literacy classes. Payne quotes Clark as stating the purpose of the schools was "'discovering local community leaders.... It is my belief that creative leadership is present in any community and only awaits discovery and development'" (75). Payne argues that the successes of the 1960s civil rights work was only possible because of the focus on building relationships and creating community support of activists a generation before, and Taylor honors that work, offering readers a space to imagine their own activism then and now. Taylor's decision to involve Cassie in grassroots mobilization of voters also contradicts the popular view of the movement as centralized protests and marches by honoring the lived experience of Black citizens who resisted unjust laws.

CENTERING BLACK AMERICAN EXPERIENCES WITH JIM CROW LAWS

Taylor's depiction of police brutality provides a counternarrative to white framing of the Black experience of the law, which usually criminalizes the Black person as justification for extralegal police violence. Cassie experiences the injustice of watching her then-boyfriend, Flynn, get arrested without cause in Los Angeles, leaving her in a white neighborhood alone on foot at night. She expresses shock that this is happening outside of the South and questions the police, explaining, "Maybe I had been studying the law too much, but I pressed them with frantic questions. 'What's he done? What are you charging him with? You need to let him go!'" (198). This only provokes the officers further, causing them to assault Flynn and threaten to arrest her, too. In showing this, Taylor shows readers the lived experience of Black communities and law enforcement, which extended beyond the Jim Crow South to California in the 1950s.

Throughout the novel, Taylor portrays the weaponizing of the law against Black people, in service of white supremacy. Cassie's lived experiences with police and the law lead her to become a lawyer in the first place, giving her a platform to fight for justice on a personal level. The United States conceives of its laws as colorblind, which is another area where Taylor resists the dominant narrative of America in the novel. Taylor resists seeing the law only through the white gaze and offers the Black experience of the law, always wielded by white men in her novel. In his study of how experiences with the law are both reflected and constructed in African American literature, scholar Jon-Christian Suggs notes: "While white American literature reserves a genre category or two for stories grounded in law—and ghettoizes those stories in separate review columns and bookstore and library sections—'classical' African American literature is universally grounded in law; in fact, all African American fiction carries the question of the legal status of blacks as its subtext" (8).

Taylor explicitly wrestles with these ideas throughout *Days* in several plotlines. In addition to the extensive documentation of the fight for voting rights and the dangers of the Jim Crow South, she weaves the subplot of Moe Turner's flight from the law in Mississippi, stemming from Turner's attack on a white boy, Statler Aames (depicted in *Road to Memphis*). In including this perpetual threat of the law coming for Moe, Taylor directly addresses the Black experience of the law not only in the South but its long reach throughout the US. Scholar Neil R. McMillen notes in his examination of Mississippians moving north in the Great Migration that while most scholars and even the migrants themselves point to the economic reasons for moving, among themselves, Black families had their own individual reasons to move, often including escaping angry mobs, plantation owners, or law enforcement (264–65, 271). Historian Isabel Wilkerson, in her exploration of the Great Migration in *The Warmth of Other Suns* (2011), observes that Black Southerners who moved and wanted to avoid extradition "back to the South over purported debts or disputes would have been wary of census takers," explaining that the number of Black people who migrated may be underestimated because of this (218). Taylor's plot captures how law enforcement, designed to uphold the hierarchies of white authority, often lacked justice for Black people. However, through her employment of Endarkened storywork, in Toliver's view, Taylor offers deeper insight into Wilkerson's claims, reinforcing through the retelling of the story among the characters how the numbers of those migrating were often hidden to protect themselves.

USING THE LOGAN FAMILY COUNTERNARRATIVES TO RESIST WHITE FRAMING

Taylor resists white framing of Black experiences with Jim Crow laws and expectations by offering the Logan family as a counternarrative. "Jim Crow" is defined as laws enacted after Reconstruction by white people in the South. African American Studies scholar Henry Louis Gates Jr. explains that Jim Crow laws developed "to maintain the country's racial hierarchy in the face of emancipation and Black citizenship. Anything but unmoored or isolated, white power was reinforced in this new era by the nation's cultural, economic, educational, legal, and violently extra-legal systems, including lynching" (37). At its core, Jim Crow legislation and customs codified and performed power and white authority. Historian Stephen A. Berrey extends this understanding, stating, "While scholars have most often understood Jim Crow as a legal and political system, it was also . . . a cultural one that revolved around daily performances of race" (3). By examining these daily performances, Berrey asserts, a different view of Black American life emerges—one that Taylor's Logan family embodies. Berrey conceptualizes Jim Crow as "a system of cultural exchange and power that was at once subtle and dynamic, intimate and volatile" and emphasizes that looking at routine and how it shapes the use of physical space makes it possible to understand how it worked in the North and the West (4–5). The Jim Crow threat to Black Mississippians echoes throughout the Logan family books.

Taylor chooses the public bus, a traditional symbol of the civil rights movement resistance, to show the limited range of options to resist, but she combines it with the unjust treatment of Black soldiers returning from World War II to highlight the dissonance many Black veterans felt returning to the Jim Crow South. The novel begins in Mississippi on a public bus. The prologue shows Cassie and her brother, Clayton Chester, formerly known as Little Man, forced to move to the back of a bus in 1944 (2). As C. Vann Woodward notes in *The Strange Career of Jim Crow*, segregated transportation provided an early win for segregationists, and the implementation and existence of this became symbolic of the Jim Crow South, reinforced by the Supreme Court's assertions about "separate but equal" facilities (140). The inclusion of this scene early in the novel provides an easily recognizable signal to readers that this is the Jim Crow South. That Clayton is now a soldier headed to Fort Hood also reflects and resists the common beliefs about the time. While the dominant American cultural narrative celebrates World War II veterans as heroes, it often leaves out the bitterness many Black veterans felt upon their return. Here, Taylor provides the reader the privilege of "listening" to these stories from her elders. In *I've Got the Light of Freedom*, Charles Payne asserts that Black veterans returning to Mississippi after World War II provided the impetus for the civil rights movement (24). Angry at being sent abroad to fight for freedom they themselves did not have at home, these soldiers led both the fight against Jim Crow and the migration to northern cities to resist segregation and laws barring employment. In grounding the text in these ideas in the prologue of *Days*, Taylor gestures toward telling a story of civil rights in Mississippi that replayed again and again. Her decision to embed the stories she heard from her family passed down from earlier generations allows readers to bear witness to this oral history through a veil of a single family, the Logans.

Throughout the scene, Taylor recounts both the invisible and the overt resistance to the bus experience. While the sidewalk rules required Black people to yield to whites whether that meant moving aside or even onto the street, the public buses allocated space depending on the needs of the white passengers. This is how Cassie and Clayton's seat literally changes from Black space to white space when the driver moves the curtain back, expanding white seating to include the seats in which Clayton and Cassie were sitting. When the driver insists they move again later in the journey because more white passengers want to board, Clayton and Cassie exit the bus rather than move a second time, and they walk home from another town miles from their stop. In this instance, the rules of which seats are Black seats change during the performance of Jim Crow rules. Berrey notes that this required additional vigilance on the part of Black riders because "on a regular basis on buses, black passengers were expected to always be watching and ready to move and to give up their seats for Whites" (46). Clayton and Cassie cannot, then, become engrossed in their conversation because they can be, and are, asked to move more than once. Berrey sums up the struggle of bus ridership for Black patrons, stating, "Thus, the segregated space of the bus called for a continual racial performance. While the White rider could relax, these circumstances could generate much tension for the black rider" (47). Taylor explores this tension more fully when Cassie and Clayton rejoin their family.

Taylor uses the intimacy of the family scene to contrast and to interrogate the deeper meaning and feelings engendered by the bus incident. When Cassie and Clayton arrive home, the family conversation shows the reader that the consequences for talking back to a white man and refusing to move could be far reaching when Papa asks, "'That driver know who you are?'" (12), intimating that there could be retribution for the family. Here again, the conversation among the characters echoes the oral storytelling practices Taylor grew up hearing. As the conversation continues, Man reveals to his family that he "'wanted to kill that man'" (13), expressing the anger many Black people felt but did not dare express. Berrey documents the case of a World War II veteran, Elport Chess, who was beaten and arrested for refusing to move seats on a Mississippi bus in 1946. The danger for Chess, as well as for the fictional Logans, restricted public expressions of anger, anger that many white people could then deny existed because it was not performed. McMillen warns, "Above all, black Mississippians were expected to avoid controversy with the dominant race. It was a breach of caste to contradict any White; an angry exchange, even when provoked, was a foolhardy act; a flash of black rage could be as dangerous as physical assault" (25). Clayton and the rest of his family understand that even if the bus driver instigated an argument, Clayton could not win, and the law would not have protected him. To speak publicly that he wanted to kill the driver would have been tantamount to Clayton signing his own death warrant. Through *Days*, Taylor can give public voice to these feelings, even in fiction, that contradict the white narrative of happy, submissive Black folks. Taylor provides a powerful counternarrative through the Endarkened storywork.

Taylor moves beyond the South in *Days* and shows Cassie resisting Jim Crow practices in other regions, beginning with the industrial Midwest, where many Black Mississippians moved during the Great Migration. While the Black exodus from Mississippi began in earnest after World War I, over three hundred thousand Black residents left Mississippi between 1940 and 1950, more than the total number of Black residents who left between 1910 and 1940 (McMillen 259). Isabel Wilkerson states in *The Warmth of Other Suns* that "[s]mall colonies of migrants from Chickasaw County, Mississippi, ended up in Toledo, Ohio" (243), as Taylor's own family did. After the Logan siblings move to Toledo, where Cassie expects she has left the Jim Crow South behind, she discovers that while some of the cultural practices are less discriminatory, such as the fact that factories will hire Black workers, many more are the same as in Mississippi.

These cultural practices offer a counternarrative to the paternalism of white people who claim not to be racist and must find a way to explain how they supported segregation laws. In Toledo, as in many Northern cities, segregation was enforced. Taylor shows Cassie overtly resisting the movie theater segregation in Toledo, which results in police escorting Cassie and Moe Turner out of the theater. Because their friend Henry calls his father, a local Black lawyer, the two do not get arrested. Here Taylor shows that Black individuals refused to accept the cultural rules that limited their freedoms and access to public spaces. In contrast, many white Southerners romanticize the past and paternalistically suggest that Black people had better lives under Jim Crow rules. In Kristen Lavelle's study of how older white Southerners construct their racial memories of the Jim Crow South, she discovered that many of the people she interviewed expressed a common theme of "acknowledging and downplaying the racial oppressions of the Jim Crow South" (10) while feeling nostalgic for the past, "inclusive of the racial arrangement" (3). While Lavelle acknowledges that part of the work the people she interviewed are doing is an attempt to "construct a White moral identity of virtuousness and racial innocence," they are also coconstructing a view of the past that confines the fight for civil rights to the past, asserting that racial equality has been achieved. This reflects Jacqueline Dowd Hall's argument that reframing the civil rights movement as something accomplished is a political act by conservatives to shift the focus from structural and systemic racism to individual acts, and it makes Taylor's reclaiming of the experiences and resistance more important. Taylor's portrayal of Cassie here and at other moments in the novel offers a counternarrative to white nostalgia and demonstrates resistance to Jim Crow norms and laws.

PERFORMING JIM CROW OUTSIDE THE AMERICAN SOUTH

The novel also allows Taylor to give voice to her experiences with Jim Crow performances, opposing the view of Jim Crow discrimination and law as being part of an American South that exists only in contrast to the enlightened North and extending it to the American West, a space for white people to tame the land they have stolen from the Indigenous people who are perceived in the American imagination as savages. "Performance" refers to the public ways Jim Crow laws and the racialization of Black people were enacted in public spaces, through custom, law, and expectations (Berrey 23). The American West lives in mainstream cultural artifacts as a space that belongs to white people, and stories of civil rights struggles are often omitted from these spaces. In the Author's Note, Taylor refers to several incidents from her own experience that she has fictionalized in the novel, including being denied table service at a restaurant in Wyoming. Here again, Taylor uses her storytelling to provide testimony, forcing the reader to bear witness to the injustices she and her family endured. In the novel, Cassie and her brothers are denied service in Wyoming, but after they point out that Clayton is a World War II veteran, the owner relents and says they can order the food to go. When he asks for them to pay ahead, Stacey asks if the other soldiers dining had to pay ahead, and the owner prepares their food without prepayment (124). The siblings discuss amongst themselves the options for resistance. After placing a large order, the Logans wait about a half hour or more and then refuse to purchase the food because they are not allowed to dine inside; the owner threatens to call the police (125). Taylor perhaps speaks through Cassie's voice when she writes: "Refusing food we had ordered might have seemed an insignificant way of fighting back, but at times, insignificant ways were all we had, all that allowed us a little dignity as human beings. We know the ways of things down home in the South but this was Wyoming. We had thought maybe things would be different here, in the great American West. We were wrong" (126).

Indeed, grave consequences often followed speaking out against a system designed to reinforce a power imbalance. In *Dark Journey*, McMillen concludes that Black people mostly "expressed their disaffections nonviolently: throughout public and private affirmations of self-worth; through daily, individual acts of passive resistance to white will; or whenever possible, through the normal channels of protest open to free people" (288). Taylor's novel captures this when the family uses nonviolence to express their anger, despite the possibility of violent consequences. Cassie tells the reader, "The romance of the West as portrayed throughout America was not for us. For us, America remained, as always, the same. *Whites Only. Colored Not Allowed.* I was learning about America" (126). Taylor's inclusion of overt resistance offers a challenge to the reader's own potential romanticized view of the American West, pushing back on narratives that erase segregation from stories of America outside the South.

The laws throughout the United States restricted Black Americans's access to residential neighborhoods, which Taylor shows when Cassie moves west. California, frequently the free West in Black imaginations during Jim Crow, also reveals to Cassie that segregation is not limited to Mississippi and the American South. A woman denies Cassie an apartment in Westwood, California, in 1949 because she is Black. At first, the woman tells her that the apartment has been rented. When Cassie tells her that is not possible, the woman tells her, "'Good luck finding a place in your own neighborhood'" (214). Cassie wants to challenge the woman further, but her husband, Flynn, tells her, "'There's nothing that says she has to rent to us,'" prompting Cassie to observe, "'Well, there ought to be'" (214). This exchange highlights that even without the codified segregation laws under which Cassie lived in Mississippi, the laws still protected white privilege and power. In this instance, Taylor is demonstrating racial prejudice as the act of an individual. However, the invisible legal structures make the all-white neighborhood possible, although it requires the complicity of white people to take action against renting or selling to Black people, in contrast to the passive engagement many white people tend to point to when discussing de facto segregation. In his history of government policy and racial housing segregation, scholar Richard Rothstein discusses Westwood's reliance on restrictive covenants to prevent African Americans from renting or purchasing housing, with exceptions for domestic servants. So in contrast to Cassie's observation that a law should protect her, laws instead were made that specifically excluded her. Rothstein retells the story of UCLA student (and later, congressman) George Brown, who circumvented the covenant by buying a property through the cooperative housing association, of which he was president, and then making a rule that "each student must contribute five hours a week of cleaning, cooking, and shopping, so the student group obtained a legal opinion that each member of the cooperative was actually a domestic servant, and an African American student was then able to join," although Rothstein states that this did not change the segregation of Westwood overall (81). Cassie's frustration at finding segregation and discrimination in California, where she had expected equality, reflects the larger experience of Black migrants there. Wilkerson notes that one man who migrated from Louisiana to California discovered that the prejudice-free California of his imagination did not exist. Wilkerson writes that "some colored people who had made the journey called it *James* Crow in California" (211). While California was not the Deep South, it still functioned by the same written and unwritten laws that enforced segregation across the country.

RECONSIDERING HOUSING AND SEGREGATION

Taylor includes discussions of housing and neighborhood segregation throughout the novel, hinting that resistance may change the laws in the future, but embedding the historical truths about segregation and access to housing in the historical time period, all while centering the marginalized viewpoint of those who endured the injustice. Cassie's observation that there "ought to be" a law requiring them to rent to Black people gestures toward the 1968 Fair Housing Act, enacted by Congress and signed by Lyndon B. Johnson as part of the "Great Society" programs. Rothstein argues that, contrary to Flynn's assertion that nothing says they have a right to rent housing where they choose, the Constitution's Fifth Amendment against the unfair treatment of citizens and the Thirteenth Amendment prohibit "actions that it deemed perpetuated the characteristics of slavery. Actions that made African Americans second-class citizens, such as racial discrimination in housing, were included in the ban" (viii). In *Let the Circle Be Unbroken*, Cassie learns about the Constitution and that it was theoretically fair but applied differently to white and Black people (198). This suggests that Cassie's sense of misplaced justice is accurate, although it is unclear whether Taylor is endorsing the view that the Constitution has always banned discrimination supported by the government.

While Taylor acknowledges the role of the Constitution in segregated housing and neighborhoods, she also explores both the dominant narratives around segregated neighborhoods and individual acts of resistance, including the dangers of integrating. When Cassie discusses housing in Jackson, Mississippi; Toledo, Ohio; Oakland, California; Los Angeles, California; Denver, Colorado; or Boston, Massachusetts, the issue of whether Black people can live where they choose or whether they are restricted to where other Black people live resurfaces. Rothstein addresses this directly, stating, "The idea that African Americans themselves don't want to integrate is a white conceit. Many thousands of African Americans risked hostility, even violence, when daring to move into predominantly white neighborhoods" (223). Taylor illustrates this concern when Stacey visits Cassie at her Boston apartment, which Cassie needed the help of her white coworkers to get, with Stacey warning her, "You're moving into some dangerous territory here. . . . You're moving into a white world, Cassie. Look at this apartment building, this white neighborhood. I was almost afraid to park my car out front the way people were staring at me" (289). Taylor gives voice to the real dangers that could occur when Black people decided to be the first to integrate a community. Again, not only is Taylor offering a counternarrative to the idea that Black residents did not want to live in white neighborhoods, but she also shows that segregation extended throughout the United States, which she experienced herself. Cassie's story again functions as testimony.

HONORING THE BLACK FAMILY

While the earlier books in the series explored history from before Taylor was born, the final book provides a context for Taylor to explore her own lived history, combined with her family stories. In doing so, she offers her book as a present-day site of resistance that embodies the civil rights struggles and Jim Crow as a way of pushing back on current anti-Black narratives in American culture. In a January 2020 interview in *O: The Oprah Magazine*, Taylor stated that she wanted to show strong Black families with two parents raising children because "[e]veryone I knew lived with their mother and father, as did we" (Haber). For Taylor, the books allowed her space to construct a counternarrative, then, of sharing stories with positive images of families often erased by the dominant culture. Strong family ties run through the entire Logan family series. In addition, Taylor notes that more than one nuclear family with two parents and children live in the Logan family house in both Mississippi and Toledo as part of the extended family, which combats Taylor's concerns about media portrayals of Black single-parent families. Throughout *Days*, as in all the books in the series, extended families gather together to share daily life of meals, domestic labor, and expenses; to celebrate holidays and togetherness and to mourn. These intimate portrayals of Black family life and communities give readers a more positive view of Black culture than Taylor felt media usually offered.

Throughout *Days*, as in the other Logan family books, Taylor focuses on the family to give insight into the historical time period and to speak back to those negative stereotypes. Cassie and her brothers leave Toledo, Ohio, for Mississippi after their mother suffers a stroke, and the visit home offers several scenes of domestic life. While preparing dinner with Big Ma, her grandmother, Cassie lists all the steps in making fried chicken, from killing it to making the batter and cooking it, reminding Big Ma, "Just saying I can do all this because of you, Big Ma. You taught me how to cook" (108). The scene honors the education and professional career of Cassie's mother, a schoolteacher, who worked outside the home, while also showing that this intergenerational family relied on each other to raise the children and now to care for the aging adults. One of the book's final scenes depicts the family holding vigil over Papa, who is dying. Taylor brings the family together, with Cassie describing the scene as Big Ma prayed, "and after her, Mama prayed. We held hands and we each prayed in turn, Uncle Hammer, Stacey, Christopher-John, Clayton Chester, and me. We prayed in a circle, holding hands, and Papa was the center of the circle as Mama and I each held one of his hands. The circle was unbroken. We held tight to each other. We prayed and we waited" (481). By placing the family at the center of key moments of the story, Taylor reclaims the Black family as whole.

Taylor builds these concepts of Black family strength and history throughout the Logan family books, and while earlier books addressed Reconstruction more specifically, her decision to include references to it in *Days* reinforces the salience of that moment in constructing the present for the characters, and by extension, the larger Black experience. These ideas also push back on narratives of Black inferiority, and instead rely on deeper cultural narratives about what it means to be a Black Southerner in the United States, including the erasure of Black people from holding positions of power during Reconstruction. Henry Louis Gates Jr. estimates that, during Reconstruction, about two thousand Black men held office from local to national posts (8). In his social history *Dark Journey: Black Mississippians in the Age of Jim Crow*, McMillen notes that while a few Black men served in state and national offices, most of them served in local roles because white men continued to control the government, although he concedes that Black men were "represented in substantial numbers" (37). Taylor shows through the character of Dee Davis, wife of the oldest Logan son, Stacey, that other Black families endured through the Jim Crow South, and Taylor details their endurance and success, noting that the Davises "were a significant family. It was even said that Dee's grandfather had served in the short-lived Mississippi legislature during Reconstruction" (*Days* 95). Taylor's inclusion of this helps restore the memory of Black elected officials in all capacities in Mississippi history, something easily overlooked when Southern Black nominees would not be elected to national office again until 1972 (Gates 8). Between 1890 and 2022, there were no Black statewide elected officials in Mississippi. Not until 2023 was a Black Republican, Rodney Hall, elected to the Mississippi House (Pittman).

CELEBRATING LAND OWNERSHIP AS RESISTANCE

In addition to pointing out the prominent place in society some Black families held, Taylor reminds readers that many Southern Black families managed to buy land during Reconstruction and to hold onto it later, another act of resistance because it removed the power of white landowners over tenant sharecroppers. Showing Black families as landowners resists cultural depictions of Black people as lazy and unfit to control land without white oversight. It's an inherent paradox in the stereotyping of Black Americans, simultaneously exploiting their labor in the guise of docile enslavement and insisting on their laziness and inability to understand how to use the land properly. In *The Strange Career of Jim Crow*, C. Vann Woodward notes that post-Reconstruction, even former abolitionists would endorse white supremacy in magazines such as *Atlantic Monthly* and *Harper's Weekly*, describing Black people's "innate inferiority, shiftlessness, and hopeless unfitness in the white man's civilization" (70). White people in the North and the South employed these stereotypes to justify their racism and exclusion of Black people. Still, General William Sherman's Special Field Order No. 15, issued following his seizure of plantations in Georgia and South Carolina, initially offered hope that the land, worked by enslaved Black labor for hundreds of years, would become the domain of the formerly enslaved during Reconstruction. Gates explains, "[I]t is difficult to imagine any act more revolutionary than the redistribution of land from the planters to the slaves in the former Confederacy," a plan dissolved by President Andrew Jackson less than a year later (31). Land ownership then and now offers a primary means of wealth building. However, this dream of land ownership continued to be a dream of many Black families. In the Mississippi Delta, where Taylor's books primarily take place, Black labor cleared and worked the land under the sharecropping system, which relied on keeping Black labor docile and cheap to maximize wealth for the white plantation owners. For many white farmers who moved to Mississippi too poor to buy their own land, sharecropping or tenant farming offered a way to survive. After the Civil War, those white farmers who could tap into credit lines and buy their own land often expanded into cotton, as well, an opportunity of which Black farmers could not take advantage because few banks loaned to Black farmers. Cotton's market value decline meant many of those white families lost their farms, putting them behind the Black farmers who held onto their land. According to historian Charles C. Bolton, "By 1900, 36 percent of all white farmers in Mississippi were either tenant farmers or sharecroppers (by comparison, 85 percent of all black farmers in 1900 did not own the land they farmed)." As a result, the tension between poor white farmers and those Black farmers who remained landowners grew, along with bitter resentment.

In *Days*, as in the rest of the series, Taylor shows the Mississippi families remaining focused on owning the land as an act of resistance. In recalling an event that happened in *Circle*, Cassie tells readers that her family, "one of the few black families in the community who owned land, was faced with losing that land" (57). McMillen documents the significant obstacles Black families overcame to both buy and keep land, including the difficulty of obtaining mortgages, paying higher fees and mortgage rates than whites, and a lack of due process enforced for the white sellers of that land to repossess it (118–20). The final images of *Days* focus on Cassie's remembrances of Papa, who has just died, her family, and the land, reasserting its importance in Taylor's family history, echoed throughout all the Logan family books.

DOCUMENTING MEDICAL RACISM

Taylor's inclusion of a subplot about Papa's medical care also offers resistance to the erasure of Black experiences with medical care in the United States. Because white doctors often mistreated or refused to treat Black patients, suspicion of the medical establishment grew. In John Hoberman's book *Black and Blue: The Origins and Consequences of Medical Racism*, the author notes that "[i]ntimidation in every social venue was the social logic of Jim Crow racism, and the social universe of American medicine was no exception to this rule" (44). In the novel, by the time Papa seeks treatment, his health has deteriorated significantly. Hoberman argues that mistrust of the medical community over generations continues to have widespread repercussions, with Black patients waiting to seek treatment (45). As a result, Black Americans are often blamed for their conditions. Medical racism continues to have far-reaching effects in America, but few structural responses have been forthcoming for a variety of reasons, according to Hoberman, who asserts, "In summary, the American medical establishment has never mobilized on behalf of a medically traumatized African American population" (23). Taylor's inclusion of the medical racism endured by the Black community for centuries restores the Black experience to the American narrative of medicine in America and challenges "colorblind" racism by showing that the failure to consider race is as destructive as denying treatment because of race.

Taylor uses Cassie's experience with the medical community to show how Cassie uses the law to resist white supremacy. When she lives in Boulder, Cassie has surgery but cannot receive follow-up treatment after the doctor who performed the surgery leaves, as the director decides it is a private practice that can exclude anyone they choose. Cassie pursues fair treatment through a lawyer, but ultimately, her lawyer tells her that while "new ground is being broken every day... [p]ossibly you could sue on the grounds of discrimination, but that costs money and you likely wouldn't win" (254). This reinforces that structural barriers, such as the cost of bringing lawsuits, prevents those who wanted access to better medical care from accessing it. When Cassie becomes a lawyer, she says, "All medical complaints involving colored people and white doctors caught my eye, and I worked them all pro bono" (356). Here, Taylor allows Cassie the activism to seek amends by helping others, turning from larger political resistance to more personal resistance.

CENTERING SEXUAL VIOLENCE AGAINST BLACK WOMEN

Taylor resists the erasure of Black women's experiences further by showing how sexual violence impacted women personally. When Cassie attempts to get a physical for a job application, a white doctor humiliates her by refusing to sign her papers if she does not consent to a pelvic exam, which he insists on doing alone without a nurse present. Ultimately, Cassie refuses the exam and decides that other white doctors would treat her similarly. Taylor also embeds the sexual stereotype of Black women through the words of the white doctor who insists on giving Cassie a pelvic exam as part of that medical evaluation. When she resists putting her feet in the stirrups, the doctor suggests she is pretending not to understand, telling her, "A pelvic exam has nothing to do with knowing the position. All you colored girls know it, married or not" (43). This reference to all Black women as sexually promiscuous dehumanizes Cassie; it is also a stereotype often used to justify sexual abuse. In historian Danielle L. McGuire's book *At the Dark End of the Street: Black Women, Rape, and Resistance—A New History of the Civil Rights Movement from Rosa Parks to the Rise of Black Power*, white men justify the sexual abuse of Black women by branding them jezebels. McGuire argues that "the civil rights movement is also rooted in African-American women's long struggle against sexual violence. ... If we understand the role rape and sexual violence played in African Americans' daily lives and with the larger freedom struggle, we have to reinterpret, if not rewrite, the history of the civil rights movement" (xx). Here, Taylor centers the lived experience of Black women as part of Cassie's motive to keep fighting for justice. Taylor addresses this dehumanization through sexual violence in other places in the book as well.

Taylor also includes a scene with a law colleague dressed as Santa who forces Cassie to sit on his lap. After flirtatious encounters with several other women, Santa says, "Don't want to discriminate!" (301). Cassie describes being "pushed forward and down on Santa's knee. I tried to get up, but strong hands on my shoulders kept me down" (301). This lack of agency over her body and men's assumption of her sexual availability, despite Cassie's protests that "this is something I don't do" and "[y]ou might think this is funny, but I don't," is only stopped when a white man intervenes and allows her to leave, although the "red-faced Santa" mocks them both for not being "fun" (302). McMillen explains this threat, stating, "In a society characterized by white dominance and black dependence, even the most virtuous black woman could be victimized with impunity. Among the most bitterly resented legacies of slavery was the white conviction, reiterated ad nauseam, that no female black above the age of puberty was chaste" (17). Here, Taylor shows the intersectional oppression of Black women, as defined by Kimberlé Crenshaw. Crenshaw notes that for Black women, interlocking systems of oppression complicate and compound their inability to seek redress or to protect themselves. Where sexual violence involves a white man and a Black woman, the law is written to protect white women, Crenshaw says, and therefore, "sexist expectations of chastity and racist assumptions of sexual promiscuity combined to create a distinct set of issues confronting Black women" (159). Crenshaw notes that part of the construction of the law, therefore, is erasing the experiences of Black women, which Taylor includes literally in the narrative by having the reader bear witness to Cassie's experience.

This sexualized violence echoes the larger threats Black women faced in the workplace, including the threat of losing their jobs, and Taylor illustrates these threats, restoring Black women's experiences, which underscore the urgency Black women felt in the civil rights movement as they sought to be recognized and protected. While Black women worked primarily in domestic servant roles, those roles also placed them in danger of sexual harassment and abuse by their white employers (McGuire 71). In addition to the stigma of Black women being seen as a Mammy or Jemima stereotype, entering the homes of white men put the domestic help in direct contact with them. In *Days*, Stacey refuses to allow his wife to take a position as a domestic, insisting, "You've never done it and I won't have you doing it!" (74). The sexual exploitation of Black women domestic servants by white men dates back to enslavement, and it is repeated throughout the Logan family history (also discussed in *Land* and *Well*). Cassie references both the possible exploitation and the commitment of her family's men to protecting the women when she notes, "None of our people had worked as a domestic since slavery and neither had Dee's" (73). While this may also reference social class, which is too complex for discussion here, it also shows the deep concerns not only of the demeaning of Black women but also of their abuse. McMillen states: "Blacks also claimed that many white men thought every day to be open season on black women, that the law effectively provided even black children no protection from white rape, and that police and white rowdies sometimes molested black women and girls on the city streets" (17–18).

The lack of legal recourse—the painting of Black women who accused white men of rape as being promiscuous themselves—provides the basis of McGuire's work: foundational to the civil rights movement was Black women's willingness to endure public humiliation and lack of redress in exchange for speaking their truth. While Taylor tempers the explicitness of the threats in her book, they are present, and they contribute to the resistance of Black women and the reframing of the civil rights movement.

INCORPORATING MISSISSIPPI'S MEDGAR EVERS

Taylor includes real-life activist Medgar Evers and the voter registration drives at several points in the book as part of her centering Mississippi in the larger civil rights movement, offering resistance to the dominant narratives of these historic events. The decision to end the book here provides additional resistance to the dominant civil rights narrative. The book also parallels the post–World War II timeline of Medgar Evers's life in Mississippi, from his return from the war in 1945 to his funeral in 1963. An icon in the Mississippi civil rights movement and the larger national embrace of it, Evers worked as the first NAACP field organizer in Mississippi, which was, as scholar Minrose Gwin notes, "a post many had called a suicide mission" (4). Taylor mentions Evers several times throughout the book, at first alongside the reference to Emmett Till's murder, which the dominant narrative often includes as part of the start of the modern civil rights movement. Taylor's entire Logan family series asserts that Black residents in Mississippi fought for equality and justice, dating back to Reconstruction, challenging this narrative overall. Mary Logan describes Medgar Evers's activism, telling Uncle Hammer: "I heard from Little Willie that he did investigative work for the NAACP checking on so-called accidents whenever colored people were killed. He even did investigative work up around Money, town where that poor Emmett Till boy was murdered. He said they're organizing for some real protests in Mississippi" (321).

Later, Cassie draws parallels between Evers's military service with Man's, saying, "Both [Medgar] and his brother had fought in World War II, but unlike Christopher-John and Clayton and many other returning Negro soldiers who could no longer tolerate the racial injustices of the South and had left, Medgar Evers, his brother Charles, and men like Little Willie had stayed" (348). The role of veterans in the civil rights movement is often left out of the dominant narrative, but fighting for freedom overseas inspired many veterans to become civil rights leaders when they returned. Payne, who argues that the 1960s civil rights movement was only possible based on the invisible activism of the previous generation (4), notes the leadership role of these pre-1960s veterans: "It was they who groomed the youngsters of the Emmett Till generation to think of themselves as the vehicles of change, who created the social and political networks later activists could exploit, who set the standards by which later activists would judge themselves, and who offered those later activists family and a tempering humanism" (404). In including Evers, Taylor reclaims the place of this generation of activists who did the foundational organizing work.

In addition, Taylor's decision to close the book with the march following Evers's funeral bears significance. Taylor avoids the dominant narrative that the civil rights movement succeeds and ends with the passage of the Civil Rights Act of 1964 or the Voting Rights Act of 1965. Instead, she leaves the Logan family and the reader thinking about what will come next. The funeral of Medgar Evers is a key moment in the Mississippi civil rights movement. Historian Keith Orejel notes that the Kennedy administration's response to the funeral and the violent clashes between protestors and police led to Evers's burial at Arlington National Cemetery and a Kennedy photo op with widow, Mrs. Myrlie Evers, where Kennedy held a "mock signing of the Civil Rights Bill" (39). However, Orejel argues that by shifting the national focus to Evers as a hero, Kennedy hampered the Mississippi civil rights movement because it also shifted "attention away from the violent nature of his death and the government's own negligence in failing to protect black activists in Mississippi" (40). By moving Evers from local agitator to World War II hero, the Kennedy administration removed the reality of Evers's death from the conversation. The administration instead "imposed a heavy-handed peace settlement on civil rights activists that required the cessation of public protests (fearing that they would produce more violent encounters), but did not grant demands for the full desegregation of [Jackson, Mississippi]" (40). Taylor's decision not to include Evers's Arlington interment keeps the focus on his sacrifice and the violence facing those carrying on the civil rights work. Orejel documents that following Evers's murder, local participation in the civil rights movement increased (46). Taylor leaves the story at this local uptick in involvement, ignoring the national story of his death in favor of keeping the work in Mississippi at the forefront.

The importance of Taylor's decision to focus on Evers has contemporary echoes, as Evers has passed from local activist into national public memory. Kristen Hoerl, a scholar of rhetoric and public culture, argues that media portrayals of the trials of Evers's killer, Byron de la Beckwith, reshaped public memory about the circumstances of the murder, instead recasting Beckwith as a lone villain whose punishment redeems Mississippi's violent racial past. The film *Ghosts of Mississippi* about the 1994 conviction of Beckwith "supplants memories of civil rights injustices with a narrative of White redemption in the present" (77). Taylor resists focusing on the white killer and instead keeps the story about the civil rights movement with Black activists at the center. Hoerl asserts that these contemporary retellings of the civil rights movement center and redeem whiteness and, in erasing the Black struggle against institutional and structural white hegemonic power, "foreclosed spaces for critical analysis of contemporary race relations" (78). This makes the work of Taylor more important in reclaiming the story for current and future readers, adding her counternarratives to the rising tide of white-centered narratives.

Further, contemporary state violence against Black bodies relies on historical context for interpretation. Knowing the civil rights story from a voice inside the movement, even if fictional, provides an important historical counternarrative for young readers, both Black and white. Law scholar Angela Onwuachi-Willig draws a clear connection between the racist tropes that motivated Emmett Till's murder and the 2012 homicide of Trayvon Martin, an unarmed teen killed while visiting a gated community in Florida. The protection of whiteness as property and the policing of perceived white spaces led to the deaths of both young men, Onwuachi-Willig argues. The connection between the two cases demonstrates that the United States "is far from becoming a bias-free society where racial stereotypes and racial bias do not result in negative consequences for African Americans and other people of color" (1185). *Days* invites readers to consider the continued dangers that the Logans would face today. The historical novel does not just describe the past; it holds a mirror to the present and asks the reader to examine the reflection.

For Taylor, history has layers—the past always echoing in the narrative present of the books themselves, the present always providing a lens for the past, and the past urging readers to reconsider their own present. The present informed Taylor's writing of *Days*, which culminates in the 1960s voter registration drives and the death of Medgar Evers. In a 2014 essay, Taylor states that she was in the middle of writing this novel when the Supreme Court ruling in *Shelby County v. Holder* essentially removed the protections of the Voting Rights Act of 1965 (in 2013), which suggests that Taylor may have been nudged to acknowledge the costs of those voting rights through *Days*. In the epilogue of the novel, Cassie says she attended Barack Obama's inauguration in 2008, showing that Taylor considered what Cassie would do throughout her life.

Through the Logan family's civil rights activism, Taylor offers a critique of the present that invites readers to examine the historical context of anti-Black racism in America. Her Endarkened storywork itself is an act of resistance, placing her own experiences and her family's history and stories in a place of privileged knowledge. In choosing to end her novel with the arrival of federal marshals in the wake of Evers's funeral, Taylor has chosen to leave on what at first glance could seem a bleak point in the civil rights movement. However, she ends the story before what the mainstream civil rights narrative sees as the movement's greatest successes: the rise of the Mississippi Freedom Democratic Party and

Fannie Lou Hamer's 1964 speech in Atlantic City, which made it impossible for the Democratic party to ignore racial violence and oppression in Mississippi; the Civil Rights Act of 1964; and the Voting Rights Act of 1965. This, according to historian Jacqueline Dowd Hall, is the dominant narrative of the civil rights movement: a decade of work in the South that culminates in these events and falls into decline (1234). However, Hall argues that this dominant narrative erases a much broader, more complete picture of the civil rights movement from the 1930s through the 1970s, which challenges assumptions of the civil rights movement ending in the 1960s (1235). Hall's proposed timeline encompasses both the Logan family narrative and Taylor's own life, including the publication of *Roll of Thunder, Hear My Cry*. This reframing also allows us to extend both the struggle and the successes of the movement to the present by honoring the work of so many present-day civil rights workers. It resists the conservative narrative currently in circulation that the civil rights movement ended and is no longer relevant. Through her final book, Taylor provides a compelling counternarrative, acknowledging struggles and gains far beyond the traditional narrative, resisting a simplistic and linear portrayal of the civil rights movement, and pushing a new generation of readers to become active in the fight.

WORKS CITED

Berrey, Stephen A. *The Jim Crow Routine: Everyday Performances of Race, Civil Rights, and Segregation in Mississippi*. U of North Carolina P, 2015. ProQuest Ebook Central.

Bolton, Charles C. "Farmers Without Land: The Plight of White Tenant Farmers and Sharecroppers." *Mississippi History Now*, Mar. 2004. https://mshistorynow.mdah.state.ms.us/articles/228/farmers-without-land-the-plight-of-white-tenant-farmers-and-sharecroppers.

Crenshaw, Kimberlé. "Demarginalizing the Intersection of Race and Sex: A Black Feminist Critique of Antidiscrimination Doctrine, Feminist Theory and Antiracist Politics." *University of Chicago Legal Forum*, vol. 1989, Article 8, 1989, pp. 139–67, https://chicagounbound.uchicago.edu/uclf/vol1989/iss1/8.

Gwin, Minrose. *Remembering Medgar Evers: Writing the Long Civil Rights Movement*. U of Georgia P, 2013.

Haber, Leigh. "*Roll of Thunder, Hear My Cry* Author Mildred D. Taylor Talks Ending the Logan Family Saga." *O: The Oprah Magazine*, Jan. 28, 2020. https://www.oprahmag.com/entertainment/books/a30535291/mildred-taylor-roll-of-thunder-hear-my-cry-interview/.

Hall, Jacquelyn Dowd. "The Long Civil Rights Movement and the Political Uses of the Past." *The Journal of American History*, vol. 91, no. 4, Mar. 2005, pp. 1233–63. JSTOR, doi:10.2307/3660172.

Hoberman, John. *Black and Blue: The Origins and Consequences of Medical Racism*. U of California P, 2012. ProQuest Ebook Central, https://ebookcentral.proquest.com/lib/rutgers-ebooks/detail.action?docID=867683.

Hoerl, Kristen. "Mississippi's Social Transformation in Public Memories of the Trial Against Byron de La Beckwith for the Murder of Medgar Evers." *Western Journal of Communication*, vol. 72, no. 1, Feb. 2008, pp. 62–82, doi:10.1080/10570310701828966.

Lavelle, Kristen M. *Whitewashing the South: White Memories of Segregation and Civil Rights*. Rowman and Littlefield, 2014.

McGuire, Danielle L. *At the Dark End of the Street: Black Women, Rape, and Resistance—A New History of the Civil Rights Movement from Rosa Parks to the Rise of Black Power*. Vintage Books, 2011.

McMillen, Neil R. *Dark Journey: Black Mississippians in the Age of Jim Crow*. U of Illinois P, 1989.

Onwuachi-Willig, Angela. "Policing the Boundaries of Whiteness: The Tragedy of Being out of Place from Emmett Till to Trayvon Martin." *Iowa Law Review*, vol. 102, no. 3, Mar. 2017, pp. 1113–86.

Orejel, Keith. "The Federal Government's Response to Medgar Evers's Funeral." *Southern Quarterly*, vol. 49, no. 2/3, pp. 37–54. *ProQuest*, https://search.proquest.com/docview/1024790093/.

Payne, Charles M. *I've Got the Light of Freedom: The Organizing Tradition and the Mississippi Freedom Struggle*. U of California P, 1997.

Pittman, Ashton. "First Black Republican Elected to the Mississippi House Since Reconstruction." *Mississippi Free Press*, Aug. 10, 2023. https://www.mississippifreepress.org/first-black-republican-elected-to-mississippi-house-since-reconstruction/.

Rothstein, Richard. *The Color of Law: A Forgotten History of How Our Government Segregated America*. Liveright Publishing Corporation, 2017.

Stone-Mediatore, Shari. *Reading across Borders: Storytelling and Knowledges of Resistance*. 1st Palgrave Macmillan ed., Palgrave Macmillan, 2003.

Suggs, Jon-Christian. *Whispered Consolations: Law and Narrative in African American Life*, U of Michigan P, 2000. ProQuest Ebook Central.

Taylor, Mildred D. *All the Days Past, All the Days to Come*. Viking, 2020.

Taylor, Mildred D. *Let the Circle Be Unbroken*. Penguin, 1981.

Taylor, Mildred D. "Tapped on the Shoulder." *World Literature Today*, vol. 88, no. 5, Oct. 2014, pp. 60–61. *JSTOR*, doi:10.7588/worllitetoda.88.5.0060.

Toliver, S. R. *Recovering Black Storytelling in Qualitative Research: Endarkened Storywork*. Routledge, 2022.

Wilkerson, Isabel. *The Warmth of Other Suns*. Vintage Books, 2011.

Woodward, C. Vann. *The Strange Career of Jim Crow*. 3rd rev. ed., Oxford UP, 2002.

List of Contributors

JENNIFER ANSBACH holds a PhD in American Studies, with a focus on the intersection of young adult literature and social justice. A public high school teacher for over twenty-five years, Jennifer works with bringing cultural and historical context to literature for young people and giving them a variety of lenses to interpret both the literature and the world. Her work has appeared in *English Journal* where she was awarded the Paul and Kate Farmer Award for best article and honorable mention for another article; *English Leadership Quarterly*; *Transformations*; *The New York Times*; and *Edutopia*. Her book *Take Charge of Your Teaching Evaluation* is published by Heinemann. When she's not teaching, reading, or writing, Jennifer can be found with her husband and four springer spaniels out in the garden.

JANI L. BARKER (she/her) is professor of English and Humanities at Southeastern Oklahoma State University, where she specializes in children's and adolescent literature. Her research focuses on historical and contemporary children's and young adult literature, with special interest in narrative strategies, historical fiction, race representation in young adult literature, and ethics. She has published papers in journals including *Children's Literature*, *Children's Literature Association Quarterly*, and *Children's Literature in Education*, and in several edited collections. She likes to grapple with critical, theoretical issues in children's literature relevant to literary scholars and teachers of children's literature alike.

MELISSA BEDFORD (she/her) is assistant professor in the School of Education at Eastern Washington University. She teaches literacy methods courses to future teachers, as well as researches various areas of education including children's and young adult (YA) literature, critical literacy, literacy-STEM integration, and culturally responsive teaching. Most recently, she has started researching multiraciality in children's and YA literature, which was inspired by her own multiracial identity as a proud Asian American. Additionally, she is an elected school board director for Spokane Public Schools and is actively involved in her local community, collaborating with local organizations to provide educational opportunities for children and adults.

HELEN BOND is a professor in the School of Education at Howard University in Washington DC. She is a Fulbright-Nehru Scholar to India, member of the Center for Women, Gender, and Global Leadership, and liaison to the Center for African Studies (CfAS). She helps organize the International Children's Literature Conference at Howard with Georgetown's Center for Contemporary Arab Studies, School of Education and the CfAS. With a PhD in human development, she is interested in how education for sustainable development can promote peace, justice, and antiracism. She published "Making Peace with Children" in *Peace Studies for Sustainable Development in Africa* in Springer's prestigious series Advances in African Economic, Social and Political Development. Her work with sustainable development connects to Howard's mission of empowering students toward creating a more sustainable and just future. Dr. Bond was inducted in the 2020 Alumni Hall of Fame by The Ohio State University-Mansfield for her work in education and human development.

WANDA M. BROOKS is professor of literacy education in the College of Education and Human Development at Temple University. She teaches courses related to literacy theories, research and instruction as well as qualitative research methods. Her research interests fall into two complementary areas. First, to better understand how readers develop literary understandings, she examines the responses of African American young adolescents to diverse children's and young adult books. Second, she carries out content analyses of African diaspora literature for youth to further situate and solidify these kinds of texts as representative of a developing literary tradition. She has published in journals such as *Research in the Teaching of English*, *Children's Literature in Education*, and *The Journal of Children's Literature*.

SUSAN BROWNE, EdD, is associate professor in the Department of Language, Literacy and Sociocultural Education at Rowan University. Dr. Browne teaches undergraduate and graduate reading courses. She serves as a research advisor to master's and EdD candidates and teaches in the Language and Literacy PhD Program. She is codirector of the Rowan University Writing Project. Dr. Browne's research interests and publications are in the areas of critical pedagogy, urban education, diverse literature for children and adolescents and reader response.

SABRINA CARNESI is a doctoral student seeking a degree in library information science at the University of Washington's Information School. She has thirty-plus years of experience in K–12 education. Her research uses qualitative interviewing and mixed methods to understand the impact literature has on youth. Her overarching perspective stems from her experiences as a school librarian, which has allowed her to grow in the knowledge of advocacy needs for school library programs, which are meant not only to support the academic needs of youth but their individual needs and interests as well. She has a specialized focus that grounds her in research and children's literature which allows BIPOC youth the opportunity to experience powerful impacts with text without compromising their identity.

EMILY CARDINALI CORMIER is assistant professor-in-residence in the Department of English at the University of Connecticut, Storrs, where she teaches children's literature, young adult literature, and popular literature. Her research interests include literature about agricultural communities, ecocriticism, and the poetry of Marilyn Nelson.

Y. "FALAMI" DEVOE also known as "Dr. Falami" is a holistic human development strategist, public speaker, educator, poet, and self-proclaimed self-care ritualist. She is passionate about centering the voices of Black women and curates intentional spaces for authentic dialogue, self-reflection, and community building. Dr. Falami specializes in community conversations with higher education institutions, public school systems, and nonprofits. Her conversations focus on a holistic approach to the development of one's authentic self and strategies for cultivating a person's freedoms and opportunities helping them to thrive wherever they may lead and serve. She has facilitated training for hundreds of participants across the United States focusing on self and collective care, leading from within, and mindfulness.

BAHAR ESHRAQ, PhD in Translation Studies at Allameh Tabataba'i University; her dissertation is *Translation and Cultural Memory in Roald Dahl's Texts of Childhood*. She is an independent scholar in the translation of children's literature and has attended different congresses such as SUCCLS, IBBY, and IRSCL. Her main area of research is translation criticism, translation semiotics, and cultural memory in translated children's literature. She is head of the acquisition department of the reference library at the Institute for Intellectual Development of Children and YA (IIDCYA) and an academic tutor at Shahid Beheshti University. She is translator of children's and YA books such as *The Bolds*, and the author of scholarly articles in magazines such as *Translation*

Studies Journal, Pazhuhešnameh-ye Adabiât-e Koodak va Nojavân, Nârenj, and *Bookbird*. She has also contributed to writing a commentary on the translation of Jabberwocky in Persian in *Jabberwocky in Translation*.

LATRICE FERGUSON is concluding her doctoral studies in literacy studies from University of Pennsylvania's Graduate School of Education before joining the faculty at East Carolina program in library and information sciences. Prior to beginning her doctoral studies, she earned an MA in children's literature at Kansas State University. Additionally, Latrice worked nearly a decade in public and school libraries serving children and teens. It was in the library that she discovered the power of sharing and discussing incredible literature with youth. Her dissertation explores the relationship between play, identity, and literacy in the library.

CATHARINE KANE received her MA in children's literature and MFA in writing for children from Simmons University in 2016. She is interested in portrayals of violence, trauma, and healing in children's and YA media, especially media released in the late 1990s and early 2000s. She is currently working on a paper exploring how SF graphic novels engage with posthumanism. She has been in love with Mildred D. Taylor's work since reading *Song of the Trees* at age eight.

SARAH LAYZELL (they/she) is a writer and editor with a PhD in children's literature. Their research looks at depictions of economics, race, class, and questions of agency, choice, consumption, growth, scarcity, and waste. Sarah is coeditor of *Healthcare in Children's Media* with Naomi Lesley and coeditor of the special section of the *International Journal of Young Adult Literature* on diversity and inclusion in YA sports media with Carla Plieth. Sarah's debut novel, *Cottonopolis*, in part inspired by Mary Logan's history lesson in *Roll of Thunder, Hear My Cry*, was published by Northodox Press in 2024.

MICHELLE H. MARTIN has been the Beverly Cleary Endowed Professor in Children and Youth Services in the Information School at the University of Washington since 2016. From 2011–June 2016, she was the inaugural Augusta Baker Endowed Chair in Childhood Literacy at the University of South Carolina. She teaches children's and young adult literature and has published *Brown Gold: Milestones of African-American Children's Picture Books, 1845–2002* (Routledge 2004) and coedited (with Claudia Nelson) *Sexual Pedagogies: Sex Education in Britain, Australia, and America, 1879–2000* (Palgrave, 2003). Martin's current project, *Dream Keepers for Children of the Sun*, examines the collaborative and individual works that Arna Bontemps and Langston Hughes wrote for children during their forty-year friendship and collaborative working relationship. Martin is a 2024 Kirkus Prize judge.

DEVIKA MEHRA is the 2024 early career fellow at the School of Advanced Study, University of London. She is the 2022 Inclusion, Participation, and Engagement Fellow (School of Advanced Study, University of London) for a research project investigating the role of children's literature archives, museums, and libraries in promoting diversity. She has worked as a postdoctoral research associate on the British Academy-funded project team at Newcastle University investigating Black British children's literature archives and the role of young people's voices in increasing representation in children's prize culture. Her areas of interest include twentieth-century and contemporary children's literature and film in global contexts, critical archival studies and digital humanities, book history and children's publishing, and participatory research methods. She has presented internationally and published in these areas. Her current interdisciplinary project explores the history and evolution of children's print cultures and publishing in India.

TAMMY L. MIELKE, PhD, first became interested in Mildred D. Taylor's work as an adolescent reader, and then as an elementary school teacher. As a PhD student, Dr. Mielke's work centered on African American children's literature in the 1930s and how authors looked back and wrote about the 1930s after 1968. Dr. Mielke has also published on the use of dialect and music as cultural markers in children's and adolescent literature. Having spent fifteen years in academia, Dr. Mielke returned to the middle school classroom in 2021 as an English language arts specialist and is once again teaching students about Taylor and her amazing Logan family series.

NGOZI ONUORA is the incoming Chair of the Teaching, Learning, and Foundations Department in the College of Education at Eastern Illinois University. Prior to this role, she taught literacy courses in early childhood and elementary education such as children's literature and reading methods at Millikin University. Her research interests focus on multicultural representation in children's literature. Dr. Onuora earned an EdD in Curriculum and Instruction from the University of Illinois at Urbana-Champaign.

LAUREN RIZZUTO holds a PhD in English from Tufts University, where she wrote her dissertation on Black American contributions to environmental writing for children, and an MA in Children's Literature from Simmons University. In summer 2022, she was a Research Fellow at the Internationale

Jugendbibliothek in Munich, Germany. She is now a high school teacher in New Orleans, Louisiana.

SHELLY SHAFFER is associate professor of literacy in the School of Education at Eastern Washington University, Cheney, WA. She is the coeditor of the 2019 book *Contending with Gun Violence in the English Language Classroom* and has published in *Journal of Adolescent and Adult Literacy*, *The ALAN Review*, *Voices from the Middle*, and *English Journal*, as well as written several chapters in recent young adult-focused volumes. Her current research interests are young adult literature analysis and pedagogy, and reading motivation.

BRYANNA SOMERS is a PhD student in English Studies at Illinois State University. Her research centers on representations of activism in youth literature with a focus on activist rhetoric, queer theory, and feminist care ethics. Her poetry chapbook *Fake Magic* is out from Press 254.

ANN VAN WIG is associate professor at Eastern Washington University. Since her days as a reading teacher, she has maintained using literature as a way for students to see the world. Dr. Van Wig teaches literacy methods classes to undergraduate and graduate students. She is an active member of the Literacy Research Association and works with many teacher educators in collaborative research focused on preservice and in-service literacy education.

ANNETTE WANNAMAKER is professor in the Department of English Language and Literature at Eastern Michigan University where she serves as coordinator of the Children's Literature Program. She served ten years as North American editor-in-chief of *Children's Literature in Education*, has edited several collections of academic essays, and is the author of *Boys in Children's Literature and Popular Culture: Masculinity, Abjection, and the Fictional Child*. Her book *How to Read Like an Anti-Fascist: Storytelling and Narrative Literacy for Young People* is forthcoming in 2025.

RAEN PARKER WASHINGTON holds a PhD in language and literacy education specializing in literacies and children's literature and a certificate in interdisciplinary qualitative studies. She has a master's in early childhood education and a passion for teaching, lifelong learning, and the arts—including prose poetry and SpokenWord. As an education researcher and independent scholar, she uses poetry, narrative, and arts-based inquiry in the service of her research. Use of these approaches informs her current works based on Appalachia familial roots and a critical literacy framework on a dehistoricized movement: The Great Migration. (The Taylor works are drawn from that historical period).

Index

Page numbers in *italics* indicate illustrations.

Abrams, Jasmine, 34
Acevedo, Elizabeth, 91
activism: anger as tool, 272; antiracist, 76–77, 84; Black Lives Matter movement, 6, 177–78, 191, 243, 246, 257, 277; children's literature as, 246–49, 258, 262; and environmental justice, 182; grassroots, 281; "movement building," 162; and relational care, 271, 276–77; and violence, relationship with, 274. *See also* civil rights movement
adaptation, filmic, 111–14
African American history, 6, 53, 120–21, 138, 206, 251
African American literature, 17; anger, role of, 192; and antiblackness, 162–64; impact of, 78–79
African Americans: Africana womanism, 34–35, 45–46, 47; artistic expressions of culture, 93–94; Black joy, 252; family films, 116; family histories, 15–16; family histories, silence on, 16–17; and identity formation, 56; lived experience and storytelling, 63; nature, relationship with, 185; oral traditions in Black communities, 17, 57; struggle for racial progress, 28–29
African spiritualism, 186
Afrofuturism, 280

Afro Indigenous farming practices, 219
Afro-pessimism, 163
agency as theme: and activism, 281; agency of Black children, 56, 62; in nature, 184; in *Roll of Thunder* film adaptation, 109–10, 114, 115, 116, 120–21, 126–27; in *The Land*, 21; semiotics of, 127, 144
agrarian traditions: Black Agrarianism, 204–6, 209, 214; communities, 208–9; farming novels, 215–19
Alexander, Kwame, 6, 95
Allen, Autumn, 225, 229
All the Days Past, All the Days to Come (Taylor), 5; activism and resistance, 281; analysis of, 37; Black family structures, 289–90; Cassie Logan and womanism, 35; children, education vs. protection, 264–65; critical race theory, 70–73; inclusion of real-life events, 295–98; Jim Crow laws, 281–86; Jim Crow laws outside the South, 286–88; land ownership and sharecropping, 292; medical racism, 292–93; police brutality, 281–82; race and implied audiences, 78–85; racial education in, 73–78; racism, North vs. South, 44–48; return to South, 25; sexual violence against women, 293–95; "the Veil," 64; and white supremacy, 171

307

Althusser, Louis, 120
American Library Association Children's Literature Legacy Award, 9
American Library Association interview, 63
American West, 286–87
Amistad (film), 95
Anderson, Rodino, 53
Angelou, Maya, 16–17, 29
anger: and care ethics, 272–75; racism and environmental justice, 191–95
Ansāri, Košneviss, 147
Ansbach, Jennifer, 8, 279–98
antiracism: antiracist teaching, 223, 251–53; laws restricting, 253n1; protest movements, 257. *See also* racism
Arbery, Ahmaud, 163, 277
art. *See* cover art, books
Art and Imagination of W. E. B. Du Bois, The (Rampersad), 53
Artist Magazine, The, 94
Assembly on Literature for Adolescents of NCTE (ALAN) Award, 60, 161
At the Dark End of the Street (McGuire), 293
autobiography: definitions of, 16–17; power of, 54
Autobiography of an Ex-Colored Man, The (Johnson), 53

Babington, Bruce, 113, 114
Bader, Barbara, 188
Baldwin, James, 187–88
Bang, Molly, 92, 97, 98, 102
Barad, Karen, 54
Barker, Jani L., 8, 68–85, 118, 225, 228, 234, 254nn9–10
Barlow, Charnelle Pinkney, 93
Batch of Books blog, 91
Beckwith, Byron de la, 296
Bedford, Melissa, 8, 31–50
Behrouzi, Ali Naqi, 147
Belgrave, Faye, 34
Bell, Derrick, 70
Belonging (hooks), 215
Bernstein, Robin, 250, 254n8
Berrey, Stephen A., 283
Berry, Wendell, 211–12, 214, 219n1

Between Voice and Silence (Gilligan), 272
Beyond Forty Acres and a Mule (Reid), 206
Beyond Heroes and Holidays (Lee), 223
Biden, Joe, 241
biracial identities, 207
Birth of a Nation (film), 112
Bishop, Rudine Sims, 49, 78–79, 84, 226–27
Black Agrarianism, 204–6, 209, 214, 216
Black Americans. *See* African Americans
Black and Blue (Hoberman), 292
Black Arts Movement, 192
Black feminism, 34, 259–61, 271–72. *See also* care ethics
Black Independent cinema, 110
Black joy, 252
Black Lives Matter movement, 6, 177–78, 191, 243, 246, 257, 277
Black Panther Ten-Point program, 247–48
Black resistance: *All the Days Past, All the Days to Come*, 75, 279, 281, 286–87; everyday acts of, 114, 181, 295; land ownership as, 291–92; language of, 131–32, 140–41, 151–52. *See also* activism
Black Skin, White Masks (Fanon), 54
"Black Woman Speaks, A" (Richards), 251
"Black Women and the Wilderness" (White), 193
Blake, Jacob, 163
Blaxploitation films, 110, 117
Bloomfield, Maureen, 94
Bolton, Charles C., 291
Bond, Helen, 8, 52–65
Booker, Keith M., 115
Bookstagrammers, 90
Born a Crime (Noah), 228
Bosmajian, Hamida, 39, 118, 122, 125, 228, 229
Boym, Svetlana, 207, 217–18, 219
Breathe: A Letter to My Sons (Perry), 165
Brooks, Wanda, 8, 70, 161–78
Brown, George, 287
Brown, Lyn Mikel, 272
Brown, Michael, 234–35, 257
Brown, Noel, 113, 114, 115
Browne, Susan, 8, 161–78
Brown Girl Dreaming (Woodson), 16
Brownies' Book, The (Du Bois), 56, 63

Bud, Not Buddy (Curtis), 6
Bullard, Robert, 182
Burnett, Frances Hodgson, 193

Caldecott awards, 190
Capshaw, Kate, 254n8
Carbado, Devon, 36
care ethics, 259–61; anger as care, 272–75; caring relationships, parents and children, 262–65; critique of, 276–77; ethical ideals, 276–77; generational care, 267–72; inclusion and subversion, 267–72; institutions and care dynamics, 262–67
Caring: A Feminine Approach to Ethics and Moral Education (Noddings), 259
Carnesi, Sabrina, 8, 89–105
Carver, George Washington, 215
Caste: The Origins of Our Discontent (Wilkerson), 166
Chandler, Karen, 204
Charlotte's Web (White), 193
Chavis, Benjamin, 182
Chesnutt, Charles, 182–83
children: and agency, 123–25; child-signifiers in filmic adaptations, 117–20; innocence vs. racial education, 249–51, 262, 265, 266–67; mission to, 84–85. *See also* family structures
Children's Book Council (Iran), 133, 134
children's literature: and activism, 246–49, 258, 262; and feminist care ethics, 260–61; impact on gender roles, 34; impact on social awareness, 226; multiracial audiences for, 250–51; need for multiethnic, 228; nostalgia and farm novels, 215–19; pastoral influences, 193; picture book as art form, 188–89; racial education vs. childhood innocence, 249–51; selection of texts for translation, 133–34; "white canon," 7
Children's Literature Legacy Award (ALA), 9, 57
Children's Literature Review, 138
Children's Novels and the Movies (Street), 111–12

Childress, Alice, 116
Chiles, Mari, 257
Chipko protests, 200–201n9
Christian, Robert, 116
Citizenship Schools, 281
Civil Rights Act, 296, 298
civil rights movement: activism, 39, 49, 83, 84–85, 280, 281–86, 295–98; Black Agrarianism, 205–6, 209; Black women's experience, 293–95; education on, 73–78, 244, 248; filmic portrayals, 110. *See also* activism
Clark, Septima, 281
Clark, Stephon, 234–35
Cobb, Cicely, 170, 172
COINTELPRO, 222
Collins, Patricia Hill, 261
"color line," 56. *See also* "Veil, the" (Du Bois)
community: equitable, and care ethics, 260; "radical community care," 219; and shared history, 122
"concord of sensibilities" (Ellison), 163
Connolly, Holly, 90
Contemporary Authors interview, 6
Cooper, Brittney, 23
Coretta Scott King Award, 95, 144
Cormier, Emily Cardinali, 8, 204–19
counterstorytelling/counternarratives, 33, 163–64, 177–78, 283–86. *See also* critical race theory (CRT)
cover art, books: criteria for quality, 91–92; *The Friendship*, 101–2; illustrators, prominent, 93–95; impact of, 90–91, 104–5; *The Land*, 95–96; *Let the Circle Be Unbroken*, 102–3; *Mississippi Bridge*, 99–100; *Road to Memphis*, 103–4; *Roll of Thunder, Hear My Cry*, 100–101; semiotic aspects, 144; *Song of the Trees*, 98–99, 189, *198*; visual rhetoric, 92–93; *The Well*, 96–98
COVID-19 pandemic, 277
Cowdery, Randi, 34
Craft, Jerry, 6
Crenshaw, Kimberlé, 36, 294
Crisis (NAACP magazine), 56

"critical consciousness," 252–53
critical race theory (CRT): children's literature as teaching tool, 246–47; context of and resistance to, 245–46; expressed in fiction, 242–43; and justice in *To Kill a Mockingbird*, 225; as lens on *All the Days Past, All the Days to Come*, 70–73; overview, 32–33; realists vs. idealists, 70–71, 72; *Roll of Thunder, Hear My Cry*, 242; tenets of, 33; in *The Hate U Give*, 243–45; and white supremacy, 163
Crossover, The (Alexander), 6
Crowe, Chris, 200n2
Cullors, Patrisse, 6
Cultivation and Catastrophe (Postmentier), 206–7
"cultural adaptation," 132
Curtis, Christopher Paul, 6

Dadashova, Shafag, 54
Dahl, Roald, 142
Dark Journey (McMillen), 287, 290
Dark Voices (Zamir), 55
Darkwater: Voices from Within the Veil (Du Bois), 53
Davis, Pamela, 62
DeBlasio, Alyssa, 134
DeCuir, Jessica, 32–33
Delgado, Richard, 70, 75, 79–80
Delta State University, 279
Democracy in Chains (MacLean), 254n6
Descriptive Anthology of the YA Characters (Aftābgardān Press), 141
design. *See* cover art, books
Devoe, Y. Falami, 3–4
dialogic situations/relationships, 111, 132, 135–37
DiAngelo, Robin, 80
dignity, as theme, 9, 62, 78–79, 118–19, 211
diverse books, need for, 104–5
Dixson, Adrienne, 32–33
domestication technique, 132, 145–46, 152
domestic space, 121, 126, 127
"dominant gaze," 112–13
Donelson, Kenneth L., 138, 143

double consciousness (Du Bois), 53, 55, 58–59
Douglass, Frederick, 213, 214
DreamWorks Studio, 94–95
duality of experience, 54. *See also* "Veil, the" (Du Bois)
Du Bois, W. E. B., 214; *The Brownies' Book*, 56, 63; childhood and background, 55–56; double consciousness, 53, 55, 58–59; impact on Taylor, 62; *The Negro*, 61; outsider vision, 59–61. *See also* "Veil, the" (Du Bois)
Dumas, Michael J., 163, 173
Dunbar, Paul Lawrence, 54
Dust Tracks on a Road (Hurston), 17

Eastern Michigan University (EMU), 252, 255n11
ecocriticism, 192, 208
economic systems and oppression, 211–12
Education Publishing Center (Iran), 133
Ellington Was Not a Street (Shange), 95
Ellison, Ralph, 163
El Paso, Texas mass shooting (2019), 163
Elsie Dinsmore novels, 226
Emerson, Ralph Waldo, 188
empowerment: Black empowerment/white fear, 234; Black pride and education, 56, 122; and land ownership, 62
Endarkened epistemologies/storywork, 280, 297
engrossment, principle of, 259, 263, 267, 275
entanglement, concept of, 54, 234
Environmental Justice Movement, 182
environmental movement: environmental justice, 181–86; white environmentalism and racism, 194, 200n3
Epstein, Mikhail, 134
Eshraq, Bahar, 8, 131–53
ethics of care. *See* care ethics
Ethics of Care, The (Held), 273
Evans, Mei Mei, 201n14
Evers, Medgar, 76, 280, 295–96
Evers, Myrlie, 296
experiential knowledge, 33. *See also* critical race theory (CRT)

INDEX

Fair Housing Act (1968), 288
family films, 115–16, 117; generic elements, 127–28
family structures: Black families, 78–79, 102–3, 144–45, 218–19, 263, 289–90; childrearing within racist structures, 18–19; family histories/narratives, 15–17; family storytellers, 161, 280, 283–85; film portrayals, 109–10, 113–28; Logan family over time, 23–28, 52, 57, 68–69, 279; violence against families, 123–24. *See also* children
Fanon, Frantz, 54
farming. *See* agrarian traditions; sharecropping
feminism: Black, 34, 259–61, 271–72; ethics of care, 258
Ferguson, Latrice, 7–8, 15–29
Ferguson, Yvonne, 15
Ferngully: The Last Rainforest (Young), 184
Field, Kendra, 16, 25
Fielder, Brigitte, 250
film adaptations. See *Roll of Thunder, Hear My Cry* (film adaptation)
Finding Your Roots (PBS series), 15
Finley, Martha, 226
Fisher, Leona, 173
Fiskio, Janet, 205
Floyd, George, 163, 221, 230, 243, 257, 277
Foner, Eric, 53
Ford, Jennifer Anne, 92
foreignization, 132–33
Freedom Riders, 28, 76, 280, 281
Freeman, Morgan, 116
Freewater (Luqman-Dawson), 6
Freyfogle, Eric, 212
Friendship, The (Taylor): cover art, 101–2; translation of, 139, 142, 144; and white supremacy, 165, 169–70, 173–75
From the Mixed-up Files of Mrs. Basil E. Frankweiler (film), 109

Gannon, Susan, 189
Garner, Eric, 243, 257
Gates, Henry Louis, Jr., 53, 283, 290, 291
Geisel, Theodor, 196–97

gender roles, 25; perceptions of, 34. *See also* men's roles; women's roles
gender schema theory (GST), 34–36, 45–46
genealogy/family histories, 15–16
Genre and New Hollywood (Neale), 111
Ghosts of Mississippi (film), 296
Gilligan, Carol, 259–60, 272
Ginsburg, Max, 93, 94; *The Friendship* cover, 101; *The Land* cover, 95–96; *Let the Circle Be Unbroken* cover, 102; *Mississippi Bridge* cover, 99; *Road to Memphis* cover, 103; *Roll of Thunder, Hear My Cry* cover, 98, 100–101; *The Well* cover, 97
Giroux, Henry, 80–81
Gold Cadillac, The (Taylor), 267
Great Migration, 25, 58, 73, 213–14, 280, 282, 285
Great Society programs, 288
grief, silencing of, 23–24
Griffith, D. W., 112
Growing Up with the Country (Field), 16
Gwin, Minrose, 295

Hall, Jacqueline Dowd, 286, 298
Hall, Rodney, 290
Hamer, Fannie Lou, 298
Hamilton, Virginia, 6, 89
Hampton, Fred, 222
Han, Hyejung, 133, 134
Hardstaff, Sarah (Layzell), 62, 83–84, 119–20, 166
Harper, Mary Turner, 122, 141
Harris, Cheryl, 41
Harris, Marla, 224, 226, 228, 229
Hartman, Saidiya, 180, 197; on "black noise," 181–82
Hate U Give, The (Thomas), 242, 243–45; anger, role of, 273–75; care ethics, 262, 269; children, education vs. protection, 266–67; ethical decision-making, 276; literature as activism, 246–49; police brutality, 267; racial education vs. childhood innocence, 249–50; Taylor's influence on, 257–58; teaching in classroom, 252
Hawkins, Tom, 55

Hegel, Georg Wilhelm Friedrich, 55
Heinemann, Arthur, 109
Held, Virginia, 260, 273
Henderson, Mae Gwendolyn, 17
Heritage Foundation, 245
Hero Ain't Nothin but a Sandwich, A (film), 109, 116
Heyer, Heather, 163
"hidden transcripts," 16, 25
Higgenbotham, Evelyn Brooks, 23
Hine, Darlene Clark, 23
historical fiction: accuracy of, 224; children's, 182; role of, 5–6
history: antiracist approaches, 223; counterpoints to white, 181; definitions of, broadening, 229; nationalistic, 241; racial in US, 235–36. *See also* historical fiction
Hoberman, John, 292
Hoerl, Kristen, 296–97
Holiday, Billie, 17
Hollywood: 1960s–1970s, 110–11; and children's cinema, 113; family film genre, 123; genre system, 112; rating systems and codes, 110
"Homemade Love" (Washington/poetic tribute), 11–12
hooks, bell, 211–12, 215, 217–18, 252–53
Hope Draped in Black (Winters), 28
Horn Book, The: "Our Modern Minstrelsy," 29; "What Makes a Good Book Cover?," 91
Hudson-Weems, Clenora, 34
Hughes, Langston, 54, 221
Hurston, Zora Neale, 17

identity formation, 120–21, 206
I Know Why the Caged Bird Sings (Angelou), 16
I'll Take My Stand: The South and the Agrarian Tradition (Kline), 205
implied readers, 69, 76; *All the Days Past, All the Days to Come*, 78–85; white, 82–84
In a Different Voice (Gilligan), 259
Indigenous storywork, 280
Institute for the Intellectual Development of Children and YA (Iran), 133, 134

interest convergence, 33; and "passing," 40; and voter suppression, 40. *See also* critical race theory (CRT)
interracial relationships/marriage, 41, 82–83
intersectionality, 36; and Black men's roles in *Let the Circle Be Unbroken*, 42–44; and Black men's roles in *The Road to Memphis*, 43; Black women in *The Land*, 20–25; and "passing" in *Let the Circle Be Unbroken*, 40–42; race and gender, 31, 49, 294; and voting rights in *Let the Circle Be Unbroken*, 38–40
Iran: children's literature, 133; history of, 139–40, 152. *See also* translation
Iser, Wolfgang, 69
I've Got the Light of Freedom (Payne), 281, 284

Jackson, Mississippi, 5
Jacques, Wesley S., 260, 261, 271, 276
January 6 insurrection (2021), 222
Jefferson, Thomas, 205
Jenkins, Jessica, 94
Jeong, Wooseob, 133, 134
Jezebel trope, 22–23, 293
Jim Crow laws, 281–86; outside the South, 286–88
John Henry (Lester/Pinkney), 190
Johnson, James Weldon, 53
Johnson, Lyndon B., 288
Jones, Montgomery, 253n2
justice: environmental, 181–86; justice system in *To Kill a Mockingbird*, 225. *See also* racial justice
"Justice" (Hughes), 221

Kakbāzān, Ali, 139
Kane, Catharine, 8, 221–36
Kātami, Mohammad, 142
Kidd, Kenneth, 242, 253n3
King, Amy Sarig, 184
King, Deborah, 61
King, Katrina Quisumbing, 205, 209, 212
King, Martin Luther, 76
Kirshner, Jonathan, 113
Klingberg, Gote, 132, 133
Kohlberg, Lawrence, 259

Kourdis, Evangelos, 131
Ku Klux Klan, 233, 270

LaDuke, Winona, 185
Lady Sings the Blues (Holiday), 17
land: connections with, 184–85, 207–15; and dignity, 119; farming traditions in *The Land*, 204–19; and identity formation, 120–21; and independence, 214–15; ownership and liberation, 268; ownership and white supremacy, 206; ownership as resistance, 291–92; ownership systems, 62, 210–11, 213, 217; property rights, 70; spiritual connections, 207–8, 215
Land, The (Taylor): Black agrarian traditions, 204–19; children, education vs. protection, 262; cover art, 95–96; critical race theory analysis of, 70; environmental justice, 183–84; land, connections with, 207–15; and nostalgia, 215–19; women's roles, 20–25
Larbalestier, Justine, 90–91
LA Rebellion films, 110–11
Lavelle, Kristen, 285–86
Learning Tree, The (film), 117
Lee, Enid, 223
Lee, Harper, 222. See also *To Kill a Mockingbird* (Lee)
L'Engle, Madeleine, 260–61
Leonardo, Zeus, 177
Let the Circle Be Unbroken (Taylor): analysis of, 37; antiracism, 223–24; biracial characters, 228; cover art, 102–3; intersectionality in, 38–40; justice, search for, and systemic racism, 231–32; law, written and unwritten, 233–35; masculinity and traditional male roles, 25–26, 27; and segregation, 288–89; systemic racism, 223; "the Veil," 63
Lewis, David Levering, 53
Liar (Larbalestier), 90–91
liberalism, critique of, 33. See also critical race theory (CRT)
Lion and the Mouse, The (Rose/Pinkney), 190
literacy, 209; Citizenship Schools, 281; in *The Land*, 20; and liberation, 268

Little Women (film), 109
Logan Family Saga: Black American family histories, 15–16; Cassie Logan character, arc of development, 31–32, 35, 49, 68, 184–86, 229, 230; chronology of novels, 207; connections between novels, 31–32, 68; cover art, 89–105; 40th anniversary redesign, 104–5; recurring elements, 69; rural Mississippi, depictions of, 279; silence vs. voice, 17, 28–29; systemic racism, 228; and white supremacy, 162
Lorax, The (Geisel/Seuss), 196–97
Lorde, Audre, 24, 191, 272, 273
Lose Your Mother (Hartman), 180
Lotman, Yuri M., 131, 134–35, 136–37, 137, 151
Love, Bettina, 23–24
Lupack, Barbara, 126
Luqman-Dawson, Amina, 6
lynchings, 148, 176–77, 193, 270, 283

MacLachlan, Janet, 116–17, 127
MacLean, Nancy, 254n6
Magoon, Kekla, 6, 29
Major, William, 211, 216, 217–18
Martin, Michelle H., 5–9, 35, 118, 192, 200n2, 228, 265–66, 267–68
Martin, Trayvon, 234–35, 257, 297
masculinity. See men's roles
Maxwell, Morgan, 34
McCallum, Robyn, 112
McDowell, Kelly, 121, 254n5
McGuire, Danielle L., 293
M. C. Higgins, the Great (Hamilton), 6
McIntosh, Peggy, 251
McMillen, Neil R., 282, 285, 287, 290, 292, 294
McMurdie, Dena, 91
McNeil, Claudia, 116–17
Me and Marvin Gardens (King), 184
medical racism, 292–93
Meeropol, Aber, 201n12
Meeting at the Crossroads (Brown), 272
Mehdizādeh, Fahimeh, 139, 142
Mehra, Devika, 8, 109–29
men's roles: in *Let the Circle Be Unbroken*, 25–26, 42–44; male dominance, 35–36;

in oppressive states, 26–27; in *Song of the Trees*, 25, 26; in *The Road to Memphis*, 43; traditional male roles, 27
Meredith, James, 77, 280
"Mirrors, Windows, and Sliding Glass Doors" (Bishop), 49, 84, 104
Mirzāi, Behnāz A., 147
Mississippi: contemporary political climate, 290; Mississippi Freedom Democratic Party, 297–98
Mississippi Bridge (Taylor): cover art, 99–100; white narrator, 99
Moran, Mary Jeanette, 260–61
Morrison, Toni, 249
Moses, Wilson Jeremiah, 54
Mother Emanuel AME Church, Charleston, 163, 222
motherhood role, 20, 34. *See also* women's roles
"movement building," 162
Moynihan Report, 27
Muller, Anja, 117

narrator-reader relationships, 68–69
Nash, Jennifer, 261
National Association for the Advancement of Colored People (NAACP), 56, 76
National Housing Act (1934), 221
National Women's Studies Association, 191
nature and pastoral literature, 193
Neale, Steve, 111
Negro, The (Du Bois), 61
Nelson, Kadir, 90, 93, 94–95; *The Friendship* cover, 101–2; *The Land* cover, 96; *Let the Circle Be Unbroken* cover, 102; *Mississippi Bridge* cover, 99–100; *Road to Memphis* cover, 103–4; *Roll of Thunder, Hear My Cry* cover, 99, 101; *The Well* cover, 97–98
New Agrarianism, 204–5, 209, 211
Newbery Award, 6, 7, 68, 162, 258; Taylor's acceptance speech, 31, 83
New Deal programs, 223
New Kid (Craft), 6
Nikolajeva, Maria, 133, 134
Nilsen, Allen Pace, 138, 143

Noah, Trevor, 228
Noddings, Nel, 259–60, 263, 266, 275
nostalgia: and children's farm novels, 215–19; restorative/reflective, 207, 217–18
"Not the Color Purple" (Thompson), 272

Obama, Barack, 28, 75, 297
Onuora, Ngozi, 8, 89–105
Onwuachi-Willig, Angela, 297
Orejel, Keith, 296
Oriki (Yoruba praise poem), 3–4
Osa, Osayimwense, 186
O: The Oprah Magazine, 289
"Our Modern Minstrelsy" (Magoon), 29
outsider vision, 55, 59–61, 62

"passing," 40–42
patriotism and nationalism, 241
Payne, Charles, 281, 284, 295–96
Pellerin, Marquita, 35
Penniman, Leah, 219
People of Color Environmental Leadership Summit (PoCELS), 182–83
peritextual analysis, 143–45
Perry, Imani, 165
Persian translation. *See* translation
Phenomenology of Mind (Hegel), 55
Picture This: How Pictures Work (Bang), 98
Pinkney, Andrea Davis, 93
Pinkney, Brian, 93
Pinkney, Gloria Jean, 93
Pinkney, Jerry, 93–94, 181, 188–91; *Roll of Thunder, Hear My Cry* cover, 98, 100; *Song of the Trees*, 198–99
Pinkney, Myles, 93
Pinkney, Sandra L., 93
Pinkney, Scott, 93
Pinkney, Troy, 93
Pinsent, Pat, 83
Plato's Cave, 55
Poet X, The (Acevedo), 91
police brutality, 266–67, 277; in *All the Days Past, All the Days to Come*, 281–82
Port Chicago Fifty, 223
"Po' Sandy" (Chesnutt), 182–83

Postmentier, Sonya, 206–7
Presenting Mildred Taylor (Crowe), 200n2
Prude, Daniel, 163
Purdy, Jebediah, 200n3
Puutinen, Tiina, 133

Qezelayāq, Soryā, 139, 140–41

racial education: in *All the Days Past, All the Days to Come*, 73–78; for teachers, 246, 250–51
racial justice: boundaries and place, 165–66; linked with environmental justice, 182–83
racial norms, Southern, 41
racism: in *All the Days Past, All the Days to Come*, 71; and anger, 191–95; antiblackness, 162–64; environmental, 187–91; impact on Taylor, 5–6; institutionalized, 70; internalized, 74; land ownership systems, 210–11, 217; medical racism, 292–93; North vs. South, 44–48, 58–59, 73–74; permanence of, 33, 40; resistance, language of, 131–32, 151–52. *See also* critical race theory (CRT); systemic racism; white supremacy
Railway Children, The (film), 109
Rampersad, Arnold, 53
Rankine, Claudia, 26
rape/sexual assault, 22
reception, principle of, 263–64, 265
reception process, 131–32, 135–39, 142, 152
Reese, Debbie, 84
"reflective nostalgia," 218–19
Reid, Debra A., 206
Reid, Mark, 115–16, 117
relational ethics, 259. *See also* care ethics
resistance. *See* Black resistance
respectability as tool, 22–23
Richards, Beah, 251
Rizzuto, Lauren, 8, 180–99
Road to Memphis, The (Taylor): analysis of, 37; cover art, 103–4; and critical race theory, 33; womanist identities, 47
Robinson, Eugene, 235
Robinson, Fiona, 260

Roll of Thunder, Hear My Cry (film adaptation), 109–29; children/family/entangled agency, 123–25; child-signifier and witnessing, 117–20; in context of film adaptation, 111–14; in context of Hollywood (1960s–1970s), 110–11; scriptwriting process, 114–17; spatial dynamics and childhood, 120–23; text, adaptation of, 128–29; text, faithfulness to, 126–28; voiceover, 118
Roll of Thunder, Hear My Cry (Taylor), 6; agency as theme, 62; anger, role of, 272–73, 274; and Black American family histories, 15–16; care and relationality, 269–72; and care ethics, 261; children, education vs. protection, 262, 265; cover art, 100–101; educational methods reflected in, 268–69; imagery, 279–80; impact of, 257–58; intergenerational narratives, 57; literature as activism, 246–49; Mississippi social structures, 17–20; multiracial audiences for, 250; *The Negro*, 61; outsider vision, 59, 60; and revisionist history, 241–42; silence, acts of resistance to, 27; teaching in classroom, 252; translation, Persian, 139, 140–42, 144; translation, Persian, cover art, 153; translation and peritextual analysis, 143–44; "the Veil," 60–61, 63–64; and white supremacy, 168–69, 172–73, 176–77
Romatowski, Jane, 34
Roof, Dylann, 222
Roosevelt, Franklin D., 223
Rosenberg, Julius and Ethel, 201n12
Rothstein, Richard, 287–89
rural South. *See* Black Agrarianism; Southern culture
Russell, Margaret M., 112–13

Šʻabāni, Dāvud, 139, 142
Saul, Wendy, 251
Savannah, Georgia, 28–29
second sight. *See* outsider vision
Secret Garden, The (Burnett), 193

segregation: age, 252; in bathrooms, 46–47; housing, 287–89; neighborhood development under New Deal, 223
semiospheres, 131, 135–37, *137*; American, 138
semiotic systems, 131–32, 134–35
sense of belonging, 79
"1776 Commission," 241
sexual exploitation, 82
sexuality: Black women, stereotypes, 22–23
sexual violence, 293–95
Shadow and Substance (Sims), 226–27
Shaffer, Shelly, 8, 31–50
Shapoval, Mariana, 146
sharecropping, 63, 209, 214, 233, 291–92
Shelby County v. Holder, 297
Sherman, William, 291
Shohat, Ella, 111
Sibert Medal, 95
silence: in Black American family histories, 16–17; decisions to be silent, 19–20; in face of Black death, 26; grief, silencing of, 23–24; between men and women, 26–27; in nature, 187–91; in oral histories, 17; resistance to, 27–28; and white supremacy, 18–19. *See also* voice
slavery: enslaver/enslaved power relationships, 20–21; enslavers' treatment of enslaved Black women, 44–45; legacy and impact, 163, 171–72, 180
Sleeter, Christine, 32–33
Smight, Jack, 109
Smith, Kimberly K., 213
Smithsonian National Museum of African American History and Culture, 95
social conscience books, 226–27
social media, 90
Solórzano, Daniel, 164
Somers, Bryanna, 8, 257–77
Song of the South (film), 112
Song of the Trees (Taylor), 6; children, education vs. protection, 262; cover art, 98–99; and environmental justice, 180–99; men's roles, 25, 26; Pinkney's illustrations, 188–91; violence, role of, 274
Soul Fire Farm, 219

Souls of Black Folk, The (Du Bois), 53, 54–55, 56
Sounder (film), 109, 116, 117, 127
Southern culture: agrarian traditions, 205; and Black roots, 25, 213–14; racial norms, 41; rural Mississippi, 54, 181, 186, 192–93, 258, 279
Southgate, Minoo, 147
space: children's habitation of, 120–21; domestic, 121, 126, 127; private vs. public, 118
Spade, Dean, 222–23
Spielberg, Steven, 95
Stam, Robert, 111
Starr, Christine, 34
Stefancic, Jean, 70, 75
stereotypes: of anger, 272; Black women's sexuality, 22–23; hypersexuality, 231–32; Jezebel trope, 22–23, 293; representations in art, 112–13; women's roles, 127
Stone-Mediatore, Shari, 280
Stop and Frisk policies, 222
storytelling: and Black cultural knowing, 280; educational functions of, 69; family storytellers, 161; intergenerational narratives, 57, 252; and psychic self-preservation, 79; as tool in critical race theory, 70. *See also* counterstorytelling/counternarratives
Stowe, Harriet Beecher, 131
Strange Career of Jim Crow, The (Woodward), 283, 291
"Strange Fruit" (song), 192, 201n12
Street, Douglas, 111–12
Sturgeon, Noel, 184
sugar cane plantations, 234
Suggs, Jon-Christian, 282
sweet gum trees, 185, 200n7
systemic racism: childrearing, impact on, 263–64; children's literature as teaching tool, 246–47; denial of, 222–23; in *To Kill a Mockingbird*, 227–30. *See also* critical race theory (CRT); racism

Tait, Althea, 249–50
Taliaferro Baszile, Denise, 162, 163–64
Tarkington, Rockne, 116–17

Taylor, Breonna, 163, 257, 277
Taylor, Mildred D.: ALAN Award, 60; childhood and family background, 5, 186; critical reception, 6–7; Du Bois, impact of, 62; historical fiction, goals for, 48; land ownership in Colorado, 218; legacy and impact, 6, 9, 50, 93, 104; moves and journeys, 64; Newbery Award acceptance speech, 31; *O: The Oprah Magazine* interview, 289; personal brand, 104; storytelling and Veil work, 57; themes, 52; writing routine, 104. *See also specific novels*
Tending to the Past (Chandler), 204
terrorism, 176–77. *See also* violence
Theory for Beginners (Kidd), 253n3
Thirteenth Amendment, 288
Thomas, Angie, 6, 242, 243–44. *See also Hate U Give, The* (Thomas)
Thomas, Ebony Elizabeth, 255n12
Thompson, Audrey, 260, 263, 266, 270, 272, 276
Till, Emmett, 192–93, 249, 280, 295, 297
Tinker, George, 185
To Kill a Mockingbird (Lee), 222–30; criticism of, 224–25; and justice, 230–31; popularity of, 224; as social conscience book, 226–27; and systemic racism, 227–30; systemic racism not acknowledged, 222–23
Toledo, Ohio, 5, 285
Toliver, Stephanie, 280
Torop, Peeter, 134–35, 145–46
translation: and cultural adaptation, 132; criticism, 143; domestication, 132; equivalence approaches, 133; foreignization, 132–33; peritextual analysis, 143–45; Persian, 131–53; selection of texts for, 133–34; semiosphere of source texts, 138–39; stages of, 135–36; synonymous substitution, 146–47; textual analysis, 145–51
Trepanier-Street, Mary, 34
Trites, Roberta Seelinger, 261
Tronto, Joan, 260
Trump, Donald, 241
Twenty-First-Century Feminisms in Children's and Young Adult Literature (Trites), 261
Tyson, Cicely, 116

UCLA Film School, 110–11
Uncle Tom's Cabin (Stowe), 7, 53, 131
Undefeated, The (Alexander), 95
United States: Constitution, 221, 288; racism as founding principle, 5–6
Unite the Right rally, Charlottesville, Virginia, 163, 222
"Uses of Anger, The" (Lorde), 272

Van Wig, Ann, 8, 31–50
"Veil, the" (Du Bois), 52; definitions, 53–55; origins and development of concept, 55–56; in *Roll of Thunder, Hear My Cry*, 60–61; storytelling as Veil work, 56–58; Taylor's Veil work, 57. *See also* double consciousness
"Venus in Two Acts" (Hartman), 180
Venuti, Lawrence, 132
violence: and activism, relationship with, 274; against the family, 123–24; and intergenerational trauma, 171–72; lynchings, 148, 176–77, 193, 270, 283; physical, 71–72; police brutality, 266–67, 277, 281–82; racial, 124–25; sexual, 22, 293–95; and trauma, 176–77
visual appeal of books, 90–91. *See also* cover art, books
visual rhetoric, 92–93
voice: Cassie Logan's voice, 35, 54, 57, 58, 62, 173, 286–87; contrasted with nature, 143; contrasted with silence, 17; and storytelling, 64, 70. *See also* silence
voting rights, 38–40, 233, 281
Voting Rights Act, 296, 297, 298

Wallace, Kendra, 251
Wallace, Walter, Jr., 163
Wannamaker, Annette, 8, 241–53, 258
Warmth of Other Suns, The (Wilkerson), 282, 285
Washington, Booker T., 214
Washington, Rachelle, 35
Washington, Raen Parker, 11–12
We Are the Ship (Nelson), 95
Well, The (Taylor): children, education vs. protection, 262; cover art, 96–98;

environmental justice, 184; silence, acts of resistance to, 27–28; storytelling as Veil work, 57–58; translation of, 139, 144; and white supremacy, 166–68, 170–71, 175–76
West, Cornel, 26
Westwood, California, 287–88
We Want to Do More Than Survive (Love), 23–24
White, E. B., 193
White, Evelyn C., 193
"white canon" in children's literature, 7
"white flight," 72
whiteness, 80–81; decentering in education, 251–53; as property, 297; and racial innocence, 285–86; white fragility, 83–84; white privilege, 252; white readers, 79–80
Whiteness as Property (Harris), 41
"White Noise: Toward a Pedagogy of Whiteness" (Giroux), 80–81
"White Privilege" (McIntosh), 251
white supremacy, 161–62; communities built upon, 212; counternarratives, 177–78; and enforced silence, 18–19; false narratives, 177–78; as founding principle of US, 5–6; and Jim Crow laws, 281–83; and land ownership, 206; in Mississippi history, 17–18; narratives of white dominance, 165–69; in Reconstruction period, 291; subjugation and brutality, 173–77; superiority, feelings of, 234; and women's vulnerability, 22–23. *See also* racism
Wilkerson, Isabel, 166, 282, 285, 288
Winant, Howard, 62
Winfield, Paul, 116
Winfrey, Oprah, 16
Winters, Joseph R., 28
Wollman-Bonilla, Julie, 83
women's roles: as burden, 18–19, 23–24; filmic representations of, 126–27; motherhood, 20, 34; respectability as tool, 22–23; safety/vulnerability in *The Land*, 21–22; sexual violence against women, 293–95
Wood, Robin, 128

Woodson, Jacqueline, 6, 50; Taylor's impact on, 15–16
Woodward, C. Vann, 283, 291
Wright, Daunte, 163

Yokota, Junko, 9
Yoo, Hjun-Joo, 168
Yosso, Tara, 164

Zamir, Shamoon, 55
Zeely (Hamilton), 89
Zimmerman, George, 235, 257
Zinn Education Project, 253
Zowkāi, Mohammad Said, 140, 142
Zurbriggen, Eileen, 34